The Rosicrucian Cosmo-Conception

Or, Mystic Christianity

*An Elementary Treatise Upon Man's Past Evolution,
Present Constitution and Future Development*

By Max Heindel

Published by Pantianos Classics

ISBN-13: 978-1-78987-236-1

First published in 1909

Contents

Creed or Christ

No man loves God who hates his kind,
   Who tramples on his brother's heart and soul;
Who seeks to shackle, cloud, or fog the mind
   By fears of hell has not perceived our goal.

God-sent are all religions blest;
   And Christ, the Way, the Truth, the Life,
To give the heavy-laden rest
   And peace from sorrow, sin, and strife.

Behold the Universal Spirit came
   To *all* the churches, not to one alone;
On Pentecostal morn a tongue of flame
   Round *each* apostle as a halo shone.

Since then, as vultures ravenous with greed,
   We oft have battled for an empty name,
And sought by dogma, edict, cult, or creed,
   To send each other to the quenchless flame.

Is Christ then twain? Was Cephas, Paul,
   To save the world, nailed to the tree?
Then why divisions here at all?
   Christ's love enfolds both you and I.

His pure sweet love is not confined
   By creed which segregate and raise a wall.
His love enfolds, embraces human kind,
   No matter what ourselves or Him we call.

Then why not take Him at His word?
   Why hold to creeds which tear apart?
But one thing matters, be it heard
   That brother love fill every heart.

There's but one thing the world has need to know.
   There's but one balm for all our human woe:
There's but one way that leads to heaven above--
   That way is human sympathy and love.

Max Heindel.

A Word to the Wise

The founder of the Christian Religion stated an occult maxim when He said: "Whosoever shall not receive the kingdom of God as a little child shall not enter therein" (Mark X:15). All occultists recognize the far-reaching importance of this teaching of Christ, and endeavor to "live" it day by day.

When a new philosophy is presented to the world it is met in different ways by different people.

One person will grasp with avidity any new philosophical effort in an endeavor to ascertain how far *it supports his own ideas*. To such a one the philosophy itself is of minor importance. Its prime value will be its vindication of *his* ideas. If the work comes up to expectation in that respect, he will enthusiastically adopt it and cling to it with a most unreasoning partisanship; if not, he will probably lay the book down in disgust and disappointment, feeling as if the author had done him an injury.

Another adopts an attitude of skepticism as soon as he discovers that it contains something which *he* has not previously read, heard, or originated in his own thought. He would probably resent as extremely unjustified the accusation that his mental attitude is the acme of self-satisfaction and intolerance; such is nevertheless the case; and thus he shuts his mind to any truth which may possibly be hidden in that which he off-hand rejects.

Both these classes stand in their own light. "Set" ideas render them impervious to rays of truth. "A little child" is the very opposite of its elders in that respect. It is not imbued with an overwhelming sense of superior knowledge, nor does it feel compelled to look wise or to hide its nescience of any subject by a smile or a sneer. It is frankly ignorant, unfettered by preconceived opinions and therefore *eminently teachable*. It takes everything with that beautiful attitude of trust which we have designated "child-like faith," wherein there is not the shadow of a doubt. There the child holds the teaching it receives until proven or disproven.

In all occult schools the pupil is first taught to forget all else when a new teaching is being given, to allow neither preference nor prejudice to govern, but to keep the mind in a state of calm, dignified waiting. As skepticism will blind us to truth in the most effective manner, so this calm, trustful attitude of the mind will allow the intuition, or "teaching from within," to become aware of the truth contained in the proposition. That is the only way to cultivate an absolutely certain perception of truth.

The pupil is not required to believe off-hand that a given object which he has observed to be white, is really black, when such a statement is made to him; but he must cultivate an attitude of mind which "believeth all things" *as possible*. That will allow him to put by for the time being even what are generally considered "established facts," and investigate if perchance there be another viewpoint hitherto unobserved by him whence the object referred to would appear black. Indeed, he would not allow himself to look upon anything as *"an established fact,"* for he realizes thoroughly the importance of keeping his mind in the fluidal state of *adaptability* which characterizes the little child. He realizes in every fiber of his being that "now we see through a glass, darkly," and Ajax-like he is ever on the alert, yearning for "Light, more Light."

The enormous advantage of such an attitude of mind when investigating any given subject, object or idea must be apparent. Statements which appear positively and unequivocally contradictory, which have caused an immense amount of feeling among the advocates of opposite sides, may nevertheless be capable of perfect reconciliation, as shown in one such instance mentioned in the present work. *The bond of concord is only discovered by the open mind*, however, and though the present work may be found to differ from others, the writer would bespeak an impartial hearing as the basis of *subsequent* judgment. If the book is "weighed and found wanting," the writer will have no complaint. He only fears a hasty judgment based upon lack of knowledge of the system he advocates--a hearing wherein the judgment is "wanting" in consequence of having been denied an impartial "weighing." He would further submit, that the only opinion worthy of the one who expresses it *must be based upon knowledge.*

As a further reason for care in judgment we suggest that to many it is exceedingly difficult to retract a hastily expressed opinion. Therefore it is urged that the reader withhold all expressions of either praise or blame until study of the work has reasonably satisfied him of its merit or demerit.

The Rosicrucian Cosmo-Conception is not dogmatic, neither does it appeal to any other authority than the reason of the student. It is not controversial, but is sent forth in the hope that is may help to clear some of the difficulties which have beset the minds of students of the deeper philosophies in the past. In order to avoid serious misunderstanding, it should be firmly impressed upon the mind of the student, however, that there is no infallible revelation of this complicated subject, which includes everything under the sun and above it also.

An infallible exposition would predicate omniscience upon the part of the writer, and even the Elder Brothers tell us that they are sometimes at fault in their judgment, so a book which shall say the last word on the World-Mystery is out of the question, and the writer of the present work does not pretend to give aught but the most elementary teachings of the Rosicrucians.

The Rosicrucian Brotherhood has the most far-reaching, the most logical conception of the World-Mystery of which the writer has gained any knowledge during the many years he has devoted exclusively to the study of this subject. So far as he has been able to investigate, their teachings have been found in accordance with facts as he knows them. Yet he is convinced that *The Rosicrucian Cosmo-Conception* is far from being the last word on the subject; that as we advance greater vistas of truth will open to us and make clear many things which we now "see through a glass, darkly." At the same time he firmly believes that all other philosophies of the future will follow the same main lines, for they appear to be absolutely true.

In view of the foregoing it will be plain that this book is not considered by the writer as the Alpha and Omega, the ultimate of occult knowledge, and even though is entitled *"The Rosicrucian Cosmo-Conception,"* the writer desires to strongly emphasize that is not to be understood as a "faith once for all delivered" to the Rosicrucians by a founder of the Order or by any other individual. It is emphatically stated that *this work embodies only the writer's understanding of the Rosicrucian teachings* concerning the World-Mystery, strengthened by his personal investigations of the inner Worlds, the antenatal and post-mortem states of man, etc. The responsibility upon one who wittingly or unwittingly leads others astray is clearly realized by the writer, and he wishes to guard as far as possible against that contingency, and also to guard others against going wrong inadvertently.

What is said in this work is to be accepted or rejected by the reader according to his own discretion. All care has been used in trying to make plain the teaching; great pains have been taken to put it into words that shall be easily understood. For that reason only one term has been used throughout to convey each idea. The same word will have the same meaning wherever used. When any word descriptive of an idea is first used, the clearest definition possible to the writer is given. None but English terms and the simplest language have been used. The writer has tried to give as exact and definite descriptions of the subject under consideration as possible; to eliminate all ambiguity and to make everything clear. How far he has succeeded must be left to the student to judge; but having used every possible means to convey the teaching, he feels obliged to guard also against the possibility of this work being taken as a verbatim statement of the Rosicrucian teachings. Neglect of this precaution might give undue weight to this work in the minds of some students. That would not be fair to the Brotherhood nor to the reader. It would tend to throw the responsibility upon the Brotherhood for the mistakes which must occur in this as in all other human works. Hence the above warning.

There is an Indian story which says that anyone who has two semi-circular lines on the palm-side of the outer joint of the thumb "carries a grain of rice with him." They assert that such an one will always be well-received, hospitably treated and befriended wherever he goes. The writer has the mark mentioned, and the prognostication has been marvelously true in his case. Friends have met him everywhere and have treated him in such a way that he has been literally overwhelmed with kindness at every turn. So also in the work upon this book. Dr. von Brandis furnished the means whereby he first came into contact with the Rosicrucian teachings. Kingsmill Commander and Jessie Brewster loyally helped him in a literary sense, Mrs. M. E. Rath Merrill and Miss Allene Merrill executed a number of the drawings, and Wm. M. Patterson has given to the writer not only personal services but financial aid *to enable him to publish at cost of printing and handling.* This work has been produced for Love's sake. No one connected with it from first to last has received or will receive a penny of recompense. All have given freely of time and money. Therefore the writer wishes to express his heartfelt gratitude to them all, and the earnest hope that they may find other and greater opportunities for the exercise of unselfish service.

Max Heindel

During the four years which have elapsed since the foregoing paragraphs were written, the writer has continued his investigations of the invisible worlds, and experienced the expansion of consciousness relative to these realms of nature which comes by practice of the precepts taught in the Western Mystery School. Others also who have followed the method of soul-unfoldment herein described as particularly suited to the Western peoples, have likewise been enabled to verify for themselves many things here taught. Thus the writer's understanding of what was given by the Elder Brothers has received some corroboration and seems to have been substantially correct, therefore he feels it a duty to state this for the encouragement of those who are still unable to see for themselves.

If we said that the vital body is built of *prisms* instead of points, it would have been better, for it is by refraction through these minute prisms that the colorless solar fluid changes to a rosy hue as observed by other writers beside the author.

Other new and important discoveries have also been made; for instance, we know now that the Silver Cord is grown anew in each life, that one part sprouts from the seed atom of the desire body in the great vortex of the liver, that the other part grows out of the seed atom of the dense body in the heart, that both parts meet in the seed atom of the vital body in the solar plexus, and that this union of the higher and lower vehicles causes the quickening. Further development of the cord between the heart and solar plexus during the first seven years has an important bearing on the mystery of child life, likewise its fuller growth from the liver to the solar plexus, which takes place during the second septenary period, is a contributory cause of adolescence. Completion of the Silver Cord marks the end of child life, and from that time the solar energy which enters through the spleen and is tinted by refraction through the prismatic seed atom of the vital body located in the solar plexus, commences to give a distinctive and individual coloring to the aura which we observe in adults.

THE FOUR KINGDOMS.

Pure Spirit		WILL IMAGINATION	THE ONE UNIVERSAL SPIRIT			
			Mineral Group Spirit	Plant Group Spirit	Animal Group Spirit	Human Ego
World of Thought	Ego	Abstract Thought				
	Mind	The Focus of Mind — Concrete Thought				
Desire World	Desire Body	Higher Desires — Feeling — Lower Desires				
Physical World	Vital Body	Reflecting-Ether Memory — Light-Ether The-Senses — Life-Ether Propagation — Chemical Assimilation				
	Dense Body	Gas Breath — Liquid Blood — Solid Bone	Mineral	Plant	Animal	Man

Part One – Man's Present Constitution and Method of Development

Chapter One - The Visible and Invisible Worlds

The first step in Occultism is the study of the invisible Worlds. These Worlds are invisible to the majority of people because of the dormancy of the finer and higher senses whereby they may be perceived, in the same way that the Physical World about us is perceived through the physical senses. The majority of people are on a similar footing in regard to the super-physical Worlds as the man who is born blind is to our world of sense; although light and color are all about him, he is unable to see them. To him they are non-existent and incomprehensible, simply because he lacks the sense of sight wherewith to perceive them. Objects he can feel; they seem real; but light and color are beyond his ken.

So with the greater part of humanity. They feel, and see objects and hear sounds in the Physical World, but the other realms, which the clairvoyant calls the higher Worlds, are as incomprehensible to them as light and color are to the blind man. Because the blind man cannot see color and light, however, is no argument against their existence and reality. Neither is it an argument, that because most people cannot see the super-physical Worlds no one can do so. If the blind man obtains his sight, he will see light and color. If the higher senses of those blind to the super-physical Worlds are awakened by proper methods, they also will be able to behold the Worlds which are now hidden from them.

While many people make the mistake of being incredulous concerning the existence or reality of the super-sensuous Worlds, there are also many who go to the other extreme, and, having become convinced of the verity of invisible Worlds, think that when a person is clairvoyant all truth is at once open to him; that when one can "see," he at once "knows all about" these higher Worlds.

This is a great mistake. We readily recognize the fallacy of such a contention in matters of everyday life. We do not think that a man who was born blind, but has obtained his sight, at once "knows all about" the Physical World. Nay, more; we know that even those of us who have been able to see the things about us all our lives are far from having a universal knowledge of them. We know that it requires arduous study and years of application to know about even that infinitesimal part of things that we handle in our daily lives, and reversing the Hermetic aphorism, "as above, so below," we gather at once that it must be the same in the other Worlds. At the same time it is also true that there are much greater facilities for acquiring knowledge in the super-physical Worlds than in our present dense physical condition, but not so great as to eliminate the necessity for close study and the possibility of making a mistake in observation. In fact, all the testimony of reliable and qualified observers prove that much more care in observation is needed there than here.

Clairvoyants must first be trained before their observations are of any real value, and the more proficient they become the more modest they are about telling of what they see; the more they defer to the versions of others, knowing how much there is to learn and realizing how little the single investigator can grasp of all the detail incident to his investigations.

This also accounts for the varied versions, which superficial people think are an argument against the existence of the higher Worlds. They contend that if these Worlds exist, investigators must necessarily bring back identical descriptions. If we take an illustration from everyday life, the fallacy of this becomes apparent.

Suppose a newspaper sends twenty reporters to a city with orders to "write it up." Reporters are, or ought to be, trained observers. It is their business to see everything and they should be able to give as good descriptions as can be expected from any source. Yet it is certain that of the twenty reports, no two would be exactly alike. It is much more likely that they would be totally different. Although some of them might contain leading features in common, others might be unique in quality and quantity of description.

Is it an argument against the existence of the city that these reports differ? Certainly not! It is easily accounted for by the fact that each saw the city from his own particular point of view and instead of these varying reports being confusing and detrimental, it is safe to say that a perusal of them all would give a fuller, better understanding and description of the city than if only one were read and the others were thrown in the wastebasket. Each report would round out and complement the others.

The same is true regarding accounts made by investigators of the higher Worlds. Each has his own peculiar way of looking at things and can describe only what he sees from his particular point of view. The account he gives may differ from those of others, yet all be equally truthful from each individual observer's viewpoint.

It is sometimes asked, Why investigate these Worlds? Why is it not best to take one World at a time; to be content for the present time with the lessons to be learned in the Physical World, and, if there are invisible Worlds why not wait until we reach them before investigating? "Sufficient unto the day is the evil thereof!" Why borrow more?

If we knew without doubt that at some time, sooner or later, each one of us must be transported to a far country where, under new and strange conditions, we must live for many years, is it not reasonable to believe that if we had an opportunity to learn of that country in advance of our removal to it we would gladly do so? Knowledge would render it much easier for us to accommodate ourselves to new conditions.

There is only one certainty in life and that is--Death! As we pass into the beyond and are confronted by new conditions, knowledge of them is sure to be of the greatest help.

But that is not all. To understand the Physical World, which is the world of effects, it is necessary to understand the super-physical World, which is the world of causes. We see street cars in motion and we hear the clicking of telegraph instruments, but the mysterious force which causes phenomena remains invisible to us. We say it is electricity, but the name gives us no explanation. We learn nothing of the force itself; we see and hear only its effects.

If a dish of cold water be placed in an atmosphere of a sufficiently low temperature ice crystals immediately begin to form and we can see the process of their formation. The lines along which the water crystallizes were in it all the time as lines of force but they were invisible until the water congealed. The beautiful "frost flowers" on a windowpane are visible manifestations of currents of the higher Worlds which operate upon us all the time, unrecognized by most of us, but none the less potent.

The higher Worlds are thus the worlds of causes, of forces; and we cannot really understand this lower World unless we know the others and realize the forces and causes of which all material things are but the effects.

As to the reality of these higher Worlds compared with that of the Physical World, strange as it may seem, these higher Worlds, which to the majority appear as mirages, or even less substantial, are, in truth, much more real and the objects in them more lasting and indestructible than the objects in the Physical World. If we take an example we shall readily see this. An architect does not start to build a house by procuring the material and setting the workmen to laying stone upon stone in a haphazard way, without thought or plan. He "thinks the house out." Gradually it takes form in his mind and final-

12

ly there stands a clear idea of the house that is to be--a thought-form of a house.

This house is yet invisible to all but the architect. He makes it objective on paper. He draws the plans and from this objective image of the thought-form the workmen construct the house of wood, iron, or stone, accurately corresponding to the thought-form originated by the architect.

Thus the thought-form becomes a material reality. The materialist would assert that it is much more real, lasting and substantial that the image in the architect's mind. But let us see. The house could not have been constructed without the thought-form. The material object can be destroyed by dynamite, earthquake, fire, or decay, but the thought-form will remain. It will exist as long as the architect lives and from it any number of houses similar to the one destroyed may be constructed. Not even the architect himself can destroy it. Even after his death this thought-form can be recovered by those who are qualified to read the memory of nature, which will be dealt with later.

Having thus seen the reasonableness of such Worlds existing around and about us, and having satisfied ourselves of their reality, their permanency, and of the utility of a knowledge concerning them, we shall now examine them severally and singly, commencing with the Physical World.

Chemical Region of the Physical World

In the Rosicrucian teaching the universe is divided into seven different Worlds, or states of matter, as follows:

1. World of God. 2. World of Virgin Spirits. 3. World of Divine Spirit. 4. World of Life Spirit. 5. World of Thought. 6. Desire World. 7. Physical World.

The division is not arbitrary but necessary, because the substance of each of these Worlds is amenable to laws which are practically inoperative in others. For instance, in the Physical World, matter is subject to gravity, contraction and expansion. In the Desire World there is neither heat nor cold, and forms levitate as easily as they gravitate. Distance and time are also governing factors of existence in the Physical World, but are almost non-existent in the Desire World.

The matter of these worlds also varies in density, the Physical World being the densest of the seven.

Each World is subdivided into seven Regions or subdivisions of matter. In the Physical World, the solids, liquids and gases form the three denser subdivisions, the remaining four being ethers of varying densities. In the other Worlds similar subdivisions are necessary, because the matter of which they are composed is not of uniform density.

There are still two further distinctions to be made. The three dense subdivisions of the Physical World--the solids, liquids and gases--constitute what is termed the Chemical Region. The substance in this Region is the basis of all dense Form.

13

The Ether is also physical matter. It is not homogeneous, as material science alleges, but exists in four different states. It is the medium of ingress for the quickening spirit which imparts *vitality* to the Forms in the Chemical Region. The four finer or etheric subdivisions of the Physical World constitute what is known as the Etheric Region.

In the World of Thought the three higher subdivisions are the basis of abstract thought, hence they, collectively, are called the Region of Abstract Thought. The four denser subdivisions supply the mind-stuff in which we embody and concrete our ideas and are therefore termed the Region of Concrete Thought.

The careful consideration given by the occultist to the characteristics of the Physical World might seem superfluous were it not that he regards all things from a view point differing widely from that of the materialist. The latter recognizes three states of matter--solids, liquids, and gases. These are all chemical, because derived from the chemical constituents of Earth. From this chemical matter all the *forms* of mineral, plant, animal, and man have been built, hence they are as truly chemical as the substances which are commonly so termed. Thus whether we consider the mountain or the cloud that envelops its top, the juice of the plant or the blood of the animal, the spider's thread, the wing of the butterfly or the bones of the elephant, the air we breathe or the water we drink--all are composed of the same chemical substance.

What is it then which determines the conformation of this basic substance into the multiplex variety of Forms which we see about us? It is the One Universal Spirit, expressing Itself in the visible world as four great streams of Life, at varying stages of development. This fourfold spiritual impulse molds the chemical matter of the Earth into variegated forms of the four Kingdoms--mineral, plant, animal, and man. When a form has served its purpose as a vehicle of expression for the three higher streams of life, the chemical forces disintegrate that form so that the matter may be returned to its primordial state, and thus made available for the building of new forms. The spirit or life which molds the form into an expression of itself is, therefore, as extraneous to the matter it uses as a carpenter is apart from and personally independent of the house he builds for his own occupancy.

As all the forms of mineral, plant, animal, and man are chemical, they must logically be as dead and devoid of feeling as chemical matter in it primitive state, and the Rosicrucian asserts that they are.

Some scientists contend that there is feeling in all tissue, living or dead, to whatever kingdom it belongs. They include even the substances ordinarily classed as mineral in their category of objects having feeling, and to prove their contentions they submit diagrams with curves of energy obtained from tests. Another class of investigators teach that there is no feeling even in the human body, except in the brain, which is the *seat* of feeling. They say it is the brain and not the finger which feels the pain when the latter is injured. Thus is the house of Science divided against itself on this as on most other

14

points. The position taken by each is partly right. It depends upon what we mean by "feeling." If we mean simply response to impacts, such as the rebound of a rubber ball that is dropped to the ground, of course it is correct to attribute feeling to mineral, plant, and animal tissue; but if we mean pleasure and pain, love and hate, joy and sorrow, it would be absurd to attribute them to the lower forms of life, to detached tissue, to minerals in their native state, or even to the brain, because such feelings are expressions of the self-conscious immortal spirit, and the brain is only the keyboard of the wonderful instrument upon which the human spirit plays its symphony of life, just as the musician expresses himself upon his violin.

As there are people who are quite unable to understand that there must be and are higher Worlds, so there are some who, having become slightly acquainted with the higher realms, acquire the habit of undervaluing this Physical World. Such an attitude is as incorrect as that of the materialist. The great and wise Beings who carry out the will and design of God placed us in this physical environment to learn great and important lessons which could not be learned under other conditions, and it is our duty to use our knowledge of the higher Worlds in learning to the best of our ability the lessons which this material world has to teach us.

In one sense the Physical World is a sort of model school or experiment station to teach us to work correctly in the others. It does this whether or not we know of the existence of those other worlds, thereby proving the great wisdom of the originators of the plan. If we had knowledge of none but the higher Worlds, we would make many mistakes which would become apparent only when physical conditions are brought to bear as criterion. To illustrate: Let us imagine the case of an inventor working out his idea of a machine. First he builds the machine in thought, and in his mind he sees it complete and in operation, performing most beautifully the work it is designed to do. He next makes a drawing of the design, and in doing so perhaps finds that modifications in his first conception are necessary. When, from the drawings, he has become satisfied that the plan is feasible, he proceeds to build the actual machine from suitable material.

Now it is almost certain that still further modifications will be found necessary before the machine will work as intended. It may be found that it must be entirely remodeled, or even that it is altogether useless in its present form, must be discarded and a new plan evolved. But mark this, for here is the point: the new idea or plan will be formulated for the purpose of eliminating the defects in the useless machine. Had there been no material machine constructed, thereby making evident the faults of the first idea, a second and correct idea would not have been formed.

This applies equally to all conditions of life--social, mercantile, and philanthropic. Many plans appear excellent to those conceiving them, and may even look well on paper, but when brought down in the actual test of utility they often fail. That however, should not discourage us. It is true that "we learn more from our mistakes than from our successes," and the proper light in which to regard this Physical World is as a school of valuable experience, in which we learn lessons of the utmost importance.

The Etheric Region of the Physical World

As soon as we enter this realm of nature we are in the invisible, intangible World, where our ordinary senses fail us, hence this part of the Physical World is practically unexplored by material science.

Air is invisible, yet modern science knows that it exists. By means of instruments its velocity as wind can be measured; by compression it can be made visible as liquid air. With either, however, that is not so easy. Material science finds that it is necessary to account in some way for the transmission of electricity, with or without wires. It is forced to postulate some substance of a finer kind that it knows, and it calls that substance "ether." It does not really know that ether exists, as the ingenuity of the scientist has not, as yet, been able to devise a vessel in which it is possible to confine this substance, which is altogether too elusive for the comfort of the "wizard of the laboratory." He cannot measure, weigh, nor analyze it by any apparatus now at his disposal.

Truly, the achievements of modern science are marvelous. The best way to learn the secrets of nature, however, is not by inventing instruments, but by improving the investigator himself. Man has within himself faculties which eliminate distance and compensate for lack of size to a degree as much greater than the power of telescope and microscope as theirs exceeds that of the naked eye. These senses or faculties are the means of investigation used by occultists. They are their "open sesame" in searching for truth.

To the trained clairvoyant ether is as tangible as are the solids, liquids, and gases of the Chemical Region to ordinary beings. He sees that the vital forces which give life to the mineral forms of plant, animal and man flow into these forms, by means of the four states of ether. The names and specific functions of these four ethers are as follows.

Chemical Ether:

This ether is both positive and negative in manifestation. The forces which cause assimilation and excretion work through it. Assimilation is the process whereby the different nutritive elements of food are incorporated into the body of plant, animal and man. This is carried on by forces with which we shall become acquainted later. They work along the positive pole of the chemical ether and attract the needed elements, building them into the forms concerned. These forces do not act blindly nor mechanically, but in a selective way (well-known to scientists by its effects) thereby accomplishing their purpose, which is the growth and maintenance of the body.

Excretion is carried on by forces of the same kind, but working along the negative pole of the chemical ether. By means of this pole they expel from the body the materials in the food which are unfit for use, or those which have outlived their usefulness in the body and should be expurgated from the sys-

16

tem. This, like all other processes independent of man's volition, is also wide, selective, and not merely mechanical in its operation, as seen, for instance, in the case of the action of the kidneys, where only the urine is filtered through when the organs are in health; but it is known that when the organs are not in health, the valuable albumen is allowed to escape with the urine, the proper selection not being made because of an abnormal condition.

Life Ether:

As the chemical ether is the avenue for the operation of the forces the object of which is the maintenance of the individual form, so the life ether is the avenue for the operation of the forces which have for their object the maintenance of the species--the forces of propagation.

Like the chemical ether, the life ether also has its positive and negative pole. The forces which work along the positive pole are those which work in the female during gestation. They enable her to do the positive, active work of bringing forth a new being. On the other hand the forces which work along the negative pole of the life ether enable the male to produce semen.

In the work on the impregnated ovum of the animal and man, or upon the seed of the plant, the forces working along the positive pole of the life ether produce male plants, animals and men; while the forces which express themselves through the negative pole generate females.

Light Ether:

This ether is both positive and negative, and the forces which play along its positive pole are the forces which generate that blood heat in the higher species of animal and in man, which makes them individual sources of heat. The forces which work along the negative pole of the light ether are those which operate through the senses, manifesting as the passive functions of sight, hearing, feeling, tasting, and smelling. They also build and nourish the eye.

In the cold-blooded animals the positive pole of the light ether is the avenue of the forces which circulate the blood, and the negative forces have the same functions in regard to the eye as in the case of the higher animals and man. Where eyes are lacking, the forces working in the negative pole of the light ether are perhaps building or nourishing other sense organs, as they do in all that have sense organs.

In plants the forces which work along the positive pole of the light ether cause the circulation of the juices of the plant. Thus in winter, when the light ether is not charged with sunlight as in summer, the sap ceases to flow until the summer sun again invests the light ether with its force. The forces which work along the negative pole of the light ether deposit the chlorophyll, the green substance of the plant and also color the flowers. In fact, all color, in all kingdoms is deposited by means of the negative pole of the light ether. Therefore animals have the deepest color on the back and flowers are deepest colored on the side turned towards the light. In the polar regions of the earth, where the rays of the sun are weak, all color is lighter and in some cases is so sparingly deposited that in winter it is withdrawn altogether and the animals become white.

Reflecting Ether:

It has heretofore been stated that the idea of the house which has existed in the mind can be recovered from the memory of nature, even after the death of the architect. Everything that has ever happened has left behind it an ineffaceable picture in this reflecting ether. As the giant ferns of the childhood of the Earth have left their pictures in the coal beds, and as the progress of the glacier of a bygone day may be traced by means of the trail it has left upon the rocks along its path, even so are the thoughts and acts of men ineffaceably recorded by nature in this reflecting ether, where the trained seer may read their story with an accuracy commensurate with his ability.

The reflecting ether deserves its name for more than one reason, for the pictures in it are but *reflections* of the memory of nature. The real memory of nature is found in a much higher realm. In this reflecting ether no thoroughly trained clairvoyant cares to read, as the pictures are blurred and vague compared to those found in the higher realm. Those who read in the reflecting ether are generally those who have no choice, who, in fact, do not know what they are reading. As a rule ordinary psychometrists and mediums obtain their knowledge through the reflecting ether. To some slight extent the pupil of the occult school in the first stages of his training also reads in the reflecting ether, but he is warned by his teacher of the insufficiencies of this ether as a means of acquiring accurate information, so that he does not easily draw wrong conclusions.

This ether is also the medium through which thought makes an impression upon the human brain. It is most intimately connected with the fourth subdivision of the World of Thought. This is the highest of the four subdivisions contained in the Region of Concrete Thought and the home world of the human mind. There a much clearer version of the memory of nature is found than in the reflecting ether.

The Desire World

Like the Physical World, and every other realm of nature, the Desire World has the seven subdivisions called "Regions," but unlike the Physical World, it does not have the great divisions corresponding to the Chemical and Etheric Regions. Desire stuff in the Desire World persists through its seven subdivisions or regions as material for the embodiment of desire. As the Chemical Region is the realm of form and as the Etheric Region is the home of the forces carrying on life activities in those forms, enabling them to live, move and propagate, so the forces in the Desire World, working in the quickened dense body, impel it to move in this or that direction.

If there were only the activities of the Chemical and Etheric Regions of the Physical World, there would be forms having life, able to move, but *with no incentive for so doing*. This incentive is supplied by the cosmic forces active in the Desire World and without this activity playing through every fiber of the vitalized body, urging action in this direction or that, there would be no experience and no moral growth. The functions of the different ethers would take care of the growth of the form, but moral growth would entirely lacking. Evolution would be an impossibility, both as to form and life, for it is only in response to the requirements of spiritual growth that forms evolve to higher states. Thus we at once see the great importance of this realm of nature.

Desires, wishes, passions, and feelings express themselves in the matter of the different regions of the Desire World as form and feature express themselves in the Chemical Region of the Physical World. They take forms which last for a longer or shorter time, according to the intensity of the desire, wish, or feeling embodied in them. In the Desire World the distinction between the forces and the matter is not so definite and apparent as in the Physical World. One might almost say that here the ideas of force and matter are identical or interchangeable. It is not quite so, but we may say that to a certain extent the Desire World consists of force-matter.

When speaking of the matter of the Desire World, it is true that it is one degree less dense than the matter of the Physical World, but we entertain an entirely wrong idea if we imagine it is *finer* physical matter. That idea, though held by many who have studied occult philosophies, is entirely erroneous. The wrong impression is caused principally by the difficulty of giving the full and accurate description necessary for a thorough understanding of the higher worlds. Unfortunately, our language is descriptive of material things and therefore entirely inadequate to describe the conditions of the super-physical realms, hence all that is said about these realms must be taken tentatively, as similes, rather than as accurate descriptions.

Though the mountain and the daisy, the man, the horse, and a piece of iron, are composed of one ultimate atomic substance, we do not say that the daisy is a finer form of iron. Similarly it is impossible to explain in words the change or difference in physical matter when it is broken up into desire-stuff. If there were no difference it would be amenable to the laws of the Physical World, which it is not.

The law of matter of the Chemical Region is inertia-the tendency to remain *in status quo*. It takes a certain amount of force to overcome this inertia and cause a body which is at rest to move, or to stop a body in motion. Not so with the matter of the Desire World. That matter itself is almost living. It is in unceasing motion, fluid, taking all imaginable and unimaginable forms with inconceivable facility and rapidity, at the same time coruscating and scintillating in a thousand ever-changing shades of color, incomparable to anything we know in this physical state of consciousness. Something very faintly resembling the action and appearance of this matter will be seen in the play of colors on an abalone shell when held in the sunlight and moved to and fro.

That is what the Desire World is--ever-changing light and color--in which the forces of animal and man intermingle with the forces of innumerable Hierarchies of spiritual beings which do not appear in our Physical World, but are as active in the Desire World as we are here. Some of them will be dealt with later and their connection with man's evolution described.

The forces sent out by this vast and varied hose of Beings mold the ever-changing matter of the Desire World into innumerable and differing forms of more or less durability, according to the kinetic energy of the impulse which gave them birth.

From this slight description it may be understood how difficult it is for a neophyte who has just had his inner eyes opened to find his balance in the World of Desire. The trained clairvoyant soon ceases to wonder at the impossible descriptions sometimes brought through by mediums. They may be perfectly honest, but the possibilities of parallax, and of getting out of focus are legion, and of the subtlest nature, and the real wonder is that they ever communicate anything correctly. All of us had to learn to see, in the days of our infancy, as we may readily find by watching a young babe. It will be found that the little one will reach for objects on the other side of the room or the street, or for the Moon. He is entirely unable to gauge distances. The blind man who has been made to see will, at first, often close his eyes to walk from one place to another, declaring, until he has learned to use his eyes, that it is easier to walk by feeling than by sight. So the one whose inner organs of perception have been vivified must also be trained in the use of his newly acquired faculty. At first the neophyte will try to apply to the Desire World the knowledge derived from his experience in the Physical World, because he has not yet learned the laws of the world into which he is entering. This is the source of a vast amount of trouble and perplexity. Before he can understand, he must become as a little child, which imbibed knowledge without reference to any previous experience.

To arrive at a correct understanding of the Desire World it is necessary to realize that it is the world of feeling, desires, and emotions. These are all under the domination of two great forces--Attraction and Repulsion, which act in a different way in the three denser Regions of the Desire World from that in which they act in the three finer or upper Regions, while the central Region may be called neutral ground.

This central Region is the Region of feeling. Here interest in or indifference to an object or an idea sways the balance in favor of one of the two previously mentioned forces, thereby relegating the object or idea to the three higher or the three lower Regions of the Desire World, or else they will expel it. We shall see presently how this is accomplished.

In the finest and rarest substance of the three higher Regions of the Desire World the force of Attraction alone holds sway, but it is also present in some degree in the denser matter of the three lower Regions, where it works against the force of Repulsion, which is dominant there. The disintegrating force of Repulsion would soon destroy every form coming into these three lower Regions were it not that it is thus counteracted. In the densest or lowest Region, where it is strongest, it tears and shatters the forms built there in a way dreadful to see, yet it is not a fatalistic force. Nothing in nature is vandalistic. All that appears so is but working towards good. So with this force in its work in the lowest Region of the Desire World. The forms here are demoniac creations, built by the coarsest passions and desires of man and beast.

The tendency of every form in the Desire World is to attract itself all it can of a like nature and grow thereby. If this tendency to attraction were predominate in the lowest Regions, evil would grow like a weed. There would be anarchy instead of order in the Cosmos. This prevented by the preponderating power of the force of Repulsion in this Region. When a coarse desire form is being attracted to another of the same nature, there is a disharmony in their vibrations, whereby one has a disintegrating effect upon the other. Thus, instead of uniting and amalgamating evil with evil, they act with mutual destructiveness and in that way the evil in the world is kept within reasonable bounds. When we understand the working of the twin forces in this respect we are in a position to understand the occult maxim, "A lie is both murder and suicide in the Desire World."

Anything happening in the Physical World is reflected in all the other realms of nature and, as we have seen, builds its appropriate form in the Desire World. When a true account of the occurrence is given, another form is built, exactly like the first. They are then drawn together and coalesce, strengthening each other. If, however, an untrue is given, a form different from and antagonistic to the first, or true one, is created. As they deal with the same occurrence, they are drawn together, but as their vibrations are different they act upon each other with mutual destructiveness. Therefore, evil and malicious lies can kill anything that is good, if they are strong enough and repeated often enough. But, conversely, seeking for the good in evil will, in time, transmute the evil into good. If the form that is built to minimize the evil is weak, it will have no effect and will be destroyed by the evil form, but if it is strong and frequently repeated it will have the effect of disintegrating the evil and substituting the good. That effect, be it distinctly understood, is not brought about by lying, nor denying the evil, but by looking for the good. The occult scientist practices very rigidly this principle of looking for good in all things, because he knows what a power it possesses in keeping down evil.

There is a story of Christ which illustrates this point. Once when walking with His disciples they passed the decaying and ill-smelling carcass of a dog. The disciples turned in disgust, commenting upon the nauseating nature of this sight; but Christ looked at the dead body and said "Pearls are not whiter than its teeth." He was determined to find the good, because He knew the beneficial effect which would result in the Desire World from giving it expression.

The lowest Region of the Desire World is called "the Region of Passion and Sensual Desire." The second subdivision is best described by the name of

"Region of Impressionability." Here the effect of the twin forces of Attraction and Repulsion is evenly balanced. This is a neutral Region, hence all our impressions which are built of the matter of this Region are neutral. Only when the twin feelings, which we shall meet in the fourth Region, are brought to bear, do the twin forces come into play. The mere impression of anything, however, in and of itself, is entirely separate from the feeling it engenders. The impression is neutral and is an activity of the second Region of the Desire World, where pictures are formed by the forces of sense-perception in the vital body of man.

In the third Region of the Desire World, the force of Attraction, the integrating, upbuilding force, has already gained the upper hand over the force of Repulsion, with its destructive tendency. When we understand that the mainspring in this force of Repulsion is self-assertion, a pushing away of all others that it may have room, we shall understand that it gives way most easily to a desire for other things, so that the substance of the third Region of the Desire World is principally dominated by the force of Attraction towards other things, but in a selfish way, and therefore this is the Region of Wishes.

The Region of Coarse Desires may be likened to the solids in the Physical World; the Region of Impressionability to the fluids; and the fluctuating, evanescent nature of the Region of Wishes will make that compare with the gaseous portion of the Physical World. These three Regions give the substance for the forms which make for experience, soul-growth and evolution, purging the altogether destructive and retaining the materials which may be used for progress.

The fourth Region of the Desire World is the "Region of Feeling." From it comes the feeling concerning the already described forms and upon the feeling engendered by them depends the life which they have for us and also their effect upon us. Whether the objects and ideas presented are good or bad in themselves is not important this stage. It is our feeling, whether of Interest or Indifference that is the determining factor as to the fate of the object or idea.

If the feeling with which we meet an impression of an object or an idea is Interest, it has the same effect upon that impression as sunlight and air have upon a plant. That idea will grow and flourish in our lives. If, on the other hand, we meet an impression or idea with Indifference, it withers as does a plant when put in a dark cellar.

Thus from this central Region of the Desire World come the incentive to action, or the decision to refrain there from (though the latter is also action in the eyes of the occult scientist), for at the present stage of our development the twin feelings, Interest and Indifference furnish the incentive to action and are the springs that move the world. At a later stage these feelings will cease to have any weight. Then the determining factor will be *duty*.

Interest starts the forces of Attraction or Repulsion.

Indifference simply withers the object or idea against which it is directed, so far as our connection with it is concerned.

If our interest in an object or an idea generates Repulsion, that naturally causes us to expurgate from our lives any connection with the object or idea which roused it; but there is a great difference between the action of the force of Repulsion and the mere feeling of Indifference. Perhaps an illustration will make more clear the operation of the twin Feelings and the twin Forces.

Three men are walking along a road. They see a sick dog; it is covered with sores and is evidently suffering intensely from pain and thirst. This much is evident to all three men-their senses tell them that. Now Feeling comes. Two of them take an "interest" in the animal, but in the third there is a feeling of "indifference." He passes on, leaving the dog to its fate. The others remain; they are both interested, but each manifests it in a quite different way. The interest of one man is sympathetic and helpful, impelling him to care for the poor beast, to assuage pains and nurse it back to health. In him the feeling of interest has aroused the force of Attraction. The other man's interest is of a different kind. He sees only a loathsome sight which is revolting to him and wishes to rid himself and the world of it as quickly as possible. He advises killing the animal outright and burying it. In him the feeling of interest generates the destructive force of Repulsion.

When the feeling of Interest arouses the force of Attraction and it is directed toward low objects and desires, these work themselves out in the lower Regions of the Desire World, where the counteracting force of Repulsion operates, as previously described. From the battle of the twin forces-- Attraction and Repulsion--results all the pain and suffering incident to wrongdoing or misdirected effort, whether intentional or otherwise.

Thus we may see how very important is the Feeling we have concerning anything, for upon that depends the nature of the atmosphere we create for ourselves. If we love the good, we shall keep and nourish as guardian angels all that is good about us; if the reverse, we shall people our path with demons and our own breeding.

The names of the three upper Regions of the Desire World are "Region of Soul-Life," "Region of Soul-Light," and "Region of Soul-Power." In these abide Art, Altruism, Philanthropy, and all the activities of the higher soul-life. When we think of these Regions as radiating the qualities indicated by their names, into the forms of the three lower Regions, we shall understand correctly the higher and lower activities. Soul-power, however, may for a time be used for evil purposes as well as for good, but eventually the force of Repulsion destroys vice and the force of Attraction builds virtue upon its shattered ruins. All things, in the ultimate, work together for *good.*

The Physical and the Desire Worlds are not separated from each other by space. They are "closer than hands and feet." It is not necessary to move to get from one to the other, nor from one Region to the next. Just as solids, liquids, and gases are all together in our bodies, inter-penetrating one another, so are the different Regions of the Desire World within us also. We may again compare the lines of force along which ice-crystals form in water to the invis-

23

ible causes originating in the Desire World, which appear in the Physical World and give us the incentive to action, in whatever direction it may be.

The Desire World, with its innumerable inhabitants, permeates the Physical World, as the lines of force do the water--invisibly, but everywhere present and potent as the cause of everything in the Physical World.

The World of Thought

The World of Thought also consists of seven Regions of varying qualities and densities, and, like the Physical World, the World of Thought is divided into two main divisions--the Region of Concrete Thought, comprising the four densest Regions; and the Region of Abstract Thought, comprising the three Regions of finest substance. This World of Thought is the central one of the five Worlds from which man obtains his vehicles. Here spirit and body meet. It is also the highest of the three Worlds in which man's evolution is being carried forward at the present time, the two higher Worlds being practically in abeyance as yet, so far as man is concerned.

We know that the materials of the Chemical Region are used in building all physical forms. These forms are given life and the power of motion by the forces at work in the Etheric Region, and some of these living forms are stirred into activity by means of the twin Feelings of the Desire World. The Region of Concrete Thought furnishes the mind-stuff in which ideas generated in the Region of Abstract Thought clothe themselves as *thought-forms,* to act as regulators and balance wheels upon the impulses engendered in the Desire World by impacts from the phenomenal World.

Thus we see how the three Worlds, in which man is at present evolving, complement one another, making a whole that shows forth the Supreme Wisdom of the Great Architect of the system to which we belong, and Whom we reverence by the holy name of God.

Taking a more detailed view of the several divisions of the Region of Concrete Thought we find that the archetypes of *physical* form no matter to what kingdom they may belong, are found in its lowest subdivision, or the "Continental Region." In this Continental Region are also the archetypes of the continents and the isles of the world, and corresponding to these archetypes are they fashioned. Modifications in the crust of the Earth must first be wrought in the Continental Region. Not until the archetypal model has been changed can the Intelligences which we (to hide our ignorance concerning them) call the "Laws of Nature," bring about the physical conditions which alter the physical features of the Earth according to the modifications designed by the Hierarchies in charge of evolution. They plan changes as an architect plans the alteration of a building before the workmen give it concrete expression. In like manner are changes in the *flora* and *fauna* due to metamorphoses in their respective archetypes.

When we speak of the archetypes of all the different forms in the dense world it must not be thought that these archetypes are merely models in the

24

same sense in which we speak of an object constructed in miniature, or in some material other than that appropriate for its proper and final use. They are not merely likenesses nor models of the forms we see about us, but are *creative* archetypes; that is, they fashion the forms of the Physical World in their own likeness or likenesses, for often many work together to form one certain species, each archetype giving part of itself to build the required form.

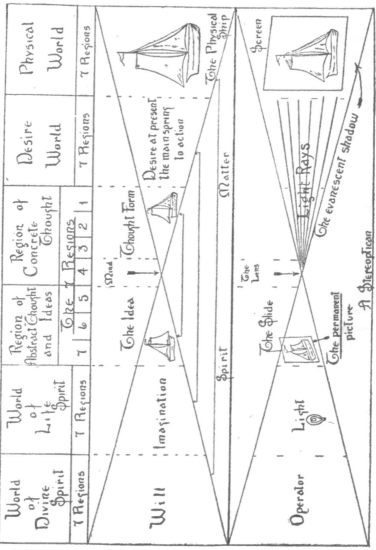

Diagram 1—The Relative Permanency of the Visible and Invisible Worlds.

(Illustrated by comparison with a stereopticon.)

25

DIAGRAM 2

THE SEVEN WORLDS			
WORLD OF GOD	Consisting of △GOD 7 Regions.		
WORLD OF VIRGIN SPIRITS	This World consists of 7 Regions and is the abode of the Virgin Spirits when they have been differentiated in God before the pilgrimage through matter.	Vehicles of Man	
WORLD OF DIVINE SPIRIT	Consists of 7 Regions and is the abode of the highest spiritual influence in man.	Divine Spirit	
WORLD OF LIFE SPIRIT	Consists of 7 Regions and is the abode of the second aspect of the threefold spirit in man.	Life Spirit	THE EGO
WORLD OF THOUGHT — REGION OF ABSTRACT THOUGHT	7th Region contains the germinal idea of form in mineral, plant, animal and man. 6th Region contains germinal idea of life in plant, animal and man. 5th Region contains germinal idea of desire and emotion in animal and man; abode of 3rd aspect of spirit in man.	Human Spirit	
REGION OF CONCRETE THOUGHT	4th Region contains the archetypal forces and the human mind.. It is the focusing point through which the spirit mirrors itself in matter. 3rd Region archetypes of desire and emotion. 2nd Region archetypes of universal vitality. 1st Region archetypes of form.	Mind	THE LINK BETWEEN
DESIRE WORLD	7th Region Soul-Power 6th Region Soul-Light 5th Region Soul-Life. } ———— Attraction 4th Region Feeling { Interest Indifference. 3rd Region Wishes 2nd Region Impressionability 1st Region Passion and Low Desire } Repulsion.	Desire Body	
PHYSICAL WORLD — ETHERIC REGION	7th Region Reflecting ether, memory of nature. 6th Region Light ether, medium of sense perception. 5th Region Life ether, medium for propagation. 4th Region Chemical ether. medium for assimilation and excretion.	Vital Body	THE PERSONALITY
CHEMICAL REGION	3rd Region Gases. 2nd Region Liquids. 1st Region Solids.	Dense Body	

The second subdivision of the Region of Concrete Thought is called the "Oceanic Region." It is best described as flowing, pulsating vitality. All the forces that work through the four ethers which constitute the Etheric Region

26

are there seen as archetypes. It is a stream of flowing life, pulsating through all forms, as blood pulsates through the body, the same life in all forms. Here the trained clairvoyant sees how true it is that "all life is one."

The "Aerial Region" is the third division of the Region of Concrete Thought. Here we find the archetype of desires, passions, wishes, feelings, and emotions such as we experience in the Desire World. Here all the activities of the Desire World appear as atmospheric conditions. Like the kiss of summer breeze come the feelings of pleasure and joy to the clairvoyant sense; as the sighing of the wind in the tree-tops seem the longings of the soul and like flashes of lighting the passions of warring nations. In this atmosphere of the Region of Concrete Thought are also pictures of the emotions of man and beast.

The "Region of Archetypal Forces" is the fourth division of the Region of Concrete Thought. It is the central and most important region in the five Worlds wherein man's entire evolution is carried on. On the one side of this Region are the three higher Regions of the World of Thought, the World of Life Spirit and the World of Divine Spirit. On the other side of this Region of Archetypal Forces are the three lower Regions of the World of Thought, the Desire and the Physical Worlds. Thus this Region becomes a sort of "crux," bounded on one side by the Realms of Spirit, on the other by the Worlds of Form. It is a focusing point, where Spirit reflects itself in matter.

As the name implies, this Region is the home of the Archetypal Forces which direct the activity of the archetypes in the Region of Concrete Thought. From this Region Spirit works on matter in a formative manner. Diagram 1 shows the idea in a schematic way the forms in the lower World being reflections of the Spirit in the higher Worlds. The fifth Region, which is the one nearest to the focusing point on the Spirit side, reflects itself in the third Region, which is nearest the focusing point on the Form side. The sixth Region reflects itself in the second and the seventh reflects itself in the first.

The whole of the Region of Abstract thought is reflected in the World of Desire; the World of Life Spirit in the Etheric Region of the Physical World; and the World of Divine Spirit in the Chemical Region of the Physical World.

Diagram 2 will give a comprehensive idea of the seven Worlds which are the sphere of our development, but we must carefully keep in mind that these Worlds are not placed one above another, as shown in the diagram. They inter-penetrate--that is to say, that as in the case where the relation of the Physical World and the Desire World was compared, where we likened the Desire World to the lines of force in freezing water and the water itself to the Physical World, in the same way we may think of the lines of force as being any of the seven Worlds, and the water, as in our illustration, would correspond to the next denser World in the scale. Another illustration may perhaps make the subject clearer.

Let us use a spherical sponge to represent the dense earth--the Chemical Region. Imagine that sand permeates every part of the sponge and also forms a layer outside the sponge. Let the sand represent the Etheric Region, which

27

in a similar manner permeates the dense earth and extends beyond its atmosphere.

Let us further imagine this sponge and sand immersed in a spherical glass vessel filled with clear water, and a little larger than the sponge and sand. We place the sponge and sand in the center of the vessel as the yolk is placed in the center of an egg. We have now a space of clear water between the sand and the vessel. The water as a whole will represent the Desire World, for just as the water percolates between the grains of sand, through every pore of the sponge, and forms that clear layer, so the Desire World permeates both the dense Earth and the ether and extends beyond both of these substances.

We know there is air in water, and if we think of the air in the water (in our illustration), as representing the World of Thought, we shall have a firm mental picture of the way in which the World of Thought, being finer and more subtle, inter-penetrates the two denser Worlds.

Finally, imagine that the vessel containing the sponge, sand and water is placed in the center of a large spherical vessel; then the air in the space between the two vessels would represent that part of the World of Thought which extends beyond the Desire World.

Each of the planets in our solar system has three such inter-penetrating Worlds, and if we think of each of the planets consisting of three Worlds as being individual sponges, and of the fourth World, the World of Life Spirit, as being the water in a large vessel where these three cold separate sponges swim, we shall understand that as the water in the vessel fills the space between the sponges and percolates through them, so the World of Life Spirit pervades inter-planetary space and inter-penetrates the individual planets. It forms a common bond between them, so that as it is necessary to have a boat and be able to control it, if we wish to sail from America to Africa, so it is necessary to have a vehicle correlated to the World of Life Spirit under our conscious control in order to be able to travel from one planet to another.

In a manner similar to that in which the World of Life Spirit correlates us to the other planets in our own solar system does the World of Divine Spirit correlate us to the other solar systems. We may regard the solar systems as separate sponges, swimming in a World of Divine Spirit, and thus it will be apparent that in order to travel from one solar system to another it would be necessary to be able to function consciously in the highest vehicle of man, the Divine Spirit.

Chapter Two - The Four Kingdoms

The three Worlds of our planet are at present the field of evolution for a number of different kingdoms of life, at various stages of development. Only four of these need concern us at present, viz.: the mineral, plant, animal, and human kingdoms.

These four kingdoms are related to the three Worlds in different ways, according to the progress these groups of evolving life have made in the school of experience. So far as form is concerned the dense bodies of all the kingdoms are composed of the same chemical substances--the solids, liquids, and gases of the Chemical Region. The dense body of a man is as truly a chemical compound as is the stone, although the latter is ensouled by mineral life only. But even when speaking from the purely physical standpoint, and laying aside all other considerations for the time being, there are several important differences when we compare the dense body of the human being with the mineral of the Earth. Man moves, grows, and propagates his species--the mineral, in its native state, does none of these things.

Comparing man with the forms of the plant kingdom, we find that both plant and man have a dense body, capable of growth and propagation. But Man has faculties not possessed by the plant. He feels, has the power of motion, and the faculty of perceiving things exterior to himself.

When we compare man with the animal we see that both have the faculties of feeling, motion, growth, propagation, and sense-perception. In addition, man has the faculty of speech, a superior structure of the brain, and also hands--which are a very great physical advantage. We may note especially the development of the thumb, which makes the hand much more valuable than even that of the anthropoid. Man has also evolved a definite language in which to express his feelings and thoughts, all of which places the dense body of the human being in a class by itself, beyond the three lower kingdoms.

To account for these differences in the four kingdoms we must go to the invisible Worlds, and seek the causes which give one kingdom that which is denied to another.

To function in any world, and express the qualities peculiar to it, we must first possess a vehicle made of its material. In order to function in the dense Physical World it is necessary to have a dense body, adapted to our environment. Otherwise we should be ghosts, as they are commonly called, and be invisible to most physical beings. So we must have a vital body before we can express life, grow, or externalize the other qualities peculiar to the Etheric Region.

To show feeling and emotion it is necessary to have a vehicle composed of the materials of the Desire World, and a mind formed of the substance of the Region of Concrete Thought is necessary to render thinking possible.

When we examine the four kingdoms in relation to the Etheric Region, we find that the mineral does not possess a separate vital body, and at once we see the reason why it cannot grow, propagate, or show sentient life.

As an hypothesis necessary to account for other known facts, material science holds that in the densest solid, as in the rarest and most attenuated gas, no two atoms touch each other; that there is an envelope of ether around each atom; that the atoms in the universe float in an ocean of ether.

The occult scientist knows this to be true of the Chemical Region and that the mineral does not possess a separate vital body of ether. And as it is the planetary ether alone which envelops the atoms of the mineral, that makes the difference described. It is necessary, as we have shown, to have a separate, vital *body*, desire *body*, etc., to express the qualities of a particular realm, because the atoms of the World of Desire, of the World of Thought and even of the Higher Worlds, inter-penetrate the Mineral as well as the dense human body, and if the inter-penetration of the planetary ether, which is the ether that envelops the atoms of the mineral, were enough to make it feel and propagate its inter-penetration by the planetary World of Thought would also be sufficient to make it think. This it cannot do, because it lacks a *separate* vehicle. It is penetrated by the planetary ether only, and is therefore incapable of individual growth. Only the lowest of the four states of ether--the chemical--is active in the mineral. The chemical forces in minerals are due to that fact.

When we consider plant, animal, and man in relation to the Etheric Region we note that each has a separate, vital body, in addition to being penetrated by the planetary ether which forms the Etheric Region. There is a difference, however, between the vital bodies of the plants and the vital bodies of animal and man. In the vital body of the plant only the chemical and the life ethers are fully active. Hence the plant can grow by the action of the chemical ether and propagate its species through the activity of the life ether of the separate, vital body which it possesses. The light ether is present, but is partially latent or dormant and reflecting ether is lacking. Therefore it is evident that the faculties of sense-perception and memory, which are the qualities of these ethers, cannot be expressed by the plant kingdom.

Turning our attention to the vital body of the animal we find that in it the chemical, life and light ethers are dynamically active. Hence the animal has the faculties of assimilation and growth, caused by the activities of the chemical ether; and the faculty of propagation by means of the life ether--these being the same as in plants. But in addition, it has the faculties of generating internal heat and of sense-perception. The fourth ether, however, is inactive in the animal, hence it has no thought nor memory. That which appears as such will be shown later to be of a different nature.

When we analyze the human being, we find that in him all four ethers are dynamically active in the highly organized vital body. By means of the activities of the chemical he is able to assimilate food and to grow; the forces at work in the life ether enable him to propagate his species; the forces in the light ether supply the dense body with heat, work on the nervous system and muscles, thus opening the doors of communication with the outside world by way of the senses; and the reflecting ether enables the spirit to control its vehicle by means of thought. This ether also stores past experience as memory.

The vital body of plant, animal, and man, extends beyond the periphery of the dense body as the Etheric Region, which is the vital body of a planet, extends beyond its dense part, showing again the truth of the Hermetic axiom "As above, so below." The distance of this extension of the vital body of man is about an inch and a half. The part which is outside the dense body is very luminous and about the color of a new-blown peach-blossom. It is often seen by persons having very slight involuntary clairvoyance. The writer has found, when speaking with such persons, that they frequently are not aware they see anything unusual and do not know what they see.

The dense body is built into the matrix of this vital body during ante-natal life, and with one exception, it is an exact copy, molecule for molecule, of the vital body. As the lines of force in freezing water are the avenues of formation for ice crystals, so the lines of force in the vital body determine the shape of the dense body. All through life the vital body is the builder and restorer of the dense form. Were it not for the etheric heart the dense heart would break quickly under the constant strain we put upon it. All the abuses to which we subject the dense body are counteracted, so far as lies in its power, by the vital body, which is continually fighting against the death of the dense body.

The exception mentioned above is that the vital body of a man is female or negative, while that of a woman is male or positive. In that fact we have the key to numerous puzzling problems of life. That woman gives way to her emotions is due to the polarity noted, for her positive, vital body generates an excess of blood and causes her to labor under an enormous internal pressure that would break the physical casement were not a safety-valve provided in the periodical flow, and another in the tears which relieve the pressure on special occasions--for tears are "white bleeding."

Man may have and has as strong emotions as woman, but he is usually able to suppress them without tears, because his negative vital body does not generate more blood than he can comfortably control.

Unlike the higher vehicles of humanity, the vital body (except under certain circumstances, to be explained when the subject of "Initiation" is dealt with) does not ordinarily leave the dense body until the death of the latter. Then the chemical forces of the dense body are no longer held in check by the evolving life. They proceed to restore the matter to its primordial condition by disintegration so that it may be available for the formation of other forms in the economy of nature. Disintegration is thus due to the activity of the planetary forces in the chemical ether.

In texture the vital body may be crudely compared to one of those picture frames made of hundreds of little pieces of wood which interlock and present innumerable points to the observer. These points enter into the hollow centers of the dense atoms, imbuing them with vital force that sets them vibrating at a higher rate than that of the mineral of the earth which is not thus accelerated and ensouled.

When a person is drowning, or falling from a height, or freezing, the vital body leaves the dense body, the atoms of which become temporarily inert in consequence, but at resuscitation it re-enters the dense body and the "points" are again inserted in the dense atoms. The inertia of the atoms caus-es them to resist the resumption of vibration and that is the cause of the in-tense prickly pain and the tingling sensation noted at such times, but not or-dinarily, for the same reason that we become conscious of the starting or stopping of a clock, but are oblivious to its tick when it is running.

There are certain cases where the vital body partly leaves the dense body, such as when a hand "goes to sleep." Then the etheric hand of the vital body may be seen hanging below the dense arm like a glove and the points cause the peculiar pricking sensation felt when the etheric hand re-enters the dense hand. Sometimes in hypnosis the head of the vital body divides and hangs outside the dense head, one half over each shoulder, or lies around the neck like the collar of a sweater. The absence of prickly sensation at awaken-ing in cases like this is because during the hypnosis part of the hypnotist's vital body had been substituted for that of the victim.

When anesthetics are used the vital body is partially driven out, along with the higher vehicles, and if the application is too strong and the life ether is driven out, death ensues. This same phenomenon may also be observed in the case of materializing mediums. In fact the difference between a material-izing medium and an ordinary man or woman is just this: In the ordinary man or woman the vital body and the dense body are, at the present stage of evolution, quite firmly interlocked, while in the medium they are loosely connected. It has not always been so, and the time will come again when the vital body may normally leave the dense vehicle, but that is not normally ac-complished at present. When a medium allows his or her vital body to be used by entities from the Desire World who wish to materialize, the vital body generally oozes from the left side--through the spleen, which is its par-ticular "gate." Then the vital forces cannot flow into the body as they do normally, the medium becomes greatly exhausted, and some of them resort to stimulants to counteract the effects, in time becoming incurable drunk-ards.

The vital force from the sun, which surrounds us as a colorless fluid, is ab-sorbed by the vital body through the etheric counterpart of the spleen, wherein in undergoes a curious transformation of color. It becomes pale rose-hued and spreads along the nerves all over the dense body. It is to the nervous system what the force of electricity is to a telegraph system. Though there be wires, instruments, and telegraph operators all in order, if the elec-tricity is lacking, no message can be sent. The Ego, the brain, and the nervous system may be in seemingly perfect order, but if the vital force be lacking to carry the message of the Ego through the nerves to the muscles, the dense body will remain inert. This is exactly what happens when part of the dense body becomes paralyzed. The vital body has become diseased and the vital force can no longer flow. In such cases, as in most sickness, the trouble is with the finer invisible vehicles. In conscious or unconscious recognition of this fact, the most successful physicians use suggestion--which works upon the higher vehicles--as aid to medicine. The more a physician can imbue his patient with faith and hope, the speedier disease will vanish and give place to perfect health.

During the health the vital body specializes a superabundance of vital force, which, after passing through a dense body, radiates in straight lines in every direction from the periphery thereof, as the radii of a circle do from the center; but during ill-health, when the vital body becomes attenuated, it is not able to draw to itself the same amount of force and in addition the dense body is feeding upon it. Then the lines of the vital fluid which pass out from the body are crumpled and bent, showing the lack of force behind them. In health the great force of these radiations carries with it germs and microbes which are inimical to the health of the dense body, but in sickness, when the vital force is weak, these emanations do not so readily eliminate disease germs. Therefore the danger of contracting disease is much greater when the vital forces are low than when one is in robust health.

In cases where parts of the dense body are amputated, only the planetary ether accompanies the separated part. The separate vital body and the dense body disintegrate synchronously after death. So with the etheric counterpart of the amputated limb. It will gradually disintegrate as the dense member decays, but in the meantime the fact that the man still possesses the etheric limb accounts for his assertion that he can feel his fingers or suffers pain in them. There is also a connection with a buried member, irrespective of distance. A case is on record where a man felt severe pain, as if a nail had been driven into the flesh of an amputated limb, and he persisted until the limb was exhumed, when it was found that a nail had been driven into it at the time it was boxed for burial. The nail was removed and the pain instantly stopped. It is also in accordance with these facts that people complain of pain in a limb for perhaps two or three years after the amputation. The pain will then cease. This is because the disease remains in the still undetached etheric limb, but as the amputated part disintegrates, the etheric limb follows suit and thus the pain ceases.

Having noted the relations of the four kingdoms to the Etheric Region of the Physical World, we will next turn our attention to their relation to the Desire World.

Here we find that both minerals and plants lack a separate desire body. They are permeated only by the planetary desire body, the Desire World. Lacking the separate vehicle, they are incapable of feeling, desire, and emotion, which are faculties pertaining to the Desire World. When a stone is broken, it does not feel; but it would be wrong to infer that there is no feeling connected with such an action. That is the materialistic view, or the view taken by the uncomprehending multitude. The occult scientist knows that there is no act, great or small, which is not felt throughout the universe, and even though the stone, because it has no separate desire body, cannot feel, the Spirit of the Earth feels because it is Earth's desire body that permeates the stone. When a man cuts his finger, the finger, having no separate desire body, does not feel the pain, but the man does, because it is his desire body

33

which permeates the finger. If a plant is torn up by the roots, it is felt by the Spirit of the Earth as a man would feel if a hair were torn from his head. This Earth is a living, feeling body, and all the forms which are without separate desire bodies through which their informing spirits may experience feeling, are included in the desire body of the Earth and *that* desire body has feeling. The breaking of a stone and the breaking off of flowers are productive of pleasure to the Earth, while the pulling out of plants by the root causes pain. The reason is given in the latter part of this work, for at this stage of our study the explanation would be incomprehensible to the general reader.

The planetary Desire World pulsates through the dense and vital bodies of animal and man in the same way that it penetrates the mineral and plant, but in addition to this, animal and man have separate desire bodies, which enable them to feel desire, emotion and passion. There is a difference, however. The desire body of the animal is built entirely of the material of the denser regions of the Desire World, while in the case of even the lowest of human races a little matter of the higher Regions enters into the composition of the desire body. The feelings of animals and the lowest human races are almost entirely concerned with the gratification of the lowest desires and passions which find their expression in the matter of the lower Regions of the Desire World. Hence, in order that they may have such emotions to educate them for something higher, it is necessary that they should have the corresponding materials in their desire bodies. As man progresses in the school of life, his experiences teach him, and his desires become purer and better. Thus by degrees the material of his desire body undergoes a corresponding change. The purer and brighter material of the higher Regions of the Desire World replaces the murky colors of the lower part. The desire body also grows in size, so that in a saint it is truly a glorious object to behold, the purity of its colors and its luminous transparency being beyond adequate simile. It must be seen to be appreciated.

At present the materials of both the lower and the higher Regions enter into the composition of the desire bodies of the great majority of mankind. None are so bad that they have not some good trait. This is expressed in the materials of the higher Regions which we find in their desire bodies. But, on the other hand, very, very few are so good that they do not use some of the materials of the lower Regions.

In the same way that the planetary vital and desire bodies inter-penetrate the dense material of the Earth, as we saw in the illustration of the sponge, the sand and the water, so the vital and desire bodies inter-penetrate the dense body of plant, animal, and man. But during the life of man his desire body is not shaped like his dense and vital bodies. After death it assumes that shape. During life it has the appearance of a luminous ovoid which, in waking hours, completely surrounds the dense body, as the albumen does the yolk of an egg. It extends from twelve to sixteen inches beyond the dense body. In this desire body there are a number of sense centers, but, in the great majority of people, they are latent. It is the awakening of these centers of perception that corresponds to the opening of the blind man's eyes in our former illustration. The matter in the human desire body is in incessant motion of inconceivable rapidity. There is in it no settled place for any particle, as in the dense body. The matter that is at the head one moment may be at the feet in the next and back again. There are no organs in the desire body, as in the dense and vital bodies, but there are centers of perception, which, when active, appear as vortices, always remaining in the same relative position to the dense body, most of them about the head. In the majority of people they are mere eddies and are of no use as centers of perception. They may be awakened in all, however, but different methods produce different results.

In the involuntary clairvoyant developed along improper, negative lines, these vortices turn from right to left, or in the opposite direction to the hands of a clock--counterclockwise.

In the desire body of the properly trained voluntary clairvoyant, they turn in the same direction as the hands of a clock--clockwise, glowing with exceeding splendor, far surpassing the brilliant luminosity of the ordinary desire body. These centers furnish him with means for the perception of things in the Desire World and he sees, and investigates as he wills, while the person whose centers turn counter-clockwise is like a mirror, which reflects what passes before it. Such a person is incapable of reaching out for information. The reason for this belongs to a later chapter, but the above is one of the fundamental differences between a medium and a properly trained clairvoyant. It is impossible for most people to distinguish between the two; yet there is one infallible rule that can be followed by anyone: *No genuinely developed seer will ever exercise this faculty for money or its equivalent; nor will he use it to gratify curiosity; but only to help humanity.*

No one capable of teaching the proper method for the development of this faculty will ever charge so much a lesson. Those demanding money for the exercise of, or for giving lessons in these things never have anything worth paying for. The above rule is a safe and sure guide, which all may follow with absolute confidence.

In a far distant future man's desire body will become as definitely organized as are the vital and dense bodies. When that stage is reached we shall all have the power to function in the desire body as we do now in the dense body, which is the oldest and best organized of these bodies of man--the desire body being the youngest.

The desire body is rooted in the liver, as the vital body is in the spleen.

In all warm-blooded creatures, which are the highest evolved, and have feelings, passions and emotions, which reach outward into the world with desire, which may be said to really live in the fuller meaning of the term and not merely vegetate--in all such creatures the currents of the desire body flow outward from the liver. The desire stuff is continually welling out in streams or currents which travel in curved lines to every point of the periphery of the ovoid and then return to the liver through a number of vortices, much as boiling water is continually welling outward from the source of heat and returning to it after completing its cycle.

The plants are devoid of this impelling, energizing principle, hence they cannot show life and motion as can the more highly developed organisms.

Where there is vitality and motion, but no *red* blood, there is no separate desire body. The creature is simply in the transition stage from plant to animal and therefore it moves entirely in the strength of the group-spirit.

In the *cold*-blooded animals which have a liver and *red* blood, there is a separate desire body and the group-spirit directs the currents *inward*, because in their case the separate spirit (of the individual fish or reptile for instance) is entirely outside the dense vehicle.

When the organism has evolved so far that the separate spirit can commence to draw into its vehicles then it (the individual spirit) commences to direct the currents *outward*, and we see the beginning of passionate existence and warm blood. It is the warm, red blood in the liver of the organism sufficiently evolved to have an Indwelling spirit which energizes the outgoing currents of desire stuff that cause the animal or the man to display desire and passion. In the case of the animal the spirit is not yet entirely *in*dwelling. It does not become so until the points in the vital body and the dense body come into correspondence, as explained in Chapter XII. For this reason the animal is not a "liver," that is, he does not live as completely as does man, not being capable of as fine desires and emotions, because not as fully conscious. The mammalia of today are on a higher plane than was man at the animal stage of his evolution, because they have warm, red blood, which man did not have at that stage. This difference in status is accounted for by the spiral path of evolution, which also accounts for the fact that man is a higher type of humanity than the present Angels were in their human stage. The present mammalia, which have in their animal stage attained to the possession of warm, red blood, and are therefore capable of experiencing desire and emotion to some extent will, in the Jupiter Period, be a purer and better type of humanity than we are now, while from among our present humanity there will be some, even in the Jupiter Period, who will be openly and avowedly wicked. Moreover, they will not then be able to conceal their passions as is now possible, but will be unabashed about their evil doing.

In the light of this exposition of the connection between the liver and the life of the organism, it is noteworthy that in several European languages (English, German, and the Scandinavian tongues) the same word signifies the organ of the body (the liver) and also "one who lives."

When we turn our attention to the four kingdoms in their relation to the World of Thought we find that minerals, plants and animals lack a vehicle correlating them to that World. Yet we know some animals think, but they are the highest domesticated animals which have come into close touch with man for generations and have thus developed a faculty not possessed by other animals, which have not had that advantage. This is on the same principle that a highly charged wire will "induce" a weaker current of electricity in a wire brought close to it; or that a man of strong morals will arouse a like tendency in a weaker nature, while one morally weak will be overthrown if brought within the influence of evil characters. All we do, say, or are, reflects itself in our surroundings. This is why the highest domestic animals think. They are the highest of their kind, almost on the point of individualization, and man's thought vibrations have "induced" in them a similar activity of a lower order. With the exceptions noted, the animal kingdom has not acquired the faculty of thought. They are not *individualized*. This is the great and cardinal difference between the human and other kingdoms. Man is an individual. The animals, plants and minerals are divided into species. They are not individualized in the same sense that man is.

It is true that we divide mankind into races, tribes and nations; we note the difference between the Caucasian, the Negro, the Indian, etc.; but that is not to the point. If we wish to study the characteristics of the lion or the elephant or any other species of the lower animals, all that is necessary is to take any member of that species for that purpose. When we learn the characteristics of one animal, we know the characteristics of the species to which it belongs. All members of the same animal tribe are alike. That is the point. A lion, or its father, or its son, all look alike; there is no difference in the way they will act under like conditions. All have the same likes and dislikes; one is the same as another.

Not so with human beings. If we want to know about the characteristics of Negroes, it is not enough that we examine one single individual. It would be necessary to examine each individually, and even then we will arrive at no knowledge concerning Negroes as a whole, simply because that which was a characteristic of the single individual does not apply to the race collectively.

If we desire to know the character of Abraham Lincoln it will avail us nothing to study his father, his grandfather, or his son, for they would differ entirely. Each would have his own peculiarities quite distinct from the idiosyncrasies of Abraham Lincoln.

On the other hand, minerals, plants, and animals are described if we devote our attention to the description of one of each species; while there are as many species among human beings as there are individuals. Each individual person is a "species," a law unto himself, altogether separate and apart from any other individual, as different from his fellow men as one species in the lower kingdom is from another. We may write the biography of a man, but an animal can have no biography. This is because there is in each man an individual, *indwelling* spirit which dictates the thoughts and actions of each individual human being; while there is one "group-spirit" *common to all* the different animals or plants of the same species. The group-spirit works on the all *from the outside*. The tiger which roams in the wilds of the Indian jungle and the tiger penned up in the cage of a menagerie are both expressions of the same group-spirit. It influences both alike from the Desire World, distance being almost annihilated in the inner Worlds.

The group-spirits of the three lower kingdoms are variously located in the higher Worlds, as we shall see when we investigate the consciousness of the different kingdoms; but to properly comprehend the positions of these group-spirits in the inner Worlds it is necessary to remember and to clearly understand what has been said about all the forms that are in the visible world having crystallized from models and ideas in the inner Worlds, as illustrated by the architect's house and the inventor's machine. As the juices of the soft body of the snail crystallize into the hard shell which it carries upon its back, so the Spirits in the higher Worlds have, in a similar manner, crystallized out from themselves the dense, material bodies of the different kingdoms.

DIAGRAM 3

Showing the vehicles of each kingdom, and the manner in which such vehicles are correlated to the different worlds.

WORLD	KINGDOM			
	Mineral	Plant	Animal	Man
Region of Abstract Thought .... and	Group-spirit and Ego	Group-spirit and Ego	Group-spirit and Ego	Ego
Region of Concrete Thought	No vehicle	No vehicle	No vehicle	Mind
Desire World..........	No vehicle	No vehicle	Desire body	Desire body
Physical World; includes the Etheric Region........ and the	No vehicle	Vital body	Vital body	Vital body
Chemical Region	Dense body	Dense body	Dense body	Dense body

Thus the so-called "higher" bodies, although so fine and cloudy as to be invisible, are not by any means "emanations" from the dense body, but the dense vehicles of all kingdoms correspond to the shell of the snail, which is crystallized from its juices, the snail representing the spirit; and the juices of its body in their progress towards crystallization representing the mind, desire body and vital body. *These various vehicles were emanated by the spirit from itself* for the purpose of gaining experience through them. It is the spirit that moves the dense body where it will, as the snail moves its house, and not the body that controls the movements of the spirit. The more closely the spirit is able to enter into touch with its vehicle the better can it control and express itself through that vehicle, and vice versa. That is the key to the different states of consciousness in the different kingdoms. A study of diagram 3 and diagram 4 should give a clear understanding of the vehicles of each kingdom, the manner in which they are correlated to the different Worlds and the resulting state of consciousness.

38

DIAGRAM 4

Showing the state of consciousness appertaining to each kingdom.

WORLD	KINGDOM				State of Consciousness
	Mineral	Plant	Animal	Man	
Region of Abstract Thought......	Group-spirit and Ego				Trance-like
and Region of Concrete Thought......		Group-spirit and Ego			Dreamless Sleep
Desire World			Group-spirit and Ego		Dream Consciousness
Physical World; includes the Etheric Region......... and the Chemical Region.......	Dense body	Vital body Dense body	Desire body Vital body Dense body	Ego Mind Desire body Vital body Dense body	Waking Consciousness

From diagram 3 we learn that the separate Ego is definitely segregated within the Universal Spirit in the Region of Abstract Thought. It shows that only man possesses the complete chain of vehicles correlating him to all divisions of the three Worlds. The animal lacks one link of chain--the mind; the plant lacks two links; the mind and the desire body; and the mineral lacks three links of the chain of the vehicles necessary to function in a self-conscious manner in the Physical World--the mind, the desire and the vital bodies.

The reason for the various deficiencies is that the Mineral Kingdom is the expression of the latest stream of evolving life; the Plant Kingdom is ensouled by a life wave that has been longer upon the path of evolution; the life wave of the animal kingdom has a still longer past; while Man, that is to say, the life now expressing itself in the human form, has behind it the longest journey of all the four kingdoms, and therefore leads. In time, the three life-waves which now animate the three lower kingdoms will reach the human, and we shall have passed to higher stages of development.

To understand the degree of consciousness which results from the possession of the vehicles used by the life evolving in the four kingdoms, we turn our attention to diagram 4, which show that man, the Ego, the Thinker, has descended into the Chemical Region of the Physical World. Here he has marshaled all his vehicles, thereby attaining the state of waking consciousness. He is learning to control his vehicles. The organs of neither the desire body nor the mind are yet evolved. The latter is not yet even a body. At present it is simply a link, a sheath for the use of the Ego as a focusing point. It is the

39

last of the vehicles that have been built. The spirit works gradually from finer into coarser substance, the vehicles also being built in finer substance first, then in coarser and coarser substance. The dense body was built first and has now come into its fourth stage of density; the vital body is in its third stage and the desire body in its second, hence it is still cloud-like, and the sheath of mind is filmier still. As those vehicles have not, as yet, evolved any organs, it is clear that they *alone* would be useless as vehicles of consciousness. The Ego, however, enters *into* the dense body and connects these organless vehicles with the physical sense centers and thus attains the waking state of consciousness in the Physical World.

The student should particularly note that it is because of their connection with the splendidly organized mechanism of the dense body that these higher vehicles become of value at present. He will thus avoid a mistake frequently made by people who, when they come into the knowledge that there are higher bodies, grow to despise the dense vehicle; to speak of it as "low" and "vile"--turning their eyes to heaven and wishing that they might soon be able to leave this earthly lump of clay and fly about in their "higher vehicles."

These people generally do not realize the difference between "higher" and "perfect." Certainly, the dense body is the lowest vehicle in the sense that it is the most unwieldy, correlating man to the world of sense with all the limitations thus implied. As stated, it has an enormous period of evolution back of it; is in its fourth state of development and has now reached a great and marvelous degree of efficiency. It will, in time, reach perfection, but even at present it is the best organized of man's vehicles. The vital body is in its third stage of evolution, and less completely organized than the dense body. The desire body and the mind are, as yet, mere clouds--almost entirely unorganized. In the very lowest human beings these vehicles are not even definite ovoids; they are more or less undefined in form.

The dense body is a wonderfully constructed instrument and should be recognized as such by everyone pretending to have any knowledge of the constitution of man. Observe the femur, for instance. This bone carries the entire weight of the body. On the outside it is built of a thin layer of compact bone, strengthened on the inside by beams and cross-beams of cancellated bone, in such a marvelous manner that the most skilled bridge or construction engineer could never accomplish the feat of building a pillar of equal strength with so little weight. The bones of the skull are built in a similar manner, always the least possible material is used and the maximum of strength obtained. Consider the wisdom manifested in the construction of the heart and then question if this superb mechanism deserves to be despised. The wise man is grateful for his dense body and takes the best possible care of it, because he knows that it is the most valuable of his present instruments.

The animal spirit has in its descent reached only the Desire World. It has not yet evolved to the point where it can "enter" a dense body. Therefore the animal has no individual *in*dwelling spirit, but a group-spirit, which directs it *from without.* The animal has the dense body, the vital body and the desire body, but the group-spirit which directs it is outside. The vital body and the desire body of an animal are not entirely within the dense body, especially where the head is concerned. For instance, the etheric head of a horse projects far beyond and above the dense physical head. When, as in rare cases it happens, the etheric head of a horse draws into the head of the dense body, that horse can learn to read, count and work examples in elementary arithmetic. To this peculiarity is also due the fact that horses, dogs, cats and other domesticated animals sense the Desire World, though not always realizing the difference between it and the Physical World. A horse will shy at the sight of a figure invisible to the driver; a cat will go through the motions of rubbing itself against invisible legs. The cat sees the ghost, however without realizing that it has no dense legs available for frictional purposes. The dog, wiser than a cat or horse, will often sense that there is something he does not understand about the appearance of a dead master whose hands it cannot lick. It will howl mournfully and slink into a corner with its tail between its legs. The following illustration may perhaps be of service to show the difference between the man with his indwelling spirit and the animal with its group-spirit.

Let us imagine a room divided by means of a curtain, one side of the curtain representing the Desire World and the other the Physical. There are two men in the room, one in each division; they cannot see each other, nor can they get into the same division. There are, however, ten holes in the curtain and the man who is in the division representing the Desire World can put his ten fingers through these holes into the other division, representing the Physical World. He now furnishes an excellent representation of the group-spirit which is in the Desire World. The fingers represent the animals belonging to one species. He is able to move them as he wills, but he cannot use them freely nor as intelligently as the man who is walking about in the Physical division uses his body. The latter sees the fingers which are thrust through the curtain and he observes that they all move, but he does not see the connection between them. To him it appears as if they were all separate and distinct from one another. He cannot see that they are fingers of the man behind the veil and are governed in their movements by his intelligence. If he hurts one of the fingers, it is not only the finger that he hurts, but chiefly the man on the other side of the curtain. If an animal is hurt, it suffers, but not to the degree that the group-spirit does. The finger has no individualized consciousness; it moves as the man dictates--so do the animals move as the group-spirit dictates. We hear of "animal instinct" and "blind instinct." There is no such vague, indefinite thing as "blind" instinct. There is nothing "blind" about the way the group-spirit guides its members--there is Wisdom, spelled with capitals. The trained clairvoyant, when functioning in the Desire World, can communicate with these spirits of the animal species and finds them much more intelligent than a large percent of human beings. He can see the marvelous insight they display in marshaling the animals which are their physical bodies.

It is the spirit of the group which gathers its flocks of birds in the fall and compels them to migrate to the south, neither too early nor too late to escape the winter's chilly blast; that directs their return in the spring, causing them to fly at just the proper altitude, which differs for the different species.

The group-spirit of the beaver teaches it to build its dam across a stream at exactly the proper angle. It considers the rapidity of the flow, and all the circumstances, precisely as a skilled engineer would do, showing that it is as up-to-date in every particular of the craft as the college-bred, technically-educated man. It is the wisdom of the group-spirit that directs the building of the hexagon cell of the bee with such geometrical nicety; that teaches the snail to fashion its house in an accurate, beautiful spiral; that teaches the ocean mollusk the art of decorating its iridescent shell. Wisdom, wisdom everywhere! So grand, so great that one who looks with an observant eye is filled with amazement and reverence.

At this point the thought will naturally occur that if the animal group-spirit is so wise, considering the short period of evolution of the animal as compared with that of man, why does not the latter display wisdom to a much greater degree and why must man be taught to build dams and geometrize, all of which the group spirit does without being taught?

The answer to that question has to do with the descent of the Universal Spirit into matter of ever-increasing density. In the higher Worlds, where its vehicles are fewer and finer, it is in closer touch with cosmic wisdom which shines out in a manner inconceivable in the dense Physical World, but as the spirit descends, the light of wisdom becomes temporarily more and more dimmed, until in the densest of all the Worlds, it is held almost entirely in abeyance.

An illustration will make this clearer. The hand is man's most valuable servant; its dexterity enables it to respond to his slightest bidding. In some vocations, such as bank teller, the delicate touch of the hand becomes so sensitive, that it is able to distinguish a counterfeit coin from a genuine in a way so marvelous that one would almost think the hand were endowed with individual intelligence.

Its greatest efficiency is perhaps reached in the production of music. It is capable of producing the most beautiful, soul-stirring melodies. The delicate, caressing touch of the hand elicits the tenderest strains of soul-speech from the instrument, telling of the sorrows, the joys, the hopes, the fears and the longings of the soul in a way that nothing but music can do. It is the language of the heaven world, the spirit's true home, and comes to the divine spark imprisoned in flesh as a message from its native land. Music appeals to all, regardless of race, creed, or other worldly distinction. The higher and more spiritual the individual the plainer does it speak to him and even "the savage breast" is not unmoved by it.

Let us now imagine a master musician putting on thin gloves and trying to play his violin. We note at once that the delicate touch is less subtle; the soul of the music is gone. If he puts another and a heavier pair of gloves over the first pair, his hand is hampered to such an extent that he may occasionally create a discord instead of the former harmony. Should he at last put on, in addition to the two pairs of gloves already hampering him, a pair of still heavier mittens, he would, temporarily, be entirely unable to play, and one who had not heard him play previously to the time he put on the gloves and the mittens, would naturally think that he had never been able to do so, especially if ignorant of the hampering of his hands.

So it is with the Spirit; every step down, every descent into coarser matter is to it what the putting on of a pair of gloves would be to the musician. Every step down limits its power of expression until it has become accustomed to the limitations and has found its focus, in the same way that the eye must find its focus after we enter a house on a bright summer day. The pupil of the eye contracts to its limit in the glare of the sun and on entering the house all seems dark; but, as the pupil expands, and admits the light, the man is enabled to see as well in the dimmer light of the house as he did in the sunlight.

The purpose of man's evolution here is to enable him to find his focus in the Physical World, where at present the light of wisdom seems obscured. But when in time we have "found the light," the wisdom of man will shine forth in his actions, and far surpass the wisdom expressed by the group-spirit of the animal.

Besides, a distinction must be made between the group spirit and the virgin spirits of the life wave now expressing itself as animals. The group-spirit belongs to a different evolution and is the guardian of the animal spirits.

The dense body in which we function is composed of numerous cells, each having separate cell-consciousness, though of a very low order. While these cells form part of our body they are subjected to and dominated by *our* consciousness. An animal group-spirit functions in a *spiritual body*, which is its lowest vehicle This vehicle consists of a varying number of virgin spirits imbued for the time being with the consciousness of the group-spirit. The latter directs the vehicles built by the virgin spirits in its charge, caring for them and helping them to evolve their vehicles. As its wards evolve, the group-spirit also evolves, undergoing a series of metamorphoses, in a manner similar to that in which we grow and gain experience by taking into our bodies the cells of the food we eat, thereby also raising their consciousness by enduing them with ours for a time.

Thus while a separate, self-conscious Ego is within each human body and dominates the actions of its particular vehicle, the spirit of the separate animal is not yet individualized and self-conscious, but forms part of the vehicle of a self-conscious entity belonging to a different evolution--the group-spirit.

The group-spirit dominates the actions of the animals in harmony with cosmic law, until the virgin spirits in its charge shall have gained self-consciousness and become human. Then they will gradually manifest wills of their own, gaining more and more freedom from the group-spirit and becoming responsible for their own actions. The group-spirit will influence them, however (although in a decreasing degree), as race, tribe, community, or

43

family spirit until each individual has become capable of acting in full harmony with cosmic law. Not until that time will the Ego be entirely free and independent of the group-spirit, which will then enter a higher phase of evolution.

The position occupied by the group-spirit in the Desire World gives to the animal a consciousness different from that of man, who has a clear, definite waking consciousness. Man sees things *outside* of himself in sharp, distinct outlines. Owing to the spiral path of evolution, the higher domestic animals, particularly the dog, horse, cat and elephant see objects in somewhat the same way, though perhaps not so clearly defined. All other animals have an internal "picture consciousness" similar to the dream-state in man. When such an animal is confronted by an object, a picture is immediately perceived *within*, accompanied by a strong impression that the object is inimical or beneficial to its welfare. If the feeling is one of fear, it is associated with a suggestion from the group-spirit how to escape the threatened danger. This negative state of consciousness renders it easy for the group-spirit to guide the dense bodies of its charges by suggestion, as the animals have no will of their own.

Man is not so easily managed from without, either with or without his consent. As evolution progresses and man's will develops more and more, he will become non-amenable to outside suggestion and free to do as he pleases regardless of suggestions from others. This is the chief difference between man and the other kingdoms. They act according to law and the dictates of the group-spirit (which we call instinct), while man is becoming more and more a law unto himself. We do not ask the mineral whether or not it will crystallize, nor the flower whether it will or will not bloom, nor the lion whether it will or will not cease to prey. They are all, in the smallest as in the greatest matter, under the absolute domination of the group-spirit, being without free will and initiative which, in some degree, are possessed by every human being. All animals of the same species look nearly alike, because they emanate from the same group-spirit, while among the fifteen hundred millions of human beings who people the Earth no two look exactly alike, not even twins when adolescent, because the stamp that is put upon each by the indwelling individual Ego makes the difference in appearance as well as in character.

That all oxen thrive on grass, and all lions eat flesh, while "one man's meat is another man's poison" is another illustration of the all-inclusive influence of the group-spirit as contrasted with the Ego which makes each human being require a different proportion of food from every other. Doctors note with perplexity the same peculiarity in administering medicine. Its acts differently upon different individuals, while the same medicine will produce identical effects on two animals of the same species, owing to the fact that animals all follow the dictates of the group-spirit and Cosmic Law--always act similarly in identical circumstances. Man alone is, in some measure, able to follow his own desires within certain limits. That his mistakes are many

44

and grievous, is granted, and to many it might seem better if he were forced into the right way, but if this were done, he would never learn to do right. Lessons of discrimination between good and evil cannot be learned unless he is free to choose his own course and has learned to eschew the wrong as a veritable "womb of pain." If he did right only because he had no choice, and had no chance to do otherwise, he would be but an automaton and not an evolving God. As the builder learns by his mistakes, correcting past errors in future buildings, so man, by means of his blunders, and the pain they cause him, is attaining to a higher (because self-conscious) wisdom than the animal, which acts wisely because it is impelled to action by the group-spirit. In time the animal will become human, have liberty of choice and will make mistakes and learn by them as we do now.

Diagram 4 shows that the group-spirit of the plant kingdom has its lowest vehicle in the Region of Concrete Thought. It is two steps removed from its dense vehicle and consequently the plants have a consciousness corresponding to that of *dreamless sleep*. The group-spirit of the mineral has it slowest vehicle in the Region of Abstract Thought and it is, therefore, three steps removed from its dense vehicle; hence it is in a state of deep unconsciousness similar to the *trance* condition.

We have now shown that man is an individual indwelling spirit, an Ego separate from all other entities, directing and working in one set of vehicles from *within*, and that plants and animals are directed from *without* by a group-spirit having jurisdiction over a number of animals or plants in our Physical World. They are separate only in appearance.

The relations of plant, animal and man to the life currents in the Earth's atmosphere are symbolically represented by the cross. The Mineral Kingdom is not represented, because as we have seen, it possesses no individual vital body, hence cannot be the vehicle for currents belonging to the higher realms. Plato, who was an Initiate, often gave occult truths. He said "The World-Soul is crucified."

The lower limb of the cross indicates the plant with its root in the chemical mineral soil. The group-spirits of plants are at the center of the Earth. They are (it will be remembered) in the Region of Concrete Thought, which interpenetrates the Earth, as do all the other Worlds. From these group-spirits flow streams or currents in all directions to the periphery of the Earth, passing outward through the length of plant or tree.

Man is represented by the upper limb; his is the *inverted plant*. The plant takes its food through the root. Man takes his food through the head. The plant stretches its generative organs towards the sun. Man, the inverted plant, turns his towards the center of the earth. The plant is sustained by the spiritual currents of the group-spirit in the center of the earth, which enter into it by way of the root. Later it will be shown that the highest spiritual influence comes to man from the sun, which sends its rays through man, the inverted plant, from the head downwards. The plant inhales the poisonous

45

carbon-dioxide exhaled by man and exhales the life-giving oxygen used by him.

The animal, which is symbolized by the horizontal limb of the cross, is between the plant and the man. Its spine is in a horizontal position and through it play the currents of the animal group-spirit which encircle the Earth. No animal can be made to remain constantly upright, because in that case the currents of the group-spirit could not guide it, and if it were not sufficiently individualized to endure the spiritual currents which enter the vertical human spine, it would die. It is necessary that a vehicle for the expression of an individual Ego shall have three things--an upright walk, that it may come into touch with the currents just mentioned; an upright larynx, for only such a larynx is capable of speech (parrots and starlings are examples of this effect of the upright larynx); and, owing to the solar currents, it must have warm blood. The latter is of the utmost importance to the Ego, which will be logically explained and illustrated later. These requisites are simply mentioned here as the last words on the status of the four kingdoms in relation to each other and to the Worlds.

THE SEVENFOLD CONSTITUTION OF MAN.

World or Region.			Corresponding Vehicle.		
5..World of Divine Spirit........		Divine Spirit	The Threefold Spirit	The Ego	
4..World of Life Spirit.........		Life Spirit			
3 {	World of	Region of Abstract Thought......			
		.... Human Spirit			
	Thought	Region of Concrete Thought..Mind..	(The Mind is the mirror through which the threefold spirit reflects itself in the threefold body; the focussing - point. See Diagr. 1.)		

2..Desire World...........		Desire Body	The Three-fold Body; the Shadow of the Threefold Spirit.		
1 {	Phys-ical	Etheric Region..	Vital Body		
	World	Chemical Region.	Dense Body		

Chapter Three - Man and the Method of Evolution, Activities of Life; Memory and Soul-Growth

Our study thus far of the seven Worlds or states of matter has shown us that each serves a definite purpose in the economy of nature, and that God, the Great Spirit, *in* Whom we actually and in fact "live and move and have our being," is the Power that permeates and sustains the whole Universe with Its Life; but while that Life flows into and is immanent in every atom of the six lower Worlds and all contained therein, in the Seventh--the highest--the Triune God alone *is.*

The next highest or sixth realm is the World of Virgin Spirits. Here those sparks from the divine "Flame: have their being before they commence their long pilgrimage through the five denser Worlds for the purpose of developing latent potentialities into dynamic powers. As the seed unfolds its hidden possibilities by being buried in the soil, so these virgin spirits will, in time, when they have passed through matter (the school of experience), also become divine "Flames," capable of bringing forth universes from themselves.

The five Worlds constitute the field of man's evolution, the three lower or denser being the scene of the present phase of his development. We will now consider his as related to these five Worlds by means of his appropriate vehicles, remembering the two grand divisions into which two of these Worlds are divided, and than man has a vehicle for each of these divisions.

In the waking state these vehicles are all together. They inter-penetrate one another as the blood, the lymph, and other juices of the body inter-penetrate. Thus is the Ego enabled to act in the Physical World.

We ourselves, as Egos, function directly in the subtle substance of the Region of Abstract Thought, which we have specialized within the periphery of our individual aura. Thence we view the impressions made by the outer world upon the vital body through the senses, together with the feelings and emotions generated by them in the desire body, and mirrored in the mind.

From these mental images we form our conclusions, in the substance of the Region of Abstract Thought, concerning the subjects with which they deal. Those conclusions are ideas. By the power of will we project an idea through the mind, where it takes concrete shape as a thought-form by drawing mind-stuff around itself from the Region of Concrete Thought.

The mind is like the projecting lens of a stereopticon. It projects the image in one of three directions, according to the will of the thinker, which ensouls the thought-form.

1. It may be projected against the desire body in an endeavor to arouse feeling which will lead to immediate action.

    a. If the thought awakens Interest, one of the twin forces, Attraction or Repulsion, will be stirred up.

If Attraction, the centripetal force, is aroused, it seizes the thought, whirls it into the desire body, endows the image with added life and clothes it with desire-stuff. Then the thought is able to act on the etheric brain, and propel the vital force through the appropriate brain centers and nerves to the voluntary muscles which perform the necessary action. Thus the force in the thought is expended and the image remains in the ether of the vital body as memory of the act and the feeling that caused it.

    b. Repulsion is the centrifugal force and if that is aroused by the thought there will be a struggle between the spiritual force (the will of the man) within the thought-form, and the desire body. This is the battle between conscience and desire, the higher and the lower nature. The spiritual force, in spite of resistance will seek to clothe the thought-form in the desire-stuff needed to manipulate the brain and muscles.

47

The force of Repulsion will endeavor to scatter the appropriated material and oust the thought. If the spiritual energy is strong it may force its way through to the brain centers and hold its clothing of desire-stuff while manipulating the vital force, thus compelling action, and will then leave upon the memory a vivid impression of the struggle and the victory. If the spiritual energy is exhausted before action has resulted, it will be overcome by the force of Repulsion, and will be stored in the memory, as are all other thought-forms when they have expended their energy.

c. If the thought-form meets the withering feeling of Indifference it depends upon the spiritual energy contained in it whether it will be able to compel action, or simply leave a weak impress upon the reflecting ether of the vital body after its kinetic energy has been exhausted.

2. Where no immediate action is called for by the mental images of impacts from without, these may be projected directly upon the reflecting ether, together with the thoughts occasioned by them, to be used at some future time. The spirit, working through the mind, has instant access to the storehouse of conscious memory and may at any time resurrect any of the pictures found there, endue them with new spiritual force, and project them upon the desire body to compel action. Each time such a picture is thus used it will gain in vividness, strength and efficiency, and will compel action along its particular line grooves, and produces the phenomenon of thought, "gaining" or "growing" upon us by repetition.

3. A third way of using a thought-form is when the thinker projects it toward another mind to act as a suggestion, to carry information, etc., as in thought-transference, or it may be directed against the desire body of another person to compel action, as in the case of a hypnotist influencing a victim at a distance. It will then act in precisely the same manner as if it were the victim's own thought. If in line with his proclivities it will act as per paragraph 1a. If contrary to his nature, as described in 1b or 1c.

When the work designed for such a projected thought-form has been accomplished, or its energy expended in vain attempts to achieved its object, it gravitates back to its creator, bearing with it the indelible record of the journey. It success or failure is imprinted on the negative atoms of the reflecting ether of its creator's vital body, where it forms that part of the record of the thinker's life and action which is sometimes called the sub-conscious mind.

This record is much more important than the memory to which we have conscious access, for the latter is made up from imperfect and illusive sense-perceptions and is the voluntary memory or conscious mind.

The involuntary memory or sub-conscious mind comes into being in a different way, altogether beyond our control at present. As the ether carries to the sensitive film in the camera an accurate impression of the surrounding landscape, taking in the minutest detail regardless of whether the photographer has observed it or not, so the ether contained in the air we inspire carries with it an accurate and detailed picture of all our surroundings. Not only of material things, but also the conditions existing each moment within our aura. The slightest thought, feeling or emotion is transmitted to the lungs, where it is injected into the blood. The blood is one of the highest products of the vital body as it is the carrier of nourishment to every part of the body, and the direct vehicle of the Ego. The pictures it contains are impressed upon the negative atoms of the vital body, to serve as arbiters of the man's destiny in the *post mortem* state.

The memory (or so-called mind), both conscious and sub-conscious, relates *wholly* to the experiences of this life. It consists of impressions of events on the vital body. These may be changed or even eradicated, as noted in the explanation concerning the forgiveness of sins which is given a few pages further on, which change or eradication depends upon the elimination of these impressions from the ether of the vital body.

There is also a superconscious memory. That is the storehouse of all faculties acquired and knowledge gained in previous lives, though perhaps latent in the present life. This record is indelibly engraven on the life spirit. It manifests ordinarily, though not to the full extent, as conscience and character which ensoul all thought-forms, sometimes as counselor, sometimes compelling action with resistless force, even contrary to reason and desire.

In many women, in whom the vital body is positive, and in advanced people of either sex where the vital body has been sensitized by a pure and holy life, by prayer and concentration, this superconscious memory inherent in the life spirit is occasionally, to some extent, above the necessity of clothing itself in mind stuff and desire matter in order to compel action. It does not always need to incur the danger of being subjected to and perhaps overruled by a process of reasoning. Sometimes, in the form of intuition or teaching from within, it impresses itself directly upon the reflecting ether of the vital body. The more readily we learn to recognize it and follow its dictates, the oftener it will speak, to our eternal welfare.

By their activities during waking hours the desire body and the mind are constantly destroying the dense vehicle. Every thought and movement breaks down tissue. On the other hand, the vital body faithfully endeavors to restore harmony and build up what the other vehicles are tearing down. It is not able, however, to entirely withstand the powerful onslaughts of the impulses and thoughts. It gradually loses ground and at last there comes a time when it collapses. Its "points" shrivel-up, so to say. The vital fluid ceases to flow along the nerves is sufficient quantity; the body becomes drowsy, the Thinker is hampered by its drowsiness and forced to withdraw, taking the desire body with him. This withdrawal of the higher vehicle leaves the dense body interpenetrated by the vital body in the senseless state we call sleep.

Sleep, however, is not by any means an inactive state, as people generally suppose. If it were, the body would be no different on awakening in the morning from its condition when it went to sleep at night; its fatigue would

49

be just as great. On the contrary, sleep is a period of intense activity and the more intense it is the greater its value, for it eliminates the poisons resulting from tissue destroyed by the mental and physical activities of the day. The tissues are re-built and the rhythm of the body restored. The more thoroughly this work is done the greater the benefit accruing from sleep.

The Desire World is an ocean of wisdom and harmony. Into this the Ego takes the mind and the desire body when the lower vehicles have been left to sleep. There the first care of the Ego is the restoration of the rhythm and harmony of the mind and the desire body. This restoration is accomplished gradually as the harmonious vibrations of the Desire World flow through them. There is an essence in the Desire World corresponding to the vital fluid which permeates the dense body by means of the vital body. The higher vehicles, as it were, steep themselves in this elixir of life. When strengthened, they commence work on the vital body, which was left with the sleeping dense body. Then the vital body begins to specialize the solar energy anew, rebuilding the dense body, using particularly the chemical ether as its medium in the process of restoration.

It is this activity of the different vehicles during sleep which forms the basis for the activity of the following day. Without that there would be no awakening, for the Ego was forced to abandon his vehicles because their weariness rendered them useless. If the work of removing that fatigue were not done, the bodies would remain asleep, as sometimes happens in natural trance. It is just because of this harmonizing, recuperative activity that sleep is better than doctor or medicine in preserving health. Mere rest is nothing is comparison with sleep. It is only while the higher vehicles are in the Desire World that there is a total suspension of waste and an influx of restoring force. It is true that during rest the vital body is not hampered in its work by tissue being broken down by active motion and tense muscles, but still it must contend with the wasting energy of thought and it does not then receive the *outside* recuperative force from the desire body as during sleep.

It happens, however, that at times the desire body does not fully withdraw, so that part of it remains connected with the vital body, the vehicle for sense perception and memory. The result is that restoration is only partly accomplished and that the senses and actions of the Desire World are brought into the physical consciousness as dreams. Of course most dreams are confused as the axis of perception is askew, because of the improper relation of one body to another. The memory is also confused by this incongruous relation of the vehicles and as a result of the loss of the restoring force, dream-filled sleep is restless and the body feels tired on awakening.

During the life the threefold spirit, the Ego, works on and in the threefold body, to which it is connected by the link of mind. This work brings the threefold soul into being. The soul is the spiritualized product of the body.

Diagram 5 shows the Tenfold Constitution of Man.

Man Is a threefold Spirit, possessing a Mind by means of which be governs a threefold Body, which he emanated from himself to gather experience. This threefold body he transmutes into a threefold Soul, upon which he nourishes himself from Impotence to omnipotence.

The Divine Spirit	emanates	The Dense Body	extracting	Conscious Soul
The Life Spirit	from	The Vital Body	as	Intellectual Soul
The Human Spirit	Itself	The Desire Body	pabulum	Emotional Soul

The mirror of Mind also contributes increasingly to spiritual growth as the thoughts which it transmits to and from the Spirit polish it to greater brightness, sharpening and intensifying its focus more and more to a single point, perfectly flexible and under the control of the Spirit.

As proper food feeds the body in a material sense, so the activity of the spirit in the dense body, which results in *right action*, promotes the growth of the Conscious Soul. As the forces from the sun play in the vital body and nourish it, that it may act on the dense body, so the *memory* of actions done in the dense body-the desires, feelings and emotions of the desire body and the thoughts and ideas in the mind-cause the growth of the Intellectual Soul. In like manner the *highest desires and emotions* of the desire body form the Emotional Soul.

This threefold soul in turn enhances the consciousness of the threefold spirit.

The Emotional Soul, which is the extract of the desire body, adds to the efficiency of the Human Spirit, which is the spiritual counterpart of the desire body.

The Intellectual Soul gives added power to the Life Spirit, because the Intellectual Soul is extracted from the vital body, which is the material counterpart of the Life Spirit.

51

The Conscious Soul increases the consciousness of the Divine Spirit because it (the Conscious Soul) is the extract of the dense body, which latter is the counterpart of the Divine Spirit.

Death and Purgatory

So man builds and sows until the moment of death arrives. Then the seed-time and the periods of growth and ripening are past. The harvest time has come, when the skeleton specter of Death arrives with his scythe and hour-glass. That is a good symbol. The skeleton symbolizes the relatively permanent part of the body. The scythe represents the fact that this permanent part, which is about to be harvested by the spirit, is the fruitage of the life now drawing to a close. The hour-glass in his hand indicates that the hour does not strike until the full course has been run in harmony with unvarying laws. When that moment arrives a separation of the vehicles takes place. As his life in the Physical World is ended for the time being, it is not necessary for man to retain his dense body. The vital body, which as we have explained, also belongs to the Physical World, is withdrawn by way of the head, leaving the dense body inanimate.

The higher vehicles--vital body, desire body and mind-are seen to leave the dense body with a spiral movement, taking with them the *soul* of one dense atom. Not the atom itself, but *the forces* that played through it. The results of the experiences passed through in the dense body during the life just ended have been impressed upon this particular atom. While all the other atoms of the dense body have been renewed from time to time, this permanent atom has remained. It has remained stable, not only through one life, but it has been a part of every dense body ever used by a particular Ego. It is withdrawn at death only to reawaken at the dawn of another physical life, to serve again as the nucleus around which is built the new dense body to be used by the same Ego. It is therefore called the "Seed-Atom." During life the seed-atom is situated in the left ventricle of the heart, near the apex. At death it rises to the brain by way of the pneumogastric nerve, leaving the dense body, together with the higher vehicles, by way of the sutures between the parietal and occipital bones.

When the higher vehicles have left the dense body they are still connected with it by a slender, glistening, silvery cord shaped much like two figure sixes reversed, one upright and one horizontally placed, the two connected at the extremities of the hooks. (See diagram 5 1/2.)

One end is fastened to the heart by means of the seed-atom, and it is the rupture of the seed-atom which causes the heart to stop. The cord itself is not snapped until the panorama of the past life, contained in the vital body, has been reviewed.

Care should be taken, however, not to cremate or embalm the body until at least three days after death, for while the vital body is with the higher vehicles, and they are still connected with the dense body by means of the silver cord, any *post mortem* examination or other injury to the dense body will be felt, in a measure, by the man.

Cremation should be particularly avoided in the first three days after death, because it tends to disintegrate the vital body, which should be kept intact until the panorama of the past life has been etched into the desire body.

The silver cord snaps at the point where the sixes unite, half remaining with the dense body and the other half with the higher vehicles. From the time the cord snaps the dense body is quite dead.

In the beginning of 1906 Dr. McDougall made a series of experiments in the Massachusetts General Hospital, to determine, if possible, whether anything not ordinarily visible left the body at death. For this purpose he constructed a pair of scales capable of registering differences of one-tenth of an ounce.

The dying person and his bed were placed on one of the platforms of the scale, which was then balanced by weights placed on the opposite platform. In every instance it was noted that at the precise moment when the dying person drew the last breath, the platform containing the weights dropped with startling suddenness, lifting the bed and the body, thus showing that something invisible, but having weight, had left the body. Thereupon the newspapers all over the country announced in glaring headlines that Dr. McDougall had "weighed the soul."

Occultism hails with joy the discoveries of modern science, as they invariably corroborate what occult science has long taught. The experiments of Dr. McDougall showed conclusively that something invisible to ordinary sight left the body at death, as trained clairvoyants had seen, and as had been stated in lectures and literature for many years previous to Dr. McDougall's discovery.

But this invisible "something" is not the soul. There is a great difference. The reporters jump at conclusions when they state that the scientists have "weighed the soul." The soul belongs to higher realms and can never be weighed on physical scales, even though they registered variations of one-millionth part of a grain instead of one-tenth of an ounce.

It was the vital body which the scientists weighed. It is formed of the four ethers and they belong to the Physical World.

As we have seen, a certain amount of this ether is "superimposed" upon the ether which envelops the particles of the human body and is confined there during physical life, adding in a slight degree to the weight of the dense body of plant, animal and man. In death it escapes; hence the diminution in weight noticed by Dr. McDougall when the persons with whom he experimented expired.

Dr. McDougall also tried his scales in weighing dying animals. No diminution was found here, though one of the animals was a St. Bernard dog. That was taken to indicate that animals have no souls. A little later, however, Professor La V. Twining, head of the Science Dept. of the Los Angeles Polytechnic School, experimented with mice and kittens, which he enclosed in hermetically sealed glass flasks. His scales were the most sensitive procurable and were enclosed in a glass case from which all moisture had been removed. It was found that all the animals observed lost weight at death. A good-sized mouse, weighing 12.886 grams, suddenly lost 3.1 milligrams at death.

A kitten used in another experiment lost one hundred milligrams while dying and at its last gasp it suddenly lost an additional sixty milligrams. After that it lost weight slowly, due to evaporation.

Thus the teaching of occult science in regard to the possession of vital bodies by animals was also vindicated when sufficiently fine scales were used, and the case where the rather insensitive scales did not show diminution in the weight of the St. Bernard dog shows that the vital bodies of animals are proportionately lighter than in man.

When the "silver cord" is loosened in the heart, and man has been released from his dense body, a moment of the highest importance comes to the Ego, and it cannot be too seriously impressed upon the relatives of a dying person that it is a great crime against the departing soul to give expression to loud grief and lamentations, for it is just then engaged in a matter of supreme importance and a great deal of the value of the past life depends upon how much attention the soul can give to this matter. This will be made clearer when we come to the description of man's life in the Desire World.

It is also a crime against the dying to administer stimulants which have the effect of forcing the higher vehicles back into the dense body with a jerk, thus imparting a great shock to the man. It is not torture to pass out, but it is torture to be dragged back to endure further suffering. Some who have passed out have told investigators that they had, in that way, been kept dying for hours and had prayed that their relatives would cease their mistaken kindness and let them die.

When the man is freed from the dense body, which was the heaviest clog upon his spiritual power (like the heavy mitten on the hand of the musician in our previous illustration), his spiritual power comes back in some measure, and he is able to read the pictures in the negative pole of the reflecting ether of his vital body, which is the seat of the sub-conscious memory.

The whole of his past life passes before his sight like a panorama, the events being presented *in reverse order*. The incidents of the days immediately preceding death come first and so on back through manhood or womanhood to youth, childhood and infancy. Everything is remembered.

The man stands as a spectator before this panorama of his past life. He sees the pictures as they pass and they impress themselves upon his higher vehicles, but he has no feeling about them at this time. That is reserved until the time when he enters into the Desire World, which is the world of feeling and emotion. At present he is only in the Etheric Region of the Physical World.

This panorama lasts from a few hours to several days, depending upon the length of time the man could keep awake, if necessary. Some people can keep awake only twelve hours, or even less; others can do so, upon occasion, for a number of days, but as long as the man can remain awake, the panorama lasts.

This feature of life after death is similar to that with takes place when one is drowning or falling from a height. In such cases the vital body also leaves the dense body and the man sees his life in a flash, because he loses consciousness at once. Of course the "silver cord" is not broken, or there could be no resuscitation.

When the endurance of the vital body has reached its limit, it collapses in the way described when we were considering the phenomenon of sleep. During physical life, when the Ego controls its vehicles, this collapse terminates the waking hours; after death the collapse of the vital body terminates the panorama and forces the man to withdraw into the Desire World. The silver cord breaks at the point where the sixes unite (see diagram 5 1/2), and the same division is made a during sleep, but with this important difference, that thought the vital body returns to the dense body, it no longer interpenetrates it, but simply hovers over it. It remains floating over the grave, decaying synchronously with the dense vehicle. Hence, to the trained clairvoyant, a graveyard is a nauseating sight and if only more people could see it as he does, little argument would be necessary to induce them to change from the present unsanitary method of disposing of the dead to the more rational method of cremation, which restores the elements to their primordial condition without the objectionable features incident to the process of slow decay.

In leaving the vital body the process is much the same as when the dense body is discarded. The life forces of one atom are taken, to be used as a nucleus for the vital body of a future embodiment. Thus, upon his entrance into the Desire World the man has the seed-atoms of the dense and the vital bodies, in addition to the desire body and the mind.

If the dying man could leave all desires behind, the desire body would very quickly fall away from him, leaving him free to proceed into the heaven world, but that is not generally the case. Most people, especially if they die in the prime of life, have many ties and much interest in life on earth. They have not altered their desires because they have lost their physical bodies. In fact often their desires are even augmented by a very intense longing to return. This acts in such a manner as to bind them to the Desire World in a very unpleasant way, although unfortunately, they do not realize it. On the other hand, old and decrepit persons and those who are weakened by long illness and are tired of life, pass on very quickly.

The matter may be illustrated by the ease with which the seed falls out of the ripe fruit, no particle of the flesh clinging to it, while in the unripe fruit the seed clings to the flesh with the greatest tenacity. Thus it is especially hard for people to die who were taken out of their bodies by accident while at the height of their physical health and strength, engaged in numerous ways in the activities of physical life; held by the ties of wife, family, relatives, friends, pursuits of business and pleasure.

The suicide, who tries to get away from life, only to find that he is as much alive as ever, is in the most pitiable plight. He is able to watch those whom he has, perhaps, disgraced by his act, and worst of all, he has an unspeakable feeling of being "hollowed out." The part in the ovoid aura where the dense body used to be is empty and although the desire body has taken the form of the discarded dense body, it feels like an empty shell, because the creative archetype of the body in the Region of Concrete Thought persists as an empty mold, so to speak, as long as the dense body should properly have lived. When a person meets a natural death, even in the prime of life, the activity of the archetype ceases, and the desire body adjusts itself so as to occupy the whole of the form, but in the case of suicide that awful feeling of "emptiness" remains until the time comes when, in the natural course of events, his death would have occurred.

As long as the man entertains the desires connected with earth life he must stay in his desire body and as the progress of the individual requires that he pass on to higher Regions, the existence in the Desire World must necessarily become purgative, tending to purify him from his binding desires. How this is done is best seen by taking some radical instances.

The miser who loved his gold in earth life loves it just as dearly after death; but in the first place he cannot acquire any more, because he has no longer a dense body wherewith to grasp it and worst of all, he cannot even keep what he hoarded during life. He will, perhaps, go and sit by his safe and watch the cherished gold or bonds; but the heirs appear and with, it may be, a stinging jeer at the "stingy old fool" (whom they do not see, but who both sees and hears them), will open his safe, and though he may throw himself over his gold to protect it, they will put their hands through him, neither knowing nor caring that he is there, and will then proceed to spend his hoard, while he suffers in sorrow and impotent rage.

He will suffer keenly, his sufferings all the more terrible on account of being entirely mental, because the dense body dulls even suffering to some extent. In the Desire World, however, these sufferings have full sway and the man suffers until he learns that gold may be a curse. Thus he gradually becomes contented with his lot and at last is freed from his desire body and is ready to go on.

Or take the case of the drunkard. He is just as fond of intoxicants after death as he was before. It is not the dense body that craves drink. It is made sick by alcohol and would rather be without it. It vainly protests in different ways, but the desire body of the drunkard craves the drink and forces the dense body to take it, that the desire body may have the sensation of pleasure resulting from the increased vibration. That desire remains after the death of the dense body, but the drunkard has in his desire body neither mouth to drink not stomach to contain physical liquor. He may and does get into saloons, where he interpolates his body into to bodies of the drinkers to get a little of their vibrations by induction, but that is too weak to give him much satisfaction. He may and also does sometimes get inside a whiskey cask, but that is of no avail either for there are in the cask no such fumes as are generated in the digestive organs of a tippler. It has no effect upon him and he is like a man in an open boat on the ocean. "Water, water everywhere, but not a drop to drink;" consequently he suffers intensely. In time, however, he learns the uselessness of longing for drink which he cannot obtain. As with so many of our desires in the Earth life, all desires in the Desire World die for want of opportunity to gratify them. When the drunkard has been purged, he is ready, so far as this habit is concerned, to leave this state of "purgatory" and ascend into the heaven world.

Thus we see that it is not an avenging Deity that makes purgatory or hell for us, but our own individual evil habits and acts. According to the intensity of our desires will be the time and suffering entailed in their expurgation. In the cases mentioned it would have been no suffering to the drunkard to lose his worldly possessions. If he had any, he did not cling to them. Neither would it have caused the miser any paid to have been deprived of intoxicants. It is safe to say that he would not have cared if there were not a drop of liquor in the world. But he did care about his gold, and the drunkard cared about his drink and so the unerring law gave to each that which was needed to purge him of his unhallowed desires and evil habits.

This is the law that is symbolized in the scythe of the reaper, Death; the law that says, "whatsoever a man soweth, that shall he also reap." It is the law of cause and effect, which rules all things in the three Worlds, in every realm of nature--physical, moral and mental. Everywhere it works inexorably, adjusting all things, restoring the equilibrium wherever even the slightest action has brought about a disturbance, as all action must. The result may be manifested immediately or it may be delayed for years or for lives, but sometime, somewhere, just and equal retribution will be made. The student should particularly note that its work is absolutely impersonal. There is in the universe neither reward nor punishment. All is the result of invariable law. The action of this law will be more fully elucidated in the next chapter, where we shall find it associated with another Great Law of the Cosmos, which also operates in the evolution of man. The law we are now considering is called the law of Consequence.

In the Desire World it operates in purging man of the baser desires and the correction of the weaknesses and vices which hinder his progress, by making him suffer in the manner best adapted to that purpose. If he had made others suffer, or has dealt unjustly with them, he will be made to suffer in that identical way. Be it noted, however, that if a person has been subject to vices, or has done wrong to others, but has overcome his vices, or repented and, as far as possible, made right the wrong done, such repentance, reform and restitution have purged him of those special vices and evil acts. The equilibrium has been restored and the lesson learned during that embodiment, and therefore will not be a cause of suffering after death.

In the Desire World life is lived about three times as rapidly as in the Physical World. A man who has lived to be fifty years of age in the Physical World would live through the same life events in the Desire World in about sixteen years. This is, of course, only a general gauge. There are persons who remain in the Desire World much longer than their term of physical life. Others again, who have led lives with few gross desires, pass through in a much shorter period, but the measure above given is very nearly correct for the average man of present day.

It will be remembered that as the man leaves the dense body at death, his past life passes before him in pictures; but at that time he has no feeling concerning them.

During his life in the Desire World also these life pictures roll backwards, as before; but not the man has all the feelings that it is possible for him to have as, one by one, the scenes pass before him. Every incident in his past life is now lived over again. When he comes to a point where he has injured someone, he himself feels the pain as the injured person felt it. He lives through all the sorrow and suffering he has caused to others and learns just how painful is the hurt and how hard to bear is the sorrow he has caused. In addition there is the fact already mentioned that the suffering is much keener because he has no dense body to dull the pain. Perhaps that is why the speed of life there is tripled--that the suffering may lose in duration what it gains in sharpness. Nature's measures are wonderfully just and true.

There is another characteristic peculiar to this phase of post-mortem existence which intimately connected with the fact (already mentioned) that distance is almost annihilated in the Desire World. When a man dies, he at once seems to swell out in his vital body; he appears to himself to grow into immense proportions. This feeling is due to the fact, not that the body really grows, but that the perceptive faculties receive so many impressions from various sources, all seeming to be close at hand. The same is true of the desire body. The man seems to be present with all the people with whom on earth he had relations of a nature which require correction. If he has injured one man in San Francisco, another in New York, he will feel as if part of him were in each place. This gives him a peculiar feeling of being cut to pieces.

The student will now understand the importance of the panorama of the past life during the purgative existence, where this panorama is realized in definite feelings. If it lasted long and the man were undisturbed, the full, deep, clear impression etched into the desire body would make life in the Desire World more vivid and conscious and the purgation more thorough than if, because of distress at the loud outbursts of grief on the part of his relatives, at the death bed and during the three-day period previously mentioned the man had only vague impression of his past life. The spirit which has etched a deep clear record into its desire body will realize the mistakes of the past life so much more clearly and definitely than if the pictures were blurred on account of the individual's attention being diverted by the suffering and grief around him. His feeling concerning the things which cause his present suffering in the Desire World will be much more definite if they are drawn from a distinct panoramic impression than if the duration of the process were short.

This sharp, clear-cut feeling is of immense value in future lives. It stamps upon the seed-atom of the desire body an ineffaceable impression of itself.

The experiences will be forgotten in succeeding lives, but the Feeling remains. When opportunities occur to repeat the error in later lives, this Feeling will speak to us clearly and unmistakably. It is the "still, small voice" which warns us, though we do not know why; but the clearer and more definite the panoramas of past lives has been, the oftener, stronger and clearer shall we hear this voice. Thus we see how important it is that we leave the passing spirit in absolute quietness after death. By so doing we help it to reap the greatest possible benefit from the life just ended and to avoid perpetuating the same mistakes in future lives, while our selfish, hysterical lamentations may deprive it of much of the value of the life it has just concluded.

The mission of purgatory is to eradicate the injurious habits by making their gratification impossible. The individual suffers exactly as he has made others suffer through his dishonesty, cruelty, intolerance, or what not. Because of this suffering he learns to act kindly, honestly, and with forbearance toward others in future. Thus, in consequence of the existence of this beneficent state, man learns virtue and right action. When he is reborn he is free from evil habits, at least every evil act committed is one of free will. The tendencies to repeat the evil of past lives remain, for we must learn to do right consciously and of our own will. Upon occasion these tendencies tempt us, thereby affording us an opportunity of ranging ourselves on the side of mercy and virtue as against vice and cruelty. But to indicate right action and to help us resist the snares and wiles of temptation, we have the feeling resulting from the expurgation of evil habits and the expiation of the wrong acts of past lives. If we heed that feeling and abstain from the particular evil involved, the temptation will cease. We have freed ourselves from it for all time. If we yield we shall experience keener suffering than before until at last we have learned to live by the Golden Rule, because the way of the transgressor is hard. Even then we have not reached the ultimate. To good to others because we want them to do good to us is essentially selfish. In time we must learn to do good *regardless* of how we are treated by others; as Christ said, we must love even our enemies.

There is an inestimable benefit in knowing about the method and object of this purgation, because we are thus enabled to forestall it by living our purgatory here and now day by day, thus advancing much faster than would otherwise be possible. An exercise is given in the latter part of this work, the object of which is purification as an aid to the development of spiritual sight. It consists of thinking over the happenings of the day after retiring at night. We review each incident of the day, in reverse order, taking particular note of the moral aspect, considering whether we acted rightly or wrongly in each particular case regarding actions, mental attitude and actions, mental attitude and habits. By thus judging ourselves day by day, endeavoring to correct mistakes and wrong actions, we shall materially shorten or perhaps even eliminate the necessity for purgatory and be able to pass to the first heaven directly after death. If in this manner, we consciously overcome our weaknesses, we also make a very material advance in the school of evolution.

Even if we fail to correct our actions, we derive an immense benefit from judging ourselves, thereby generating aspirations toward good, which in time will surely bear fruit in right action.

In reviewing the day's happenings and blaming ourselves for wrong, we should not forget to impersonally approve of the good we have done and determine to do still better. In this way we enhance the good by approval as much as we abjure the evil by blame.

Repentance and reform are also powerful factors in shortening the purgatorial existence, for nature never wastes effort in useless processes. When we realize the wrong of certain habits or acts in our past life, and determine to eradicate the habit and to redress the wrong committed, we are expunging the pictures of them from the sub-conscious memory and they will not be there to judge us after death. Even though we are not able to make restitution for a wrong, the sincerity of our regret will suffice. Nature does not aim to "get even," or to take revenge. Recompense may be given to our victim in other ways.

Much progress ordinarily reserved for future lives will be made by the man who thus takes time by the forelock, judging himself and eradicating vice by reforming his character. This practice is earnestly recommended. It is perhaps the most important teaching in the present work.

The Borderland

Purgatory occupies the three lower Regions of the Desire World. The first heaven is in the upper Regions. The central Regions is a sort of borderland--neither heaven nor hell. In this Region we find people who are honest and upright; who wronged no one, but were deeply immersed in business and thought nothing of the higher life. For them the Desire World is a state of the most indescribable monotony. There is no "business" in that world nor is there, for a man of that kind, anything that will take its place. He has a very hard time until he learns to think of higher things than ledgers and drafts. The men who thought of the problem of life and came to the conclusion that "death ends it all;" who denied the existence of things outside the material-sense world--these men also feel this dreadful monotony. They had expected annihilation of consciousness, but instead of that they find themselves with an augmented perception of persons and things about them. They had been accustomed to denying these things so vehemently that they often fancy the Desire World an hallucination, and may frequently be heard exclaiming in the deepest despair, "When will it end? When will it end?"

Such people are really in a pitiable state. They are generally beyond the reach of any help whatever and suffer much longer than almost anyone else. Besides, they have scarcely any life in the Heaven world, where the building of bodies for future use is taught, so they put all their crystallizing thoughts into whatsoever body they build for a future life, and thus a body is built that has the hardening tendencies we see, for instance, in consumption. Some-

60

times the suffering incident to such decrepit bodies will turn the thoughts of the entities ensouling them to God, and their evolution can proceed; but in the materialistic mind lies the greatest danger of losing touch with the spirit and becoming an outcast. Therefore the Elder Brothers have been very seriously concerned for the last century regarding the fate of the Western World and were it not for their special beneficent action in its behalf, we should have had a social cataclysm compared with which the French Revolution were child's play. The trained clairvoyant can see how narrowly humanity has escaped disasters of a nature so devastating that continents would have been swept into the sea. The reader will find a more extended and thorough exposition of the connection of materialism with volcanic outbursts in Chapter XVIII, where the list of the eruptions of Vesuvius would seem to corroborate the statement of such a connection, unless it is credited to "coincidence," as the skeptic generally does when confronted with facts and figures he cannot explain.

The First Heaven

When the purgatorial existence is over the purified spirit rises into the first heaven, which is located in the three highest Regions of the Desire World, where the results of its sufferings are incorporated in the seed-atom of the desire body, thus imparting to it the quality of right feeling, which acts as an impulse to good and a deterrent from evil in the future. Here the panorama of the past again unrolls itself backward, but this time it is the good acts of life that are the basis of feeling. When we come to scenes where we helped others we realize anew all the joy of helping which was ours at the time, and in addition we feel all the gratitude poured out to us by the recipient of our help. When we come to scenes where we were helped by others, we again feel all the gratitude that we then felt toward our benefactor. Thus we see the importance of appreciating the favors shown us by others, because gratitude makes for soul-growth. Our happiness in heaven depends upon the joy we gave others, and the valuation we placed upon what others did for us.

It should be ever borne in mind that the power of giving is not vested chiefly in the monied man. Indiscriminate giving of money may even be an evil. It is well to give money for a purpose we are convinced is good, but service is a thousandfold better. As Whitman says,

Behold! I do not give lectures, or a little charity; When I give, I give myself.

A kind look, expression of confidence, a sympathetic and loving helpfulness--these can be given by all regardless of wealth. Moreover, we should particularly endeavor to help the needy one to help himself, whether physically, financially, morally, or mentally, and not cause him to become dependent upon us or others.

The ethics of giving, with the effect on the giver as a spiritual lesson, are most beautifully shown in Lowell's "The Vision of Sir Launfal." The young and ambitious knight, Sir Launfal, clad in shining armor and astride a splendid charger, is setting out from his castle to seek The Holy Grail. On his shield gleams the cross, the symbol of the benignity and tenderness of Our Savior, the meek and lowly One, but the knight's heart is filled with pride and haughty disdain for the poor and needy. He meets a leper asking alms and with a contemptuous frown throws him a coin, as one might cast a bone to a hungry cur, but

The leper raised not the gold from the dust,
"Better to me the poor man's crust,
Better the blessing of the poor,
Though I turn empty from his door.
That is not true alms which the hand can hold;
He gives only worthless gold
Who gives from a sense of duty;
But he who gives from a slender mite,
And gives to that which is out of sight--
That thread of all-sustaining Beauty
Which runs through all and doth all unite,--
The hand cannot clasp the whole of his alms,
The heart outstretches its eager palms,
For a god goes with it and makes it store
To the soul that was starving in darkness before.

On his return sir Launfal finds another in possession of his castle, and is driven from the gate.

An old bent man, worn out and frail,
He came back from seeking the Holy Grail;
Little he recked of his earldom's loss,
No more on his surcoat was blazoned the cross,
But deep in his heart the sign he wore,
The badge of the suffering and the poor.

Again he meets the leper, who again asks alms. This time the knight responds differently.

And Sir Launfal said: "I behold in thee
An image of Him Who died on the tree;
Thou also hast had thy crown of thorns,
Thou also hast had the world's buffets and scorns,
And to thy life were not denied
The wounds in the hands and feet and side;
Mild Mary's Son, acknowledge me;
Behold, through him I give to Thee!"

A look in the leper's eye brings remembrance and recognition, and

The heart within him was ashes and dust;
He parted in twain his single crust,
He broke the ice on the streamlet's brink,
And gave the leper to eat and drink.

A transformation takes place:

The leper no longer crouched by his side,
But stood before him glorified,
. . . .
And the Voice that was softer that silence said,

62

"Lo, it is I, be not afraid!
In many lands, without avail,
Thou has spent thy life for the Holy
Grail;
Behold, it is here!--This cup which thou
Did'st fill at the streamlet for me but
now;
This crust is my body broken for thee,
This water the blood I shed on the tree;

The Holy Supper is kept, indeed,
In what so we share with another's
need;
Not what we give, but what we share--
For the gift without the giver is bare;
Who gives himself with his alms feeds
three--
Himself, his hungering neighbor, and
me."

The first heaven is a place of joy without a single drop of bitterness. The spirit is beyond the influence of the material, earthly conditions, and assimilates all the good contained in the past life as it lives it over again. Here all ennobling pursuits to which the man aspired are realized in fullest measure. It is a place of rest, and the harder has been the life, the more keenly will rest be enjoyed. Sickness, sorrow, and pain are unknown quantities. This is the Summerland of the spiritualists. There the thoughts of the devout Christian have built the New Jerusalem. Beautiful houses, flowers, etc., are the portion of those who aspired to them; they build them themselves by thought from the subtle desire stuff. Nevertheless these things are just as real and tangible to them as our material houses are to us. All gain here the satisfaction which earth life lacked for them.

There is one class there who lead a particularly beautiful life--the children. If we could but see them we would quickly cease our grief. When a child dies before the birth of the desire body, which takes place about the fourteenth year, it does not go any higher than the first heaven, because it is not responsible for its actions, any more than the unborn child is responsible for the pain it causes the mother by turning and twisting in her womb. Therefore the child has not purgatorial existence. That which is not quickened cannot die, hence the desire body of a child, together with the mind, will persist until a new birth, and for that reason such children are very apt to remember their previous life as instanced in the case cited elsewhere.

For such children the first heaven is a waiting-place where they dwell from one to twenty years, until an opportunity for a new birth is offered. Yet it is more than simply a waiting-place, because there is much progress made during this interim.

When a child dies there is always some relative awaiting it, or, failing that there are people who loved to "mother" children in the earth life who find delight in taking care of a little waif. The extreme plasticity of the desire stuff makes it easy to form the most exquisite living toys for the children, and their life is one beautiful play; nevertheless their instruction is not neglected. They are formed into classes according to their temperaments, but quite regardless of age. In the Desire World it is easy to give object-lessons in the influence of good and evil passions on conduct and happiness. These lessons are indelibly imprinted upon the child's sensitive and emotional desire body, and remain with it after rebirth, so that many a one living a noble life owes much of it to the fact that he was given this training. Often when a weak spirit is born, the Compassionate ones (the invisible Leaders who guide our evolution) cause it to die in early life that it may have this extra training to fit it for what may be perhaps a hard life. This seems to be the case particularly where the etching on the desire body was weak in consequence of a dying person having been disturbed by the lamentations of his relatives, or because he met death by accident or on the battle-field. He did not under those circumstances experience the appropriate intensity of feeling in his *post mortem* existence, therefore, when he is born and dies early life, the loss is made us as above. Often the duty of caring for such a child in the heaven life falls to those who were the cause of the anomaly. They are thus afforded a chance to make up for the fault and to learn better. Or perhaps they become the parents of the one they harmed and care for it during the few years it lives. It does not matter then if they do lament hysterically over its death, because there would be no pictures of any consequence in a child's vital body.

This heaven is also a place of progression for all who have been studious, artistic, or altruistic. The student and the philosopher have instant access to all the libraries of the world. The painter has endless delight in ever-changing color combinations. He soon learns that his thought blends and shapes these colors at will. His creations glow and scintillate with a life impossible of attainment to one who works with the dull pigments of Earth. He is, as it were, painting with living, glowing materials and able to execute his designs with a facility which fills his soul with delight. The musician has not yet reached the place where his art will express itself to the fullest extent. The Physical World is the world of *Form*. The Desire World, where we find purgatory and the first heaven, is particularly the world of *Color*; but the World of Thought, where the second and third heavens are located, is the sphere of *Tone*. Celestial music is a fact and not a mere figure of speech. Pythagoras was not romancing when spoke of the music of the spheres, for each one of the heavenly orbs has its definite tone and together they sound the celestial symphony which Goethe also mentions in the prolog to his "Faust," where the scene is laid in heaven. The Archangel Raphael says,

The Sun intones his ancient song
'Mid rival chant of brother spheres.
His prescribed course he speeds along
In thund'rous way throughout the years.

Echoes of that heavenly music reach us even here in the Physical World. They are our most precious possession, even though they are as elusive as a will-o'-the-wisp, and cannot be permanently created, as can other works of art--a statue, a painting, or a book. In the Physical World tone dies and vanishes the moment after it is born. In the first heaven these echoes are, of course, much more beautiful and have more permanency, hence there the musician hears sweeter strains than ever he did during earth life.

The experiences of the poet are akin to those of the musician, for poetry is the soul's expression of it innermost feelings in words which are ordered according to the same laws of harmony and rhythm that govern the outpouring of the spirit in music. In addition, the poet finds a wonderful inspiration in the pictures and colors which are the chief characteristics of the Desire World. Thence he will draw the material for use in his next incarnation. In like manner does the author accumulate material and faculty. The philanthropist works out his altruistic plans for the upliftment of man. If he failed in one life, he will see the reason for it in the first heaven and will there learn how to overcome the obstacles and avoid the errors that made his plan impracticable.

In time a point is reached where the result of the pain and suffering incident to purgation, together with the joy extracted from the good actions of the past life, have been built into the seed-atom of the desire body. Together these constitute what we call conscience, that impelling force which warns us against evil as productive of pain and inclines us toward good as productive of happiness and joy. Then man leaves his desire body to disintegrate, as he left his dense body and vital body. He takes with him the forces only of the seed-atom, which are to form the nucleus of future desire bodies, as it was the persistent particle of his past vehicles of feeling.

As stated above, the forces of the seed-atom are withdrawn. To the materialist force and matter are inseparable. The occultist knows differently. To him they are not two entirely distinct and separate concepts, but the two poles of one spirit.

Matter is crystallized spirit. *Force* is the same spirit not yet crystallized.

This has been said before, but it cannot be too strongly impressed upon the mind. In this connection the illustration of the snail is very helpful. Matter, which is crystallized spirit, corresponds to the snail's house, which is crystallized snail. The chemical force which moves matter, making it available for the building of form, and the snail which moves its house are also good correspondences. That which is now the snail will in time become the house, and that which is now force will in time become matter when it has crystallized further. The reverse process of resolving matter back into spirit is also going on continually. The coarser phase of this process we see as decay when a man is leaving his vehicles behind and at that time the spirit of an atom is easily detachable from the coarser spirit which has been manifesting as matter.

The Second Heaven

At last the man, the Ego, the threefold spirit, enters the second heaven. He is clad in the sheath of mind, which contains the three seed-atoms--the quintessence of the three discarded vehicles.

When the man dies and loses his dense and vital bodies there is the same condition as when one falls asleep. The desire body, as has been explained, has no organs ready for use. It is now transformed from an ovoid to a figure resembling the dense body which has been abandoned. We can easily understand that there must be an interval of unconsciousness resembling sleep and then the man awakes in the Desire World. It not infrequently happens, however, that such people are, for a long time, unaware of what has happened to them. They do not realize that they have died. They know that they are able to move and think. It is sometimes even a very hard matter to get them to believe that they are really "dead." They realize that something is different, but they are not able to understand what it is.

Not so, however, when the change is made from the first heaven, which is in the Desire World, to the second heaven, which is in the Region of Concrete Thought. Then the man leaves his desire body. He is perfectly conscious. He passes into a great stillness. For the time being everything seems to fade away. He cannot think. No faculty is alive, yet he knows that he *is*. He has a feeling of standing in "The Great Forever;" of standing utterly alone, yet unafraid; and his soul is filled with a wonderful peace, "which passeth all understanding."

In occult science this is called *"The Great Silence."*

Then comes the awakening. The spirit is now in its home-World--heaven. Here the first awakening brings to the spirit the sound of "the music of the spheres." In our Earth life we are so immersed in the little noises and sounds of our limited environment that we are incapable of hearing the music of the marching orbs, but the occult scientist hears it. He knows that the twelve signs of the Zodiac and the seven planets form the sounding-board and strings of "Apollo's seven-stringed lyre." He knows that were a single discord to mar the celestial harmony from that grand Instrument there would be "a wreck of matter and a crash of worlds."

The power of rhythmic vibration is well known to all who have given the subject even the least study. For instance, soldiers are commanded to break step when crossing a bridge, otherwise their rhythmic tramp would shatter the strongest structure. The Bible story of the sounding of the ram's horn while marching around the walls of the city of Jericho is not nonsensical in the eyes of the occultist. In some cases similar things have happened without the world smiling in supercilious incredulity. A few years ago, a band of musicians were practicing in a garden close to the very solid wall of an old castle. There occurred at a certain place in the music a prolonged and very piercing tone. When this note was sounded the wall of the castle suddenly fell. The musicians had struck the keynote of the wall and it was sufficiently prolonged to shatter it.

When it is said that this is the world of tone, it must not be thought that there are no colors. Many people know that there is an intimate connection between color and tone; than when a certain note is struck, a certain color appears simultaneously. So it is also in the Heaven World. Color and sound are both present; but the tone is the originator of the color. Hence it is said, that this is particularly the world of tone, and it is this tone that builds all forms in the Physical World. The musician can hear certain tones in different

66

parts of nature, such as the wind in the forest, the breaking of the surf on the beach, the roar of the ocean and the sounding of many waters. These combined tones make a whole which is the key-note of the Earth--its "tone." As geometrical figures are created by drawing a violin bow over the edge of a glass plate containing sand, so the forms we see around us are the crystallized sound-figures of the archetypal forces which play into the archetypes in the Heaven World.

The work done my man in the Heaven World is many-sided. It is not in the least an inactive, dreamy not illusory existence. It is a time of the greatest and most important activity in preparing for the next life, as sleep is an active preparation for the work of the following day.

Here the quintessence of the three bodies is built into the threefold spirit. As much of the desire body as the man had worked upon during life, by purifying his desires and emotions, will be welded into the human spirit, thus giving an improved mind in the future.

As much of the vital body as the life spirit had worked upon, transformed, spiritualized, and thus saved from the decay to which the rest of the vital body is subject, will be amalgamated with the life spirit to insure a better vital body and temperament in the succeeding lives.

As much of the dense body as the divine spirit has save by right action will be worked into it and will bring better environment and opportunities.

The spiritualization of the vehicle is accomplished by cultivation of the faculties of observation, discrimination and memory, devotion to high ideals, prayer, concentration, persistence and right use of the life forces.

The second heaven is the real home of man--the Ego, the Thinker. Here he dwells for centuries, assimilating the fruit of the last earth life and preparing the earthly conditions which will be best suited for his next step in progress. The sound or tone which pervades this Region, and is everywhere apparent as color, is his instrument, so to speak. It is this harmonious sound vibration which, as an elixir of life, builds into the threefold spirit the quintessence of the threefold body, upon which it depends for growth.

The life in the second heaven is an exceedingly active one, varied in many different ways. The Ego assimilates the fruits of the last earth life and prepares the environment for a new physical existence. It is not enough to say that the new conditions will be determined by conduct and action in the life just closed. It is required that the fruits of the past be worked into the World which is to be the next scene of activity while the Ego is gaining fresh physical experiences and gathering further fruit. Therefore all the denizens of the Heaven World work upon the models of the Earth, all of which are in the Region of Concrete Thought. They alter the physical features of the Earth, and bring about the gradual changes which vary its appearance, so that on each return to physical life a different environment has been prepared, wherein new experiences may be gained. Climate, *flora*, and *fauna* are altered by man under the direction of higher Beings, to be described later. Thus the world is just what we ourselves, individually and collectively, have made it; and it will be what we make it. The occult scientist sees in everything that happens a cause of a spiritual nature manifesting itself, not omitting the prevalence and alarmingly increasing frequency of seismic disturbances, which it traces to the materialistic thought of modern science.

It is true that purely physical causes can bring about such disturbances, but is that the last word on the subject? Can we always get the full explanation by merely recording what appears on the surface? Surely not! We see two men conversing on the street and one suddenly strikes the other, knocking him down. One observer may say that an angry knocked the man down. Another may scoff at this answer and declare that he saw the arm lifted, the muscles contract, the arm shooting out and coming in contact with the victim, who was knocked down. That is also true, but it is safe to say that had there not *first* been the angry thought, the blow would not have been struck. In like manner the occultist says that if materialism had not been, seismic disturbances would not have occurred.

Man's work in the Heaven World is not confined solely to the alternation of the surface of the Earth which is to be the scene of his future struggles in the subjugation of the Physical World. He is also actively engaged in learning how to build a body which shall afford a better means of expression. It is man's destiny to become a Creative Intelligence and he is serving his apprenticeship all the time. During his heaven life he is learning to build all kinds of bodies--the human included.

We have spoken of the forces which work along the positive and negative poles of the different ethers. *Man himself is part of that force.* Those whom we call dead are the ones who help us to live. They in turn are helped by the so-called "nature spirits," which they command. Man is directed in this work by Teachers from the higher creative Hierarchies, which helped him to build his vehicles before he attained self-consciousness, in the same way he himself now builds his bodies in sleep. During heaven life they teach him consciously. The painter is taught to build an accurate eye, capable of taking in a perfect perspective and of distinguishing colors and shades to a degree inconceivable among those not interested in color and light.

The mathematician has to deal with space, and the faculty for space perception is connected with the delicate adjustment of the three semi-circular canals which are situated inside the ear, each pointing in one of the three dimensions in space. Logical thought and mathematical ability are in proportion to the accuracy of the adjustment of these semi-circular canals. Musical ability is also dependent upon the same factor, but in addition to the necessity for the proper adjustment of the semi-circular canals, the musician requires extreme delicacy of the "fibers of Corti," of which there are about ten thousand in the human ear, each capable of interpreting about twenty-five gradations of tone. In the ears of the majority of people they do not respond to more than from three to ten of the possible gradations. Among ordinary musical people the greatest degree of efficiency is about fifteen sounds to each fiber; but the master musician, who is able to interpret and bring down music from the Heaven World, requires a greater range to be able to distinguish the different notes and detect the slightest discord in the most complicated chords. Persons who require organs of such exceeding delicacy for the expression of their faculties are specially taken care of, as the higher state of their development merits and demands. None other ranks so high as the musician, which is reasonable when we consider that while the painter draws his inspiration chiefly from the world of color--the nearer Desire World--the musician attempts to bring us the atmosphere of our heavenly home world (where, as spirits, we are citizens), and to translate them into the sounds of earth life. His is the highest mission, because as a mode of expression for soul life, music reigns supreme. That music is different from and higher than all the other arts can be understood when we reflect that a statue or painting, when once created, is permanent. They are drawn from the Desire World and are therefore more easily crystallized, while music, being of the Heaven World, is more elusive and must be re-created each time we hear it. It cannot be imprisoned, as shown by the unsuccessful attempts to do so partially by means of such mechanical devices as phonographs and piano-players. The music so reproduced loses much of the soul-stirring sweetness it possesses when it comes fresh from its own world, carrying to the soul memories of its home and speaking to it in a language that no beauty expressed in marble or upon canvas can equal.

The instrument through which man senses music is the most perfect sense organ in the human body. The eye is not by any means true, but the ear is, in the sense that it hears every sound without distortion, while the eye often distorts what it sees.

In addition to the musical ear, the musician must also learn to build a long, fine hand with slender fingers and sensitive nerves, otherwise he would not be able to reproduce the melodies he hears.

It is a law of nature that no one can inhabit a more efficient body that he is capable of building. He first learns to build a certain grade of body and afterwards he learns to live in it. In that way he discovers its defects and is taught how to remedy them.

All men work unconsciously at the building of their bodies during antenatal life until they have reached the point where the quintessence of former bodies--which they have saved--is to be built in. Then they work consciously. It will therefore be seen that the more a man advances and the more he works on his vehicles, thus making them immortal, the more power he has to build for a new life. The advanced pupil of an occult school sometimes commences to build for himself as soon as the work during the first three weeks (which belongs exclusively to the mother) has been completed. When the period of unconscious building has passed the man has a chance to exercise his nascent creative power, and the true original creative process--"Epigenesis"--begins.

Thus we see that man learns to *build* his vehicles in the Heaven World, and to *use* them in the Physical World. Nature provides all phases of experience in such a marvelous manner and with such consummate wisdom that as we learn to see deeper and deeper into her secrets we are more and more impressed with our own insignificance and with an ever-growing reverence for God, whose visible symbol nature is. The more we learn of her wonders, the more we realize that this world system is not the vast perpetual motion machine unthinking people would have us believe. It would be quite as logical to think that if we toss a box of loose type into the air the characters will have arranged themselves into the words of a beautiful poem by the time they reach the ground. The greater the complexity of the plan the greater the argumental weight in favor of the theory of an intelligent Divine Author.

The Third Heaven

Having assimilated all the fruits of his last life and altered the appearance of the Earth in such a manner as to afford him the necessary environment for his next step towards perfection; having also learned by work on the bodies of others, to build a suitable body through which to express himself in the Physical World and having at last resolved the mind into the essence which builds the three-fold spirit, the naked individual spirit ascends into the higher Region of the World of Thought--the third heaven, Here, by the ineffable harmony of this higher world, it is strengthened for its next dip into matter.

After a time comes the desire for new experience and the contemplation of a new birth. This conjures up a series of pictures before the vision of the spirit--a panorama of the new life in store for it. But, mark this well--this panorama contains only principal events. The spirit has free will as to detail. It is as if a man going to a distant city had a time-limit ticket, with initial choice of route. After he has chosen and begun his journey it is not sure that he can change to another route during the trip. He may stop over in as many places as he wishes, within his time limit, but he cannot go back. Thus as he proceeds on his journey, he becomes more and more limited by his past choice. If he had chosen a steam road, using soft coal, he must expect to be soiled and dusty. Had he chosen a road burning anthracite or using electricity he would have been cleaner. So it is with the man in a new life. He may have to live a hard life, but he is free to choose whether he will live it cleanly or wallow in the mire. Other conditions are also within his control, subject to limits of his past choices and acts.

The pictures in the panorama of the coming life, of which we have just spoken, begin at the cradle and end at the grave. This is the opposite direction to that in which they travel in the after-death panorama, already explained, which passes before the vision of the spirit immediately following its release from the dense body. The reason for this radical difference in the two panoramas is that in the before-birth panorama the object is to show the returning Ego how certain *causes* or acts always *produce* certain *effects*. In the case of the after-death panorama the object is the reverse, i.e., to show how each event in the past life was the *effect* of some *cause* further back in the life. Nature, or God, does nothing without a logical reason, and the further we search the more apparent it becomes to us that Nature is a wise mother, always using the best means to accomplish her ends.

But it may be asked, Why should we be reborn? Why must we return to this limited and miserable earth existence? Why can we not get experience in those higher realms without coming to Earth? We are tired of this dreary, weary earth life!

Such queries are based upon misunderstandings of several kinds. In the first place, let us realize and engrave it deep upon the tablets of our memory that *the purpose of life is not happiness, but experience.* Sorrow and pain are our most benevolent teachers, while the joys of life are but fleeting.

This seems a stern doctrine and the heart cries out passionately at even the thought that it may possibly be true. Nevertheless, it is true, and upon examination it will be found not such a stern doctrine after all.

Consider the blessings of pain. If we could place our hand upon a hot stove and feel no pain, the hand might be allowed to remain until it and perhaps the arm were burned away, without our knowing anything about it until too late to save them. It is the pain resulting from the contact with the hot stove which makes us snatch our hand away before serious damage is done. Instead of losing the hand, we escape with a blister which quickly heals. This is an illustration from the Physical World. We find that same principle applies in the Moral and Mental Worlds. If we outrage morality the pangs of conscience bring us pain that will prevent us from repeating the act and if we do not heed the first lesson, nature will give us harder and harder experiences until at last the fact is forced into our consciousness that "the way of the transgressor is hard." This will continue until at last we are forced to turn in a new direction and take a step onward toward a better life.

Experience is "knowledge of the effects which follow acts." This is the object of life, together with the development of "Will," which is the force whereby we apply the results of experience. Experience must be gained, but we have the choice whether we gain it by the hard path of personal experience or by observation of other people's acts, reasoning and reflecting thereon, guided by the light of whatever experience we have already had.

This is the method by which the occult student should learn, instead of requiring the lash of adversity and pain. The more willing we are to learn in that way, the less we shall feel the stinging thorns of "the path of pain" and the more quickly shall we gain "the path of peace."

The choice is ours, but so long as we have not learned all there is to learn in this world, we must come back to it. We cannot stay in the higher worlds and learn there until we have mastered the lessons of earth life. That would be as sensible as to send a child to kindergarten one day and to college the next. The child must return to the kindergarten day after day and spend years in the grammar school and the high school before its study has developed its capacity sufficiently to enable it to understand the lessons taught in college.

71

Man is also in school--the school of experience. He must return many times before he can hope to master all the knowledge in the world of sense. No one earth life, however rich in experience, could furnish the knowledge, so nature decrees that he must return to Earth, after intervals of rest, to take up his work where he dropped it, exactly as a child takes up its work in school each day, after the intervening sleep of night. It is not argument against this theory to say that man does not remember his former lives. We cannot recall all the events of our present lives. We do not recollect our labors in learning to write, yet we have acquired a knowledge of the art of writing, which proves that we did learn. All the faculties we possess are a proof that we acquired them sometime, somewhere. Some people do remember their past, however, as a remarkable instance related at the end of the next chapter will show, and is but one among many.

Again, if their were no return to Earth, what is the use of living? Why strive for anything? Why should a life of happiness in an eternal heaven be the reward for a good life? What benefit could come from a good life in a heaven where everybody is already happy? Surely in a place where everybody is happy and contented there is no need for sympathy, self-sacrifice or wise counsel! No one would need them here; but on Earth there are many who need those very things and such humanitarian and altruistic qualities are of the greatest service to struggling humanity. Therefore the Great Law, which works for Good, brings man back to work again in the world for the benefit to himself and others, with his acquired treasures, instead of letting them go to waste in a heaven where no one needs them.

Preparations for Rebirth

Having thus seen the necessity for repeated embodiments, we will next consider the method by which this purpose is accomplished.

Previous to taking the dip into matter, the threefold spirit is naked, having only the forces of the four seed-atoms (which are the nuclei of the threefold body and the sheath of mind). Its descent resembles the putting on of several pairs of gloves of increasing thickness, as previously illustrated. The forces of the mind of the last life are awakened from their latency in the seed-atom. This begins to attract to itself materials from the highest subdivision of the Region of Concrete Thought, in a manner similar to that in which a magnet draws to itself iron filings.

If we hold a magnet over a miscellaneous heap of filings of brass, silver, gold, iron, lead and other metals, we shall find that it selects only iron filings and that even of them it will take no more than its strength enables it to lift. Its attractive power is of a certain kind and is limited to a certain quantity of that kind. The same is true of the seed-atom. It can take, in each Region, nothing except the material for which it has an affinity and nothing beyond a certain definite quantity even of that. Thus the vehicle built around this nucleus becomes an exact counterpart of the corresponding vehicle of the last life minus the evil which has been expurgated and plus the quintessence of good which has been incorporated in the seed-atom.

The material selected by the threefold spirit forms itself into a great bell-shaped figure, open at the bottom and with the seed-atom at the top. If we conceive of the illustration spiritually we may compare it to a diving-bell descending into a sea composed of fluids of increasing density. These correspond to the different subdivisions of each World. The matter taken into the texture of the bell-shaped body makes it heavier, so that it sinks into the next lower subdivision and it takes from that its proper quota of matter. Thus it becomes still heavier and sinks yet deeper until it has passed through the four subdivisions of the Region of Concrete Thought and the sheath of the new mind of the man is complete. Next the forces in the seed-atom of the desire body are awakened. It places itself at the top of the bell, *inside*, and the materials of the seventh Region of the Desire World draw around it until it sinks to the sixth Region, getting more material there, and this process continues until the first Region of the Desire World is reached. The bell has now two layers-the sheath of mind outside and the new desire body inside.

The seed-atom of the vital body is next aroused into activity, but here the process of information is not so simple as in the case of the mind and the desire body, for it must be remembered that those vehicles were comparatively unorganized, while the vital body and the dense body are more organized and very complicated. The material, of a given quantity and quality, is attracted in the same manner and under the operation of the same law as in the case of the higher bodies, but the building of the new body and the placement in the proper environment is done by four great Beings of immeasurable wisdom, which are the Recording Angels, the "Lords of Destiny." They impress the reflecting ether of the vital body in such a way that the pictures of the coming life are reflected in it. It (the vital body) is built by the inhabitants of the Heaven World and the elemental spirits in such a manner as to form a particular type of brain. But mark this, *the returning Ego itself incorporates therein the quintessence of its former vital bodies and in addition to this also does a little original work.* This is done that in the coming life there may be some room for original and individual expression, not predetermined by past action.

It is very important to remember this fact. There is too great a tendency to think that all which now exists is the result of something that previously existed, but if that were the case there would be no margin left for new and original effort and for new causes. The chain of cause and effect is not a monotonous repetition. *There is an influx of new and original causes all the time.* That is the real backbone of evolution--the only thing that gives it meaning and makes it other than an unrolling of latent actualities. This is "Epigenesis"--the free-will that consists of the freedom the inaugurate something entirely new, not merely a choice between two courses of action. This is the important factor which alone can explain the system to which we belong in a satisfactory manner. Involution and Evolution is themselves are insufficient; but coupled with Epigenesis we have a full triad of explanation.

The fate of an individual generated under the law of Consequence, is of great complexity and involves association with Egos in and out of physical existence, at all times. Even those living at one time may not be living in the same locality, so that it is impossible for one individual's destiny to be all worked out in one lifetime or in one place. The Ego is therefore brought into a certain environment and family with which it is some way related. As regards the fate to be worked out, it is sometimes immaterial into which one of several environmental the Ego is reborn, and when such is the case, it is allowed its choice as far as possible, but once an Ego is so placed the agents of the Lords of Destiny watch unseen, that no act of free will shall frustrate the working out of the portion of fate selected. If we do aught of such as to circumvent that part, they will make another move, so as to enforce fulfillment of the destiny. It cannot be too often reiterated, however, that this does not render man helpless. It is merely the same law that governs after we have fired a pistol. We are then unable to stop the bullet, or even to deflect it from its course in any way. Its direction was determined by the position in which the pistol was held when we fired. That could have been changed at any time before the trigger was pulled, as up to that time we had full control. The same is true regarding new actions which make future destiny. We may, up to a certain point, modify or even altogether counteract certain causes already set in motion, but once started, and no further action taken, they will get beyond our control. This is called "ripe" fate and it is this kind that is meant when it is said that the Lords of Destiny check every attempt to shirk it. With regard to out past we are to a great extent helpless, but in regard to future action we have full control, except insofar as we are hampered by our past actions. By and by, however, as we learn that we are the cause of our own sorrow or joy, we shall awake to the necessity of ordering our lives more in harmony with the laws of God and thus rise above these laws of the Physical World. That is the key to emancipation; as Goethe says:

From every power that all the world enchains
Man frees himself when self-control he gains.

The vital body, having been molded by the Lords of Destiny, will give form to the dense body, organ of organ. This matrix or mold is then placed in the womb of the future mother. The seed-atom for the dense body is in the triangular head of one of the spermatozoa in the semen of the father. This alone makes fertilization possible and here is the explanation of the fact that so many times sex-unions are unfruitful. The chemical constituents of the seminal fluid and the ova are the same at all times and were these the only requirements, the explanation of the phenomenon of infertility, if sought in the material, visible world alone, would not be found. It becomes plain, however, when we understand that as the molecules of water freeze only along the lines of force in the water and manifest as ice crystals instead of freezing into a homogeneous mass, as would be the case if there were no lines of force previous to coagulation, so there can be no dense body built until there is a vital body in which to build the material; also there must be a seed-atom for the dense body, to act as gauge of the quality and quantity of the matter which is to be built into that dense body. Although at the present stage of development there is never full harmony in the materials of the body, because that would mean a perfect body, yet the discord must not be so great as to be disruptive of the organism.

Thus while heredity in the first place is true only as regards the material of the dense body and not the soul qualities, which are entirely individual, the incoming Ego also does a certain amount of work on its dense body, incorporating in it the quintessence of its past physical qualities. No body is an exact mixture of the qualities of its parents, although the Ego is restricted to the use of the materials taken from the bodies of the father and mother. Hence a musician incarnates where he can get the material to build the slender hand and the delicate ear, with it sensitive fibers of Corti and its accurate adjustment of the three semicircular canals. The arrangement of these materials, however, is, to the extent named, under the control of the Ego. It is as though a carpenter were given a pile of boards to use in building a house in which to live, but is left to his own judgment as to the kind of house he wishes to build.

Except in the case of a very highly developed being, this work of the Ego is almost negligible at the present stage of man's evolution. The greatest scope is given in the building of the desire body, very little in that of the vital body and almost none in the dense body; yet even this little is sufficient to make each individual an expression of his own spirit and different from the parents.

When the impregnation of the ovum has taken place, the desire body of the mother works upon it for a period of from eighteen to twenty-one days, the Ego remaining outside in its desire body and mind sheath, yet always in close touch with the mother. Upon the expiration of that time the Ego enters the mother's body. The bell-shaped vehicles draw themselves down over the head of the vital body and the bell closes at the bottom. From this time the Ego broods over its coming instrument until the birth of the child and the new earth life of the returning Ego commences.

Birth of the Dense Body

The vehicles of the new-born do not at once become active. The dense body is helpless for a long time after birth. Reasoning from analogy we can readily see that the same must be the case with the higher vehicles. The occult scientist sees it, but even without clairvoyance reason will show that this must be so. As the dense body is slowly prepared for the separate, individual life within the protecting cover of the womb, so the other bodies are gradually born and nurtured into activity, and while the times given in the following description are but approximate, they are nevertheless accurate enough for general purposes and show the connection between the Microcosm and the Macrocosm--the individual and the world.

In the period immediately following birth the different vehicles inter-penetrate one another, as, in our previous illustration, the sand penetrates the sponge and the water both sand and sponge. But, though they are all present, as in adult life, they are *merely present*. None of their positive faculties are active. The vital body cannot use the forces which operate along the positive pole of the ethers. Assimilation, which works along the positive pole of the chemical ether, is very dainty during childhood and what there is of it is due to the macrocosmic vital body, the ethers of which act as a womb for the child's vital body until the seventh year, gradually ripening it during that period. The propagative faculty, which works along the positive pole of the life ether, is also latent. The heating of the body--which is carried on along the positive pole of the light ether--and the circulation of the blood are due to the macrocosmic vital body, the ethers acting on the child and slowly developing it to the point where it can control these functions itself. The forces working along the negative pole of the ethers are so much the more active. The excretion of solids, carried on along the negative pole of the chemical ether (corresponding to the solid subdivision of the Chemical Region), is too unrestrained, as is also the excretion of fluid, which is carried on along the negative pole of the life ether (corresponding to the second or fluid subdivision of the Chemical Region). The passive sense-perception, which is due to the negative forces of the light ether, is also exceedingly prominent. The child is very impressionable and it is "all eyes and ears."

During the earlier years the forces operating along the negative pole of the reflecting ether are also extremely active. In those years children can "see" the higher Worlds and they often prattle about what they see until the ridicule of their elders or punishment for "telling stories" teaches them to desist.

It is deplorable that the little ones are forced to lie--or at least to deny the truth--because of the incredulity of their "wise" elders. Even the investigations of the Society for Physical Research have proven that children often have invisible playmates, who frequently visit them until they are several years old. During those years the clairvoyance of the children is of the same negative character as that of the mediums.

It is the same with the forces working in the desire body. The passive feeling of physical pain is present, while the feeling of emotion is almost entirely absent. The child will, of course, show emotion on the slightest provocation, but the duration of that emotion is but momentary. It all on the surface.

The child also has the link of mind, but is almost incapable of individual thought activity. It is exceedingly sensitive to forces working along the negative pole and is therefore imitative and teachable.

Thus it is shown that all the negative qualities are active in the new-born entity, but before it is able to use its different vehicles, the positive qualities must be ripened.

Each vehicle is therefore brought to a certain degree of maturity by the activity of the corresponding vehicle of the macrocosm, which acts as a womb for it until that degree is reached.

From the first to the seventh year the vital body grows and slowly matures within the womb of the macrocosmic vital body and because of the greater wisdom of this vehicle of the macrocosm the child's body is more rounded and well-built than in later life.

Birth of the Vital Body

While the macrocosmic vital body guides the growth of the child's body it is guarded from the dangers which later threaten it when the unwise individual vital body takes unchecked charge. This happens in the seventh year, when the period of excessive, dangerous growth begins, and continues through the next seven years. During this time the macrocosmic desire body performs the function of a womb for the individual desire body.

Were the vital body to have continual and unrestrained sway in the human kingdom, as it has in the plant, man would grow to an enormous size. There was a time in the far distant past when man was constituted like a plant, having only a dense body and a vital body. The traditions of mythology and folklore all over the world concerning giants in olden times are absolutely true, because then men grew as tall trees, and for the same reason.

Birth of the Desire Body

The vital body of the plant builds leaf after leaf, carrying the stem higher and higher. Were it not for the macrocosmic desire body it would keep on in that way indefinitely, but the macrocosmic desire body steps in at a certain point and checks further growth. The force that is not needed for further growth is then available for other purposes and is used to build the flower and the seed. In like manner the human vital body, when the dense body comes under its sway, after the seventh year, makes the latter grow very rapidly, but about the fourteenth year the individual desire body is born from the womb of the macrocosmic desire body and is then free to work on its dense body. The excessive growth is then checked and the force theretofore used for that purpose becomes available for propagation, that the human plant may flower and bring forth. Therefore the birth of the personal desire body marks the period of puberty. From this period the attraction towards the opposite sex is felt, being especially active and unrestrained in the third septenary period of life--from the fourteenth to the twenty-first year, because the restraining mind is then still unborn.

Birth of the Mind

After the fourteenth year, the mind is in turn brooded over and nurtured by the macrocosmic mind, unfolding its latent possibilities and making it capa-

77

ble of original thought. The forces of the individual's different vehicles have now been ripened to such a degree that he can use them all in his evolution, therefore at the twenty-first year the Ego comes into possession of its complete vehicle. It does this by means of the blood-heat and by developing individual blood. This is done in connection with the full development of the light ether.

The Blood the Vehicle of the Ego

In infancy, and up to the fourteenth year, the red marrow-bones do not make all the blood corpuscles. Most of them are supplied by the thymus gland, which is largest in the fetus and gradually diminishes as the individual blood-making faculty develops in the growing child. The thymus gland contains, as it were, a supply of blood corpuscles given by the parents, and consequently the child, which draws its blood from that source, does not realize its individuality. Not until the blood is made by the child does it think of itself as "I," and when the thymus gland disappears, at the age of fourteen, the "I" feeling reaches its full expression, for then the blood is made and dominated entirely by the Ego. The following will make clear the idea and its logic:

It will be remembered that assimilation and growth depend upon the forces working along the positive pole of the vital body's chemical ether. That is set free at the seventh year, together with the balance of the vital body. Only the chemical ether is fully ripe at that time; the other parts need more ripening. At the fourteenth year the life ether of the vital body, which has to do with propagation, is fully ripe. In the period from seven to fourteen years of age the excessive assimilation has stored up an amount of force which goes to the sex organs and is ready at the time the desire body is set free.

This force of sex is stored in the blood during the third of the seven-year periods and in that time the light ether, which is the avenue for the blood-heat, is developed and controls the heart, so that the body is neither too hot nor too cold. In early childhood the blood very often rises to an abnormal temperature. During the period of excessive growth it is frequently the reverse, but in the hot-headed, unrestrained youth, passion and temper very often drive the Ego out by over-heating the blood. We very appropriately call this an ebullition or boiling over of temper and describe the effect as causing the person to "lose his head," i.e., become incapable of thought. That is exactly what happens when passion, rage, or temper overheats the blood, thus drawing the Ego outside the bodies. The description is accurate when, of a person in such a state, we say, "He has lost control of himself." The Ego is outside of his vehicles and they are running amuck, bereft of the guiding influence of thought, part of the work of which is to act as a brake on impulse. The great and terrible danger of such outbursts is that before the owner re-enters his body some disembodied entity may take possession of it and keep him out. This is called "obsession." Only the man who keeps cool and does not allow excess of heat to drive him out can think properly. As proof of the assertion that the Ego cannot work in the body when the blood is either tool hot or too cold we will call attention to the well-known fact that excessive heat makes one sleepy and, if carried beyond a certain point, it drives the Ego out, leaving the body in a faint, that is, unconscious. Excessive cold has also a tendency to make the body sleepy or unconscious. It is only when the blood is at or near the normal temperature that the Ego can use it as a vehicle of consciousness.

To further show the connection of the ego with the blood we may mention the burning blush of shame, which is an evidence of the manner in which the blood is driven to the head, thus over-heating the brain and paralyzing thought. Fear is the state when the Ego wants to barricade himself against some outside danger. He then drives the blood to the center and grows pale, because the blood has left the periphery of the body and has lost heat, thus paralyzing thought. His blood "freezes," he shivers and his teeth chatter, as when the temperature is lowered by atmospheric conditions. In fever the excess of heat causes delirium.

The full-blooded person, when the blood is not too hot, is active in body and mind, while the anemic person is sleepy. In one the Ego has better control; in the other less. When the Ego wants to think it drives blood, at the proper heat, to the brain. When a heavy meal centers the activity of the Ego upon the digestive tracts, the man cannot think; he is sleepy.

A · LIFE-CYCLE

Mind·Essence of Right Thought "Soul·Essence of "Right Feeling" built into Spirit as basis for Future Right Acts	3rd Heaven	Desire for Experience and Soul·Growth draws the Ego To Re-Birth	World of Abstract
Good in past Life built into the Mind as Right Thought also work on New Environment	2nd Heaven	It Gathers Materials for A New Mind	and Concrete Thought
Essence of Pain built into Soul as Right Feeling / Suffering purges Soul	1st Heaven Purgatory	A New Desire-Body	Desire World
Soul views panorama of past Life ___Death	The Ether	A New Vital·Body Birth of Dense Body	The
Prime of Mentality	43 Life	Birth of Vital Body-Growth	Phys-
Change of Life	42 on Earth 14	Birth of Desire Body Puberty	ical
Prime of Life 2nd Growth	35 28 21	Birth of Mind-Majority	World
Beginning of Serious Life			

79

The old Norsemen and the Scots recognized that the Ego is in the blood. No stranger could become associated with them as a relative until he had "mixed blood" with them and thus become one of them. Goethe, who was an Initiate, also showed this in his "Faust." Faust is about to sign the compact with Mephistopheles and asks, "Why not sign with ordinary ink? Why use blood?" Mephisto answers, "Blood is a most peculiar essence." He knows, that who has the blood has the man; that without the warm blood, no Ego can find expression.

The proper heat for the real expression of the Ego is not present until the mind is born from the macrocosmic Concrete Mind, when the individual is about twenty-one years old. Statutory law also recognizes this as the earliest age when the man is deemed fit to exercise a franchise.

At the present stage of human development the man goes through these principal stages in each life cycle, from one birth to the next.

Chapter Four - Rebirth and the Law of Consequence

Only three theories worthy of note have ever been brought forward to solve the riddle of Life and Death.

In the previous chapter we have, to some extent, explained one of these three theories--that of Rebirth, together with its companion law, the law of Consequence. It may not be out of place to compare the theory of Rebirth with the other two theories advanced, with a view to ascertaining their relative foundation in nature. To the occultist there can be no question. He does not say that he "believes" in it any more than we need to say that we "believe" as to the blooming of the rose or the flowing of the river, or the operation of any of the visible workings of the material world, which are continually going on before our eyes. We do not say of these things that we "believe;" we say that we "know," because we see them. So the occult scientist can say "I know" in regard to Rebirth, the law of Consequence and their corollaries. He sees the Ego and can trace its path after it has passed out of the dense body at death until it has reappeared on earth through a new birth. Therefore to him no "belief" is necessary. For the satisfaction of others, however, it may be well to examine these three theories of life and death in order to arrive at an intelligent conclusion.

Any great law of nature must necessarily be in harmony with all her other laws. Therefore it may be very helpful to the inquirer to examine these theories in their relation to what are admitted by all parties to be "known laws of nature," as observed in that part of our universe with which we are more familiar. To this end we will first state the three theories:

1.   **The Materialistic Theory** holds that life is a journey from the womb to the tomb; that mind is the result of certain correlations of matter; than man is the highest intelligence in the Cosmos; and, that his intelligence perishes when the body disintegrates at death.

2. **The Theory of Theology** asserts that at each birth a newly-created soul enters the arena of life fresh from the hand of God, passing from an invisible state through the gate of birth into visible existence; that at the end of one short span of life in the material world it passes out through the gate of death into the invisible beyond, whence it returns no more; that its happiness or misery there is determined for all eternity by its actions during the infinitesimal period intervening between birth and death.

3. **The Theory of Rebirth** teaches that each soul is an integral part of God, enfolding all divine possibilities as the seed enfolds the plant; that by means of repeated existences in an earthly body of gradually improving quality, the latent possibilities are slowly developed into dynamic powers; that none are lost by this process, but that all mankind will ultimately attain the goal of perfection and re-union with God.

The first of these theories is monistic. It seeks to explain all facts of existence as processes within the material world. The two other theories agree in being dualistic, that is, they ascribe some of the facts and phases of existence to a super-physical, invisible state, but they differ widely on other points.

Bringing the materialistic theory into comparison with the known laws of the universe, we find that the continuity of force is as well established as the continuity of matter and both are beyond the need of elucidation. We also know that matter and force are inseparable in the Physical World. This is contrary to the materialistic theory, which holds that mind perishes at death. When nothing can be destroyed, mind must be included. Moreover we know that mind is superior to matter, for it molds the fact, so that it becomes a reflection or mirror of the mind. We have discovered that the particles of our bodies are constantly changing; that at least once in seven years there is a change in every atom of matter composing them. If the materialistic theory were true, the consciousness ought also to undergo an entire change, with no memory of that which preceded, so that at no time could man remember any event more than seven years. We know that is not the case. We remember the events of our childhood. Many of the most trivial incidents though forgotten in ordinary consciousness, have been distinctly recalled in a swift vision of the whole life by drowning persons, who have related the experience after resuscitation. Similar experiences in states of trance are also common. Materialism is unable to account for these phases of sub- and super-consciousness. It ignores them. At the present stage of scientific investigation, where leading scientists have established beyond a doubt the existence of these phenomena, the policy of ignoring them is a serious defect in a theory claiming to solve the greatest problem of life--Life itself.

We may therefore safely pass from the materialistic theory as being inadequate to solve the mystery of life and death and turn to a consideration of the next theory.

One of the greatest objections to the orthodox theological doctrine, as it is expounded, is its entire and confessed inadequacy. Of the myriads of souls which have been created and have inhabited this Globe since the beginning of existence, even if that beginning dates back no further than six thousand years, the insignificant number of only "one hundred and forty and four thousand" are to be saved! The rest are to be tortured forever and ever! The devil gets the best of it all the time. One cannot help saying with Buddha, "If God permits such misery to exist He cannot be good, and if He is powerless to prevent it, He cannot be God."

Nothing in nature is analogous to such a method of creation in order that destruction may follow. It is represented that God desires ALL should be saved and is averse to the destruction of any, having for their salvation "given His only Son," and yet this "glorious plan of salvation" fails to save!

If a trans-Atlantic liner with two thousand souls on board sent a wireless message that she was sinking just off Sandy Hook, would it be regarded as a "glorious plan of salvation" if a fast motor-boat capable of rescuing only two or three people, were sent to her aid? Certainly not! It would more likely be denounced as a "plan of destruction" if adequate means were not provided for the saving of at least the majority of those in danger.

But the theologians' plan of salvation is vastly worse than this, because two or three of two thousand is an immensely greater proportion than the orthodox theological plan of saving only 144,000 out of all the myriads of souls created. We may safely reject this theory also, as being untrue, because unreasonable. If God were all-wise He would have evolved a more efficacious plan. So He has, and the above is only the theory of the theologian. The teaching of the Bible is very different, as will appear later.

We turn now to consider the doctrine of Rebirth, which postulates a slow process of development, carried on with unwavering persistence through repeated embodiments in forms of increasing efficiency whereby all are, in time, brought to a height of spiritual splendor at present inconceivable to us. There is nothing unreasonable nor difficult to accept in such a theory. As we look about us we find everywhere in nature this striving for perfection in a slow, persistent manner. We find no sudden process of creation or destruction, such as the theologian postulates, but we do find "Evolution."

Evolution is "the history of the progression of the Spirit in Time." Everywhere, as we see about us the varied phenomena in the universe, we realize that the path of evolution is a spiral. Each loop of the spiral is a cycle. Each cycle merges into the next, as the loops of the spiral are continuous, each cycle being the improved product of those preceding it and the creator of those more developed states which succeed it.

A straight line is but the extension of a point. It occupies but one dimension in space. The theory of the materialist and that of the theologian would be analogous to this line. The materialist makes the line of life start at birth, and to be consistent, the death hour must terminate it. The theologian commences his line with the creation of the soul just previous to birth. After death the soul lives on, its fate irretrievably determined by the deeds of a few short years. There is no coming back to correct mistakes. The line runs straight on, implying a modicum of experience and no elevation for the soul after death.

Natural progression does not follow a straight line such as these two theories imply; nor even a circular path, for that would imply a never-ending round of the same experiences and the use of only two dimensions in space. All things move in progressive cycles and in order to take full advantages of all the opportunities for advancement offered by our three-dimensional universe, it is necessary that the evolving life should take the three-dimensional path--the spiral--which goes ever onward and upward.

Whether we look at the modest little plant in our garden, or go to the redwood district of California and examine one of the giant Sequoias with its thirty-foot diameter, it is always the same--every branch, twig or leaf will be found growing in either a single or a double spiral, or in opposite pairs, each balancing either, analogous to ebb and flow, day and night, life and death and other *alternating* activities in nature.

Examine the vaulted arch of the sky and observe the fiery nebulae or the path of the Solar-Systems--everywhere the spiral meets the eye. In the spring the Earth discards its white blanket and emerges from its period of rest its winter sleep. All activities are exerted to bring forth new life everywhere. Time passes. The corn and the grape are ripened and harvested. Again the busy summer fades into the silence and inactivity of the winter. Again the snowy coverlet enwraps the Earth. But her sleep is not forever; she will wake again to the song of the new spring, which will mark for her a little further progress along the pathway of time.

So with the Sun. He rises in the morning of each day, but each morning he is further along on his journey through the year.

Everywhere the spiral--*Onward, Upward, Forever!*

Is it possible that this law, so universal in all other realms, should be inoperative in the life of man? Shall the earth wake each year from its winter sleep; shall the tree and the flower live again and man die? It cannot be! The same law that wakes the life in the plant to new growth will wake the human being to new experience, to further progress toward the goal of perfection. Therefore the theory of Rebirth, which teaches repeated embodiment in gradually improving vehicles, is in perfect accord with evolution and the phenomena of nature, which the other two theories are not.

Regarding life from an ethical viewpoint, we find that the law of Rebirth coupled with the companion law of Consequence, is the only theory that will satisfy a sense of justice, in harmony with the facts of life as we see them about us.

It is not easy for the logical mind to understand how a "just and loving" God can require the same virtues from the milliards whom He has been "pleased to place in differing circumstances" according to no apparent rule nor system, but willy-nilly, according to His own capricious mood. One lives in luxury; the other on "kicks and crusts." One has a moral education and an atmosphere of high ideals; the other is placed in squalid surroundings and taught to lie and steal and that the more he does of both, the more of a success he is. It is just to require the same of both? Is it right to reward one for living a good life when he was placed in an environment that made it extremely difficult for him to go astray, or to punish the other, who was handicapped to such an extent that he never had an idea of what constitutes true morality? Surely not! Is it not more logical to think that we may have misinterpreted the Bible than to impute to God such a monstrous plan and method of procedure?

It is useless to say that we must not inquire into the mysteries of God; that they are past our finding out. The inequalities of life can be satisfactorily explained by the twin laws of Rebirth and Consequence and made to harmonize with the conception of a just and loving God, as taught by Christ Himself.

Moreover, by means of these twin laws a way to emancipation from present undesirable position or environment is shown, together with the means of attaining to any degree of development, no matter how imperfect we may be now.

What we are, what we have, all our good qualities are the result of our own actions in the past. What we lack in physical, moral, or mental excellence may yet be ours in the future.

Exactly as we cannot do otherwise than take up our lives each morning where we laid them down the preceding night, so by our work in previous lives have we made the conditions under which we now live and labor, and are at present creating the conditions of our future lives. Instead of bemoaning the lack of this or that faculty which we covet, we must set to work to acquire it.

If one child plays beautifully on a musical instrument, with hardly an effort at learning, while another, despite persistent effort, is a poor player in comparison, it merely shows that one expended the effort in a previous life and is easily regaining a former proficiency, while the efforts of the other have been started only in the present life, and in consequence we see the uphill work. But, if the latter persist, he may, even in the present life, become superior to the former unless the former constantly improves.

That we do not remember the effort made in acquiring a faculty by hard work is immaterial, it does not alter the fact that the faculty remains with us.

Genius is the hall-mark of the advanced soul, which by hard work in many previous lives has developed itself in some way beyond the normal achievements of the race. It reveals a glimpse of the degree of attainment which will be the common possession of the coming Race. It cannot be accounted for by heredity, which applies only in part to the dense body and not to qualities of the soul. If genius could be accounted for by heredity, why is there not a long line of mechanical ancestry previous to Thomas Edison, each more capable than his predecessor? Why does not genius propagate itself? Why is not Siegfried the son, greater than Richard Wagner, the father?

In cases where the expression of genius depends upon the possession of specially constructed organs, requiring ages of development, the Ego naturally is reborn in a family the Egos of which have, for generations, labored to build a similar organism. That is why twenty-nine musicians of more or less genius were born in the Bach family during a period of two hundred and fifty years. That genius is an expression of the soul and not of the body is shown by the fact that it did not gradually improve and reach efflorescence in the person of John Sebastian Bach, but that the proficiency which reached its highest expression in him towered high above ancestors and descendants alike.

The body is simply an instrument, the work it yields being dependent upon the Ego which guides it, as the quality of the melody is dependent upon the musician's skill, aided by the *timbre* of the instrument. A good musician cannot fully express himself on a poor instrument, and even upon the same instrument, all musicians do not and cannot play alike. Because an Ego seeks rebirth as the son of a great musician it does not necessarily follow that he must be a still greater genius, as would be the case if the physical heredity were a fact and genius were not a soul-quality.

The "Law of Attraction" accounts in quite as satisfactory a manner for the facts we ascribe to heredity. We know that people of like tastes will seek another. If we know that a friend is in a certain city, but are ignorant of his address, we will naturally be governed by the law of association in our efforts to find him. If he is a musician, he will most likely be found where musicians are wont to assemble; if he is a student inquiry will be made at public libraries, reading-rooms and book stores, or if he is a sporting man we would seek him at race tracks, pool-rooms or saloons. It is not probable that the musician or the student would frequent the latter places and it is safe to say that our search for the sporting man would not be successful if we sought him in a library or at a classical concert.

Similarly, the Ego ordinarily gravitates to the most congenial associations. It is constrained to do so by one of the twin forces of the Desire World--the force of Attraction.

The objection may be urged that there are people of entirely opposite tastes, or bitter enemies even, in the same family, and if the law of Association governed why should they be attracted thereto?

The explanation of such cases is that during the Ego's earth lives many relations have been established with various people. These relations were pleasant or otherwise, involving on one hand obligations which were not liquidated at the time; or on the other involving the infliction of an injury and a feeling of very strong hate between the injured and his enemy. The law of Consequence requires an exact adjustment of the score. Death does not "pay it all" any more than moving to another city will liquidate a monetary debt. The time comes when the two enemies will meet again. The old hate has brought them together in the same family, because it is the purpose of God that all shall love one another; therefore hate must be transformed into love and though, perchance, they may spend many lives "fighting it out," they will at some time learn the lesson and become friends and mutual benefactors instead of enemies. In such cases the Interest these people had in one another set in action the force of Attraction, and that brought them together. Had

85

they simply been mutually Indifferent they could not have become associated.

Thus do the twin laws of Rebirth and Consequence solve, in a rational manner, all the problems incident to human life as man steadily advances toward the next stage in evolution--the Superman. The trend of humanity's progress is onward and upward forever, says this theory--not as some people think who have confounded the doctrine of Rebirth with the foolish teaching of some Indian tribes who believe that man is reborn in animals or plants. That would be retrogression. No authority for this doctrine of retrogression can be found in nature or in the sacred books of any religion. In one (and one only) of the religious writings of India is it touched upon. In the Kathopanishad (chapter. v, verse 9) it is stated that "Some men, according to their deeds, go into the womb and others into the 'sthanu.'" "Sthanu" is a Sanskrit word, which means "motionless," but it also means "a pillar," and has been interpreted to mean that some men, because of their sins, go back to the motionless plant kingdom.

Spirits incarnate only to gain experience; to conquer the world; to overcome the lower self and attain self-mastery. When we realize this we shall understand that there comes a time when there is no further need for incarnation because the lessons have all been learned. The teaching of the Kathopanishad indicates that instead of remaining tied to the wheel of birth and death, man will at some time go into the motionless state of "Nirvana."

In the Book of Revelation we find these worlds: "Him that overcometh will I make a *pillar* in the temple of my God *and he shall go no more out*," referring to entire liberation from concrete existence. Nowhere is there any authority for the doctrine of the transmigration of souls. A man who has evolved so far as to have an individual, separate soul cannot turn back in his progress and enter the vehicle of animal or plant, which are under a group-spirit. The individual spirit is a higher evolution than the group-spirit and the lesser cannot obtain the greater.

Oliver Wendell Holmes, in his beautiful poem, "The Chambered Nautilus," has embodied this idea of constant progression in gradually improving vehicles, and final liberation. The nautilus builds its spiral shell in chambered sections, constantly leaving the smaller ones, which it has outgrown, for the one last built:

Year after year beheld the silent toil
That spread his lustrous coil;
Still, as the spiral grew,
He left the past year's dwelling for the new,
Stole with soft step its shining archway through,
Built up its idle door,
Stretched in his last-found home, and knew the old no more.
Thanks for the heavenly message brought by thee,
Child of the wandering sea,

Cast from her lap forlorn!
From thy dead lips a clearer note is born
Than ever Triton blew from wreathed horn!
While on mine ear it rings,

Through the deep caves of thought I hear a voice that sings:

Build thee more stately mansions, O my soul!
As the swift seasons roll!
Leave thy low-vaulted past!
Let each new temple, nobler than the last,
Shut thee from heaven with a dome more vast,
'Till thou at length art free,
Leaving thine outgrown shell by life's unresting sea!

The necessity, previously referred to, of obtaining an organism of a specific nature, brings to mind an interesting phase of the twin laws of Rebirth and Consequence. These laws are connected with the motion of the Cosmic bodies, the Sun, the planets and the signs of the Zodiac. All move in harmony with these laws, guided in their orbits by their indwelling spiritual Intelligences--the Planetary Spirits.

On account of the precession of the equinoxes the Sun moves backward through the twelve signs of the Zodiac at the rate of approximately one degree of space in 72 years, and through each sign (30 degrees of space) in about 2,100 years, or around the whole circle in about 26,000 years.

This is due to the fact that the Earth does not spin upon a stationary axis. Its axis has a slow, swinging motion of its own (just like the wobble of a spinning top that has almost spent its force), so that it describes a circle in space and thus one star after another becomes Pole Star.

Because of this wobbling motion the Sun does not cross the equator in the same place every year, but a few hundred rods further back, hence the name, the "precession of the equinoxes," because the equinox "precedes"-- comes too early.

All happenings on the Earth in connection with the other Cosmic bodies and their inhabitants are connected with this and other Cosmic movements. So are also the laws of Rebirth and Consequence.

As the Sun passes through the different signs in the course of the year, the climatic and other changes affect man and his activities in different ways. Similarly the passage of the Sun by the procession of the equinoxes, through the twelve signs of the Zodiac--which is called a World-year, brings about conditions on the Earth of a far greater variety. It is necessary to the growth of the soul that it should experience them all. In fact, as we have seen, the man himself makes these conditions while in the Heaven World between births. Therefore, every Ego is born twice during the time the Sun is passing through one sign of the Zodiac; and, as the soul itself is necessarily double-sexed, in order to obtain all experiences, it is reborn alternately in a male and a female body. This is because the experience of one sex differs widely from that of the other. At the same time, the outside conditions are not greatly altered in one thousand years and therefore permit the entity to receive experience in the same identical environment from the standpoint of both man and woman.

These are the general terms upon which the law of Rebirth operates, but as it is not a blind law, it is subject to frequent modifications, determined by the Lords of Destiny, the Recording Angels, as, for instance, in a case where an Ego needs a sensitive eye or ear and there is an opportunity for giving it the required instrument in a family with which relations have previously been established. The time for the re-embodiment of the Ego in question may lack, perhaps, two hundred years of being ripe according to the average period, but it is seen by the Lords of Destiny that unless this opportunity is embraced, the Ego will perhaps have to spend four or five hundred years in heaven in excess of the time required, before another chance will present itself. Therefore the Ego is brought to rebirth ahead of schedule time, so to speak, the deficiency of rest in the third heaven being made up at another time. So we see that, not only do the departed work on us from the Heaven World, but we also work on them, attracting or repelling them. A favorable opportunity for procuring a suitable instrument may attract an Ego to rebirth. Had no instrument been available, he would have been kept longer in heaven and the surplus time deducted from his succeeding heaven lives.

The law of Consequence also works in harmony with the stars, so that *a man is born at the time when the positions of the bodies in the solar system will give the conditions necessary to his experience and advancement in the school of life.* That is why Astrology is an absolutely true science, though even the best astrologer may misinterpret it, because, like all other human beings, he is fallible. The stars show accurately the time in a man's life when the debt which the Lords of Destiny have selected for payment is due, and to evade it is beyond the power of man. Yes, they show the very day, although we are not always able to read them correctly.

Perhaps the most striking instance known to the writer of this inability to escape what is written in the stars, though perfectly cognizant of it, occurred in Los Angeles, California, in 1906. Some instructions in astrology were given to Mr. L., a well-known lecturer. Mr. L.'s own horoscope was taken up, because a pupil will be more interested in that than in the nativity of a stranger. He is also enabled to check the accuracy of the interpretation of the signs which are given to him. The horoscope revealed a liability to accidents and Mr. L. was shown how accidents and other events in the past figured to the time of occurrence. In addition, he was told that another accident would befall him and that it would occur on the twenty-first of the following July, or the seventh day after, i.e., on the twenty-eighth, the latter day being regarded as the more dangerous. He was warned against conveyances of any kind and the place of the threatened injury was designated as the breast, shoulders, arms and lower part of the head. He was thoroughly convinced of the danger and promised to remain at home on that day.

The writer went north to Seattle and a few days before the critical time wrote to Mr. L. and again warned him. Mr. L. answered that he remembered the warning and would act accordingly.

The next communication in regard to the matter came from a mutual friend, who stated that on the 29th of July Mr. L. had gone to Sierra Madre on an electric car which had collided with a railroad train, Mr. L. sustaining injuries of the exact description mentioned and also having a tendon cut in the left leg.

The question was why Mr. L., having entire faith in the prediction, had disregarded the advice. The explanation came three months later, when he had recovered sufficiently to write. The letter said, "I thought the 28th was the 29th."

There is no question in the writer's mind that this was a piece of "ripe" fate, impossible to escape, which was accurately foreshown by the stars.

The stars may therefore be called the "Clock of Destiny." The twelve signs of the Zodiac correspond to the dial; the Sun and the planets to the hour hand, indicating the month of the year when the different items in the score of ripe fate allotted to each life are due to work themselves out.

It cannot be sufficiently emphasized, however, that though there are some things that cannot be escaped, man has a certain scope of free will in modifying causes already set going. A poet puts it thus:

One ship sails east and another sails west
With the self-same winds that blow.
'Tis the set of the sail and not the gale
Which determines the way they go.
As the winds of the sea are the ways of fate
As we voyage along through life,
'Tis the act of the soul that determines the goal,
And not the calm or the strife.

The great point to grasp is that our present actions determine future conditions.

Orthodox religionists and even those who profess no religion at all, often bring forward as one of their strongest objections to the law of Rebirth that it is taught in India to the "ignorant heathen," who believe in it. If it is a natural law, however, there is no objection strong enough to invalidate it or make it inoperative. Before we speak of "ignorant heathen," or send missionaries to them, it might be well to examine our own knowledge a little. Educators everywhere complain of superficiality on the part of our students. Professor Wilbur L. Cross, of Yale, mentions among other startling cases of ignorance, the fact that in a class of forty students, *not one could "place" Judas Iscariot!*

89

It would seem as though the labors of missionaries could profitably be diverted from "heathen" countries and from slum work to enlighten the college-bred individuals of our own country, on the principle that "charity begins at home," and "as God will not let the *ignorant* heathen perish" it would seem better to leave him in ignorance where he is sure of heaven, than to enlighten him and so render his chances of going to hell legion. Surely, this is a case of "Where ignorance is bliss 'tis folly to be wise." We would be doing ourselves and the heathen a signal service by letting him alone and looking after the ignorant Christian nearer home.

Moreover, to call this a heathen doctrine does not disprove it. Its assumed priority in the East is not more an argument against it than the accuracy of the solution of a mathematical problem is invalidated because we do not happen to like the person who first solved it. The only question is: Is it correct? If so, it is absolutely immaterial whence the solution first came.

All other religions have been but leading up to the Christian religion. They were Race Religions and contain only in part that which Christianity has in fuller measure. The real Esoteric Christianity has not yet been taught publicly, not will it be so taught until humanity has passed the materialistic stage and becomes fitted to receive it. The laws of Rebirth and Consequence have been secretly taught all the time, but, *by the direct Command of Christ Himself,* as we shall see, these two laws have not been *publicly* taught in the Western world for the past two thousand years.

Wine as a Factor in Evolution

To understand the reason for this omission and the means employed to obscure these teachings, we must go back to the beginning of man's history and see how, for his good, he has been led by the Great Teacher of humanity.

In the teaching of occult science the stages of development on the earth are divided into periods called "Epochs." There have been four of these Epochs, which are designated as follows, respectively: The Polarian, the Hyperborean, the Lemurian, the Atlantean. The present Epoch is called the Aryan Epoch.

In the First or Polarian Epoch, what is now humanity had only a dense body, as the minerals have now, hence he was mineral-like.

In the Second or Hyperborean Epoch, a vital body was added and man-in-the-making possesses a body constituted as are those of plants. He was not a plant, but was plantlike.

In the Third or Lemurian Epoch, he obtained his desire body and became constituted like the animal--an animal-man.

In the Fourth or Atlantean Epoch, mind was unfolded and now, so far as his principles are concerned, he steps upon the stage of physical life as *man.*

In the present, the Fifth or Aryan Epoch, man will in some degree unfold the third or lowest aspect of his threefold spirit--the Ego.

The student is requested to strongly impress upon his mind the emphatic statement that in the process of evolution up to the time when man gained self-consciousness, *absolutely nothing was left to chance.*

After self-consciousness there is a certain scope for the exercise of man's own individual will to enable him to unfold his Divine spiritual powers.

The great Leaders of mankind take everything into consideration, the food of man included. This has a great deal to do with his development. "Tell me what you eat and I will tell you what you are" is not a far-fetched idea, but a great truth in nature.

The man of the first Epoch was ethereal. That does not contradict the statement that he was mineral-like, for all gases are mineral. The Earth was still soft, not yet having solidified. In the Bible man is called Adam and it is said that he was made of earth.

Cain is described as an agriculturist. He symbolizes the man of the Second Epoch. He had a vital body like the plants which sustained him.

In the Third Epoch food was obtained from living animals to supplement the former plant food. Milk was the means used for evolving the desire body, which made the mankind of that time animal-like. This is what is meant by the Bible statement that "Abel was a shepherd." It is nowhere stated that he killed animals.

In the Fourth Epoch man had evolved beyond animals--he had Mind. Thought breaks down nerve cells: kills, destroys and causes decay. Therefore the food of the Atlantean was, by analogy, carcasses. He killed to eat and that is why the Bible states that "Nimrod was a mighty hunter." Nimrod represents the man of the Fourth Epoch.

In the meanwhile, man had descended deeper and deeper into matter. His former ethereal body formed the skeleton within and had become solid. He had also lost by degrees the spiritual perception which was possessed by him in the earlier Epochs. Thus it was designed. He is destined to get it back at a higher stage, plus the self-consciousness which he did not then possess. He had, however, during the first four Epochs, a greater knowledge of the spiritual world. He knew he did not die and that when one body wasted away it was like the drying of a leaf from the tree in the autumn--another body would grow to take its place. Therefore he had no real appreciation of the opportunities and advantages of this Earth life of concrete existence.

But it was necessary that he should become thoroughly awake to the great importance of this concrete existence, so that he might learn from it all that could be learned. So long as he felt that he was a citizen of the higher Worlds and knew for a certainty that physical life is but a small part of real existence he did not take it seriously enough. He did not apply himself to the cultivation of the opportunities for growth which are found only in the present phase of existence. He dallied his time away without developing the resources of the world, as do the people of India today, for the same reason.

The only way in which an appreciation of concrete physical existence could be aroused in man was by depriving him of the memory of his higher, spiritual existence for a few lives. Thus, during his Earth life, he came to hold no positive knowledge of any other than the one present physical life, and was in this way impelled to earnestly apply himself to living it.

There had been religions previous to Christianity which had taught Rebirth and the law of Consequence, but the time had now come when it was no longer conducive to man's advancement that he should know this doctrine, and ignorance concerning it came to be regarded as a sign of progress. This one single life was to be made paramount. Therefore we find that the Christian Religion, as publicly taught, does not embody the laws of Consequence and Rebirth. Nevertheless, as Christianity is the religion of the most advanced Race, it must be the most advanced Religion, and because of the elimination of this doctrine from its *public* teachings, the conquest of the world of matter is being made by the Anglo-Saxon and Teutonic races, in which this phase has been carried furthest.

As some new addition to or change in the food of man has been made in every Epoch to meet its conditions and accomplish its purposes, we now find added to the food of the previous Epochs a new article--*wine.* It was needed on account of its benumbing effect upon the spiritual principle in man, because no religion, in and of itself, could have made man forget his nature as a spirit and have caused him to think of himself as "a worm of the dust," or made him believe that "we walk with the same force with which we think"--indeed, it was never intended that he should go so far as that.

Hitherto only water had been used as a drink and in the ceremonies of the Temple service, but after the submergence of Atlantis--a continent which once existed between Europe and America, where the Atlantic Ocean now lies--those who escaped destruction began to cultivate the vine and make wine, as we find narrated in the Bible story of Noah. Noah symbolizes the remnant of the Atlantean Epoch, which became the nucleus of the Fifth Race --therefore our progenitors.

The active principle of alcohol is a "spirit" and as the humanity of the earlier Epochs used the articles of food best suited to their vehicles, so this spirit was, in the Fifth Epoch, added to the foods previously used by evolving humanity. It acts upon the spirit of the Fifth Epoch man, temporarily paralyzing it, that it may know, esteem and conquer the physical world and value it at its proper worth. Thus man forgets, for the time being, his spiritual home, clinging to this form of existence, which he has previously despised, with all the tenacity born of a feeling that this is all there is--or at least, preferring the certainty of this world to taking chances on a heaven which, in his present muddled state, he does not understand.

Water only had been used in the Temples, but now this is altered. "Bacchus," a god of wine, appears and under his sway the most advanced nations forget that there is a higher life. None who offer tribute to the *counterfeit* spirit of wine or any alcoholic liquor (the product of fermentation and decay) can ever know anything of the higher Self--the *true* Spirit which is the very source of life.

All this was preparatory to the coming of Christ, and it is of the highest significance that *His first act* was to change "water into wine." (John ii:11.)

In private He taught Rebirth to His disciples. He not only taught them in words, but He took them "into the mountain." This is a mystic term meaning a place of Initiation. In the course of Initiation they see for themselves that Rebirth is a fact, for there Elijah appeared before them, who, they are told, is also John the Baptist. Christ, in unequivocal terms, had previously told them, when speaking of John the Baptist, "this is Elijah who was for to come." He reiterates this at the transfiguration scene, saying, "Elijah has come already and they knew him not, but have done to him whatsoever they listed." And following this, it is said that "they understood He spake of John the Baptist." (Matt. xvii:12-13). On this occasion, and also at the time when Rebirth was discussed between Him and His disciples, they told Him that some thought He was Elijah and others that He was one of the prophets who had been reborn. He commanded them to "tell no man." (Matt. xvii:9; Like ix:21). This was to be, for thousands of years, an esoteric teaching, to be known only among the few pioneers who fitted themselves for the knowledge, pushing ahead to the stage of development when these truths will again be known to man.

That Christ taught Rebirth and also the law of Consequence is perhaps shows in not other place as clearly as in the case of the man who had been born blind, where His disciples asked, "Who did sin, this man or his parents, that he was born blind?" (John ix:2).

Had Christ not taught Rebirth and the Law of Consequence, the natural answer would have been, "Nonsense! How could a man have sinned *before he was born*, and have brought blindness upon himself as a result? But Christ does not answer in that way. He is not surprised at the question, nor does He treat it as being at all unusual, showing that it was quite in harmony with His teachings. He explains, "Neither hath this man sinned, nor his parents; but that the works of (the) God should be made manifest in him."

The orthodox interpretation is that the man was born blind in order that Christ might have the opportunity of performing a miracle to show His power. It would have been a strange way for a God to obtain glory-- capriciously condemning a man to many years of blindness and misery that He might "show off" at a future time! We would consider a man who acted in such a manner a monster of cruelty.

How much more logical to think that there may be another explanation. To impute to God conduct which, in a human being, we would denounce in the strongest terms, is surely unreasonable.

Christ differentiates between the physically blind body of the man and the God within, which is the Higher Self.

The dense body has committed no sin. The God within has done some deed which manifests in the particular affliction from which he is suffering. It is not stretching a point to call a man a God. Paul says, "know ye not that ye are

93

Gods? and he refers to the human body as the "temple of God," the indwelling spirit.

Finally, although most people do not remember their past lives, there are some who do, and all may know if they will live the life necessary to attain the knowledge. This requires great strength of character, because such knowledge will carry with it a knowledge of impending fate that may be hanging black and sinister over one, which will manifest in dire disaster. Nature has graciously hidden the past and the future from us, that we may not be robbed of peace of mind by suffering in anticipation of the pain in store for us. As we attain greater development we shall learn to welcome all things with equanimity, seeing in all troubles the result of past evil and feeling thankful that the obligations incurred thereby are being annulled, knowing that so much less stands between us and the day of liberation from the wheel of birth and death.

When a person dies in childhood in one life, he or she not infrequently remembers that life in the next body, because children under 14 years do not journey around the entire life cycle, which necessitates the building of a complete set of new vehicles. They simply pass into the upper Regions of the Desire World and there wait for a new embodiment, which usually takes place in from one to twenty years after death. When they return to birth, they bring with them the old mind and desire body, and if we listened to the prattle of children, we should often be able to discover and reconstruct such stories as the following:

A Remarkable Story

One day in Santa Barbara, Cal., a man by the name of Roberts came to a trained clairvoyant who is also a lecturer on Theosophy and asked for help in a perplexing case. Mr. Roberts had been walking in the street the previous day when a little three-year old girl came up to him and put her arms around his knees, calling him papa. Mr. Roberts was indignant, thinking that someone was trying to father the child on him. But the mother of the child, who came up directly, was equally put out and tried to get the child away. The child, however, kept on clinging to Mr. R., insisting that he was her father. On account of circumstances to be told later Mr. R. could not put it out of his mind, and sought out the clairvoyant, who accompanied him to the house of the child's parents. Where the girl at once ran up to Mr. R. and again called him papa. The clairvoyant, whom I call X, first took the child over to the window to note whether the iris of the eye would expand and contract when he turned her to and from the light, in order to see whether another entity than the rightful owner was in possession of the child's body, for the eye is the window of the soul and no "obsessing" entity can secure control of that part. Mr. X. found however, that the child was normal and next proceeded to question the little one carefully. After patient work carried on intermittently during the afternoon, so as not to tire the child, this is the story she told:

She had lived with her papa, Mr. Roberts, and another mamma in a little house that stood all alone, where no other house could be seen; there was a little brook close to the house where some flowers grew (and here she ran out and brought in some "pussy-willows") and there was a plank across the brook which she was cautioned against crossing, for fear she might fall into the brook. One day her papa had left her mother and herself and had not returned. When their supply of food was exhausted her mamma lay down on the bed and became so still. At last she said quaintly, "then I also died, but I didn't die. I came here."

Mr. Roberts next told his story. Eighteen years before he lived in London, where his father was brewer. He fell in love with their servant girl. His father objected, so he eloped with her to Australia after they had first been married. Here he went out into the bush and cleared a little farm, where he erected a small cabin by a brook, just as described by the little girl. A daughter was born to them there, and when she was about two years old he left the house one morning and went to a clearing some distance from the house, and while there a man with a rifle came up to him, saying that he arrested him in the name of the law for a bank robbery committed on the night Mr. R. had left England. The officer had tracked him here, thinking him the criminal. Mr. R. begged to be allowed to go to his wife and child, but, thinking this a ruse to entrap him into the hands of confederates, the officer refused and drove him to the coast at the point of the gun. He was taken to England and tried and his innocence proven.

First then did the authorities take heed of his constant ravings about his wife and child, whom he knew must starve in that wild and lonely country. An expedition was sent out to the cabin, when it was found that only the skeletons of the wife and child remained. Mr. Roberts' father had died in the meantime, and though he had disinherited Mr. R. his brothers divided with him and he came to America a broken man.

He then produced photographs of himself and his wife, and at the suggestion of Mr. X. they were mixed with a number of other photographs and shown to the little girl, who unhesitatingly picked out the photographs of both her alleged parents, although the photograph shown was very different from the present appearance of Mr. Roberts.

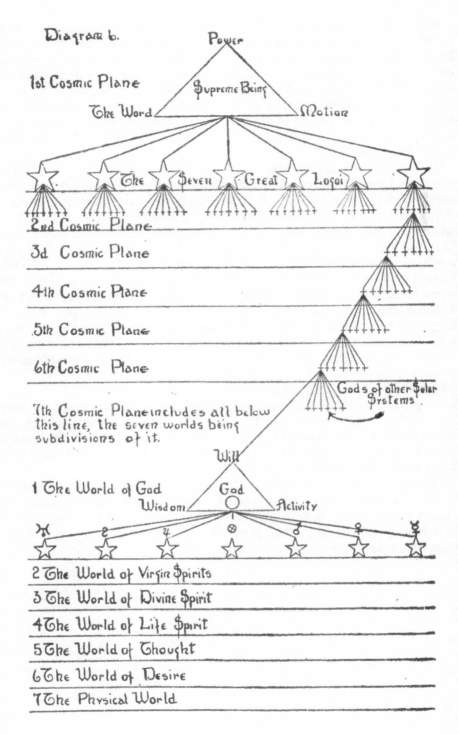

Diagram b.

1st Cosmic Plane

Power

The Word — Supreme Being — Motion

The Seven Great Logoi

2nd Cosmic Plane

3d Cosmic Plane

4th Cosmic Plane

5th Cosmic Plane

6th Cosmic Plane

Gods of other Solar Systems.

7th Cosmic Plane includes all below this line, the seven worlds being subdivisions of it.

Will

1 The World of God

Wisdom — God — Activity

2 The World of Virgin Spirits

3 The World of Divine Spirit

4 The World of Life Spirit

5 The World of Thought

6 The World of Desire

7 The Physical World

96

Part Two – Cosmogenesis and Anthropogenesis

Chapter Five - The Relation of Man to God

In the preceding chapters we have been considering man in relation to three of the five Worlds which form the field of his evolution. We have partly described these Worlds and noted the different vehicles of consciousness by means of which he is correlated to them. We have studied his relation to the other three Kingdoms--mineral, plant and animal--noting the difference in vehicles, and consequent difference in consciousness, between man and each of these Kingdoms. We have followed man through one life cycle in the three Worlds and have examined the operation of the twin laws of Consequence and Rebirth in their bearing upon the evolution of man.

In order to understand further details as to the progress of man, it now becomes necessary to study his relation to the Grand Architect of the Universe--to God and to the Hierarchies of Celestial Beings which stand upon the many different rungs of the Jacob's ladder of attainment that stretches from man to God and beyond.

This is a task of the utmost difficulty, rendered still more so by the indefinite conceptions of God which exist in the minds of the majority of the readers of literature dealing with this subject. It is true that names, in and of themselves, are not important, but it matters greatly that we know what we mean by a name; otherwise misunderstanding will result, and if a common nomenclature is not agreed upon by writers and teachers, the present confusion will be worse confounded. When the name "God" is used it is always uncertain whether The Absolute, the One Existence, is meant; or The Supreme Being, Who is the Great Architect of the Universe; or God, Who is the Architect of our Solar system.

The division of the Godhead into "Father," "Son" and "Holy Ghost" is also confusing. Although the Beings designated by these names are immeasurably above man and worthy of all the reverence and worship he is capable of rendering to his highest conceptions of Divinity, yet They are different from one another in actual fact.

Diagram 6 and diagram 11 will perhaps make the subject clear. It must be kept in mind that the Worlds and Cosmic Planes are not one above another in space, but that the seven Cosmic Planes inter-penetrate each other and all the seven Worlds. They are states of spirit-matter, permeating one another, so that God and the other great Beings who are mentioned are not far away in space. They pervade every part of their own realms and realms of greater density than their own. They are all present in our world and are actually and *de facto* "nearer than hands and feet." It is a literal truth when we say " in Him we live and move and have our being." For none of us could exist outside these great Intelligences Who pervade and sustain our world with Their Life. It has been shown that the Etheric Region extends beyond the atmosphere of our dense Earth; that the Desire World extends out into space further than the Etheric Region; also that the World of Thought extends further into inter-planetary Space than either of the others. Of course, the Worlds of rarer substance occupy a larger space than the denser World, which has crystallized and condensed, thus occupying less space.

The same principle is operative in the Cosmic Planes. The densest of them is the seventh (counting from the top downward). It is represented in the diagram as larger than any of the others, the reason being that it is the plane with which we are most intimately concerned, and it was desired to indicate its principle subdivisions. In reality, however, it occupies less space than any of the other Cosmic Planes, although it must be borne in mind that, even with this comparatively restrictive qualification as to its extent, it is still immeasurably vast, far beyond the utmost power of the human mind to conceive, comprising within its limits millions of Solar Systems similar to our own, which are the fields for the evolution of many grades of beings of approximately our own status.

Of the six Cosmic Planes above our own we know nothing, save that we are told they are the fields of activity of great Hierarchies of Beings of indescribable splendor.

Proceeding from our Physical World to the inner and finer worlds and up through the Cosmic Planes, we find that God, the Architect of our Solar System, the Source and goal of our existence, is found in the highest division of the seventh Cosmic Plane. This is His World.

His realm includes the systems of evolution carried on in the other planets which belong to our system--Uranus, Saturn, Jupiter, Mars, Earth, Venus, Mercury, and their satellites.

The great Spiritual Intelligences designated as the Planetary Spirits, which guide these evolutions, are called the "Seven Spirits before the Throne." They are His Ministers, each presiding over a certain department of the Kingdom of God--which is our solar System. The Sun is also the field of evolution of the most exalted Beings in our Cosmos. They alone can endure and advance by means of the terrific solar vibrations. The Sun is the nearest approach we have to a visible symbol of God, yet it is but a veil for That which is behind. What That is cannot be uttered publicly.

When we try to discover the origin of the Architect of our Solar System, we find that we must pass to the highest of the seven Cosmic Planes. We are then in the Realm of the Supreme Being, Who emanated from the Absolute.

The Absolute is beyond comprehension. No expression nor simile which we are capable of conceiving can possibly convey any adequate idea. Manifestation implies limitation. Therefore, we may at best characterize the Absolute as Boundless Being; as the Root of Existence.

From the Root of Existence--The Absolute--proceeds the Supreme Being, at the dawn of manifestation. This is *The One.*

98

In the first chapter of John this Great Being is called God. From this Supreme Being emanates The Word, the Creative Fiat "without whom was not anything made," and this Word is the alone-begotten Son, born of His father (the Supreme Being) before all worlds--but positively *not* Christ. Grand and glorious as is Christ, towering high above mere human nature, He is not this Exalted Being. Truly "the Word was made flesh," but not in the limited sense of the flesh of one body, but the flesh of all that is, in this and millions of other solar Systems.

The first Aspect of the Supreme Being may be characterized as *power*. From this proceeds the Second Aspect, *the Word;* and from both of these proceeds the Third, Aspect, *motion.*

From this threefold Supreme Being proceed the seven Great Logoi. They contain within Themselves all the great Hierarchies which differentiate more and more as they diffuse through the various Cosmic Planes. (See diagram 6). There are forty-nine Hierarchies on the second Cosmic Plane; on the third there are 343 Hierarchies. Each of these is capable of septenary divisions and subdivisions, so that in the lowest Cosmic Plane, where the Solar System manifest, the number of divisions and subdivisions is almost infinite.

In the Highest World of the seventh Cosmic Plane dwells the God of our Solar Systems in the Universe. These great Beings are also threefold in manifestation, like The Supreme Being. Their three aspects are Will, Wisdom and Activity.

Each of the seven Planetary Spirits which proceeds from God and has charge of the evolution of life on one of the seven planets, is also threefold and differentiates within itself Creative Hierarchies which go through a septenary evolution. The evolution carried on by one Planetary Spirit differs from the methods of development inaugurated by each of the others.

It may be further stated that, at least in the particular planetary scheme to which we belong, the entities farthest evolved in the earliest stages, who had reached a high stage of perfection in previous evolutions, assume the functions of the original Planetary Spirit and continue the evolution, the original Planetary Spirit withdrawing from active participation, but guiding its Regents.

The foregoing is the teaching relative to all the Solar Systems, but coming down to the particular System to which we belong, the following is the teaching which the sufficiently trained Seer can obtain for himself by personal investigation of the memory of nature.

Chapter Six - The Scheme of Evolution, The Beginning

In harmony with the Hermetic axiom "As above, so below" and *vice versa,* Solar Systems are born, die and come to birth anew in cycles of activity and rest, as does man.

There is a constant flaming out and dying down of activity in every department of nature, corresponding to the alternations of ebb and flow, day and night, summer and winter, life and death.

In the beginning of a Day of Manifestation it is taught that a certain Great Being (designated in the Western World by the name of God, but by other names in other parts of the earth) limits Himself to a certain portion of space, in which He elects to create a Solar System for the evolution of added self-consciousness. (See diagram 6).

He includes in His own Being hosts of glorious Hierarchies of, to us, immeasurable spiritual power and splendor. They are the fruitage of past manifestations of this same Being and also other Intelligences, in descending degrees of development down to such as have not reached a stage of consciousness as high as our present humanity, and therefore these latter will not be able to finish their evolution in this System. In God--this great collective Being--there are contained lesser beings of every grade of intelligence and stage of consciousness, from omniscience to an unconsciousness deeper than that of the deepest trance condition.

During the period of manifestation with which we are concerned, these various grades of beings are working to acquire more experience than they possessed at the beginning of this period of existence. Those who, in previous manifestations, have attained to the highest degree of development work on those who have not yet evolved any consciousness. They induce in them a stage of self-consciousness from which they can take up further work themselves. Those who had started their evolution in a former Day of Manifestation, but had not progressed far at the close, now take up their task again, just as we take up our daily work in the morning where we left off the previous night.

All the different Beings, however, do not take up their evolution at the early stages of a new manifestation. Some must wait until those who precede them have made the conditions which are necessary for their further development. There are no instantaneous processes in nature. All is an exceedingly slow unfolding, a development which, though so exceedingly slow, is yet absolutely certain to attain ultimate perfection. Just as there are progressive stages in the human life--childhood, youth, manhood or womanhood, and old age--so in the macrocosm there are different stages corresponding to these various periods of the microcosmic life.

A child cannot take up the duties of fatherhood or motherhood. Its undeveloped mental and physical condition render it incapable of doing such work. The same is true of the less evolved beings in the beginning of manifestation. They must wait until the higher evolved have made the proper conditions for them. The lower the grade of the intelligence of the evolving being, the more it is dependent upon outside help.

At the Beginning, then, the highest Beings--those who are the farthest evolved--work upon those who have the greatest degree of unconsciousness. Later, they turn them over to some of the less evolved entities, who are then

100

able to carry the work a little further. At last self-consciousness is awakened. The evolving life has become Man.

From the point where the self-conscious individual Ego has come into being he must go on and expand his consciousness without outside help. Experience and thought are then to take the place of outside teachers and the glory, power and splendor he may attain are limitless.

The period of time devoted to the attainment of self-consciousness and to the building of the vehicles through which the spirit in man manifests, is called "Involution."

The subsequent period of existence, during which the individual human being develops self-consciousness into divine omniscience, is called "Evolution."

The Force within the evolving being which makes evolution what it is and not a mere unfoldment of latent germinal possibilities; which makes the evolution of each individual differ from that of every other; which provides the element of originality and gives scope to the creative ability which the evolving being is to cultivate that he may become a God--that Force is called "Genius," and as previously explained, its manifestation is "Epigenesis."

Many of the advanced philosophies of modern times recognize involution and evolution. Science recognizes only the latter, because it (Science) deals only with the Form side of manifestation. Involution belongs to the Life side; but the most advanced scientists regard Epigenesis as a demonstrable fact. The Rosicrucian Cosmo-Conception combines all three as necessary to full understanding of the past, present and future development of the System to which we belong.

The Seven Worlds

We might use a homely instance to illustrate the building of a Cosmos. Suppose a man wants to establish a home in which to live. He first selects a suitable location and then proceeds to build a house, dividing it into various rooms to serve certain purpose. He makes a kitchen, dining-room bedrooms and bathroom, and furnishes them all to suit the special purpose they are intended to serve.

When God desires to create, He seeks out an appropriate place in space, which He fills with His aura, permeating every atom of the cosmic root-substance of that particular portion of space with His Life, thus awakening the activity latent within every *in*separate atom.

This Cosmic Root-substance is an expression of the negative pole of the Universal Spirit, while the great Creative Being we call God (of whom we, as spirits, are part) is an expression of the positive energy of the same Universal Absolute Spirit. From the work of one upon the other, all that we see about us in the Physical World has resulted. The oceans, the Earth, everything we see manifesting as mineral, plant, animal, and human forms--all are *crystallized space*, emanated from this negative Spirit-substance, which alone existed at the dawn of Being. As surely as the hard and flinty house of the snail is the solidified juices of its soft body, so surely all *forms* are crystallizations around the negative pole of Spirit.

God draws from the Cosmic Root-substance outside His immediate sphere; thus the substance within the nascent cosmos becomes denser than it is in Universal space, between Solar Systems.

When God has thus prepared the material for His Habitation, He next sets it in order. Every part of the system is pervaded by His consciousness, but a different modification of that consciousness in each part of division. The Cosmic Root-substance is set in varying rates of vibration and is therefore differently constituted in its various divisions, or regions.

The above is the manner in which the Worlds come into being and are fitted to serve different purposes in the evolutionary scheme, the same as the various rooms in the house are fitted to serve the purpose of everyday life in the Physical World.

We have already seen that there are seven Worlds. These Worlds have each a different "measure" and rate of vibration. In the densest World (the Physical) the measure of vibration, though in the case of light-waves reaching a rate of hundreds of millions per second, is nevertheless infinitesimal when compared to the rapidity of the vibration in the Desire World, which is next to the Physical. To get some conception of the meaning and rapidity of vibration, perhaps the easiest way is to watch the heat vibrations rising from a very hot stove, or from a steam radiator near a window.

It must be borne constantly in mind that these Worlds are not separated by space or distance, as is the earth from the other planets. They are states of matter, of varying density and vibration, as are the solids, liquids and gases of our Physical World. These Worlds are not instantaneously created at the beginning of a day of Manifestation, nor do they last until the end; but as a spider spins its web thread by thread, so god differentiates one after another of the worlds within Himself, as the necessity arises for new conditions in the scheme of evolution in which He is engaged. Thus have all the seven Worlds been gradually differentiated as they are at present.

The highest Worlds are created first, and as involution is to slowly carry the life into denser and denser matter for the building of forms, the finer Worlds gradually condense and new Worlds are differentiated within God to furnish the necessary links between Himself and the Worlds which have consolidated. In due time the point of greatest density, the nadir of materiality, is reached. From that point the life begins to ascend into higher Worlds, as evolution proceeds. That leaves the denser Worlds depopulated, one by one. When the purpose has been served for which a particular World was created, God ends its existence, which has become superfluous, by ceasing within Himself the particular activity which brought into being and sustained that World.

The highest (finest, rarest, most ethereal) Worlds are the first created and the last eliminated, while the three densest Worlds, in which our present phase of evolution is carried on, are but comparatively evanescent phenomena incident to the spirit's dip into matter.

The Seven Periods

The evolutionary scheme is carried through these five Worlds in seven great Periods of Manifestation, during which the virgin spirit, or evolving life, becomes first, man--then, a God.

At the beginning of Manifestation God differentiates *within* (not *from*) Himself these virgin spirits, as sparks from a Flame, of the same nature, capable of being fanned into Flames themselves. Evolution is the fanning process which is to accomplish that end. In the virgin spirits are enfolded all the possibilities of their Divine Father, including the germ of independent Will, which makes them capable of originating new phases, not latent in them. The latent *possibilities* are transformed into dynamic powers and available faculties during evolution, while the independent Will institutes new and original departures--or Epigenesis.

Prior to the beginning of the pilgrimage through matter the virgin spirit is in the World of Virgin Spirits, the next to the highest of the seven Worlds. It has Divine Consciousness, but *not Self-* consciousness. That, Soul-power, and the Creative Mind, are faculties or powers attained to by evolution.

When the virgin spirit is immersed in the World of Divine Spirit, it is blinded and rendered utterly unconscious by that matter. It is as oblivious to outside conditions as is man when in the deepest trance. This state of unconsciousness prevails during the first period.

In the Second Period it rises to the dreamless sleep state; in the third Period it reaches the dream stage, and in the middle of the Fourth Period, at which we have now arrived, the full waking consciousness of man is attained. This is a consciousness pertaining to only the lowest one of the seven Worlds. During the remaining half of this Period, and the entire three remaining Periods, man must expand his consciousness so as to include all of the six Worlds above this Physical World.

When man passed through these Worlds in his descent his energies were directed by higher Beings, who assisted him to turn unconscious energy *inward* for the building of proper vehicles. At last, when he was far enough advanced and equipped with the threefold body as a necessary instrument, these higher Beings "opened his eyes" and turned his gaze *outward* upon the Chemical Region of the Physical World, that his energies might conquer it.

When he has fitted himself by his work in the Chemical Region, his next step in progress will be toward an expansion in consciousness that will include the Etheric Region; then the Desire World, etc., etc.

In the Rosicrucian terminology, the names of the seven Periods are as follows:

1. The Saturn Period
2. The Sun Period
3. The Moon Period
4. The Earth Period
5. The Jupiter Period
6. The Venus Period
7. The Vulcan Period

103

These periods are successive Rebirths of our Earth.

It must not be thought that the above mentioned Periods have anything to do with the planets which move in their orbits around the sun in company with the earth. In fact, it cannot be too emphatically stated that there is no connection whatever between these planets and the periods. The Periods are simply past, present or future incarnations of our Earth, "conditions" through which it has passed, is now passing, or will pass in the future.

The three first mentioned Periods (the Saturn, Sun and Moon Periods) have been passed through. We are now in the fourth, or Earth Period. When this Earth Period of our Globe has been completed, we and it shall pass in turn through the Jupiter, Venus and Vulcan conditions before the great septenary Day of Manifestation comes to an end, when all that now is will once more be merged in the Absolute for a period of rest and assimilation of the fruits of our evolution, to re-emerge for further and higher development at the dawn of another Great Day.

The three and one-half Periods already behind us have been spent in gaining our present vehicles and consciousness. The remaining three and one-half Periods will be devoted to perfecting these different vehicles and expanding our consciousness into something akin to omniscience.

The journey made by the virgin spirit from unconsciousness to omniscience, unfolding its latent possibilities into a kinetic energy, is a process of marvelous complexity and only the roughest outline will at first be given. As we progress in our present study, however, more details will be filled in, until the picture is as complete as the writer is capable of making it. The attention of the student is called to the definition of terms that are given as new ideas are being presented. He is earnestly importuned to familiarize himself with them, as the intention is to simplify the matter by using only one familiar English name for the same idea throughout the work. The name will be as descriptive as possible of the idea to be conveyed, in hopes that thereby much of the confusion arising from a multiplex terminology may be avoided. By paying strict attention to definition of terms, it should not be too difficult for any person of average intelligence to acquire a knowledge of at least the outlines of the scheme of evolution.

That such a knowledge is of the utmost importance will, we think, be conceded by every intelligent individual. We live in this world, governed by the laws of nature. Under these laws we must live and work, and we are powerless to change them. If we know them and intelligently cooperate with them, these nature-forces become most valuable servants, e.g., electricity and the expansive force of steam. If, on the other hand, we do not understand them and in our ignorance work contrary to them, they become most dangerous enemies, capable of terrible destruction.

Therefore, the more we know of the working methods of nature, which latter is but the visible symbol of the invisible God, the better able we shall be to take advantage of the opportunities it offers for growth and power; for emancipation from bondage and for elevation to mastery.

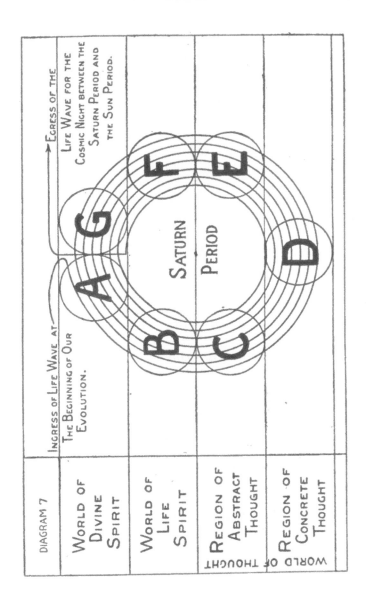

DIAGRAM 7

EGRESS OF THE LIFE WAVE FOR THE COSMIC NIGHT BETWEEN THE SATURN PERIOD AND THE SUN PERIOD.

INGRESS OF LIFE WAVE AT THE BEGINNING OF OUR EVOLUTION.

SATURN PERIOD

WORLD OF DIVINE SPIRIT

WORLD OF LIFE SPIRIT

REGION OF ABSTRACT THOUGHT

REGION OF CONCRETE THOUGHT

WORLD OF THOUGHT

Chapter Seven - The Path of Evolution

A word of warning in regard to diagrams used for purposes of illustration may not be out of place. The student should remember that anything that is reduced into another dimension can never be accurate. The picture of a house would mean little or nothing to us if we had never seen a house. In that case we would see in the picture only lines and blotches. It would convey no meaning to us. Diagrams used to illustrate super physical matters are much less true representations of the reality, for the simple reason that in the case of the picture, the three-dimensional house is only reduced to two dimensions, while in the case of diagrams of the Periods, Worlds and Globes, the realities possess from four to seven dimensions, and the diagrams of two dimensions by which it is endeavored to represent them are thus so much further removed from the possibility of correctly portraying them. We must constantly bear in mind that these Worlds inter-penetrate, that the Globes inter-penetrate, and that the way they are shown in the diagram is analogous to taking all the wheels of a watch and laying them side by side in order to show how the watch keeps time. If these diagrams are to be of any use to the student they must be spiritually conceived. Otherwise they will be confusing instead of enlightening.

Revolutions and Cosmic Nights

The Saturn Period is the first of the seven Periods, and at this early stage the virgin spirits take their first step towards the evolution of Consciousness and Form. By reference to diagram 7 it will be seen that the evolutionary impulse travels seven times around the seven Globes, A, B, C, D, E, F and G, the arrows showing the direction.

First, a part of the evolution is accomplished on Globe A, situated in the World of Divine Spirit, the rarest of the five Worlds which form our field of evolution. Then, gradually the evolving life is transferred to Globe B, which is located in the somewhat denser World of Life Spirit. Here another stage of evolution is passed through. In due time the evolving life is ready to enter the arena on Globe C, which is situated in and formed of the yet denser substance of the Region of Abstract Thought. After learning the lessons peculiar to that stage of existence, the life wave travels onward to Globe D, which is located in and formed of the substance of the Region of Concrete Thought. This is the densest degree of matter reached by the life wave during the Saturn Period.

From this point the life wave is carried upward again to Globe E, which is situated in the Region of Abstract Thought, as is Globe C, yet the conditions are not the same as on Globe C. This is the Involutionary stage, and the substance of the Worlds is getting denser all the time. The tendency in everything is to become denser and more solid as times goes on; also, as the path of evolution is a spiral, it will be clear that, though the same points are gone over, the conditions are never the same, but are on a higher and more advanced plane.

When the work on Globe E has been completed, the next step is taken on Globe F, which is situated in the World of Life Spirit, the same as Globe B; thence it mounts to Globe G. When the work there is done, the life wave has traveled once around all the seven Globes; once down and up through the four respective Worlds. This journey of the life wave is called a Revolution, and seven Revolutions make one Period. During one Period the life wave travels seven times down and up through the four Worlds.

106

When the life wave has traveled its full complement of seven times around the seven Globes, completing the seven Revolutions, the first Day of Creation closes and there follows a Cosmic Night of rest and assimilation, after which the Sun Period dawns.

Like the night of sleep between two days of human life and the interval of rest between two earth lives, this Cosmic Night of rest after the completion of the Saturn Period is not a time of passive repose, but a season of preparation for the activity to be unfolded in the coming Sun Period, where man-in-the-making is to take a further dip into matter. Therefore, new Globes are necessary, the positions of which in the seven Worlds are different from those occupied by the Worlds of the Saturn Period. The providing of these new Globes, and other subjective activities, occupy the evolving spirits during the interval between Periods--the Cosmic Night. The manner of procedure is as follows:

When the life wave has left Globe A in the Saturn Period for the last tine, the Globe begins to slowly disintegrate. The forces which built it are transferred from the World of Divine Spirit (where Globe A is located during the Saturn Period) to the World of Life Spirit (where Globe A is located during the Sun Period). This is shown on diagram 8.

When the life wave has left Globe B in the Saturn Period for the last time, it also commences to disintegrate, and the forces thereof, like the seed-atom of a human vehicle, are used as a nucleus for Globe B in the Sun Period, this Globe being then located in the Region of Abstract Thought.

In like manner the forces of Globe C are transferred to the Region of Concrete Thought and draw upon the substance of that Region for the material wherewith to build a new Globe C for the coming Sun Period. Globe D is similarly transmuted and placed in the Desire World. Globes E, F, and G, in order named, are analogously transferred. The result is (as reference to diagram 8 will show) that in the Sun Period all the Globes are located one step further down into denser matter that they were in the Saturn Period, so that the life wave, upon its emergence from the Cosmic Night of Rest intervening between the last activity on Globe G of the Saturn Period and the renewed activity on Globe A of the Sun Period finds a new environment, with the opportunity thus afforded for new experiences.

The life wave now circles seven times around the seven Globes during the Sun Period, traversing seven times down and up the four Worlds or Regions in which these Globes are located. It makes seven Revolutions in the Sun Period, as it did in the Saturn Period.

When the life wave leaves Globe A in the Sun Period for the last time, that Globe begins to disintegrate. Its forces are transferred to the denser Region of Abstract Thought, where they form a planet to be used during the Moon Period. In the same way, the forces of the other Globes are transferred and serve as nuclei for the Globes of the Moon Period, as shown in diagram 8, the process being exactly the same as when the Globes are removed from their locations in the Saturn Period to the positions they occupied during the Sun

Period. Thus the Globes of the Moon Period are placed one step further down in matter that they were during the Sun Period, the lowest (Globe D) being situated in the Etheric Region of the Physical World.

After the interim of Cosmic Night between the Sun Period and the Moon Period, the life wave starts its course on Globe A of the latter, completing in due time its seven Revolutions, as before. Then there is another Cosmic Night, during which the Globes are again transferred one step further down, and this time the densest Globe is located in the Chemical Region of the Physical World, as reference to diagram 8 will show.

This, then, is the Earth Period and the lowest and densest Globe (Globe D) is our present Earth.

The life wave here, as usual, started on Globe A, after the Cosmic Night succeeding the Moon Period. In the present Earth Period it has circled three times around the seven globes and is now on Globe D, in its fourth Revolution.

Here on earth and in this present fourth Revolution, the greatest density of matter--the nadir of materiality--was reached a few millions years ago. The tendency henceforth will be upward into rarer substance. During the three and one-half Revolutions which remain to complete this Period, the condition of the Earth will gradually become more and more ethereal, and in the next--the Jupiter Period--Globe D will again be located in the Etheric Region, as it was in the Moon Period, the other Globes being also elevated correspondingly.

In the Venus Period they will be located in the same Worlds as were the Globes of the Sun Period. The Globes of the Vulcan Period will have the same density and be located in the same Worlds as were the Globes of the Saturn Period. This is all shown on diagram 8.

When the life wave has completed its work in the Earth Period and the Cosmic Night which follows is past, it will go through its seven Revolutions on the Globes of the Jupiter Period. Then will come the usual Cosmic Night, with its subjective activities; after which the seven Revolutions of the Venus Period; then another rest, succeeded by the last of the Periods of the present scheme of evolution--the Vulcan Period. The life wave also makes its seven Revolutions here, and at the end of the last Revolution all the Globes are dissolved and the life wave is reabsorbed by God, for a period of time equal in duration to that occupied by all the seven Periods of activity. God Himself then merges into the Absolute during the Universal Night of assimilation and preparation for another Great Day.

Other and grander evolutions will then follow, but we can deal only with the seven Periods described.

Diagram 8—The 777 Incarnations

or

Pilgrimage of the Virgin Spirits

7 Revolutions around the 7 Globes of the 7 World Periods.

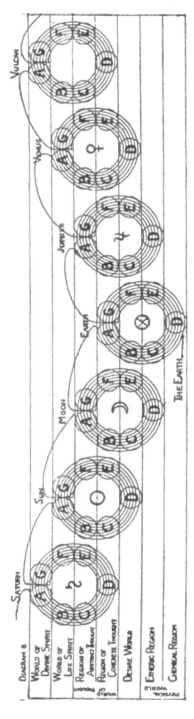

Chapter Eight - The Work of Evolution

Ariadne's Thread

Having become acquainted with the Worlds, the Globes and the Revolutions which constitute the path of evolution during the seven Periods, we are now in a position to consider the work which is done in each Period, as well as the methods employed to accomplish it.

The "Ariadne's thread" which will guide us through the maze of Globes, Worlds, Revolutions and Periods will be found when it is remembered and kept steadily in mind that the virgin spirits which constitute the evolving life wave became entirely *unconscious* when they commenced their evolutionary pilgrimage through the five Worlds of substance denser than the World of Virgin Spirits. The purpose of evolution is to make them fully conscious and able to master the matter of all the Worlds, therefore the conditions embodied in Globes, Worlds, Revolutions and Periods are ordered with that end in view.

During the Saturn, Sun and Moon Periods and the past half of the present Earth Period, the virgin spirits have unconsciously built their different vehicles under the direction of exalted Beings who guided their progress, and have gradually awakened until they have attained the present state of waking consciousness. This period is called "Involution".

From the present time to the end of the Vulcan Period, the virgin spirits, who are now our humanity, will perfect their vehicles and expand their consciousness in the five Worlds by their own efforts and genius. This period is called "Evolution."

The above is the key to the understanding of what follows.

A thorough comprehension of the scheme of planetary evolution which has been outlines in the preceding pages is of immense value to the student. Although some believers in the laws of Consequence and Rebirth seem to think that the possession of such knowledge is quite non-essential and of little use, it is nevertheless of very great importance to the earnest student of these two laws. It trains the mind in abstract thought and elevates it above the sordid things of concrete existence, helping the imagination to soar beyond the hampering toils of self-interest. As stated in our study of the Desire World, Interest is the mainspring to action, yet at our present stage of progress, Interest is generally aroused by selfishness. It is sometimes of a very subtle nature, but it spurs to action of various kinds. All action inspired by Interest generates certain effects which act on us, and in consequence we are bound by action having to do with the concrete Worlds. But, if our minds are occupied with such subjects as mathematics or study of the planetary phases of evolution, we are in the Region of purely Abstract Thought, beyond the influence of Feeling, and the mind is directed upward towards the spiritual realism and liberation. When we are extracting cube root, or multiplying figures, or thinking of Periods, Revolutions, etc., we have no Feeling about it. We do not quarrel about twice two being four. If our feelings were involved we should perhaps try to make it five and quarrel with the one who, for personal reasons, said it was but three, but in mathematics Truth is most clearly apparent and Feeling is eliminated. Therefore, to the average man, desiring to live in the feelings, mathematics is dry and uninteresting. Pythagoras taught his pupils to live in the World of Eternal Spirit and he demanded that those who desired instruction from him should first study mathematics. A mind capable of understanding mathematics is above the average and is capable of rising into the World of Spirit, because it is not fettered in the World of Feeling and Desire. The more we accustom ourselves to think in terms of the Spiritual Worlds, the better we shall be able to rise above the illusions which surround us in this concrete existence, where the twin feelings, Interest and Indifference, obscure the Truth and bias us, as the reflection of the light rays through the Earth's atmosphere gives us incorrect ideas of the position of the luminary emitting them.

Therefore the student who wishes to know Truth; to enter and investigate the realms of Spirit; to free himself from the toils of the flesh, as rapidly as is consistent with safety and proper growth, is earnestly advised to study what follows as thoroughly as possible; to assimilate it and draw mental conceptions of these Worlds, Globes and Periods. If he wishes to progress in this way, the study of mathematics and of Hinton's "The Fourth Dimension" are also admirable exercises in abstract thought. This work of Hinton's (though basically incorrect, because the four-dimensional Desire World cannot be actually found by three-dimensional methods), has opened the eyes of several persons who have studied it, and made them clairvoyant. Moreover, remembering that logic is the best teacher in any world, it is certain that the individual who succeeds in entering into the super-physical World by means of such studies in abstract thought, will not become confused but will be able to give a good account of himself under all circumstances.

A stupendous scheme is here unfolded, and as more and more detail is filled in, its complexity becomes almost inconceivable. Anyone capable of comprehending it will be well rewarded for taking the utmost pains to do so. Therefore, the student should read slowly, repeat often, think deeply and much.

This book, particularly this chapter, cannot be read in a casual manner. Every sentence has weight and bearing upon what follows, and presupposes a knowledge of what precedes it. If the books is not studied thoroughly and systematically, it will grown more and more incomprehensible and confusing with every page. On the other hand, if it is studied and well thought out as the student proceeds, it will be found that each page is illuminated by the increased knowledge gained by study of what went before.

No work of this kind, dealing with the deepest phases of the Great World Mystery that the human mind, at its present stage of development, is capable of grasping, can be written in such a manner that it will be light reading. Yet the deepest phases now comprehensible to use are but the A B C of the scheme as it will be revealed to us when our minds have become capable of understanding more, in later stages of our development as Supermen.

The Saturn Period

The Globes of the Saturn Period consisted of much rarer and finer substances than our Earth, as will be evident from a study of diagram 7 and diagram 8, which the student is advised to keep close at hand for frequent reference while studying this subject. The densest Globe of that Period was located in the same portion of the World of Thought occupied by the rarest of Globes of the present Period--the Region of Concrete Thought. These Globes had no consistency such as we can sense. "Warmth" is the only word that approximates the idea of the ancient Saturn Period. It was dark; and if a person could have entered into the space it occupied, he would have seen nothing. All about him would have been darkness, but he would have felt its warmth.

To the materialist it will, of course, seem insanity to call such a condition a "Globe", and to assert that it was the field of evolution of Form and Life. Yet, when we consider the Nebular Theory, we can realize that the nebula must have been dark before it glowed with light, and that it must have been hot before it could become fiery. This heat must have been brought about by motion, and motion is life.

We may say that the virgin spirits who were to evolve consciousness and form were embedded in this Globe, or perhaps better, that the whole Globe was composed of virgin spirits, as a raspberry is made of a great number of small raspberries. They were incorporated in the Globe, as the life ensouling the mineral is in our Earth. Therefore it is said among occult scientists that in the Saturn Period man went through the mineral stage.

Outside this "warmth-Globe"--in its atmosphere, we might say--were the great creative Hierarchies, who were to help the evolving virgin spirits to develop form and consciousness. There were many Hierarchies, but for the present we shall concern ourselves with the principal ones only--those which did the most important work of the Saturn Period.

In the Rosicrucian terminology these are called "Lords of the Flame," because of the brilliant luminosity of their bodies and their great spiritual powers. They are called "Thrones" in the Bible, and worked on man of their own free will. They were so far advanced that this evolutionary manifestation could give them no new experiences, and therefore no added wisdom, and the same may be said of two still higher order of Hierarchies, to be named later. The rest of the creative Hierarchies, in order to complete their own evolutions, were compelled to work on, in and with man.

These Lords of the Flame were outside the dark Saturn Globe and their bodies emitted a strong light. They, so to say, projected their pictures upon the surface of that ancient Saturn Globe, which was so impressionable that it reflected, in a multiple or echo-like manner, everything that came in contact with it, giving back the images manifolded. (This is told in the Greek myth wherein it is said that Saturn destroyed his children.)

However, by repeated efforts during the first Revolution, the Lords of the Flame succeeded in implanting in the evolving life the germ which has developed our present dense body. This germ was somewhat developed during the remainder of the first six Revolutions, being given the capacity for developing the senses organs, particularly the ear. Therefore, the ear is the most highly developed organ we possess. It is the instrument which carries with the greatest accuracy the impressions of outside conditions to the consciousness. It is less subject to the illusions of the Physical World than the other sense organs.

The consciousness of the evolving life of that Period was like that of the mineral of today--a state of unconsciousness similar to that attained by mediums in the deepest trance--yet during the first six Revolutions, the evolving life worked on the germ of the dense body under the direction and with the help of the different creative Hierarchies. In the middle of the seventh Revolution the Lords of the Flame, Who had been inactive since They gave the germ of the dense body in the first Revolution, again become active, this time to awaken the highest spiritual principle. They aroused the initial activity of the divine spirit in man.

Thus, man owes his highest and lowest vehicles--the divine spirit and the dense body, to the evolution of the Saturn Period. These, the Lords of the Flame of their own free will helped him to manifest, not being under the slightest compulsion to do so.

The work of the various creative Hierarchies is not started on Globe A, at the commencement of a Period or a Revolution. It commences in the middle of one Revolution, growing in strength and reaching its highest efficiency in the middle of the Cosmic Night--which is between Revolutions, as well as between Periods. Then it gradually declines, as the life wave sweeps on to the middle of the next Revolution.

Thus the work of the Lords of the Flame in awakening the germinal consciousness, was most active and efficient during the rest Period between the Saturn and Sun Periods.

We reiterate that a Cosmic Night is not to be regarded as a time of inactivity. It is not inert existence, as we saw in the case of the individual passing from death to a new birth. So with the great death of all the Globes of a Period. It is a cessation of active manifestation, that a proportionately keener subjective activity may be unfolded.

Perhaps the best idea of the nature of this subjective activity may be gained by observing what happens when a ripe fruit is buried in the ground. Fermentation and decay of the flesh sets in, but out of that chaos comes the new plant, sprouting forth into the air and sunshine. So, when a Period is past, all is resolved into conglomerate chaos, apparently incapable of being reduced to order. At the proper time, however, the Globes of a new period are formed

113

and made ready for occupancy as man-bearing Worlds. Hither the evolving life is transferred from five dark Globes which it traverses during the Cosmic Night, to commence the activities of a new creative day in an altered environment, prepared and externalized during the activities of the Cosmic Night. As the forces of fermentation in the fruit stimulate the seed and fertilize the soil in which it grows, so the Lords of the Flame stimulated the germ of divine spirit, particularly during the Cosmic Night between the Saturn and Sun Periods, continuing their activities until the middle of the first Revolution of the Sun Period.

Recapitulation

Before the activity in any Period can be started, there is a recapitulation of all that has been gone through before. Owing to the spiral path of evolution, this activity takes place each time on a higher scale that the stage in progression which it rehearses. The necessity will become apparent when the actual work in recapitulation is described.

The first Revolution of any Period is a recapitulation of the work upon the dense body in the Saturn Period, and is spoken of among Rosicrucians as the "Saturn Revolution."

The Second Period is the Sun Period, and therefore the second Revolution of any Period subsequent to the Sun Period would be the "Sun Revolution."

The third Period is the Moon Period, therefore the third Revolution of any subsequent Period will be a recapitulation of the work done in the Moon Period, and is called the "Moon Revolution."

Not until after the recapitulatory Revolutions does the proper work of a Period begin. For instance, in the present Earth Period, we have passed through three and one-half Revolutions. That means that in the first, or Saturn Revolution of the Earth Period, the work done in the Saturn Period was repeated, but on an advanced scale. In the second, or Sun Revolution, the work of the Sun Period was gone through again. In the third, or Moon Revolution, the work of the Moon Period was repeated; and it was only in the fourth--the present Revolution--that the real work of the Earth Period commenced.

In the last of the seven Periods--the Vulcan Period--only the last Revolution will be concerned with real Vulcan work. In the preceding six Revolutions the work of the preceding six Periods will have been recapitulated.

Moreover (and this will particularly help the student to remember), a Saturn Revolution in any Period has always to do with the development of some new feature of the dense body, because that was started in a first Revolution; and *any* seventh, or Vulcan Revolution, has for its particular work some activity in connection with the divine spirit, because that was started in a seventh Revolution. In the same way, we shall see that there is a connection between the different Revolutions and all the vehicles of man.

114

The Sun Period

Conditions during the Sun Period differed radically from those of the Saturn Period. Instead of the "warmth-Globes" of the latter, the Sun Period Globes were glowing light-balls, of the consistency of gas. These great gas balls contained all that had been evolved in the Saturn Period, and similarly, in the atmosphere were the creative Hierarchies.

Instead of the echo-like, reflecting quality of the Saturn Period, these Globes, to some extent, had the quality of absorbing and working over sight or sound projected against their surfaces. They, as it were, "sensed" things. The Earth does not seem to do this, and a materialist would scoff at the idea, yet the occultist knows that the Earth feels everything on and in it. This lighter Globe was much more sensitive that the Earth, because it was not limited and bound in such hard and fast conditions of materiality as is our present habitat.

The life, of course, was different, because no forms such as we know could have existed there. But life can express itself in forms of fiery gas as well as-- in fact better than--in forms of hard chemical matter such as the present dense forms of mineral, plant, animal and man.

As the evolving life appeared upon Globe A in the first or Saturn Revolution of the Sun Period, it was still in charge of the Lords of the Flame who, in the middle of the last Revolution of the Saturn Period, awakened in man the germ of the divine spirit.

They had previously given the germ of the dense body and, in the first half of the Saturn Revolution of the Sun Period, were concerned with certain improvements to be made upon it.

In the Sun Period the formation of the vital body was to be commenced, with all thereby implied of capability for assimilation, growth, propagation, glands, etc.

The Lords of the Flame incorporated in the germ of the dense body only the capability of evolving sense organs. At the time now under consideration it became necessary to change the germ in such a way as to allow of interpenetration by a vital body, also capability of evolving glands and an alimentary canal. This was done by the joint action of the Lords of the Flame, who gave the original germ, and the Lords of Wisdom, who took charge of material evolution in the Sun Period.

The Lords of Wisdom, who were not so highly evolved as the Lords of the Flame, worked to complete their own evolution; therefore they received the assistance of an order of exalted Beings who, like the Lords of the Flame, acted of their own free will. In esoteric parlance they are called the Cherubim. These exalted Beings did not, however, become active in the work until it was necessary to awaken the germ of the second spiritual principle of our man-in-the-making, as the Lords of Wisdom were quite capable of doing the work connected with the vital body which was to be added to the constitution of man in the Sun Period, but not of awakening the second spiritual principle.

When the Lords of the Flame and the Lords of Wisdom had, in the Saturn Revolution of the Sun Period, conjointly reconstructed the germinal dense body, the Lords of Wisdom, in the second Revolution, started the proper work of the Sun Period, by radiating from their own bodies the germ of the vital body, making it capable of inter-penetrating the dense body and giving to the germ the capability of furthering growth and propagation and of exciting the sense centers of the dense body and causing it to move. In short, they gave, germinally, to the vital body all the faculties which it is now unfolding to become a perfect and pliable instrument for the use of the spirit.

This work occupied the second, third, fourth and fifth Revolutions of the Sun Period. In the sixth Revolution the Cherubim entered and awakened the germ of the second aspect of the threefold spirit in man--the life spirit. In the seventh and last Revolution the newly awakened germ of the life spirit was linked to the germinal divine spirit, and this was still further worked upon.

We remember that in the Saturn Period our consciousness was similar to the trace condition. By the activity of the Sun Period this was modified until it became like the consciousness of dreamless sleep.

Evolution in the Sun Period added to the constitution of the evolving embryonic man, the next highest and the next lowest of his present vehicles. As the result of the Saturn Period he possessed a germinal dense body and divine spirit. At the end of the Sun Period he possessed a germinal dense body, vital body, divine spirit and life spirit, i.e., a twofold spirit and a twofold body.

We also note that, as the first, or Saturn Revolution, of any Period is concerned with work in the dense body (because that was started in a first Revolution), so the second, or Sun Revolution, of any Period is concerned with improvements on the vital body, because it was started in a second Revolution. In like manner, the sixth Revolution of any Period is dedicated to some work on the life spirit, and any seventh Revolution is particularly concerned with matters connected with the divine spirit.

In the Saturn Period man-in-the-making went through a mineral stage of existence. That is to say, he had a dense body only in the sense as had the mineral. His consciousness was also similar to that of the present mineral.

In the same way, and for analogous reasons, it may be said that in the Sun Period man went through the plant existence. He had a dense body and a vital body, as plants have, and his consciousness, like theirs, was that of dreamless sleep. The student will fully grasp this analogy by referring to diagram 4 in the chapter on the four kingdoms, where the vehicles of consciousness possessed by mineral, plant, animal and man are schematically shown, with the particular consciousness resulting from their possession in each case.

When the Sun Period was past there came another Cosmic Night of assimilation, together with the subjective activity necessary before the opening of the Moon Period. This was equal in length to the preceding Period of objective manifestation.

116

The Moon Period

As the chief characteristic feature of the dark Saturn Globes was described by the term "warmth," and that of the Sun Period Globes as "light" or glowing heat, so the chief characteristic feature of the Globes of the Moon Period may be best described by the term "moisture." There was no air such as we know. In the center was the hot fiery core. Next to that, and consequent upon contact with the cold of outside space, there was dense moisture. By contact with the fiery central core the dense moisture was changed into hot steam, which rushed outward to cool, and sink again toward the center. Therefore the occult scientist calls the Globes of the Moon Period "water" and describes the atmosphere of that time as "fire-fog." That was the scene of the next forward step of the evolving life.

The Moon Period work was that of acquiring the germ of a desire body and starting the germinal activity of the third aspect of the threefold spirit in man--the human spirit--the Ego.

In the middle of the seventh Revolution of the Sun Period, the Lords of Wisdom took charge of the germinal life spirit given by the Cherubim in the sixth Revolution of the Sun Period. They did this for the purpose of linking it to the divine spirit. Their greatest activity in this work was reached in the Cosmic Night intervening between the Sun and Moon Periods. In the first dawn of the Moon Period, as the life wave started upon its new pilgrimage, the Lords of Wisdom reappeared, bearing with them the germinal vehicles of the evolving man. In the first or Saturn Revolution of the Moon Period, they co-operated with the "Lords of Individuality," who had special charge of the material evolution of the Moon Period. Together they reconstructed the germ of the dense body, brought over from the Sun Period. This germ had unfolded embryonic sense organs, digestive organs, glands, etc., and was inter-penetrated by a budding vital body which diffused a certain degree of life into the embryonic dense body. Of course, it was not solid and visible as it is now, yet in a crude sort of way it was somewhat organized and is perfectly distinguishable to the trained clairvoyant sight of the competent investigator who searches the memory of nature for scenes in that far-off past.

In the Moon Period it was necessary to reconstruct the dense body to make it capable of being inter-penetrated by a desire body, and also capable of evolving a nervous system, muscle, cartilage and a rudimentary skeleton. This reconstruction was the work of the Saturn Revolution of the Moon Period.

In the second, or Sun Revolution, the vital body was also modified to render it capable of being inter-penetrated by a desire body, also of accommodating itself to the nervous system, muscle, skeleton, etc. The Lords of Wisdom, who were the originators of the vital body, also helped the Lords of Individuality with this work.

In the third Revolution the proper Moon work commenced. The Lords of Individuality radiated from themselves the substance which they helped the unconscious, evolving man to appropriate and build into a germinal desire body. They also helped him to incorporate this germinal desire body in the compound vital body and dense body which he already possessed. This work was carried on all through the third and fourth Revolutions of the Moon Period.

As with the Lords of Wisdom, so with the Lords of Individuality; though exalted far above man, they worked on and in him to complete their own evolution. While they were capable of dealing with the lower vehicle, they were powerless in regard to the higher. They could not give the spiritual impulse necessary to the awakening of the third aspect of the threefold spirit in man. Therefore another class of Beings who were beyond the necessity of evolving in such an evolution as we are passing through--who also worked of their own free will, as did the Lords of the Flame and the Cherubim--came in during the fifth Revolution of the Moon Period, to help man. They are called "Seraphim." They awakened the germ of the third aspect of the spirit--the human spirit.

In the sixth Revolution of the Moon Period the Cherubim reappeared and co-operated with the Lords of Individuality to link the newly acquired germ of the human spirit to life spirit.

In the seventh Revolution of the Moon Period the Lords of the Flame again came to the aid of man, helping the Lords of Individuality to link the human spirit to the divine spirit. Thus the separate Ego--the threefold spirit--came into existence.

Before the beginning of the Saturn Period the virgin spirits who are now man, were in the World of Virgin Spirits, and were "All-conscious" as God in who (not from whom), they were differentiated. They were not *"self"* conscious however. The attainment of that faculty is partly the object of evolution which plunges the virgin spirits into a sea of matter of gradually increasing density which eventually shuts it from the All-consciousness.

Thus, in the Saturn Period the virgin spirits were immersed in the World of Divine Spirit and encased in the tiniest film of that substance which they partially penetrated by the help of the Lords of Flame.

In the Sun Period the virgin spirit was plunged into the denser World of Life Spirit and more effectively blinded to the All-consciousness by a second veil of the substance of the World of Life Spirit. Still, by the help of the Cherubim it partially penetrated this second veil also. The feeling of the Oneness of All was not lost either, for the World of Life Spirit is still a universal World common to and inter-penetrating all the planets of a Solar System.

In the Moon Period, however, the virgin spirits take a further dip into the still denser matter of the Region of Abstract Thought and here the most opaque of its veils, the human spirit, is added. Henceforth the All-consciousness of the virgin spirit is lost. It can no longer penetrate its veils, look *outwards* and perceive *others*, so it is forced to turn its consciousness *inwards* and there it finds its *self*, as the Ego, separated and apart from all others.

Thus the virgin spirit is encased in a threefold veil, and as its outermost veil, the human spirit, effectively blinds it to the oneness of Life, it becomes the Ego by entertaining the illusion of separateness contracted during involution. Evolution will gradually dissolve the illusion, bring back the All-consciousness, and Self-consciousness will have been added.

Thus we see that at the close of the Moon Period man possessed a threefold body in varying stages of development; and also the germ of the threefold spirit. He had dense, vital, and desire bodies, and divine, life and human spirit. All he lacked was the link to connect them.

It has been stated that man passed through the mineral stage in the Saturn Period; through the plant stage in the Sun Period, and his pilgrimage through the conditions of the Moon Period corresponds to the phase of animal existence, for the same reason that the two other similes are applicable--he had the dense, vital, and desire bodies, as have our present animals, and his consciousness was an internal picture-consciousness, such as the lower animals have today. This resembles the dream consciousness of man, save that it is perfectly rational, being directed by the group-spirit of the animals. The student is again referred to diagram 4 in the chapter on the four kingdoms, where this is shown.

These Moon beings were not so purely germinal as in the previous Periods. To the trained clairvoyant they appear suspended by strings in the atmosphere of the fire-fog, as the embryo hangs from the placenta by the umbilical cord. Currents (common to all of them), which provided some sort of nourishment flowed in and out from the atmosphere, through those cords. These currents were thus, to some extent, similar in their function to the blood of the present day. The name "blood" as applied to these currents, however, is used merely to suggest an analogy, because the Being of the Moon Period possessed nothing like our present red blood, which is one of the very latest acquisitions of man.

Towards the end of the Moon Period there was a division of the Globe which was the field of our and other evolutions, which, for the sake of greater simplicity, we have not heretofore mentioned, but with which we shall presently become acquainted.

Part of that great Globe was crystallized by man on account of his inability to keep the part which he inhabited in the high state of vibration maintained by the other beings there, and as this part became more inert the centrifugal force of the revolving Globe sent it spinning into space, where it began to circle around the glowing fiery central portion.

The spiritual reason for the throwing off of such crystallizations is that the highest beings on such a Globe require for their evolution the exceedingly rapid vibrations of fire. They are hampered by condensation, although such a condition is necessary to the evolution of other and less advanced beings required lower rates of vibration. Therefore, when part of any Globe has been consolidated by a group of evolving beings to the detriment of others, that part is thrown off to exactly the proper distance from the central mass,

119

so that it circles as a satellite around its primary. The heat vibrations which strike it are of the rate and strength suitable to the peculiar needs of the beings evolving upon that satellite. Of course the law of gravitation accounts quite satisfactorily for the phenomenon from a *physical* viewpoint. But there is always a deeper cause, that yields a more complete explanation and which we will find if we consider the spiritual side of things. As a physical action is but the visible manifestation of the invisible thought which must precede it, so is the throwing off of a planet from a central Sun simply the visible and unavoidable effect of invisible spiritual conditions.

The smaller planet which was thrown off in the Moon Period, condensed with comparative rapidity and remained the field of our evolution until the end of that Period. It was a moon to the parent planet, circling around it as our Moon circles around the Earth, but it did not show phases as our Moon does. It revolved in such a manner that one-half was always light and the other always dark, as is the case with Venus. One of its poles was pointed directly towards the large fiery Globe, as one of the poles of Venus points directly towards the Sun.

On this satellite of the Moon Period there were currents which encircled it, as the group-spirit currents encircle the Earth. The Moon beings followed those currents instinctively from the light to the dark side of this old Moon. At certain times of the year, when they were on the light side, a sort of propagation took place. We have the atavistic residue of those moon travels for propagation in the migrations of the birds of passage which, to the present day, follow the group-spirit currents around the Earth at certain seasons of the year, for identical purposes. Even the (honey)moon trips of human beings show that man himself has not yet outgrown the migratory impulse in connection with mating.

The Moon beings at this last stage were also capable of giving utterance to sounds, or cries. These were Cosmic sounds--not expressions of individual joy or sorrow, for as yet there was no individual. The development of the individual came later--in the Earth Period.

At the end of the Moon Period once more came the interval of rest, the Cosmic Night. The divided parts were dissolved and merged in the general Chaos which preceded the reorganization of the Globe for the Earth Period.

The Lords of Wisdom had now evolved so far, that they were capable of taking charge as the highest creative Hierarchy. They were given special charge of the divine spirit in man during the Earth Period.

The Lords of Individuality were also sufficiently advanced to work upon the spirit in man and the life spirit was therefore put under their charge.

Another creative Hierarchy had special care of the three germs of the dense, vital, and desire bodies as they were evolving. They were the ones who, under the direction of the higher orders, actually did the principal work on these bodies, using the evolving life as a kind of instrument. This Hierarchy is called the "Lords of Form." They were now evolved so far that they were given charge of the third aspect of the spirit in man--the human spirit--in the coming Earth Period.

There were twelve great Creative Hierarchies active in the work of evolution at the commencement of the Saturn Period. Two of these Hierarchies did some work to help at the very beginning. No information has been given as to what they did, nor anything about them, except that they helped of their own free will, and then withdrew from limited existence into liberation.

DIAGRAM 9.
The Twelve Great Creative Hierarchies.

Zodiacal Sign.	Name.	Status.
1—Aries	Nameless	The first and second
2—Taurus	Nameless	orders are said to have passed beyond the ken of anyone on Earth. It is known that they gave some assistance at the beginning of our evolution.

The three following orders worked of their own free will to help man during the three periods which preceded the Earth Period. They have also passed to liberation:

3—Gemini	Seraphim	who, in the Moon Period, aroused in man-in-the-making the germ of the human spirit—the Ego.
4—Cancer	Cherubim	who, in the Sun Period, aroused the germ of the life spirit.
5—Leo	Lords of Flame.......	who, in the Saturn Period, aroused the germ of the divine spirit and gave the germ of the dense body.

The following Seven Creative Hierarchies are active in the Earth Period:

6—Virgo	Lords of Wisdom......	who, in the Sun Period, started the vital body.
7—Libra	Lords of Individuality..	who, in the Moon Period, started the desire body.
8—Scorpio	Lords of Form........	who have special charge of human evolution in the Earth Period.
9—Saggitarius .	Lords of Mind........	the humanity of the Saturn Period.
10—Capricornus .	Archangels	the humanity of the Sun Period.
11—Aquarius ...	Angels	the humanity of the Moon Period.
12—Pisces	The Virgin Spirits....	who are the humanity of the present Earth Period.

Three more of the Creative Hierarchies followed them at the beginning of the Earth Period, the Lords of the Flame, the Cherubim and the Seraphim, leaving seven Hierarchies in active service when the Earth Period began. (Diagram 9 will give a clear idea of the twelve Creative Hierarchies and their status).

The Lords of Mind became experts at building bodies of "mind-stuff" as we are becoming experts at building bodies of chemical matter, and for a similar reason: The Region of Concrete Thought was the densest condition of matter reached during the Saturn Period where they were human and the Chemical Region is the densest state to be contacted by our humanity.

In the Earth Period the Lords of Mind reached the Creator-stage, and radiated from themselves into our being the nucleus of material from which we are now seeking to build an organized mind. They are called "Powers of Darkness" by Paul because they came from the dark Saturn Period, and are considered evil on account of the separative tendency appertaining to the plane of Reason as contrasted with the unifying forces of the World of Life Spirit; the realm of Love. The Lords of Mind work with humanity; but not with the three lower Kingdoms.

The Archangels became experts at building a body of desire-stuff: the densest matter of the Sun Period. Therefore they are able to teach and guide such less evolved beings as man and animal how to mold and use a desire-body.

The Angels are thoroughly experienced in building a vital body for in the Moon period when they were human the ether was the densest condition of matter. On account of this ability they are properly the teachers of man, animal and plant with regard to the vital functions: propagation, nutrition, etc.

Chapter Nine - Stragglers and Newcomers

In following through the preceding chapter the evolution of life, consciousness and form--the triple phase of manifestation of the virgin spirit--which is the *life* that gathers the *form* about itself and gains *consciousness* thereby, we have spoken as though there were only one class; as though the virgin spirits, without exception, had made constant and uniform progress.

This was done for the sake of simplicity, because stragglers there were, as there are in any great body or company.

In school there are, every year, those who fail to reach the standard required for promotion into a higher grade. Similarly, in every Period of Evolution, there are those who fall behind because they have not attained the standard necessary to pass onward to the next higher stage.

Even so early as the Saturn Period there were some who failed to improve sufficiently to take the next forward step. At that stage the Higher Beings were working with the life, which was itself unconscious, but that unconsciousness did not prevent the retardation of some of the virgin spirits who were not so pliable, nor so readily adaptable as others.

In that one word "Adaptability," we have the great secret of advancement or retardation. All progress depends upon whether an evolving being is flexible, adaptable and pliable, so as to be able to accommodate itself to new conditions, or whether it is crystallized, set, and incapable of alteration. Adaptability is the quality which makes for progress, whether an entity is at a high or a low stage of evolution. Lack of it is the cause of the retardation of the spirit and retrogression of the Form. This applies to the past, present and future, the division of the qualified and the unqualified, thus, being made with the exact and impersonal justice of the law of Consequence. There never was, or ever shall be any arbitrary distinction made between the "sheep" and the "goats."

The hardened unresponsive condition of some of the Saturn beings prevented the awakening of the divine spirit within them, therefore they remained simply mineral, all they had gained being the germinal dense body.

Thus there were two classes, or kingdoms, in the Sun Period, i.e., the stragglers of the Saturn Period, who were still mineral, and the pioneers of the Saturn Period, who were capable of receiving the germ of a vital body and becoming plant-like.

In addition to those two kingdoms there was also a third--a new life wave, which was just commencing its activity at the beginning of the Sun Period. (That is the life wave which now ensouls our animals).

The matter into which the new life wave entered, together with the stragglers of the Saturn Period, composed the mineral kingdom of the Sun Period. There was, however, a great difference in those two sub-divisions of the second kingdom. It is possible for the stragglers to make a "spurt" and overtake the pioneers, who are now our humanity, but impossible for the new life wave of the Sun Period to do that. It will reach a stage corresponding to the human, but under very different conditions.

The division of stragglers and pioneers took place in the seventh Revolution of the Saturn Period, when the divine spirit was awakened by the Lords of the Flame. Then it was found that some of the evolving entities were in such an unresponsive, hardened condition that it was impossible to arouse them. They therefore remained without the spark of spirit upon which their progress depended and they were obliged to remain at the same level, being unable to follow the others in whom the spiritual spark was awakened. Truly, truly, all that we are or are not is the result of our own effort, or our own inaction.

These stragglers and the newly arrived life wave formed dark spots in the otherwise glowing gas sphere which was the densest Globe of the Sun Period, and our present Sunspots are an atavistic remainder of that condition.

In the sixth Revolution of the Sun Period the life spirit was awakened by the Cherubim, and again it was found that some who had safely passed the critical point in the Saturn Period, had fallen behind in the Sun Period and were unfit to have the second aspect of the spirit vivified. Thus there were another class of stragglers, who had lagged behind the crest wave of evolution.

In the seventh Revolution of the Sun Period the Lords of the Flame reappeared to awaken the divine spirit in those who failed to qualify for it at the end of the Saturn Period, but had attained to the point where they could receive the spiritual impulse in the Sun Period. The Lords of the Flame also awakened the germ of divine spirit in as many of the new life wave entities as were ready, but here also there were stragglers.

Thus at the beginning of the Moon Period there were the following classes:

1. The Pioneers who had successfully passed through the Saturn and the Sun Periods. They had dense and vital bodies, divine and life spirit germinally active.
2. The Stragglers of the Sun Period, who had dense and vital bodies, also divine spirit--all germinal.
3. The Stragglers of the Saturn Period, who had been promoted in the seventh Revolution of the Sun Period. They had the germ of dense body and divine spirit.
4. The Pioneers of the new Life Wave, who had the same vehicles as class 3, but belong to a different scheme of evolution from ours.
5. The Stragglers of the new Life Wave, who had only the germ for the dense body.
6. The New Life Wave, which entered upon its evolution at the beginning of the Moon Period and is the life that ensouls our plants of the present day.

It is necessary to remember that Nature hastens slowly. She makes no sudden changes in forms. To her, time is nothing; the attainment of perfection is everything. A mineral does not change to a plant at one bound, but by gradual, almost imperceptible degrees. A plant does not become an animal in a night. It requires millions of years to bring about the change. Thus at all times there are all stages and gradations to be found in nature. The Ladder of Being stretches without break from protoplasm to God.

Therefore we have to deal, not with six different kingdoms corresponding to the above six classes which entered the arena of evolution at the beginning of the Moon Period, but with three kingdoms only--mineral, plant and animal.

The lowest class in the Moon Period composed the new life stream which there commenced its evolution. It formed the hardest mineral part, yet it must be borne in mind that it was by no means as hard as the mineral of the present time, but only about as dense as our wood.

This statement does not contradict former ones which described the Moon as watery, nor does it conflict with diagram 8, showing the densest Globe in the Moon Period as located in the Etheric Region, which is etheric. As before stated, the fact that the path of evolution is spiral prevents any condition ever being duplicated. There are similarities, but never reproductions of identical conditions. It is not always possible to describe conditions in exact terms. The best available term is used to convey an idea of the conditions existing at the time under consideration.

Class 5 in our list was nearly mineral, yet on account of having passed through and beyond the mineral condition during the Sun Period, it had some plant characteristics.

Class 4 was almost plant and did evolve to a plant before the close of the Mood Period. It was, however, more nearly allied to the mineral kingdom that the next two classes, which formed the higher kingdom. We may therefore group classes 4 and 5 together, as forming a sort of half step, a "mineral-plant" kingdom, which composed the surface of the ancient planet of the Moon Period. It was something like our present peat, which is also a state between the mineral and the plant. It was soggy and wet, consistent with the statement that the Moon Period was watery.

Thus the fourth, fifth and sixth classes composed the different gradations of the mineral kingdom in the Moon Period--the highest being nearly plant and the lowest the hardest mineral substance of that time.

Classes 2 and 3 formed the plant kingdom, though they were both really more than plants, yet were not quite animal. They grew in the mineral-plant soil; they were stationary like plants; yet they could not have grown in a purely mineral soil, as our plants do now. Good examples of what they were like may be found in our parasitic plants, which cannot grow in a purely mineral soil, but seek the food already specialized by the real plant or tree.

Class 1 was composed of the pioneers of the life wave of virgin spirits. In the Moon Period they were going through a sort of animal-like existence. Yet they were like the animals of our time only in so far as they had the same vehicles and were under the control of a group-spirit, which included the whole human family. In appearance they were very different from our present animals, as shown by the partial description given in the previous chapter. They did not touch the surface of the planet, but floated suspended by umbilical-like cords. Instead of lungs they had a gill-like apparatus through which they breathed the hot steamy "fire-fog." These features of the Moon existence are still recapitulated by the embryo during the period of gestation. At certain stages of development it has the gills. The Moon beings at that time had also the horizontal spine of the animal.

During the Moon Period several more divisions of classes occurred than in the preceding periods, because there were, of course, stragglers who failed to keep abreast of the crestwave of evolution. As a result there were, at the beginning of the Earth Period, 5 classes, some of them containing several divisions, as diagram 10 will show. These divisions occurred at the following times and for the following reasons:

In the middle of the fifth Revolution of the Moon Period, when the Seraphim bestowed the germ of the human spirit upon the pioneers who had fitted themselves to pass on, some were found wanting when weighed in the balance and therefore unfit to receive the spiritual impulse which awakened the threefold spirit.

In the sixth Revolution of the Moon Period the Cherubim reappeared and vivified the life spirit of those who had been left behind in the Sun Period but had since reached the necessary stage of development (Class 2 in our previous list), and also in those stragglers of the Sun Period who had now evolved a vital body during their plant existence in the Moon Period. (These latter were class 3 in the previous list.)

Class 4 in the previous list had been going through a low stage of plant existence; nevertheless the majority of them had evolved the vital body sufficiently to allow of the awakening of the life spirit.

DIAGRAM 10

Showing the different classes of the several life waves which are evolving in the four kingdoms of the earth; their status *at the beginning of the earth period* and the vehicles they *then* possessed; also their present status.

CLASS	VEHICLES		PRESENT STATE
1—Pioneers of the Saturn, Sun and Moon Periods......	Divine ⎱ Life ⎰ Human ⎰ spirit	Dense ⎱ Vital ⎰ body Desire ⎰	The Aryan Races
2—The Stragglers of the Moon Period...	Divine ⎱ Life ⎰ spirit	Dense ⎱ Vital ⎰ body Desire ⎰	The Mongolians, Africans, and all lower Races
3—(a) The Stragglers of the Saturn Period	Divine ⎱	Dense ⎱	
(b) The Stragglers of the Sun Period..	Life ⎰ spirit	Vital ⎰ body	Anthropoids
All the	above belong to our		life wave
(c) Pioneers of the new Sun life wave.	Same as 3a and 3b..............		Animals
4—(a) Stragglers of the new Sun life wave	Divine spirit	Dense body	Plant Kingdom —— Trees and perennials
(b) Pioneers of the new Moon life wave	Same as 4a		Flowers and grasses
5—(a) Stragglers of the new Moon life wave	Dense body only..............		Mineral Kingdom —— Sand, soft soils, etc.
(b) The new life wave of the Earth Period	Dense body only; same as 5a...		Mountains, rocks, etc.

Thus, the three last named all possessed the same vehicles at the beginning of the Earth Period, although only the two first named (class 3a and 3b in diagram 10) belong to our life wave, and have a chance of even yet overtaking us if they pass the critical point which will come in the next Revolution of the Earth Period. Those who cannot pass that point will be held over until some future evolution reaches a stage where they can drop in and proceed with their development in a new human period. They will be debarred from going forward with our humanity because it will be advanced so far beyond their status that it would prove a serious clog to our progress to drag them along. They will not be destroyed, but simply held in waiting for another period of evolution.

Progression with our present wave of evolution is what is meant when "salvation" is spoken of in the Christian religion, and it is something to be earnestly sought, for though the "eternal damnation" of those who are not "saved" does not mean destruction nor endless torture, it is nevertheless a very serious matter to be held in a state of inertia for inconceivable milliards of years, before a new evolution shall have progressed to such a stage that those who fail here can have an opportunity to proceed. The spirit is not conscious of the lapse of time, but it is none the less a serious loss, and there must also be feeling of unhomelikeness when at last such spirits find themselves in a new evolution.

So far as the present humanity is concerned, that possibility is so small as to be almost negligible. It is said, however, that of the total number of virgin spirits which started evolution in the Saturn Period, only about three-fifths will pass that critical point in the next Revolution and go on to the end.

The greatest apprehension of occult scientists is materialism, which if carried too far, not only prevents progress but will destroy all the seven vehicles of the virgin spirit, leaving it naked. Such an one will then have to commence at the very beginning of the new evolution. All the work it has done since the dawn of the Saturn Period will have been utterly wasted. For this reason, the present period is to our humanity, the most critical of all. Therefore occult scientists speak of the Sixteen Races, of which the Germano-Anglo-Saxon is one, as "the sixteen possibilities for destruction." May the reader safely pass them all, for their grip is worse than the retardation in the next Revolution.

Speaking generally, class 5 in the foregoing list was given the germ of the divine spirit during the seventh Revolution, when the Lords of Flame reappeared. Therefore they were pioneers of the last life wave, entering evolution at the Moon Period. They passed their mineral existence there. The stragglers of that life wave were thus left with only the germ of a dense body.

In addition to the above, there was also a new life wave (our present mineral kingdom) entering upon its evolution at the beginning of the Earth Period.

At the end of the Moon Period these classes possessed the vehicles as they are classified in diagram 10, and started with them in the beginning of the Earth Period. During the time which has elapsed since then, the human kingdom has been evolving the link of mind, and has thereby attained full waking consciousness. The animals have obtained a desire body, the plants a vital body; the stragglers of the life wave which entered evolution in the Moon Period have escaped the hard and fast conditions of rock soils; while the life wave that entered evolution here in the Earth Period forms the hard rocks and stones.

Thus have the different classes obtained the vehicles ascribed to them in diagram 3, to which the reader is referred.

Chapter Ten - The Earth Period

The Globes of the Earth Period are located in the four densest states of matter--the Region of Concrete Thought, the Desire World, the Etheric, and the Chemical Regions (See Diagram 8). The densest Globe (Globe D) is our present Earth.

When we speak of "the *densest* Worlds" or "the *densest* states of matter," the term must be taken in a relative sense. Otherwise it would imply a limitation in the absolute, and that is absurd. Dense and attenuated, up and down, east and west, are applicable only relatively to our own status and position. As there are higher, finer Worlds than those touched by our life wave, so there are also denser states of matter which are the field of evolution for other classes of beings. Nor must it be thought that these denser worlds are elsewhere in space; they are interpenetrated by our worlds in a manner similar to that in which the higher Worlds interpenetrate this Earth. The fancied solidity of the Earth and the forms we see are no bar to the passage of a denser body any more than our solid dense walls bar the passage of a human being clothed in his desire body. Neither is solidity synonymous with density, as may be illustrated by aluminum, a solid which is less dense than the fluidic mercury; nevertheless the latter, in spite of its density, will evaporate or exude through many solids.

This being the fourth Period, we have at present four elements. In the Saturn Period there was but one element, Fire--i.e., there was warmth, or heat, which is incipient fire. In the second, or Sun Period, there were to elements, Fire and Air. In the third, or Moon Period, there were three elements, Water being added; and in the fourth, or Earth Period, was added the fourth element, Earth. Thus it will be seen that a new element was added for each Period.

In the Jupiter Period an element of a spiritual nature will be added, which will unite with the speech so that words will invariable carry with them understanding--not misunderstanding, as is frequently the case now. For instance, when one says "house," he may mean a cottage, while the hearer may get the idea of a tenement flat building.

To this environment of the four elements, as specified above, the different classes mentioned in diagram 10 were brought over by the Hierarchies in charge of them. We remember that in the Moon Period these classes formed three kingdoms--animal, animal-plant and plant-mineral. Here on Earth, however, the conditions are such that there can be no large half-way classes. There must be four distinctly different kingdoms. In this crystallized phase of existence the lines between them must be more sharply drawn than was the case in former Periods, where one kingdom gradually merged into the next.

Therefore some of the classes mentioned in diagram 10 advanced one-half step, while others went back a half a step.

Some of the mineral-plants advanced completely into the plant kingdom and became the verdure of the fields. Others went down and became the purely mineral soil in which the plants grew. Of the plant-animals some advanced into the animal kingdom, ahead of time, and those species have yet the colorless plant-blood and some, like star-fishes, have even the five points like the petals of flowers.

All of class 2 whose desire bodies could be divided into two parts (as was the case with all of class 1) were fitted to become human vehicles and were therefore advanced into the human group.

We must carefully remember that in the above paragraphs we are dealing with Form, not with the Life which dwells in the Form. The instrument is graded to suit the life that is to dwell in it. Those of class 2, in whose vehicles the above mentioned division could be made were raised to the human kingdom, but were given the indwelling spirit at a point in time later than class 1. Hence, they are not now so far evolved as class 1, and are therefore the lower races of mankind.

Those whose desire bodies were incapable of division were put into the same division as classes 3a and 3b. They are our present anthropoids. They may yet overtake our evolution if they reach a sufficient degree of advancement before the critical point already mentioned, which will come in the middle of the fifth Revolution. If they do not overtake us by that time, they will have lost touch with our evolution.

It was said that man had built his threefold body by the help of others higher than he, but in the previous Period there was no coordinating power; the threefold spirit, the Ego, was separate and apart from its vehicles. Now the time had come to unit the spirit and the body.

Where the desire body separated, the higher part become somewhat master over the lower part and over the dense and vital bodies. It formed a sort of animal-soul with which the spirit could unite by means of the link of mind. Where there was no division of the desire body, the vehicle was given over to desires and passions without any check, and could therefore not be used as a vehicle *within* which the spirit could dwell. So it was put under the control of a group-spirit which ruled if from *without*. It became an animal body, and that kind has now degenerated into the body of the anthropoid.

Where there was a division of the desire body, the dense body gradually assumed a vertical position, thus taking the spine out of the horizontal currents of the Desire World in which the group-spirit acts upon the animal through the horizontal spine. The Ego could then enter, work in and express itself through the vertical spine and build the vertical larynx and brain for its adequate expression in the dense body. A horizontal larynx is also under the domination of the group-spirit. While it is true that some animals, as the starling, raven, parrot, etc., previously mentioned, are able, because of the possession of a vertical larynx, to *utter* words, they cannot use them understandingly. *The use of words to express thought is the highest human privilege* and can be exercised only by a reasoning, thinking entity like man. If the student will keep this in mind, it will be easier to follow the different steps which lead up to this result.

The Saturn Revolution of the Earth Period

This is the Revolution during which, in each Period. the dense body is reconstructed. This time it was given the ability to form a brain and become a vehicle for the germ of mind which was to be added later. This addition constituted the final reconstruction of the dense body, rendering it capable of attaining the highest degree of efficiency possible to such a vehicle.

Unspeakable Wisdom has been employed in its construction. It is a marvel. It can never be sufficiently impressed upon the mind of the student what immeasurable facilities for the gaining of knowledge are contained in this instrument, and what a great boon it is to man; how much he should prize it and how thankful he should be to have it.

Some examples of the perfection of construction and intelligent adaptability displayed in this instrument have previously been given, but in order to further impress this great truth upon the mind of the student, it might not be out of place to illustrate more fully this Wisdom, also the work of the Ego in the blood.

It is generally know, in a vague kind of way, that the gastric juice acts upon the food to promote assimilation; but only a very few people, outside of the medical profession, are aware that there are many different gastric juices, each appropriate to the treatment of a certain kind of food. The researches of Pavlov, however, have established the fact beyond doubt, that there is one kind of juice for the digestion of meat, another for milk, another for acid fruit, etc. That fact, by the way, is the reason why all foods do not mix well. Milk, for instance, requires a gastric juice that is widely different from almost any other kind except that required for the digestion of starchy foods, and is not readily digested with any food other than cereals. This alone would show marvelous wisdom; that the Ego working subconsciously is able to select the different juices which are appropriate to the different kinds of food taken into the stomach, making each of just the right strength and quantity to digest the food. What makes the matter still more wonderful, however, is the fact that the gastric juice is poured into the stomach in *advance* of the food.

We do not consciously direct the process of mixing this fluid. The great majority of people know nothing of metabolism or any other phrase of chemistry. So it is not enough to say that, as we taste what is coming, we direct the process by means of signals through the nervous system.

When this fact of the selection of juices was first proven, scientists were sorely puzzled trying to learn how the right kind of juice was selected and caused to enter the stomach *before* the food. They thought the signal was given along the nervous system. But it was demonstrated beyond doubt that

130

the proper juice was poured into to the stomach even though the nervous system was blocked.

At last Starling and Bayliss, in a series of experiments of brilliant ingenuity, proved that infinitesimal parts of the food are taken up by the blood as soon as the food enters the mouth, go in advance to the digestive glands and cause a flow of the proper juice.

This again, is only the physical side of the phenomena. To understand the whole wonderful connection, we must turn to occult science. That alone explains why the signal is carried by the blood.

The blood is one of the highest expressions of the vital body. The Ego guides and controls its dense instrument by means of the blood, therefore the blood is also the means used to act on the nervous system. During some of the time that digestion is going on, it acts partially through the nervous system, but (especially at the commencement of the digestive process) it acts directly upon the stomach. When, during scientific experiments, the nerves were blocked, the direct way through the blood was still open and the Ego derived the necessary information in that way.

It will also be seen that the blood is driven to wherever the Ego unfolds the greatest activity at any time. If a situation requires sudden though and action, the blood is promptly driven to the head. If a heavy meal is to be digested the greater portion of the blood leaves the head, centering around the digestive organs. The Ego concentrates its efforts on ridding the body of the useless food. Therefore a man cannot think well after a heavy meal. He is sleepy because so much blood has left the brain that the residue is insufficient to carry on the functions necessary to full waking consciousness, besides, nearly all the vital fluid or solar energy specialized by the spleen is absorbed by the blood rushing through that organ after a meal in greater volume than between meals. Thus the rest of the system is also deprived of the vital fluid in a large measure during digestion. It is the Ego that drives the blood into the brain. Whenever the body goes to sleep, the table will invariably tip towards the feet, raising the head. During coition the blood is centered in the sex organs, etc. All these examples tend to prove that during the waking hours, the Ego works in and controls the dense body by means of the blood. The larger portion of the total amount goes to that part of the body where at any given time, the Ego unfolds any particular activity.

The reconstruction of the dense body in the Saturn Revolution of the Earth Period was for the purpose of rendering it capable of inter-penetration by the mind. It gave the first impulse to the building of the frontal part of the brain; also the incipient division in the nervous system which has since become apparent in its subdivisions--the voluntary and the sympathetic. The latter was the only one provided for in the Moon Period. The voluntary nervous system (which has transformed the dense body from a mere automaton acting under stimuli from without, to an extraordinary adaptable instrument capable of being guided and controlled by an Ego from within) was not added until the present Earth Period.

The principal art of the reconstructive work was done by the Lords of Form. They are the Creative Hierarchy which is most active in the Earth Period, as were the Lords of Flame in the Saturn Period, the Lords of Wisdom in the Sun Period, and the Lords of Individuality in the Moon Period.

The Earth Period is pre-eminently the Period of Form, for there the form or matter side of evolution reaches its greatest and most pronounced state. Here spirit is more helpless and suppressed and Form is the most dominant factor--hence the prominence of the Lords of Form.

The Sun Revolution of the Earth Period

During this Revolution the vital body was reconstructed to accommodate the germinal mind. The vital body was fashioned more in the likeness of the dense body, so that it could become fitted for use as the densest vehicle during the Jupiter Period, when the dense body will have become spiritualized.

The Angels, the humanity of the Moon Period, were aided by the Lords of Form in reconstruction. The organization of the vital body is now next in efficiency to the dense body. Some writers on this subject call the former a link, and contend that it is simply a mold of the dense body, and not a separate vehicle.

While not desiring to criticize, and admitting that this contention is justified by the fact that man, at his present stage of evolution, cannot *ordinarily* use the vital body as a separate vehicle--because it always remains with the dense body and to extract it *in toto* would cause death of the dense body--yet there was a time when it was not so firmly incorporated with the latter, as we shall presently see.

During those epochs of our Earth's history which have already been mentioned as the Lemurian and the Atlantean, man was involuntarily clairvoyant, and it was precisely this looseness of connection between the dense and the vital bodies that made him so. (The Initiators of that time helped the candidate to loosen the connection still further, as in the voluntary clairvoyant.)

Since then the vital body has become much more firmly interwoven with the dense body in the majority of people, but in all sensitives it is loose. It is that looseness which constitutes the difference between the psychic and the ordinary person who is unconscious of all but the vibrations contacted by means of the five senses. All human beings have to pass through this period of close connection of the vehicles and experience the consequent limitation of consciousness. There are, therefore, two classes of sensitives, those who have not become firmly enmeshed in matter, such as the majority of the Hindus, the Indians, etc., who possess a certain low grade of clairvoyance, or are sensitive to the sounds of nature, and those who are in the vanguard of evolution. The latter are emerging from the acme of materiality, and are again divisible into two kinds, one of which develops in a passive, weak-willed manner. By the help of others they re-awaken the solar plexus or other organs in connection with the involuntary nervous system. These are therefore involuntary clairvoyants, mediums who have no control of their faculty. They have retrograded. The other kind is made up of those who by their own wills unfold the vibratory powers of the organs now connected with the voluntary nervous system and thus become trained occultists, controlling their own bodies and exercising the clairvoyant faculty as they will to do. They are called voluntary or trained clairvoyants.

In the Jupiter Period man will function in his vital body as he now does in his dense body; and as no development in nature is sudden, the process of separating the two bodies has already commenced. The vital body will then attain a much higher degree of efficiency than the dense body of today. As it is a much more pliable vehicle, the spirit will then be able to use it in a manner impossible of realization in the case of the present dense vehicle.

The Moon Revolution of the Earth Period

Here the Moon Period was recapitulated, and much the same conditions prevailed (on an advanced scale) as obtained on Globe D of that Period. There was the same kind of fire-fog atmosphere; the same fiery core; the same division of the Globe into two parts, in order to allow the more highly evolved beings a chance to progress at the proper rate and pace, which it would be impossible for beings such as our humanity to equal.

In that Revolution the Archangels (humanity of the Sun Period) and the Lords of Form took charge of the reconstruction of the desire body, but they were not alone in that work. When the separation of the Globe into two parts occurred, there was a similar division in the desire bodies of some of the evolving beings. We have already noted that where this division took place, the form was ready to become the vehicle of an *in*dwelling spirit, and in order to further this purpose the Lords of Mind (humanity of the Saturn Period) took possession of the higher part of the desire body and implanted in it the separate selfhood, without which the present man with all his glorious possibilities, could never have existed.

Thus in the latter part of the Moon Revolution the first germ of separate personality was implanted in the higher part of the desire body by the Lords of Mind.

The Archangels were active in the lower part of the desire body, giving it the purely animal desires. They also worked in the desire bodies where there was no division. Some of these were to become the vehicles of the animal group-spirits, which work on them from without, but do not enter wholly into the animal forms, as the individual spirit does into the human body.

The desire body was reconstructed to render it capable of being interpenetrated by the germinal mind which, during the Earth Period, will be implanted in all those desire bodies in which it was possible to make the before-mentioned division.

As has been previously explained, the desire body is an unorganized ovoid, holding the dense body as a dark spot within its center, as the white of an egg surrounds the yolk. There are a number of sense centers in the ovoid, which have appeared since the beginning of the Earth Period. In the average human being these centers appear merely as eddies in a current and are not now awake, hence his desire body is of no use to him as a *separate* vehicle of consciousness; but when the sense centers are awakened they look like whirling vortices.

Rest Periods Between Revolutions

Hitherto we have noted only the Cosmic Nights between Periods. We saw that there was an interval of rest and assimilation between the Saturn and the Sun Periods; another Cosmic Night between the Sun and the Moon Periods, etc. But in addition to these, there are also rests between the Revolutions.

We might liken the Periods to the different incarnations of man; the Cosmic Nights between them to the intervals between deaths and new births; and the rest between Revolutions would then be analogous to the rest of sleep between two days.

When a Cosmic Night sets in, all manifested things are resolved into a homogenous mass--the Cosmos again becomes Chaos.

This periodical return of matter to primordial substance is what makes it possible for the spirit to evolve. Were the crystallizing process of active manifestation to continue indefinitely it would offer an insurmountable barrier to the progress of Spirit. Every time matter has crystallized to such a degree that it becomes too hard for the spirit to work in, the latter withdraws to recuperate its exhausted energy, on the same principle that a power-drill which has stopped when boring in hard metals, is withdrawn to regain its momentum. It is then able to bore its way further into the metal.

Freed from the crystallizing energy of the evolving spirits, the chemical forces in matter turn Cosmos to Chaos by restoring matter to its primordial state, that a new start may be made by the regenerated virgin spirits at the dawn of a new Day of Manifestation. The experience gained in former Periods and Revolutions enables the Spirit to build up to the point last reached, with comparative celerity, also to facilitate further progress by making such alterations as its cumulative experience dictates.

Thus at the end of the Moon Revolution of the Earth Period, all the Globes and all life returned to Chaos, re-emerging therefrom at the beginning of the fourth Revolution.

The Fourth Revolution of the Earth Period

In the exceeding complexity of the scheme of evolution, there are always spirals within spirals, *ad infinitum*. So it will not be surprising to learn that in every Revolution the work of recapitulation and rest is applied to the different Globes. When the life wave reappeared on Globe A in this Revolution, it went though the development of the Saturn Period; then after a rest which, however did not involve the complete destruction of the Globe; but only an alteration, it appeared on Globe B, where the work of the Sun Period was recapitulated. Then after a rest, the life wave passed on to Globe C, and the work of the Moon Period was repeated. Finally, the life wave arrived on Globe D, which is our Earth, and not until then did the proper work of the Earth Period begin.

Even then, the spiral within the spiral precluded its beginning immediately on the arrival of the life wave from Globe C, for the bestowal of the germ of mind did not actually take place until the fourth Epoch, the first three Epochs being still further recapitulations of the Saturn, Sun and Moon Periods, but always on a higher scale.

Chapter Eleven - The Genesis and Evolution of our Solar System

Chaos

In the previous pages nothing has been said about our Solar System, and of the different planets which compose it, because it was not until the Earth Period was reached that the present differentiation was made. The Earth Period is the acme of diversification, and although we have been speaking of only one class of virgin spirits-- those who, in the strictest and most limited sense, are concerned with the Earth evolution--there are in reality seven "Rays" or streams of life, all pursuing different evolutions, yet all belonging to the original class of virgin spirits to which our humanity belongs.

In the previous Periods all of these different sub-classes or Rays found a suitable environment for their evolution on the same planet. But, in the Earth Period, conditions became such that in order to provide for each class the degree of heat and the vibration necessary for its particular phase of evolution, they were segregated on different planets, at varying distances from the Sun--the central source of life. This is the *raison d'etre* of our System and all other Solar Systems in the Universe.

Before proceeding with the description of evolution of our humanity on the Earth after its separation from the central Sun, it is necessary for the maintenance of sequential order in the description to explain the differentiation which scattered the planets of our System in space.

Active manifestation--particularly in the Physical World--depends upon separateness; upon the limitation of life by form. But during the interim between Periods and Revolutions the marked distinction between form and life ceases. This applies not only to man and the lower kingdoms, but to the Worlds and Globes which are the basis of form for the evolving life. Only the seed-atoms and the nuclei or centers of the World-Globes remain--all else is one homogenous substance. There is but one Spirit pervading space. Life and Form, its positive and negative poles, are one.

This state of things was what Greek mythology described as "Chaos." The ancient Norsemen and the Teutonic mythology call it "Ginnungagap," which was bounded upon the northern side by the cold and foggy "Niflheim"--the land of mist and fog--and upon the south side by the fire "Muspelheim." When heat and cold entered into space which was occupied by Chaos or Ginnungagap, they caused the crystallization of the visible universe.

The Bible also gives one the idea of infinite space preceding the activity of the Spirit.

In our present materialistic period we have unfortunately lost the idea of all that lies behind that word Space. We are so accustomed to speaking of "empty" space, that we have entirely lost the grand and holy significance of the word, and are thus incapable of feeling the reverence that this idea of Space and Chaos should inspire in our breasts.

To the Rosicrucians, as to any occult school, there is no such thing as empty or void space. To them *space is Spirit* in its attenuated form; while *matter is crystallized space or Spirit*. Spirit in manifestation is dual, that which we see as Form is the negative manifestation of Spirit--crystallized and inert. The positive pole of Spirit manifests as Life, galvanizing the negative Form into action, but both Life and Form originated in Spirit, Space, Chaos!

To get an idea from everyday life which will illustrate, we may take the hatching of an egg. The egg is filled with a moderately viscous fluid. This fluid, or moisture, is subjected to heat, and out of the soft, fluidic substance comes a living chick, with hard bones and comparatively hard flesh, and with down that has a comparatively hard quill, etc.

When a living chick can come out of the inert fluid of an egg without the addition of any hardening substance from outside, is it a far-fetched idea to claim that the universe is crystallized Space or Spirit? There is no doubt that the claim will seem foolish to many; but this book is not for the purpose of convincing the world at large that these things *are*. It is intended to aid those who inherently feel that these things must be and to help them to see the light upon this great World-mystery, which the writer has been permitted to behold. The special object at present is to show that Spirit is active all the time--in one way during Manifestation, and in another during Chaos.

Modern science would sneer at the idea that life could exist upon a Globe which is in the process of formation. That is because science cannot dissociate Life and Form and cannot conceive of Form except as solid and tangible--cognizable by one of our five physical senses.

The occult scientist, in accordance with the above definitions of Life and Form, holds that life may exist independently of Concrete Form; may have Forms not perceptible to our present limited senses, and amenable to none of the laws which apply to this present concrete state of matter.

It is true that the Nebular Theory holds that all existence (which is to say all Form, the Worlds in Space and whatever Forms there may be upon them)

136

has come from the fiery nebula; but it does not recognize the further fact insisted upon by occult science--that the fiery nebula is Spirit. It does not admit that the whole atmosphere around us, the space between the worlds, is Spirit and that there is a constant interchange going on all the time--Form dissolving into Space, and Space crystallizing into Form.

Chaos is not a state which has existed in the past and has now entirely disappeared. It is all around us at the present moment. Were it not that old forms--having outlived their usefulness--are constantly being resolved back into that Chaos, which is also as constantly giving birth to new forms, there could be no progress; the work of evolution would cease and stagnation would prevent the possibility of advancement.

It is axiomatic that "The oftener we die, the better we live." The Poet-Initiate, Goethe says:

Who has not this--
Ever dying and bringing to birth--
Will aye remain a sorry guest
Upon this dismal earth.

and Paul says, "I die daily."

Therefore, as students of occult science, it is necessary to realize that even during active manifestation, *it is Chaos that is the basis of all progress.* Our life during Chaos is based upon our life in active manifestation, and *vice versa*, i.e., what we are able to achieve during active manifestation, and the ability to progress at all, is the result of the existence in Chaos. The interim between Periods and Revolutions is in reality much more important to the growth of the soul that concrete existence, though the latter is the basis of the former and therefore cannot be dispensed with. The importance of the Chaotic interim lives in the fact that during that period the evolving entities of all classes are so closely united that they are really one; consequently those which are of lower development during manifestation are in closest contact with the more highly evolved, thus experiencing and benefiting by a much higher vibration that their own. This enables them to live over and assimilate their past experiences in a manner impossible when hampered by Form.

We have seen the benefit to the spirit in man from the interim between death and a new birth. There the form still exists, though much more attenuated than the dense body; but in the Cosmic Night and intervals of rest between Periods and Revolutions, when there is perfect freedom from form, the beneficial results of past experiences can be much more effectively assimilated.

We have a word which was originally coined to convey the idea of the state of things between manifestations. This word, however, has been used in a material sense to such an extent that it has lost its primal significance. That word is Gas.

It may be thought that this is a very old word, which has nearly always existed as a synonym for a state of matter lighter than liquids, but such is not the case. The word was first used in "Physica," a work which appeared in 1633, the author of it being Helmont, a Rosicrucian.

Helmont did not call himself a Rosicrucian; no true Brother does so publicly. Only the Rosicrucian knows the brother Rosicrucian. Not even the most intimate friends or relatives know of a man's connection with the order. Those only who are Initiates themselves know the writers of the past who were Rosicrucians, because ever through their works shine the unmistakable words, phrases and signs indicative of the deep meaning that remains hidden from the non-Initiate. The Rosicrucian Fellowship is composed of students of the teachings of the Order, which are now given publicly, because the world's intelligence is growing to the necessary point of comprehension. This work is one of the first few fragments of the Rosicrucian knowledge being publicly given out. All that has been printed as such, previous to the last few years, has been the work of either charlatans or traitors.

Rosicrucians such as Paracelsus, Comenius, Bacon, Helmont and others gave hints in their works and influenced others. The great controversy concerning the authorship of Shakespeare (which has to no avail blunted so many goose-quills and wasted so much good ink that might have served useful ends) would never have arisen had it been known that the similarity in Shakespeare and Bacon is due to the fact that both were influenced by the same Initiate, who also influenced Jacob Boehme and a pastor of Ingolstadt, Jacobus Baldus, who lived subsequent to the death of the Bard of Avon, and wrote Latin lyric verse. If the first poem of Jacob Baldus is read with a certain key, it will be found that by reading down and up the lines, the following sentence will appear: "Hitherto I have spoken from across the sea by means of the drama; now I will express myself in lyrics."

In his "Physica," Helmont, the Rosicrucian wrote: "Ad huc spiritum incognitum Gas voco," i.e., "This hitherto unknown Spirit I call Gas." Further on in the same work he says, "This vapor which I have called Gas is not far removed from the Chaos the ancients spoke of."

We must learn to think of Chaos as the Spirit of God, which pervades every part of infinity; it will then be seen in its true light, as the occult maxim puts it: "Chaos is the seed-ground of the Cosmos," and we shall no longer wonder how "something can come out of nothing," because Space is not synonymous with "nothing." It holds within itself the germs of all that exists during a physical manifestation, yet not quite all; for by the wedding of Chaos with Cosmos there is something new brought forth each time, which did not exist before; something that was not foreshown and latent. The name of that something is Genius--the cause of Epigenesis.

It appears in all kingdoms. It is the expression of progressive spirit in man, animal and plant. Chaos is therefore a holy name; a name that signifies the Cause of all we see in Nature and inspires a feeling of devotion in every tried, true and trained occultist. He regards the visible sense world as a revelation of the hidden potentialities of the Chaos.

The Birth of the Planets

To express himself in the dense physical world, it was necessary for man to evolve a suitable dense body. In a world like this he must have a body with limbs, organs, a muscular system by means of which to move about; also a brain to direct and co-ordinate his movements. If the conditions had been different the body would have been modified accordingly.

It is necessary for all beings, high or low in the scale of existence, to possess vehicles for expression in any particular world in which they may wish to manifest. Even the Seven Spirits before The Throne must possess these necessary vehicles, which of course are differently conditioned for each of Them. Collectively, They are God, and make up the Triune Godhead, and He manifests in a different way through each of Them.

There is no contradiction in ascribing different numbers to God. We do not sin against the "oneness" of light because we distinguish three primary colors into which it divides itself. The white light of the Sun contains the seven colors of the spectrum. The occultists sees even twelve colors, there being five between red and violet--going one way around the circle--in addition to the red, orange, yellow, green, etc., of the visible spectrum.

THE 1.3.7 & 10 ASPECTS OF GOD & MAN

DIAGRAM II

Four of these colors are quite indescribable, but the fifth--the middle one of the five--is similar to the tint of a new blown peach blossom. It is in fact the color of the vital body. Trained clairvoyants who describe it as "bluish-gray," or "reddish-gray," etc., are trying to describe a color that has no equivalent in the physical world; and they are therefore compelled to use the nearest descriptive terms afforded by our language.

Perhaps Color will enable us to realize the oneness of God with the Seven Spirits before The Throne better than anything else. We will therefore turn to diagram 11.

We see here a white triangle looming up from a dark background. White is synthetic, containing all colors within itself, as God contains within Himself all things in the Solar System.

Within the white triangle are a blue, a red and a yellow circle. All other colors are simply combinations of these three primary colors. These circles correspond to the three aspects of God, which are without beginning, and end *in God*; though externalized only during active manifestation.

TABLE OF VIBRATIONS

WHOSE EFFECTS ARE RECOGNIZED AND STUDIED BY SCIENCE.

Number of Vibrations per second.

1st Octave	2	
2d "	4	
3d "	8	
4th "	16	
5th "	32	
6th "	64	
7th "	128	
8th "	256	Sound.
9th "	512	
10th "	1,024	
15th "	32,768	
20th "	1,047,576	Unknown.
25th "	33,554,432	
30th "	1,073,741,824	Electricity.
35th "	34,359,738,368	
40th "	1,099,511,627,776	Unknown.
45th "	35,184,372,088,832	
46th "	70,368,744,177,644	
47th "	140,737,468,355,328	Heat.
48th "	281,474,979,710,656	
49th "	562,949,953,421,312	Light.
50th "	1,125,899,906,842,624	Chemical Rays.
51st "	2,251,799,813,685,248	Unknown.
57th "	144,115,188,075,855,872	
58th "	288,230,376,151,711,744	
59th "	576,460,752,303,423,488	
60th "	1,152,921,504,606,846,976	X-Rays.
61st "	2,305,843,009,213,693,952	
62d "	4,611,686,618,427,389,004	Unknown.

When these three colors are interblended, as shown in the diagram, there appear four additional colors, the three secondary colors--each due to the blending of two primary colors--and one color (indigo) which contains the entire gamut of colors, making it in all the seven colors of the spectrum. These colors represent the Seven Spirits before the Throne. The colors are different, as are also the Seven Spirits, each having a different mission in the Kingdom of God--our Solar System.

The seven planets circling around the Sun are the dense bodies of the Seven Planetary Genii. Their names are: Uranus with one satellite, Saturn with eight moons, Jupiter with four moons, Mars with two moons, the Earth and its moon, Venus and Mercury.

Bodies are always found to suit the purpose they are made to serve, hence the dense bodies of the Seven Planetary Spirits are spherical, that form being best adapted to the enormous velocity with which they travel through space. The Earth, for instance, travels about 66,000 miles per hour in its orbit.

Man's body had a different shape in the past from that of the present, and from that which it will have in the future. During involution it was approximately spherical, as it still is during ante-natal life, because the intra-uterine development is a recapitulation of past stages of evolution. At that stage the organism developed the sphere, because during involution man's energies were directed inward, upon the building of its own vehicles, as the embryo develops within the sphere of the uterus.

Man's dense and vital bodies have straightened, but his higher vehicles still retain their ovoid form. In the dense body, the coordinating and governing brain is situated at one extremity. This is the most unfavorable position for such an organ. Too long a time is required for impulses to travel from one extremity to the other--from the brain to the feet, or for impacts on the feet to reach the brain. In cases of burns, for instance, science has demonstrated that valuable time is lost, the skin being blistered before a message can be carried from the injured place to the brain and back again.

This inefficiency would be greatly lessened if the brain were in the center of the body. Sensations and the responses thereto could be more quickly received and transmitted. In the spherical planets the Planetary Spirit directs *from the center* the movements of its vehicle. In future man will bend over, as shown in diagram 12. He will become a sphere, directing his energies outward because a spherical form affords the greatest facility for motion in all directions, and indeed, for combination of simultaneous motions.

The Rosicrucian Cosmo-Conception teaches that there is a further evolution in store for planets.

When the beings upon a planet have evolved to a sufficient degree, the planet becomes a Sun--the fixed center of a Solar System. When the beings upon it have evolved to a still greater degree, and consequently it has reached its maximum brilliancy, it breaks up into Zodiac, becoming, so to speak, the womb for a new Solar System.

Thus the great hosts of Divine Beings who, until then, were confined within that Sun, gain freedom of action upon a great number of stars, whence they can affect in different ways the system which grows up within their sphere of influence. The planets, or man-bearing worlds, within the Zodiac are constantly being worked upon by these forces, but in various ways, according to the stage they have reached in evolution.

Our Sun could not become a Sun until it had sent out from itself all the beings who were not sufficiently evolved to endure the high rate of vibration and the great luminosity of the beings who were qualified for that evolution. All the beings upon the different planets would have been consumed had they remained in the Sun.

This visible Sun, however, though it is the place of evolution for Beings vastly above man, is not by many means the Father of the other planets, as material science supposes. On the contrary, it is itself an emanation from the Central Sun, which is the invisible source of all that is in our Solar System.

Our visible Sun is but the mirror in which are reflected the rays of energy from the Spiritual Sun. The real Sun is as invisible as the real Man.

Uranus was the first planet to be thrown off from the nebula when its differentiation began in Chaos, at the dawn of the Earth Period. There was no light but the dim light of the Zodiac. The life that left with Uranus is of a rather backward strain and is said to evolve very, very slowly.

Saturn was next differentiated. It is the field of action for the life which is at the stage of evolution corresponding to the Saturn Period. This planet was differentiated before the ignition of the nebula and (like all nebulae when passing through their Saturn Period of evolution) was not a source of light, but a reflector.

Jupiter was differentiated shortly afterwards, when the nebula had become ignited. The heat of Jupiter is not so great as that of the Sun, Venus or Mercury, but on account of its immense bulk, it is capable of retaining its heat and thus remains a suitable field of evolution for very

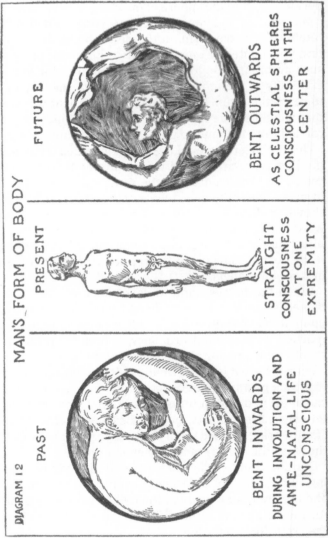

advanced beings. It corresponds to the stage which will be reached by the Earth itself in the Jupiter Period.

Mars is a mystery, and only a limited amount of information may be given out. We may say, however, that the life on Mars is of a very backward nature and that the so-called "canals" are not excavations in the surface of the plan-

142

et. They are currents such as, during the Atlantean Epoch, spread over our planet, and the remains of which can still be observed in the Aurora Borealis and the Aurora Australis. The shifting of the Martian "canals" noted by astronomers, is thus accounted for. If they were really canals, they could not possibly shift, but currents emanating from the Poles of Mars may do so.

The Earth and Moon, was next set out from the Sun, later Venus and Mercury. These and Mars will be referred to later, in connection with the evolution of man on the earth, and need not be further considered at this time.

When a planet has Moons it indicates that there are some beings in the life wave evolving on that planet who are too backward to share in the evolution of the main life wave, and they have therefore been set out from the planet to prevent them from hindering the progress of the pioneers. Such is the case with the beings inhabiting our Moon. In the case of Jupiter it is thought probable that the inhabitants of three of its moons will eventually be able to rejoin the life on the parent planet, but it is thought that at least one of the others is an eighth sphere, like our own Moon, where retrogression and disintegration of the already acquired vehicle will result from too close adherence to material existence upon the part of the evolving beings who have brought themselves to that deplorable end.

Neptune and its satellites do not properly belong to our Solar System. The other planets--or rather their Spirits-- exercise an influence over the whole of humanity, but the influence of Neptune is largely restricted to one particular class the astrologers. The writer, for instance, has several times felt its compelling influence in a marked way.

When laggards inhabiting a Moon have retrieved their position and returned to the parent planet; or, when continued retrogression has caused complete disintegration of their vehicles, the abandoned Moon also commences to dissolve. The momentum of a spiritual impulse which propelled it in a fixed orbit for eons, may endure for eons after the Moon has been vacated, and from the physical point of view it may still seem to be a satellite of the planet in encircles. As the time goes on, however, and the power of attraction exercised by the parent planet diminishes, its orbit widens, until it reaches the limit of our solar system. It is then expelled into interstellar space; dissolved in Chaos. The expulsion of these cinder-like dead worlds is analogous to the manner in which hard and foreign bodies imbedded in the human system make their way through the flesh to the skin. The Asteroids illustrate this point. They are fragments of Moons which once encircled Venus and Mercury. The beings once confined upon them are known in esotericism as "The Lords from Venus" and "The lords from Mercury;" they retrieved their lost estate in a large measure by service to our humanity, as will be later described, and are now safe on their present planet, while the Moons they inhabited have partly disintegrated, and are already far outside the earth's orbit. There are other "seeming" moons in our system, but the Rosicrucian Cosmo-Conception does not notice them, as they are outside the pale of evolution.

143

Chapter Twelve - Evolution on the Earth

The Polarian Epoch

While the material which now forms the Earth was yet a part of the Sun, it was, of course in a fiery condition; but as the fire does not burn spirit, our human evolution commenced at once, being confined particularly to the Polar Region of the Sun.

The highest evolved beings which were to become human were the first to appear. The substances which now form the Earth were all molten, and the atmosphere was gaseous, yet man recapitulated his mineral stage anew.

From that attenuated chemical substance of the sun man himself built his first mineral body, assisted by the Lords of Form. If this statement is objected to on the ground that man could not build unconsciously, the case of the mother can be cited in answer. Is she conscious of building the body of the babe in her womb? Yet surely no one will say that she has nothing to do with it! The only difference is that the mother builds unconsciously for the babe; and man built unconsciously for himself.

Man's first dense body did not even remotely resemble his present splendidly organized vehicle. That has been evolved only in the course of myriads of years. The first dense body was a large, baggy object with an opening at the top, from which an organ projected. This was a kind of organ of orientation and direction. In the course of time the dense body drew more closely together and condensed. If it came too close to places of greater heat than it could endure, it disintegrated. In time the organ grew sensitive to the condition that threatened destruction and the dense body automatically moved to a safer place.

This organ has now degenerated into what is called the pineal gland. Sometimes it is called "the third eye," but that is a misnomer, because it never was an eye, but rather the localized organ for the sensing of heat and cold, which faculty is now distributed over the entire dense body. During the Polarian Epoch this sense was thus localized, as the sense of sight is now in the eye, and that of hearing in the ear. The extension of the sense of feeling since that time indicates the manner in which the entire body will be improved, so that at some future time any part of it will be able to perceive all things. The senses of sight and hearing will be extended over the entire body, as the sense of feeling is now. Them man will be all eyes and ears. Specialized sense organs indicate limitation. Sense perception by the whole is comparative perfection.

At the early stage of which we are now speaking there was a kind of propagation. These immense baggy creatures divided in halves in a manner similar to the division of cells by fission, but the separated portions would not grow, each remaining only half as large as the original form.

The Hyperborean Epoch

At different points on the fiery globe there began in the course of time the

144

formation of crust-islands in a sea of fire.

The Lords of Form appeared, with the Angels (humanity of the Moon Period), and clothed man's dense form with a vital body. Those baggy bodies then began to increase in size by drawing to themselves material from the outside, osmosis, as it were. When they propagated, it was no longer by dividing into halves, but into two un-equal parts. Both parts grew until each had attained the original size of the parent.

As the Polarian Epoch was really a recapitulation of the Saturn Period, it may be said that during that time man passed through the mineral state; he had the same vehicle--the dense body--and a consciousness similar to the trance state. For analogous reasons, the plant state was passed through in the Hyperborean Epoch, as man had a dense and a vital body and a dreamless-sleep-consciousness.

Man began his evolution on the Earth after Mars had been thrown off from the central mass, and that which is now the Earth was yet undetached from the Sun; but at the close of the Hyperborean Epoch the incrustation had progressed so far that it had become an obstacle to the progress of some of the higher evolved beings in the Sun. The fiery condition also hindered the evolution of some of the lower grades of creatures, such as man, who at that stage required a denser world for his further development. Therefore, the part which is now the Earth was thrown off from the Sun at the end of the Hyperborean Epoch, and commenced to revolve around the parent body in a somewhat different orbit than at present. Shortly afterwards Venus and Mercury were thrown off for similar reasons.

Crystallization always commences at the pole of a planet where motion is slow. The consolidated part gradually works outwards towards the equator in obedience to the centrifugal force. If that force is stronger than the cohesive tendency the consolidated mass is thrown outwards into space.

At the time when the Earth-globe was separated from the parent-mass, it included that part which is now our Moon. On this great globe was evolving the life wave now passing through the human kingdom, also the life waves which entered evolution in the Sun, Moon, and Earth Periods, and are now evolving through the animal, plant and mineral kingdoms.

Mention has been made of the stragglers of various Periods who in later Periods were enabled to take a step upward in evolution. There were some, however, who did not take this step. They did not evolve, and were therefore left further and further behind, until they became a drag and a hindrance to the progressive ones. It became necessary to get them out of the way, that the evolution of the others might not be retarded.

In the beginning of the Lemurian Epoch, these "failures" (note that they were *failures*, not merely stragglers) had crystallized that part of the Earth occupied by them to such a degree that it become as a huge cinder or clinker, in the otherwise soft and fiery Earth. They were a hindrance and an obstruction, so they, with the part of the Earth they had crystallized, were thrown out into space beyond recall. That is the genesis of the Moon.

145

The Moon--The Eighth Sphere

The seven Globes, A to G, inclusive, are the field of Evolution. The Moon is the field of Disintegration.

If Earth had not segregated from the original Globe which is now the Sun, the rapidity of the vibrations would have disintegrated man's vehicles. He would have grown so rapidly that the growth of the mushroom would seem slow in comparison. He would have become old before he had time to pass through youth. That such is the effect of too much Sun is shown by the rapidity of growth at the tropics, where maturity and old age are reached much sooner than in the north. On the other hand had the Moon remained with the Earth, man would have crystallized into a statue. The separation of the Earth from the Sun, which now sends its rays from a far distance, enables man to live at the proper rate of vibration, to unfold slowly. The Moon-forces reach him from the exact distance necessary to enable him to build a body of the proper density. But although the latter forces are active in the building of the form, they also cause death when their continued work finally crystallizes the tissues of the body.

The Sun works in the vital body and is the force which makes for life, and wars against the death-dealing Moon force.

The Lemurian Epoch

In this Epoch appeared the Archangels (the humanity of Sun Period). and the Lords of Mind (the humanity of Saturn Period). These Hierarchies were assisted by the Lords of Form, who were given charge of the Earth Period. They helped man to build his desire body, and the Lords of Mind gave the germ of Mind to the greater part of the pioneers who formed class 1, according to the classification in diagram 10.

The Lords of Form vivified the Human spirit in as many of the stragglers of the Moon Period as had made the necessary progress in the three and one half Revolutions which had elapsed since the commencement of the Earth Period, but at that time the Lords of Mind could not give them the germ of Mind. Thus a great part of nascent humanity was left without this link between the threefold spirit and the threefold body.

The Lords of Mind took charge of the higher part of the desire body and of the germinal mind, impregnating them with the quality of separate selfhood, without which no separate, self-contained beings such as we are today would be possible.

We owe to the Lords of Mind the separate personality, with all the possibilities for experience and growth thus afforded. And this point marks the birth of the Individual.

Birth of the Individual

Diagram 1 will make clear the fact that the personality is the reflected picture of the Spirit, the mind being the mirror, or focus.

As when reflected in a pond, the images of trees appear inverted, the foliage seeming to be the deepest down in the water, so the highest aspect of the spirit (the Divine Spirit) finds its counterpart in the lowest of the three bodies (the dense body). The next highest spirit (the life spirit) is reflected in the next lowest body (the vital body). The third spirit (the human spirit) and its reflection, the third body (the desire body), appear closest of all to the reflecting mirror, which is the mind, the latter corresponding to the surface of the pond--the reflecting medium in our analogy.

The Spirit came down from the higher Worlds during involution; and by concurrent action, the Bodies were built upward in the same period. It is the meeting of these two streams in the focusing Mind that marks the point in time when the individual, the human being, the Ego, is born--when the Spirit takes possession of its vehicles.

Yet we must not suppose that this at once raised man to his present status in evolution, making him the self conscious, thinking being he is today. Before that point could be reached a long and weary road had to be traveled, for at the time we are considering, organs were in their most rudimentary stage and there was no brain that could be used as an instrument of expression. Hence the consciousness was the dimmest imaginable. In short, the man of that day was very far from being as intelligent as our present-day animals. The first step in the direction of improvement was the building of a brain to use as an instrument of mind in the Physical World. That was achieved by separating humanity into sexes.

Separation of the Sexes

Contrary to the generally accepted idea, the Ego is bisexual. Were the Ego sexless, the body would necessarily be sexless also, for the body is but the external symbol of the indwelling spirit.

The sex of the Ego does not, of course, express itself as such in the inner worlds. It manifests there as two distinct qualities--Will and Imagination. The Will is the male power and is allied to the Sun forces; Imagination is the female power and is always linked to the Moon forces. This accounts for the imaginative trend of woman and for the special power which the Moon exercises over the female organism.

When the matter of which the Earth and the Moon were afterwards formed was still a part of the Sun, the body of man-in-the-making was yet plastic, and the forces from that part which afterwards became Sun, and that part which is now Moon worked readily in all bodies, so that the man of the Hyperborean Epoch was hermaphrodite--capable of producing another being from himself without intercourse with any other.

When the Earth separated from the Sun and shortly afterwards threw off the Moon, the forces from the two luminaries did not find equal expression in all, as formerly. Some bodies become more amenable to the forces from one, and some to those from the other.

147

Influence of Mars

In the part of the Earth Period preceding the separation of the sexes--during the three and one-half Revolutions which intervened between the time when Mars was differentiated and the beginning of the Lemurian Epoch--Mars traveled in a different orbit from the present, and its aura (that part of its finer vehicles which extends beyond the dense planet) permeated the body of the central planet and polarized the iron with it.

As iron is essential to the production of warm, red blood, all creatures were cold-blooded, or rather, the fluid parts of the body were no warmer than the surrounding atmosphere.

When the Earth was set free from the Central Sun, that event changed the orbits of the planets and thus the influence of Mars over the iron in the Earth was minimized. The Planetary Spirit of Mars finally withdrew the remainder of that influence, and although the desire bodies of the Earth and Mars still penetrate, the dynamic power of Mars over the iron (which is a Mars metal) and iron has become available for use on our planet.

Iron is in reality the basis of separate existence. Without iron the red, heat-giving blood would be an impossibility, and the Ego could have no hold in the body. When red blood developed--in the latter part of the Lemurian Epoch--the body become upright and the time had come when the Ego could begin to dwell within the body and control it.

But to dwell within is not the end and aim of evolution. It is simply a means by which the Ego may better express itself through its instrument, that it may manifest in the Physical World. To that end the sense organs, the larynx, and above all, a brain, must be built and perfected. During the early part of the Hyperborean Epoch, while the Earth was still united with the Sun, the solar forces supplied man with all the sustenance he needed and he unconsciously radiated the surplus for the purpose of propagation.

When the Ego entered into possession of its vehicles it became necessary to use part of this force for the building of the brain and larynx. The latter was originally a part of the creative organ. The larynx was built while the dense body was yet bent together in the bag-like shape already described, which is still the form of the human embryo. As the dense body straightened and became upright, part of the creative organ remained with the upper part of the dense body and later became the larynx.

Thus the dual creative force which had hitherto worked is only one direction, for the purpose of the creating another being, became divided. One part was directed upward to build the brain and larynx, by means of which the Ego was to become capable of thinking and communicating thoughts to other beings. As a result of this change only one part of the force essential in the creation of another being was available to one individual, hence it became necessary for each individual to seek the co-operation of another, who possessed that part of the procreative force which the seeker lacked.

Thus did the evolving entity obtain brain consciousness of the outside world at the cost of half its creative power. Previous to that time, it used within itself both parts of that power to externalize another being. As a result of that modification, however, it has evolved the power to create and express thought. Before then, it was a creator in the physical world only; since then it has become able to create in the three worlds.

The Races and Their Leaders

Before considering in detail the evolution of the Lemurians it may be well to take a general survey of the Races and their Leaders.

Some very valuable works on Occultism, bringing before the public the teachings of the Eastern Wisdom, have nevertheless contained certain mistakes, owing to a misunderstanding of the teachings by those who were so fortunate as to receive them. All books, not written directly by the Elder Brothers, are liable to contain such errors. Considering the extreme intricacy and many complications of the subject, the wonder is not that mistakes do occur, but that they are not more frequent. Therefore the writer does not presume to criticize, recognizing that more numerous and more serious mistakes may be embodied in the present work, owing to his own misconception of the teaching. He simply sets forth in the next few paragraphs what he has received, which shows how the differing (and seemingly contradictory) teaching of two such valuable works as "The Secret Doctrine" by H. P. Blavatsky, and "Esoteric Buddhism," by A. P. Sinnett, may be reconciled.

That part of human evolution which is to be accomplished during the present sojourn of the life wave on our Earth is divisible into seven great stages or Epochs; but these cannot appropriately be called Races. Nothing to which that name could be correctly applied appears until the end of the Lemurian Epoch. From that time different Races succeed one another through the Atlantean and Aryan Epochs, and will extend slightly into the Sixth great Epoch.

The total number of Races--past, present and future--in our scheme of evolution is sixteen; one at the end of the Lemurian Epoch, seven during the Atlantean Epoch, seven more in our present Aryan Epoch and one in the beginning of the Sixth Epoch. After that time there will be nothing that can properly be called a Race.

Races did not exist in the Periods which have preceded the Earth Period and they will not exist in those Periods which follow it. It is only here, at the very nadir of material existence, that the difference is so great between man and man as to warrant the separation into Races. The immediate Leaders of humanity (apart from the creative Hierarchies) who helped man to take the first tottering steps in Evolution, after Involution had furnished him with vehicles, were Beings much further advanced than man along the path of evolution. They came on this errand of love from the two planets which are located between the Earth and the Sun--Venus and Mercury.

The Beings who inhabit Venus and Mercury are not quite so far advanced as those whose present field of evolution is the Sun, but they are very much further advanced than our humanity. Therefore they stayed somewhat longer with the central mass than did the inhabitants of the Earth, but at a certain point their evolution demanded separate fields, so those two planets were thrown off, Venus first, and then Mercury. Each was given such proximity to the central orb as insured the rate of vibration necessary for its evolution. The inhabitants of Mercury are the furthest advanced, hence are closer to the Sun.

Some of the inhabitants of each planet were sent to the Earth to help nascent humanity and are know to occult scientist as the "Lords of Venus" and the "Lords of Mercury."

The Lords of Venus were leaders of the masses of our people. They were inferior beings of the Venus evolution, who appeared among men and were know as "messengers of the Gods." For the good of our humanity they led and guided it, step by step. There was no rebellion against their authority, because man had not yet evolved an independent will. It was to bring him to the stage where he would be able to manifest will and judgment that they guided him, until he should be able to guide himself.

It was known that these messengers communed with the Gods. They were held in deep reverence and their commands were obeyed without question.

When under the tuition of these Beings mankind had reached a certain stage of progress, the most advanced were placed under the guidance of the Lords of Mercury, who initiated them into the higher truths for the purpose of making them leaders of the people. These Initiates were then exalted to kingship and were the founders of the dynasties of Divine Rulers who were indeed kings "by the grace of God," i.e., by the grace of the Lords of Venus and Mercury, who were as Gods to infant humanity. They guided and instructed the kings for the good of the people and not for self-aggrandizement and arrogation of rights at their expense.

At that time a Ruler held a sacred trust to educate and help his people; to alleviate and promote equity and well-being. He had the light of God to give him wisdom and guide his judgment. Hence, while those kings reigned, all things prospered, and it was indeed a Golden Age. Yet, as we follow the evolution of man in detail, we shall see that the present phase or period of development, though it cannot be called a golden age in any but a material sense, is nevertheless a necessary one, in order to bring man to the point where he will be able to rule himself, for *self-mastery is the end and aim of all rulership. No man can safely remain ungoverned who has not learned to govern himself,* and at the present stage of development, that is the hardest task that can be given him. It is easy to command others; it is hard to force obedience from oneself.

Influence of Mercury

The purpose of the Lords of Mercury at that time, and of all Hierophants of Mysteries since then, as also of all the occult schools of our day, was and is to teach the candidate the art of Self-Mastery. In the measure that a man has mastered himself, *and in that measure only*, is he qualified to govern others. Were the present rulers of the masses able to govern *themselves* we should again have the Millennium or Golden Age.

As the Lords of Venus worked on the masses of a long past ago, so do the Lords of Mercury now work on the Individual, fitting him for mastery over self and (incidentally only, not primarily) for mastery over others. This work on their part is but the beginning of what will be an increasing Mercurial influence during the remaining three and one-half Revolutions of the Earth Period. During the first three and one-half Revolutions Mars held sway, polarizing the iron, preventing the formation of the red blood and keeping the Ego from immuring itself in the body until the latter had attained at the requisite degree of development. During the last three- and one-half Revolutions Mercury will operate to extricate the Ego from its densest vehicle by means of Initiation. Incidentally, it may be noted that, as Mars polarized the iron, so Mercury has polarized the metal bearing its name and the workings of that metal will show very well this tendency to take the dense body away from the spirit--to liberate the latter from the former.

That dread disease, syphilis, is an example of condition were the Ego is fettered and immured in the body to a particularly cramping extent. Sufficient mercury relieves the condition, lessens the hold of the body upon the Ego and leaves the latter to that comparative freedom within the body, an overdose of mercury causes paralysis, thus taking the dense body from the man in an improper way.

The Lords of Mercury taught man to leave and re-enter the body at will; to function in his higher vehicles independent of the dense body, so that the latter becomes a cheerful dwelling house instead of a closely-locked prison-- a useful instrument instead of a clogging fetter. Therefore occult science speaks of the Earth Period as Mars-Mercury, and so it may be said truly that we have been in Mars and are going to Mercury, as taught in one of the occult works previously mentioned. It is also true, however, that we have never inhabited the planet Mars, nor are we to leave the earth at some future time to take up our abode on the planet Mercury, as the other work mentioned states, with the intention of correcting an error in the first one.

Mercury, now being in obscuration, is exercising very little influence on us, but it is emerging from a planetary rest and as time goes on its influence will be more and more in evidence as a factor in our evolution. The coming Races will have much help from the Mercurians, and the people of still later Epochs and Revolutions will have even more.

The Lemurian Race

We are now in a position to understand the information which is to follow concerning the people who lived *in the latter part* of the Lemurian Epoch, whom we may call the Lemurian Race.

151

The atmosphere of Lemuria was still very dense--somewhat like the fire-fog of the Moon Period, but denser. The crust of the Earth was just starting to become quite hard and solid in some places, while in others it was still fiery, and between islands of crust was a sea of boiling, seething water. Volcanic outbursts and cataclysms marked this time when the nether fires fought hard against the formation of the encircling wall which was to imprison them.

Upon the harder and comparatively cool spots man lived surrounded by giant fern-forests and animals of enormous size. The forms of both man and animal were yet quite plastic. The skeleton had formed, but man himself had great power in molding the flesh of his own body and that of the animals about him.

When he was born he could hear and feel, but his perception of light came later. We have analogous cases in animals like cats and dogs, the young of which receive the sense of sight some time after birth. The Lemurian had no eyes. He had two sensitive spots which were affected by the light of the Sun as it shone dimly through the fiery atmosphere of ancient Lemuria, but is was not until nearly the close of the Atlantean Epoch that he had sight as we have it today. Up to that time the building of the eye was in progress. While the Sun was within--while the Earth formed part of the light-giving mass--man need no external illuminant; he was luminous himself. But when the dark Earth was separated from the Sun it became necessary that the light should be perceived, therefore as the light rays impinged upon man, he perceived them. Nature built the eye as a light-perceiver, in response to the demand of the already-existing function, which is invariable the case, as Professor Huxley has so ably shown. The amoeba has no stomach, yet it digests. It is all stomach. The necessity for digesting food built the stomach in the course of time, but digestion took place before the alimentary canal was formed. In an analogous manner, the perception of light called forth the eye. The light itself built the eye and maintains it. Where there is no light there can be no eye. In cases where animals have withdrawn and dwelt in caves--keeping away from the light--the eyes have degenerated and atrophied because there were no light rays to maintain them and no eyes were needed in the dark caves. The Lemurian needed eyes; he had a perception of light, and the light was commencing to build the eye in response to his demand.

His language consisted of sounds like those of Nature. The sighing of the wind in the immense forests which grew in great luxuriance in that super-tropical climate, the rippling of the brook, the howling of the tempest--for Lemuria was storm-swept--the thunder of the waterfall, the roar of the vol-cano--all these were to him voices of the Gods from whom he knew himself to have descended.

Of the birth of his body he knew nothing. He could not *see* either it or anything else, but he did *perceive* his fellow beings. It was, however, an inner perception, like our perception of persons and things in dreams, but with this very important difference, that his dream-perception was clear and rational.

Thus he knew nothing at all about his body, in fact he did not know he had a body any more than we know we have a stomach when that organ is in good health. We remember its existence only when our abuse of it causes us to feel pain there. Under normal conditions we are entirely unconscious of its processes. Similarly did the body of the Lemurian serve him excellently, although he was unaware of its existence. Pain was the means of making him aware of his body and of the world without.

Everything in connection with the propagation of the race and the bringing to birth was done by direction of the Angels under the leadership of Jehovah, the Regent of the Moon. The propagative function was performed as stated times of the year when the lines of force, running from planet to planet, were focused at proper angles. Thus the creative force encountered no obstruction and parturition was painless. Man was unaware of birth, because at that time he was unconscious of the physical world as he now is during sleep. It was only in the intimate contact of sex relation that the spirit became aware of the flesh and them man "knew" his wife. That is shown is such passages of the Bible as "Adam *knew* Eve and she bore Seth"; "Elkanah *knew* Hannah and she bore Samuel"; and Mary's question, "How I shall conceive, seeing I *know* no man?" This is also the key to the meaning of the "Tree of Knowledge," the fruit of which opened the eyes of Adam and Eve, so that they came to know both good and evil. Previously they had known only good, but when they began to exercise the creative function independently, they were ignorant of stellar influences, as their descendants, and Jehovah's supposed curse was not a curse at all, but a simple statement of the result which must inevitably follow use of their generative force which failed to take into consideration the effect of the stellar rays on childbirth.

Thus the ignorant use of the generative force is primarily responsible for pain, sickness and sorrow.

The Lemurian knew no death because when, in the course of long ages, his body dropped away, he entered another, quite unconscious of the change. His consciousness was not focused in the physical world, therefore the laying aside of one body and the taking of another was no more to him than a leaf or twig drying and falling away from the tree and being replaced by a new growth.

Their language was to the Lemurians something holy. It was not a dead language like ours--a mere orderly arrangements of sounds. Each sound uttered by the Lemurian had power over his fellow-beings, over the animals and even over nature around him. Therefore, under the guidance of the Lords of Venus, who were the messengers of God--the agents of the creative hierarchies-- the power of speech was used with great reverence, as something most holy.

The education of the boys differed greatly from that of the girls. The Lemurian methods of education seem shocking to our more refined sensibilities. In

153

order to spare the reader's feelings, only the least cruel of them will be touched upon. Strenuous in the extreme as they may seen, it must be remembered that the Lemurian body was not nearly so high-strung as are the human bodies of the present day; also that it was only by the very harshest measures that the exceedingly dim consciousness could be touched at all. As time went on and the consciousness became more and more awakened, such extreme measures as those used then became unnecessary and have passed away, but at that time they were indispensable to arouse the slumbering forces of the spirit to a consciousness of the outside world.

The education of the boys was designed especially to develop the quality of Will. They were made to fight one another, and these fights were extremely brutal. They were impaled upon spits, with full power to release themselves, but by exercising the will power they were to remain there in spite of the pain. They learned to make their muscles tense, and to carry immense burdens by the exercise of the Will.

The education of the girls was intended to promote the development of the imaginative facility. They also were subjected to strenuous and severe treatment. They were put out in the great forests, to let the sound of the wind in the tree tops speak to them and to listen to the furious outbursts of flood and tempest. They thus learned to have no fear of those paroxysms of nature and to perceive only the grandeur of the warring elements. The frequent volcanic outbursts were greatly valued as a means of education, being particularly conducive to the awakening of the faculty of memory.

Such educational methods would be entirely out of the question at the present day, but they did not make the Lemurian morbid, because he had no memory. No matter what painful or terrifying experience he endured, everything was forgotten as soon as past. The above mentioned strenuous experiences were for the purpose of developing memory, to imprint these violent and constantly repeated impacts from without upon the brain, because memory is necessary that the experiences of the past may be used as guides to Action.

The education of the girls developed the first germinal, flickering memory. *The first idea of good and evil was formulated by them* because of their experiences, which worked chiefly on the imagination. Those experiences most likely to leave a recollection were thought "Good;" those which did not produce that much desired result were considered "Evil."

Thus woman become the pioneer in culture, being the first to develop the idea of "a good life," of which she became the esteemed exponent among the ancients and in that respect she has nobly led the vanguard ever since. Of course, as all Egos incarnate alternately as male and female, there is really no pre-eminence. It is simply that those who for the time being are in a dense body of the feminine gender have a positive vital body, and are therefore more responsive to spiritual impacts than when the vital body is negative as in the male.

As we have seen, the Lemurian was a born magician. He felt himself a descendant of the Gods, a spiritual being; therefore his line of advancement was by gaining not spiritual, but *material* knowledge. The Temples of Initiation for the most advanced did not need to reveal to man his high origin; to educate him to perform feats of magic; to instruct him how to function in the desire world and the higher realms. Such instruction is necessary today because now the average man has no knowledge of the spiritual world, nor can he function in superphysical realism. The Lemurian, however, in his own way, did possess that knowledge and could exercise those faculties, but on the other hand, he was ignorant of the Laws of the Cosmos of facts regarding the physical world which are matters of common, everyday knowledge with us. Therefore at the School Initiation he was taught art, the laws of Nature and facts relating to the physical universe. His will was strengthened and his imagination and memory wakened so that he could correlate experiences and devise ways and means of action when his past experiences did not serve to indicate a proper course of procedure. Thus, the Temples of Initiation in the Lemurian times were High Schools for the cultivation of Willpower and Imagination, with "post-graduate courses" in Art and Science.

Yet, though the Lemurian was a born magician, he never misused his powers because he felt himself related to the Gods. Under his direction of the Messengers of the Gods, already spoken of, his forces were directed toward the molding of forms in the animal and the plant worlds. It may be hard for the materialist to understand how he could do such work if he could not see the world about him. It is true man could not "see" as we understand the term and as he now sees objects outside in space with his physical eyes. Still, as the purest of our children are clairvoyant to this day while they remain in a state of sinless innocence, the Lemurians possessed an internal perception which gave them only a dim idea of the *outward* shape of any object; but illuminated so much the brighter its inner nature, its soul-quality, by a spiritual apperception born of innocent purity.

Innocence, however, is not synonymous with Virtue. Innocence is the child of Ignorance and could not be maintained in a universe where the purpose of evolution is the acquisition of Wisdom. To attain that end, a knowledge of good and evil, right and wrong, is essential, also choice of action.

If, having knowledge and choice, man ranges himself on the side of Good and Right he cultivates Virtue and Wisdom. If he succumbs to temptation and does wrong knowingly, he fosters vice.

God's plan is not to be brought to naught, however. Every act is a seed-ground for the Law of Consequence. We reap what we sow. The weeds of wrong action bear flowers of sorrow and suffering, and when the seeds from then have fallen into a chastened heart, when they have been watered by the tears of repentance Virtue will eventually blossom forth. What blessed assurance, that out of every evil we do, Good will eventually accrue, for in our Father's Kingdom naught but Good can endure.

Therefore, the "Fall" with its consequent pain and suffering is but a temporary state where we see through a glass darkly, but anon we shall behold again face to face the God within and without, who is ever perceived by the pure in heart.

The Fall of Man

This is kabalistically described as the experience of one pair who, of course, represent humanity. The key is given in the verse where the Messenger of the Gods says to the woman, "in sorrow thou shalt bring forth children;" the clue is also found in the sentence of death which was pronounced at that same time.

It will be observed that previous to the Fall the consciousness was not focused in the physical world. Man was unconsciousness of propagation, birth and death. The Angels who have charge of and work in the vital body (the medium of propagation) regulated the propagative function and brought the sexes together at certain seasons of the year, using the solar and the lunar forces when they produced conditions most propitious for fecundation, the union being achieved unconsciously by the participants at first, but later it produced a momentary physical cognition. Then the period of gestation caused no inconvenience and parturition was painless, the parent being plunged in deep sleep. Birth and death involved no break in the conscious and were therefore non-existent to the Lemurians.

Their consciousness was directed inward. They perceived physical things in a spiritual way, as we perceive them in a dream--at which time all that we see is within ourselves.

When "their eyes opened" and their consciousness was directed outward toward the facts of the physical world, conditions were altered. Propagation was directed, not by the Angels, but by man, who was ignorant of the operation of the Sun and Moon forces. He also abused the sex-function, using it for sense-gratification, with the result that pain attended the process of childbearing. Then his consciousness became focused in the physical world, although all things did not appear to his vision with clearly defined outlines until the latter part of the Atlantean Epoch. Still he came by degrees to know death because of the break made in his consciousness when it was shifted to the higher worlds at death and back to the physical world at rebirth.

The "opening of the eyes" was brought about in the following manner: We remember that when the sexes separated, the male became an expression for Will, which is one part of the twofold soul-force; the female expressing the other part, Imagination. If woman were not imaginative she could not build the new body in the womb and were not the spermatozoa an embodiment of the concentrated human will, it could not accomplish impregnation and so commence the germination, which results in the continued segmentation of the ovum.

These twin-forces, Will and Imagination, are both necessary to the propagation of bodies. Since the separation of the sexes, however, one of these

156

forces remains within each individual and only the part given out is available for propagation. Hence the necessity for a one-sexed being who expresses the complementary soul-force. This was previously explained; also that the part of the soul-force not used for propagation becomes available for *inner* growth. So long as man sent out the full, dual sex-force for generation, he could accomplish nothing in the direction of soul-growth for himself. But since then the part not used through the sex organ has been appropriated by the indwelling spirit to build the brain and the larynx for its expression.

Thus man built on, all through the latter part of the Lemurian Epoch and the first two-thirds of the Atlantean Epoch until, by the above mentioned use of this half of his sex-force, he became a fully-conscious, thinking, reasoning, being.

In man the brain is the link between the spirit and the outside world. He can know nothing of the outside world except through the medium of the brain. The sense organs are merely carriers to the brain of impacts from without and the brain is the instrument which interprets and coordinates those impacts. The Angels belonged to a different evolution and had never been imprisoned in a dense and cumbrously slow vehicle such as ours. They had learned to obtain knowledge without a physical brain. Their lowest vehicle is the vital body. Wisdom came to them as a gift, without the necessity of laboriously thinking it out through a physical brain.

Man, however, had to "fall into generation," and work for his knowledge. The spirit, by means of one part of the sex-force directed inward, built the brain to gather knowledge from the physical world, and the same force is feeding and building the brain today. It is subverted from its proper course inasmuch as it should have gone outward for procreation, but man retains it for selfish purposes. No so the Angels. They had experienced no division of their soul-powers, therefore they could send out the dual soul-force *without selfish reservation.*

The force that goes outward for the purpose of creating another being is Love. The Angels sent out their *whole love, without selfishness or desire* and in return, Cosmic Wisdom flowed into them.

Man sends out only part of his love; the residue he selfishly keeps and uses to build his inner organs of expression, to improve *himself;* thus does his love become selfish and sensual. With one part of his creative soul-power he selfishly loves another being because he desires co-operation in propagation. With the other part of his creative soul-power he thinks (also for selfish reasons) because he desires knowledge.

The Angels love without desire, but man had to go through selfishness. He must desire and work for wisdom selfishly, that he may reach selflessness at a higher stage.

The Angels helped him to propagate even after the subversion of part of the soul-force. They helped him to build the physical brain, but they had no knowledge that could be transmitted by means of it, because they did not know how to use such an instrument and could not speak directly to a brain being. All they could do was to control the physical expression of the love of man and guide it through the emotions in a loving, innocent way, thus saving man the pain and trouble incident to the exercise of the sex-function without wisdom.

Had that *regime* lasted, man would have remained simply a God-guided automaton and would never have become a personality--an individual. That he had become so is due to a much maligned class of entities called the Lucifer Spirits.

The Lucifer Spirits

These spirits were a class of stragglers in the life wave of the Angels. In the Moon Period they worked themselves far ahead of the great mass of those who are now the most advanced of our humanity. They have not progressed as far as the Angels who were the pioneer humanity of the Moon Period, however, but they were so much in advance of our present humanity that it was impossible for them to take a dense body as we have done; yet they could not gain knowledge without the use of an inner organ, a physical brain. They were half-way between man who has a brain and the Angels who need none--in short, they were demi-gods.

They were thus in a serious situation, The only way they could find an avenue through which to express themselves and gain knowledge was to use man's physical brain, as they could make themselves understood by a physical being endowed with a brain, which the Angels could not.

As said, in the latter part of the Lemurian Epoch man did not see the physical world as we do now. To him the desire world was much more real. He had the dream-consciousness of the Moon Period--an inner picture-consciousness; he was unconscious of the world outside himself. The Lucifers had no difficultly in manifesting to his inner consciousness and calling his attention to his outward shape, which he had not theretofore perceived. They told him how he could cease being simply the servant of external powers, and could become his own master and like unto the gods, "knowing good and evil." They also made clear to him that he need have no apprehension if his body died, inasmuch as he had within himself the creative ability to form new bodies without the mediation of the Angels. All of which information was given with the one purpose of turning his consciousness outward for the acquirement of knowledge.

This the Lucifers did that they might profit by it themselves--to gain knowledge as man acquired it. They brought to him pain and suffering where there was none before; but they also brought him the inestimable blessing of emancipation from outside influence and guidance, thereby starting him on the road to the evolution of his own spiritual powers--an evolution which will eventually enable him to upbuild himself with wisdom such as that of the Angels and other Beings Who guided him before he first exercised free will.

Before man's enlightenment by the Lucifer Spirits he had not known sickness, pain nor death. All of these resulted from the unwise use of the propagative faculty and its abuse for the gratification of the senses. Animals in their wild state are exempt from sickness and pain, because their propagation is carried on under the care and direction of the wise group spirit at only those times of the year which are propitious to that process. The sex-function is designed solely for the perpetuation of the species and under no circumstances for the gratification of sexual desire.

Had man remained a God-guided automaton, he would have known no sickness, pain, no death unto this day; but he would also have lacked the brain-consciousness and independence which resulted from his enlightenment by the Lucifer Spirits, the "light-givers," who opened the eyes of his understanding and taught him to use his then dim vision to gain knowledge of the Physical World which he was destined to conquer.

From that time there have been two forces working in man. One force is that of the Angels, who build new beings in the womb by means of Love which is turned downward for procreation; they are therefore the perpetuators of the race.

The other force is that of the Lucifers, who are the instigators of all mental activity, by means of the other part of the sex-force, which is carried upward for work in the brain.

The Lucifers are also called "serpents" and are variously represented in different mythologies. More will be said about them when we come to the analysis of Genesis. For the present enough has been said to warrant us in pursuing the main line of investigation, which leads us to follow the progress of man's evolution still further, through the Atlantean and Aryan Epochs, down to the present day.

What has been said about the enlightenment of the Lemurians applies to only a minor portion of those who lived in the latter part of that Epoch, and who became the Seed for the Seven Atlantean Races. The greater part of the Lemurians were animal-like and the *forms* inhabited by them have degenerated into the savages and anthropoids of the present day.

The student is requested to note carefully that it was the *forms* which degenerated. There is a very important distinction to be kept in mind between the bodies (or forms) of a race, and the Egos (or life) which is reborn in those race-bodies.

When a race is born, the *forms* are ensouled by a certain group of spirits and have inherent capability of evolving to a certain stage of completion and no further. There can be no standing still in nature, therefore when the limit of attainment has been reached the bodies or forms of that race begin to degenerate, sinking lower and lower until at last the race dies out.

The reason is not far to seek. New race bodies are particularly flexible and plastic, affording great scope for the Egos who are reborn in them to improve these vehicles and progress thereby. The most advanced Egos are brought to birth in such bodies and improve them to the best of their ability. These Egos,

159

however, are only apprentices as yet, and they cause the bodies to gradually crystallize and harden until the limit of improvement of that particular kind of body has been reached. Then forms for another new race are created, to afford the advancing Egos further scope for more extended experience and greater development. They discard the old race bodies for the new, their discarded bodies becoming the habitations for less advanced Egos who, in their turn, use them as stepping-stones on the path of progress. Thus the old race bodies are used by Egos *of increasing inferiority*, gradually degenerating until at last there are no Egos low enough to profit by rebirth in such bodies. The women then become sterile and the race-*forms* die.

We may easily trace this process by certain examples. The Teutonic-Anglo-Saxon race (particularly the American branch of it) has a softer, more flexible body and a more high-strung nervous system than any other race on earth at the present time. The Indian and Negro have much harder bodies and, because of the duller nervous system, are much less sensitive to lacerations, An Indian will continue to fight after receiving wounds the shock of which would prostrate or kill a white man, whereas the Indian will quickly recover. The Australian aborigines or Bushmen furnish an example of a race dying out on account of sterility, notwithstanding all that the British government is doing to perpetuate them.

It has been said by white men against the white race, that wherever it goes the other races dies out. The whites have been guilty of fearful oppression against those other races, having in many cases massacred multitudes of the defenseless and unsuspecting natives--as witness the conduct of the Spaniards towards the ancient Peruvians and Mexicans, to specify but one of many instances. The obligations resulting from such betrayal of confidence and abuse of superior intellect will be paid--yea, the last, least iota!--by those incurring them. It is equally true, however, that even had the whites not massacred, starved, enslaved, expatriated and otherwise maltreated those older races, the latter would nevertheless have died out just as surely, though more slowly, because such is the Law of Evolution--the Order of Nature. At some future time the white race-bodies when they become inhabited by the Egos who are now embodied in red, black, yellow or brown skins, will have degenerated so far that they also will disappear, to give place to other and better vehicles.

Science speaks only of evolution. It fails to consider the *lines of degeneration* which are slowly but surely destroying such bodies as have crystallized beyond possibility of improvement.

The Atlantean Epoch

Volcanic cataclysms destroyed the greater part of the Lemurian continent and in its stead rose the Atlantean continent, where the Atlantic Ocean now is.

Material scientists, impelled by the story of Plato to undertake researched regarding Atlantis, have demonstrated that there is ample foundation for the story that such a continent did exist. Occult scientists know that it existed and they also know that the conditions there were such as shall now be described.

Ancient Atlantis differed from our present world in many ways, but the greatest difference was in the constitution of the atmosphere and the water of that Epoch.

From the southern part of the planet came the hot, fiery breath of the volcanoes which were still abundantly active. From the north swept down the icy blasts of the Polar region. The continent of Atlantis was the meeting place of those two currents, consequently its atmosphere was always filled with a thick and murky fog. The water was not so dense as now, but contained a greater proportion of air. Much water was also held in suspension in the heavy, foggy Atlantean atmosphere.

Through this atmosphere the Sun never clearly shone. It appeared to be surrounded by an aura of light-mist, as do street-lamps when seen through a dense fog. It was then possible to see only a few feet in any direction and the outlines of all objects not close at hand appeared dim, hazy and uncertain. Man was guided more by internal perception than by external vision.

Not only the country, but also the man of that time was very different from anything existent on earth at the present time. He had a head, but scarcely any forehead; his brain had no frontal development; the head sloped almost abruptly back from a point just above the eyes. As compared with our present humanity; he was a giant; his arms and legs were much longer, in proportion to this body, than ours. Instead of walking, he progressed by a series of flying leaps, not unlike those of the kangaroo. He had small blinking eyes and his hair was round in section. The latter peculiarity, if no other, distinguishes the descendants of the Atlantean races who remain with us at the present day. Their hair was straight, glossy, black and *round* in section. That of the Aryan, thought it may differ in color, is always *oval* in section. The ears of the Atlantean sat much further back upon the head than do those of the Aryan.

The higher vehicles of the early Atlanteans were not drawn into a concentric position in relation to the dense body, as are ours. The spirit was not quite an *in*dwelling spirit; it was partially outside, therefore could not control its vehicles with as great facility as though it dwelt entirely inside. The head of the vital body was outside of and held a position far above the physical head. There is a point between the eyebrows and about half an inch below the surface of the skin, which has a corresponding point in the vital body. This point is not the pituitary body, which lies much deeper in the head of the dense body. It might be called "the root of the nose." When these two points in the dense and the vital bodies come into correspondence, as they do in man today, the trained clairvoyant sees then as a black spot, or rather as a vacant space, like the invisible core of a gas flame. This is the seat of the indwelling spirit in the man--the Holy of Holies in the temple of the human body, barred to all but that indwelling human Ego whose home it is. The trained clairvoyant can see with more or less distinctness, according to his capacity and training, all the different bodies which form the aura of man. This spot alone is hidden from him. This is the "Isis" whose veil none may lift. Not even the highest evolved being on earth is capable of unveiling the Ego of the humblest and least developed creature. That, and that alone upon earth, is so sacred that it is absolutely safe from intrusion.

These two points just spoken of--the one in the dense body and its counterpart in the vital body--were far apart in the men of the early Atlanteans days, as they are in the animals of our day. The head of the horse's vital body is far outside the head of its dense body. The two points are closer together in the dog than in any other animal except, perhaps, the elephant. When they come into correspondence we have an animal prodigy, able to count, spell, etc.

On account of the distance between these two points, the Atlantean's power of perception or vision was much keener in the inner Worlds than in the dense Physical World, obscured by its atmosphere of thick, heavy fog. In the fullness of time, however, the atmosphere slowly became clearer; at the same time, the point spoken of in the vital body came closer and closer to the corresponding point in the dense body. As the two approached each other, man gradually lost touch with the inner Worlds. They became dimmer as the dense Physical World became clearer in outline. Finally, in the last third of the Atlantean Epoch, the point in the vital body was united to the corresponding point in the dense body. Not until then did man become fully awake in the dense Physical World; but at the same time that full sight and perception in the Physical World were gained, the capability of perceiving the inner Worlds were gradually lost to most of the people.

In an earlier time the Atlantean did not clearly perceive the outline of an object or a person, but he saw the soul and at once knew its attributes, whether they were beneficial to him or otherwise. He knew whether the man or animal he was regarding was kindly or inimically disposed toward him. He was accurately taught by spiritual perception how to deal with others and how to escape harm. Therefore when the Spiritual World gradually faded from his consciousness, great was his sorrow at the loss.

The Rmoahals were the first of the Atlantean Races. They had but little memory and that little was chiefly connected with sensation. They remembered colors and tomes, and thus to some extend they evolved Feeling. The Lemurian had entirely lacked Feeling, in the finer signification of the word. He had the sense of touch, could feel the physical sensations of pain, ease and comfort, but not the mental and spiritual ones of joy, sorrow, sympathy and antipathy.

With memory came to the Atlanteans the rudiments of a language. They evolved words and no longer made use of mere sounds, as did the Lemurians. The Rmoahals began to give names to things. They were yet a spiritual race and, their soul-powers being like the forces of nature, they not only named the objects around them, but in their words was power over the things they named. Like the last of the Lemurians, their Feelings as spirits inspired them, and no harm was ever done to one another. To them the language was holy, as the highest direct expression of the spirit. The power was never abused or degraded by gossip or small talk. By the use of definite language the soul in this race first became able to contact the soul of things in the outside world.

The Tlavatlis were the second Atlantean Race. Already they began to feel their worth as separate human beings. They became ambitious, they demanded that their works be remembered. Memory became a factor in the life of the community. The remembrance of the deeds done by certain ones would cause a group of people to choose as their leader one who had done great deeds. This was the germ of Royalty.

This remembrance of the meritorious deeds of great men was carried even beyond the time when such leaders died. Mankind began to honor the memory of ancestors and to worship them and others who had shown great merit. That was the beginning of a form of worship which is practiced to this day by some Asiatics.

The Toltecs were the third Atlantean Race. They carried still further the ideas of their predecessors, inaugurating Monarchy and Hereditary Succession. The Toltecs originated the custom of honoring men for the deeds done by their ancestors, but there was then a very good reason for so doing. Because of the peculiar training at that time, the father had the power to bestow his qualities upon his son in a way impossible to mankind at the present time.

The education consisted of calling up before the soul of the child pictures of the different phases of life. The consciousness of the early Atlantean was, as yet, principally an internal picture-consciousness. The power of the educator to call up these pictures before the soul of the child was the determining factor upon which depended the soul qualities that would be possessed by the grown man. The instinct and not the reason was appealed to and aroused and by this method of education the son, in the great majority of cases, readily absorbed the qualities of the father. It is thus evident that there was at that time good reason for bestowing honor upon the descendants of great men, because the son almost always inherited most of his father's good qualities. Unfortunately, that is not the case in our time, although we still follow the same practices of honoring the sons of great men; but we have no reason whatever for doing so.

Among the Toltecs, experience came to be highly valued. The man who had gained the most varied experience was the most honored and sought. Memory was in them so great and accurate that our present memory is nothing in comparison. In an emergency, a Toltec of wide practical experience would be very likely to remember similar cases in the past, and suggest what action should be taken. Thus be became a valuable adviser to the community when a situation developed which none of the members had previously encountered and they were unable to think or reason from analogy as to how to

163

deal promptly with the emergency. When such an individual was not available, they were compelled to experiment in order to find what was best to do.

In the middle third of Atlantis we find the beginning of separate nations. Groups of people who discovered in one another similar tastes and habits would leave their old homes and found a new colony. They remembered old customs and followed them in their new homes as far as they suited, forming new ones to meet their own particular ideas and necessities.

The Leaders of mankind initiated great Kings at that time to rule the people, over whom they were given great power. The masses honored these kings with all the reverence due to those who were thus truly Kings "by the grace of God." This happy state, however, had in it the germ of disintegration, for in time the Kings become intoxicated with power. They forgot that it had been put into their hands by the grace of God, as a sacred trust; that they were made Kings for the purpose of dealing justly by and helping the people. They began to use their power corruptly, for selfish ends and personal aggrandizement instead of for the common good, arrogating themselves privileges and authorities never intended for them. Ambition and selfishness ruled then and they abused their high, divinely derived powers, for purposes of oppression and revenge. This was true, not only of the Kings, but also of the nobles and the higher classes, and when one considers the power possessed by them over their fellow beings of the less developed classes, it is easy to understand that its misuse would bring about terrible conditions.

The Original Turanians were the fourth Atlantean Race. They were especially vile in their abominable selfishness. They erected temples where the Kings were worshiped as gods, and caused the extreme oppression of the helpless lower classes. Black magic of the worst and most nauseating kind flourished and all their efforts were directed towards the gratification of vanity and external display.

The Original Semites were the fifth and most important of the seven Atlantean Races, because in them we find the first germ of the corrective quality of Thought. Therefore the Original Semitic Race become the "seed race" for the seven races of the present Aryan Epoch.

In the Polarian Epoch man acquired a dense body as an instrument of action. In the Hyperborean Epoch the vital body was added to give power of motion necessary to action. In the Lemurian Epoch the desire body furnished incentive to action.

The mind was given to man in the Atlantean Epoch to give purpose to action, but as the Ego was exceedingly weak and the desire nature strong, the nascent mind coalesced with the desire body, the faculty of Cunning resulted and was the cause of all the wickedness of the middle third of the Atlantean Epoch.

In the Aryan Epoch Thought and Reason were to be evolved by the work of the Ego in the mind to conduct Desire into channel leading to the attainment of spiritual perfection, which is the Goal of Evolution. This faculty of Thought and of forming Ideas was gained by man at the expense of loss of control over the vital forces-- i.e., power over Nature.

With Thought and Mind man can at present exercise power over the chemicals and minerals only, for his mind is now in the first of mineral stage of its evolution, as was his dense body in the Saturn Period. He can exercise no power over plant or animal *life*. Wood and various vegetable substances, together with different parts of the animals, are used by man in his industries. These substances are all in the final analysis chemical matter ensouled by mineral life, of which the *bodies* in all the kingdoms are composed, as previously explained. Over all these varieties of chemical mineral combinations man at his present stage may have dominion, but until he has reached the Jupiter Period, that dominion will not be extended so that he can work with life. In that Period, however, he will have the power to work with plant life as the Angels do at present in the Earth Period.

Material scientist have labored for many years in an endeavor to "create" life, but they will not succeed until they have learned that they must approach the laboratory table with the deepest reverence, as they would draw near to the altar in a Temple--with purity of heart and with holy hands, devoid of greed and selfish ambition.

Such is the wise decision of the Elder Brothers, who guard this and all the deep secrets of Nature until man shall be fit to use them for the uplifting of the race--for the glory of God and not for personal profit or self-aggrandizement.

It was, however, this very loss of power over the vital forces which the Atlanteans suffered that made it possible for man to evolve further. After that, no matter how great his selfishness became, it could not prove absolutely destructive of himself and of Nature, as would have been the case had the growing selfishness been accompanied by the great power possessed by man in his innocent former state. Thought that works only *in* man is powerless to command Nature and can never endanger humanity, as would be possible were Nature's forces under man's control.

The Original Semites regulated their desires to some extent by the mind, and instead of mere desires, came cunning and craftiness--the means by which those people sought to attain their selfish ends. Though they were a very turbulent people, they learned to curb their passions to a great extend and accomplish their purposes by the use of cunning, as being more subtle and potent than mere brute strength. They were the first to discover that "brain" is superior to "brawn."

During the existence of this Race, the atmosphere of Atlantis commenced to clear definitely, and the previously mentioned point in the vital body came into correspondence with its companion point in the dense body. The combination of events gave man the ability to see objects clearly with sharp, well-defined contours; but it also resulted in loss of sight pertaining to the inner Worlds.

Thus we see, and it may be well to definitely state it as a law: No progress is ever made that is not gained at the cost of some previously possessed faculty, which is later regained in a higher form.

Man built the brain at the expense of the temporary loss of the power to bring forth offspring from himself alone. In order to get the instrument wherewith to guide his dense body, be became subject to all the difficulty, sorrow and pain which is involved in the co-operation necessary to the perpetuation of the race; he obtained his reasoning power at the cost of the temporary loss of his spiritual insight.

While reason benefited him in many ways, it shut from his vision the soul of things which had previously spoken to him, and the gaining of the intellect which is now man's most precious possession was at first but sadly contemplated by the Atlantean, who mourned the loss of spiritual sight and power which marked its acquisition.

The exchange of spiritual powers for physical faculties was necessary, however, in order that man might be able to function, independent of outside guidance, in the Physical World which he must conquer. In time his higher powers will be regained when, by means of his experiences in his journey through the denser Physical World, he has learned to use them properly. When he possessed them, he had no knowledge of their proper use, and they were too precious and too dangerous to be used as toys, with which to experiment.

Under the guidance of a great Entity, the Original Semitic Race was led eastward from the continent of Atlantis, over Europe, to the great waste in Central Asia which is known as the Gobi Desert. There it prepared them to be the seed of the seven Races of the Aryan Epoch, imbuing them potentially with the qualities to be evolved by their descendants.

During all the previous ages--from the commencement of the Saturn Period, through the Sun and Moon Periods, and in the three and one-half Revolutions of the Earth Period (the Polarian, Hyperborean, Lemurian, and earlier part of the Atlantean Epochs)--man had been led and guided by higher Beings, without the slightest choice. In those days he was unable to guide himself, not yet having evolved a mind of his own; but at last the time had come when it was necessary for his further development that he should begin to guide himself. He must learn independence and assume responsibility for his own actions. Hitherto he had been compelled to obey the commands of his Ruler; now his thoughts were to be turned from the visible Leaders, the Lords from Venus, whom he worshiped as messengers from the gods--to the idea of the true God, the invisible Creator of the System. Man was to learn to worship and obey the commands of a God he could not see.

Their Leader therefore called the people together and delivered a soul-stirring oration, which might be thus expressed:

Hitherto, you have seen Those who led you, but there are Leaders of varying grades of splendor, higher than They, Whom you have not seen, Who guided your every tottering step in the evolution of consciousness.

166

Exalted above all these glorious Beings stands the invisible God Who has created the heaven, and the earth upon which you dwell. He has willed to give you dominion over all this land, that you may be fruitful and multiply in it.

This invisible God only must you worship, but you must worship Him in Spirit and in Truth, and not make any graven image of Him, nor use any likeness to picture Him to yourselves, because He is everywhere present, and is beyond any comparison or similitude.

If you follow His precepts, He will bless you abundantly in all good. If you stray from His ways, evil will follow. The choice is yours. You are free; *but you must endure the consequences of your own actions.*

The education of man proceeds by four great steps. First, he is worked upon from without unconsciously. Then he is placed under the Rulership of Divine Messengers and Kings whom he sees, and whose commands he must obey. Next he is taught to revere the commands of a God whom he does not see. Finally, he learns to rise above the commands; to become a law unto himself; and, by conquering himself of his own free will, to live in harmony with the Order of Nature, which is the Law of God.

Fourfold also are the steps by which man climbs upward to God.

First, through fear, he worships the God whom he begins to sense, sacrificing to propitiate Him, as do the fetish-worshipers.

Next, he learns to look to God as the *giver* of all things, and hopes to receive from Him material benefits *here and now.* He sacrifices through avarice, expecting that the Lord will repay a hundredfold, or to escape *swift* punishment by plague, war, etc.

Next, he is taught to worship God by prayer and the living of a good life; and that he must cultivate faith in a Heaven where he will be rewarded in the *future*; and to abstain from evil that he may escape a *future* punishment in Hell.

At last he comes to a point where he can do right without any thought of reward, bribe, or punishment, but simply because "it is right to do right." He loves right for its own sake and seeks to govern his conduct thereby, regardless of present benefit or injury, or of painful results at some future time.

The Original Semites had reached the second of these steps. They were taught to worship an invisible God and to expect to be rewarded by material benefits, or punished by painful afflictions.

Popular Christianity is at the third step. Esoteric Christians, and the pupils of all occult schools are trying to reach the highest step, which will be generally achieved in the Sixth Epoch, the new Galilee, when the unifying Christian religion will open the hearts of men, as their understanding is being opened now.

The Akkadians were the sixth and the Mongolians the seventh of the Atlantean Races. They evolved the faculty of thought still further, but followed lines of reasoning which deviated more and more from the main trend of the developing life. The Chinese Mongolians maintain to this day that the old ways are the best. Progress constantly requires new methods and adaptabil-

167

ity, keeping ideas in a fluid state, therefore those races fell behind and are degenerating, with the remainder of the Atlantean Races.

As the heavy fogs of Atlantis condensed more and more, the increased quantity of water gradually inundated that continent, destroying the greater part of the population and the evidences of their civilization.

Great numbers were driven from the doomed continent by the floods, and wandered across Europe. The Mongolian races are the descendants of those Atlantean refugees. The Negroes and the savage races with curly hair, are the last remnants of the Lemurians.

The Aryan Epoch

Central Asia was the cradle of the Aryan Races, who descended from the Original Semites. Thence have the different Races gone out. It is unnecessary to describe them here, as historical researches have sufficiently revealed their main features.

In the present (the Fifth or Aryan) Epoch, man came to know the use of fire and other forces, the divine origin of which was purposely withheld from him, that he might be free to use them for higher purposes or his own development. Therefore we have in this present Epoch two classes: One looks upon this Earth and upon man as being of divine origin; the other sees all things from a purely utilitarian viewpoint.

The most advanced among humanity at the beginning of the Aryan Epoch were given the higher Initiations, that they might take the place of the messengers of God, i.e. the Lords of Venus. Such human Initiates were from this time forth the only mediators between God and man. Even they did not appear publicly nor show any signs of wonders that they were Leaders and Teachers. Man was left entirely free to seek them or not, as he desired.

At the end of our present Epoch the highest Initiate will appear publicly, when a sufficient number of ordinary humanity desire, and will voluntarily subject themselves to such a Leader. They will thus form the nucleus for the last Race, which will appear at the beginning of the Sixth Epoch. After that time races and nations will cease to exist. Humanity will form one spiritual Fellowship as before the end of the Lemurian Epoch.

The names of the Races which have spread over the Earth during the Fifth Epoch, up to the present time, are as follows:

1. The Aryan, which went south to India 2. The Babylonian-Assyrian-Chaldean 3. The Persian-Greco-Latin 4. The Celtic 5. The Teutonic-Anglo-Saxon

From the mixture of the different nations now taking place in the United States will come the "Seed" for the last Race, in the beginning of the Sixth Epoch.

Two more Races will be evolved in our present Epoch, one of them being the Slav. When, in the course of a few hundred years, the Sun, because of the precession of the equinoxes, shall have entered the sign Aquarius, the Russian people and the Slav Races in general will reach a degree of spiritual development which will advance them far beyond their present condition. Music will be the chief factor in bringing this about, for on the wings of music the soul which is attuned may fly to the very Throne of God, where the mere intellect cannot reach. Development attained in that manner, however, is not permanent, because it is one-sided, therefore not in harmony with the law of evolution, which demands that development, to be permanent, must be evenly balanced--in other words, that spirituality shall evolve through, or at least equally with, intellect. For this reason the Slavic civilization will be short-lived, but it will be great and joyful while it lasts, for it is being born of deep sorrow and untold suffering, and the law of Compensation will bring the opposite in due time.

From the Slavs will descend a people which will form the last of the seven Races of the Aryan Epoch, and from the people of the United States will descend the last of all the Races in this scheme of evolution, which will run its course in the beginning of the Sixth Epoch.

The Sixteen Paths to Destruction

The sixteen Races are called the "Sixteen paths to destruction" because there is always, in each Race, a danger that the soul may become too much attached to the Race; that it may become so enmeshed in Race characteristics it cannot rise above the *Race* idea, and will therefore fail to advance; that it may, so to speak, crystallize into that Race and consequently be confined to the Race bodies when they start to degenerate, as happened to the Jews.

In Periods, Revolutions, and Epochs where there are no Races, there is much more time, and the likelihood of becoming fossilized is not so great, nor so frequent. But the sixteen Races are born and die in such a relatively short time there is grave danger that the one who gets too much attached to conditions may be left behind.

Christ is the great unifying Leader of the Sixth Epoch, and He enunciated this law when He uttered those little-understood words: "If any man come to me, and hate not his father, and mother, and wife, and children, and brethren, and sisters, yea, and his own life also, he cannot be my disciple.

"And whosoever doth not bear his cross, and come after me cannot be my disciple.

"...whosoever he be of you that forsaketh not all that he hath, he cannot be my disciple."

Not that we are to leave, nor underestimate family ties, but that we are to rise above them. Father and mother are "bodies"; all relations are part of the Race--which belongs to Form. The souls must recognize that they are not Bodies, nor Races, but Egos striving for perfection. If a man forgets this, and identifies himself with his Race--clinging to it with fanatic patriotism--he is likely to become enmeshed in and sink with it when his compeers have passed to greater heights on the Path of Attainment.

Chapter Thirteen - Back to the Bible

In our age the missionary spirit is strong. The Western churches are sending missionaries all over the world to convert the people of every nation to a belief in their creeds; nor are they alone in their proselyting efforts. The East has commenced a strong invasion of Western fields, and many Christians who have become dissatisfied with the creeds and dogmas taught by the clergy and impelled to search for truth to satisfy the demands of the intellect for an adequate explanation of the problems of life, have familiarized themselves with, and in many cases accepted, the Eastern teachings of Buddhism, Hinduism, etc.

From an occult point of view, this missionary effort, whether from East to West or *vice versa*, is not desirable, because it is contrary to the trend of evolution. The great Leaders of humanity Who are in charge of our development give us every aid necessary to that end. Religion is one of these aids, and there are excellent reasons why the Bible, containing not only one, but both the Jewish and Christian religions, should have been given to the West. If we earnestly seek for light we shall see the Supreme Wisdom which has given us this double religion and how no other religion of the present day is suitable to our peculiar needs. To this end we will in this chapter touch again upon certain points previously brought out in various places and connections.

In the Polarian, Hyperborean and Lemurian Epochs the task of leading humanity was a comparatively easy one, for man was then without mind, but when that disturbing element came in during the first part of the Atlantean Epoch, he developed Cunning, which is the product of the mind unchecked by the spirit. Cunning acts as an aid to desire, regardless of whether the desire is good or bad, whether it will bring joy or sorrow.

In the middle of the Atlantean Epoch the spirit had drawn completely into its vehicles and commenced to work in the mind to produce Thought and Reason: the ability to trace a given cause to its inevitable effect, and to deduce from a given effect the cause which produced it. The faculty of Reasoning or Logic was to become more fully developed in the Aryan Epoch, and therefore the Original Semites (the fifth race of the Atlantean Epoch) were a "chosen people," to bring out that germinal faculty to such a ripeness that it would be impregnated into the very fiber of their descendants, who would thus become the New Race.

To transmute Cunning into Reason proved no easy task. The earlier changes in man's nature had been easily brought about. He could then be led without difficulty because he had no conscious desire, nor mind to guide him, but by the time of the Original Semites he had become cunning enough to resent limitations of his liberty and to circumvent repeatedly the measures taken to hold him in line. The task of guiding him was all the more difficult because it was necessary he should have some liberty of choice, that he might in time learn self-government. Therefore a law was enacted which decreed *immedi-*

ate rewards for obedience and *instant punishment* for disregard of its provisions. Thus was man taught, coaxed and coerced into reasoning in a limited manner that "the way of the transgressor is hard," and that he must "fear God," or the Leader Who guided him.

Out of all who were chosen as "seed" for the new Race, but few remained faithful. Most of them were rebellious and, so far as they were concerned, entirely frustrated the purpose of the Leader by intermarrying with the other Atlantean Races, thus bringing inferior blood into their descendants. That is what is meant in the Bible where the fact is recorded that the sons of God married the daughters of men. For that act of disobedience were they abandoned and "lost." Even the faithful died, according to the body, in the Desert of Gobi (the "Wilderness") in Central Asia, the cradle of our present Race. They reincarnated, as their own descendants of course, and thus inherited the "Promised Land," the Earth as it is now. They are the Aryan Races, in whom Reason is being evolved to perfection.

The rebellious ones who were abandoned are the Jews, of whom the great majority are still governed more by the Atlantean faculty of Cunning than by Reason. In them the race-feeling is so strong that they distinguish only two classes of people: Jews and Gentiles. They despise the other nations and are in turn despised by them for their cunning, selfishness and avarice. It is not denied that they give to charity, but it is principally, if not exclusively, among their own people and rarely internationally, as was done in the case of the earthquake disaster in Italy, where barriers of creed, race and nationality were forgotten in the *human* feeling of sympathy.

In such cases as that and the San Francisco disaster, the inner spiritual nature of man becomes more in evidence than under any other circumstances, and the close observer may then discern the trend of evolution. The fact then becomes manifest that though in the stress of ordinary life our actions may deny it, nevertheless at heart we know and acknowledge the great truth that we are brothers and the hurt of one is really felt by all. Such incidents, therefore, point out the direction of evolution. The control of man by Reason must be succeeded by that of Love, which at present acts independent of and sometimes even contrary to the dictates of Reason. The anomaly arises from the fact that Love, at present, is rarely quite unselfish and our Reason is not always true. In the "New Galilee," the coming Sixth Epoch, Love will become unselfish and Reason will approve its dictates. Universal Brotherhood shall then be fully realized, each working for the good of all, because self-seeking will be a thing of the past.

That this much-to-be-desired end may be attained, it will be necessary to select another "chosen people" from the present stock to serve as a nucleus from which the new Race shall spring. This choosing is not to be done contrary to the will of the chosen. Each man must choose for himself; he must *willingly* enter the ranks.

Races are but an evanescent feature of evolution. Before the end of the Lemurian Epoch there was a "chosen people," different from the ordinary

171

humanity of that time, who became the ancestors of the Atlantean Races. From the fifth race of those another "chosen people" was drawn, from which the Aryan Races descended, of which there have been five and will be two more. Before a new Epoch is ushered in, however, there must be "a new Heaven and a new earth"; the physical features of the Earth will be changed and its density decreased. There will be one Race at the beginning of the next Epoch, but after that every thought and feeling of Race will disappear. Humanity will again constitute one vast Fellowship, regardless of all distinctions. Races are simply steps in evolution which must be taken, otherwise there will be no progress for the spirits reborn in them. But, though necessary steps, they are also extremely dangerous ones, and are therefore the cause of grave concern to the Leaders of mankind. They call these sixteen Races "the sixteen paths to destruction," because , while in previous Epochs the changes came after such enormous intervals that it was easier to get the majority of the entities in line for promotion, it is different with the Races. They are comparatively evanescent; therefore extra care must be taken that as few of the spirits as possible become enmeshed in the fetters of Race.

This is exactly what happened to the spirits reborn in the Jewish Race-bodies. They attached themselves so firmly to the Race that they are drawn back into it in successive births. "Once a Jew, always a Jew" is their slogan. They have entirely forgotten their spiritual nature and glory in the material fact of being "Abraham's seed." Therefore they are neither "fish nor flesh." They have no part in the advancing Aryan Race and yet they are beyond those remnants of the Lemurian and Atlantean peoples which are still with us. They have become a people without a country, an anomaly among mankind.

Because of their bondage to the Race-idea, their one-time Leader was forced to abandon them, and they became "lost." That they might cease to regard themselves as separate from other peoples, other nations were stirred up against them at various times by the Leaders of humanity and they were led captive from the country where they had settled, but in vain. They stubbornly refused to amalgamate with others. Again and again they returned in a body to their arid land. Prophets of their own Race were raised up who mercilessly rebuked them and predicted dire disaster, but without avail.

As a final effort to persuade them to cast off the fetters of Race, we have the seeming anomaly that the Leader of the coming Race, the Great Teacher Christ, appeared among the Jews. This still further shows the compassion and Wisdom of the great Beings Who guide evolution. Among all the Races of the Earth, none other was "lost" in the same sense as the Jews; none other so sorely needed help. To send them a stranger, not one of their own Race, would have been manifestly useless. It was a foregone conclusion that they would have rejected him. As the great spirit known as Booker T. Washington incarnated among the Negroes, to be received by them as one of themselves, and thus enabled to enlighten them as no white man could, so the great

172

Leaders hoped that the appearance of Christ among the Jews as one of their own might bring them to accept Him and His teachings and thus draw them out of the meshes of the Race-bodies. But sad it is to see how human prejudice can prevail. "He came unto His own and" they chose Barabbas. He did not glory in Abraham, nor any other of their ancient traditions. He spoke of "another world," of a new earth, of Love and Forgiveness, and repudiated the doctrine of "an eye for an eye." He did not call them to arms against Caesar; had He done so, they would have hailed Him as a deliverer. In that respect He was misunderstood even by His disciples, who mourned as greatly over their vanished hope of an earthly kingdom as over the Friend slain by Roman hands.

The rejection of Christ by the Jews was the supreme proof of their thralldom to Race. Thenceforth all efforts to save them *as a whole* by giving them special prophets and teachers, were abandoned and, as the futility of exiling them *in a body* had been proven, they were, as a last expedient, scattered among all the nations of the earth. Despite all, however, the extreme tenacity of this people has prevailed even to the present day, the majority being yet *orthodox*. In America, however, there is now a slight falling away. The younger generation is commencing to marry outside the Race. In time, an increasing number of bodies, with fewer and fewer of the Race characteristics, will thus be provided for the incarnating spirits of the Jews of the past. In this manner will they be saved in spite of themselves. They become "lost" by marrying into inferior Races; they will be saved by amalgamating with those more advanced.

As the present Aryan Races are reasoning human beings, capable of profiting by past experience, the logical means of helping them is by telling them of past stages of growth and the fate that overtook the disobedient Jews. Those rebels had a written record of how their Leaders had dealt with them. It set forth how they had been chosen and rebelled; were punished; but were yet hopeful of ultimate redemption. That record may be profitably used by us, that we may learn how *not* to act. It is immaterial that, in the course of ages, it has become mutilated, and that the Jews of today are still under the delusion of being a "chosen people"; the lesson that may be drawn from their experience is none the less valid. We may learn how a "chosen people" may harass their Leader, frustrate His plans, and become bound to a Race for ages. Their experience should be a warning to any future "chosen people". This Paul points out in unmistakable terms (Heb. ii. 3-4); "For if the word spoken by angels was steadfast and every transgression and disobedience received a just recompense of reward, How shall we escape if we neglect so great salvation?" and Paul was speaking to Christians, for the Hebrews to whom he wrote this were converted, had accepted Christ and were people whom he expected would, in some future life, be among the new "chosen people", who would *willingly* follow a Leader and evolve the faculty of Love and spiritual perception, the intuition which shall succeed self-seeking and Reason.

The Christian teaching of the New Testament belongs particularly to the

173

pioneer Races of the Western World. It is being specially implanted among the people of the United States, for as the object of the new Race of the Sixth Epoch will be the unification of all the Races, the United States is becoming the "melting pot" where all the nations of the earth are being amalgamated and from this amalgamation will the next "chosen people," the nucleus, be chiefly derived.

Those spirits, from all countries of the earth, who have striven to follow the teachings of the Christ, consciously or otherwise, will be reborn here, for the purpose of giving them conditions suitable for that development. Hence the American-born Jew is different from the Jew of other countries. The very fact that he has been reborn in the Western World shows that he is becoming emancipated from the Race spirit, and is consequently in advance of the crystallized Old World orthodox Jew, as were his parents, or they would not have conceived the idea of severing the old ties and moving to America. Therefore the American-born Jew is the pioneer who will prepare the path which his compatriots will follow later.

Thus we can see that the Bible contains the teaching peculiarly needed by the Western peoples, that they may be taught a lesson by the awful example of the Jewish Race as recorded in the Old Testament, and learn to live by the teachings of the Christ in the New, willingly offering up their bodies as a *living* sacrifice upon the altar of Fellowship and Love.

Chapter Fourteen - The Occult Analysis of Genesis

Limitations of the Bible

In our study thus far, previous to Chapter XIII, comparatively little reference has been made to the Bible, but we shall now devote our attention to it for some time. Not that it is intended to attempt a vindication of the Bible (in the form in which it is commonly known to us at the present day) as the only true and inspired Word of God, nevertheless it is true that it contains much valuable occult knowledge. This is, to great extent, hidden beneath interpolations and obscured by the arbitrary withholding of certain parts as being "apocryphal." The occult scientist, who knows the intended meaning, can, of course, easily see which portions are original and which have been interpolated. Yet, if we take the first chapter of Genesis even as it stands, in the best translations we possess, we shall find that it unfolds the identical scheme of evolution which has been explained in the preceding portion of this work and harmonized quite well with the occult information in regard to Periods, Revolutions, Races, Etc. The outlines given are necessarily of the briefest and most condensed character, an entire Period being covered in a score of words--nevertheless, the outlines are there.

Before proceeding with an analysis it is necessary to say that the words of the Hebrew language, particularly the old style, run into one another and are not divided as those of our language. Add to this that there is a custom of leaving out vowels from the writing, so that in reading much depends upon where and how they are inserted, and it will be seen how great are the diffi- culties to be surmounted in ascertaining the original meaning. A slight change may entirely alter the signification of almost any sentence.

In addition to these great difficulties we must also bear in mind that of the forty-seven translators of the King James version (that most commonly used in England and America), only *three* were Hebrew scholars, and of those three, two died before the Psalms had been translated! We must still further take into consideration that the Act which authorized the translation prohib- ited the translators from any rendition that would greatly deviate from or tend to disturb the already existing belief. It is evident, therefore, that the chances of getting a correct translation were very small indeed.

Nor were conditions much more favorable in Germany, for there Martin Luther was the sole translator and even he did not translate from the original Hebrew, but merely from a Latin text. Most of the versions used in Continen- tal Protestant countries today are simply translations, into the different lan- guages, of Luther's translations.

True, there have been revisions, but they have not greatly improved mat- ters. Moreover, there is a large number of people in this country who insist that the *English* text of the King James version is absolutely correct from cov- er to cover, as though the Bible had been originally written in English, and the King James version were a certified copy of the original manuscript. So the old mistakes are still there, in spite of the efforts which have been made to eradicate them.

It must also be noted that those who originally wrote the Bible did not in- tend to give out the truth in such plain form that he who ran might read. Nothing was further from their thoughts than to write an "open book of God." The great occultists who wrote the Zohar are very emphatic upon this point. The secrets of the Torah were not to be understood by all, as the following quotation will show:

"Woe to the man who sees in the Torah (the law) only simple recitals and ordinary words! Because, if in truth it contained only these, we would even today be able to compose a Torah much more worthy of admiration. But it is not so. Each word of the Torah contains an elevated meaning and a sublime mystery. . . .The recitals of the Torah are the vestments of the Torah. Woe to him who takes this vestment of the Torah for the Torah itself!. . . The simple take notice of the garments and recitals of the Torah alone. They know no other thing. They see not that which is concealed under the vestment. *The more instructed men do not pay attention to the vestment*, but to the body which it envelops."

In the preceding words, the allegorical meanings are plainly implied. Paul also unequivocally says that the story of Abraham and the two sons whom he had by Sarah and Hagar is purely allegorical (Gal. iv:22-26). Many passages are veiled; others are to be taken verbatim; and no one who has not the oc-

175

cult key is able to find the deep truth hidden in what is often a very hideous garment.

The secrecy regarding these deep matters and invariable use of allegories where the mass of the people were permitted to come in contact with occult truths will also be apparent from the practice of Christ, who always spoke to the multitude in parables, afterward privately explaining to His disciples the deeper meaning contained therein. On several occasions He imposed secrecy upon them with regard to private teachings.

Paul's methods are also in harmony with this, for he gives "milk" or the more elementary teaching to the "babes" in the faith, reserving the "meat" or deeper teaching for the "strong"--those who had qualified themselves to understand and receive them.

The Jewish Bible was originally written in Hebrew, but we do not possess one single line of the original writings. As early as 260 B.C. the Septuagint, a translation into Greek, was brought forth. Even in the time of Christ there was already the utmost confusion and diversity of opinion regarding what was to be admitted as original, and what had been interpolated.

It was not until the return from Babylonian exile that the scribes began to piece together the different writings, and not until about 500 A.D. did the Talmud appear, giving the first text resembling the present one, which, in view of the foregoing facts, cannot be perfect.

The Talmud was them taken in hand by the Masorete school, which from 590 to about 800 A.D. was principally in Tiberias. With great and painstaking labor, a Hebrew Old Testament was produced, which is the nearest to the original we have at the present time.

This Masoretic text will be used in the following elucidation of Genesis, and, not relying upon the work of one translator, it will be supplemented by a German translation, the work of three eminent Hebrew scholars-- H. Arnheim, M. Sachs, and Jul. Furst, who co-operated with a fourth, Dr. Zunz, the latter being also the editor.

In the Beginning

The opening sentence of Genesis is a very good example of what has been stated about the interpretation of the Hebrew text, which may be changed by differently placing the vowels and dividing the words in another way.

There are two well recognized methods of reading this sentence. One is: "In the beginning God created the heavens and the earth"; the other is: "Out of the ever-existing essence (of space) the twofold energy formed the double heaven."

Much has been said and written as to which of these two interpretations is correct. The difficulty is, that the people want something settled and definite. They take the stand that, if a certain explanation is true, all others must be wrong. But, emphatically, this is not the way to get at truth, which is many sided and multiplex. Each occult truth requires examination from many different points of view; each viewpoint presents a certain phase of the truth,

176

and all of them are necessary to get a complete, definite conception of whatever is under consideration.

The very fact that this sentence and many others in the vestment of the Torah can thus be made to yield many meanings, while confusing to the uninitiated, is illuminative to those who have the key, and the transcendental wisdom of the wonderful Intelligences Who inspired the Torah is thereby shown. Had the vowels been inserted, and a division made into words, there would have been only one way of reading it and these grand and sublime mysteries could not have been hidden therein. That would have been the proper method to pursue if the authors had meant to write an "open" book of God; but that was not their purpose. It was written solely for the initiated; and can be read understandingly by them only. It would have required much less skill to have written the book plainly than to have concealed its meaning. No pains are ever spared, however, to bring the information, in due time, to those who are entitled to it, while withholding it from those who have not yet earned the right to possess it.

The Nebular Theory

Regarded by the light thrown upon the genesis and evolution of our system, it is plain that both renderings of the opening sentence in the Book of Genesis are necessary to an understanding of the subject. The first tells that there was a beginning of our evolution, in which the heavens were created; the other interpretation supplements the first statement by adding that the heavens and the earth were created out of the "ever-existing essence," not out of "nothing," as is jeeringly pointed out by the materialist. The Cosmic Root-substance is gathered together and set in motion. The rings formed by the inertia of the revolving mass break away from the central part, forming planets, etc., as the modern scientist, with remarkable ingenuity, has reasoned out. Occult and modern science are in perfect harmony as to the *modus operandi*. There is nothing in these statements inconsistent with the two theories, as will presently be shown. Occult science teaches that God instituted the process of formation and is constantly guiding the System in a definite path. The modern scientist, in refutation of what he calls a foolish idea, and to demonstrate that a God is not necessary, takes a basin of water and pours a little oil into it. The water and the oil represent space and fire-mist respectively. He now commences to turn the oil around with a needle, bringing it into the form of a sphere. This, he explains, represents the Central Sun. As he turns the oil-ball faster and faster, it bulges at the equator and throws off a ring, the ring breaks and the fragments coalesce, forming a smaller ball, which circles around the Sun. Then he pityingly asks the occult scientist, "Do you not see how it is done?" There is not need for your God, or any supernatural force."

The occultist readily agrees that a Solar System may be formed in approximately the manner illustrated. But he marvels greatly that a man possessing the clear intuition enabling him to perceive with such accuracy the operation of Cosmic processes, and the intellect to conceive this brilliant demonstration of this monumental theory, should at the same time be quite unable to see that in his demonstration *he himself plays the part of God*. His was the extraneous power that placed the oil in the water, where it would have remained inert and shapeless through all eternity had he not supplied the force that set it in motion, thereby causing it to shape itself into representation of Sun and planets. His was the Thought which designed the experiment, using the oil, water and force, thus illustrating in a splendid manner the Triune God working in Cosmic substance to form a Solar System.

The attributes of God are Will, Wisdom and Activity. (See diagram 6. Note carefully what the name "God" signifies in this terminology.) The scientist has *Will* to make the experiment. He has ingenuity to supply ways and means for the demonstration. This ingenuity corresponds to *Wisdom*, the second attribute to God. He has also the muscular force necessary to perform the action, corresponding to *Activity*, which is the third attribute of God.

Further, the universe is not a vast perpetual-motion machine, which, when once set going, keeps on without any internal cause or guiding force. That also is proven by the experiment of the scientist, for the moment he ceases to turn the oil-ball the orderly motion of his miniature planets also ceases and all returns to a shapeless mass of oil floating on the water. In a corresponding manner, the universe would at once dissolve into "thin space" if God for one moment ceased to exert His all-embracing care and energizing activity.

The second interpretation of Genesis is marvelously exact in its description of a twofold formative energy. It does not specifically state that God is Triune. The reader's knowledge of that fact is taken for granted. It states the exact truth when it says that only two forces are active in the formation of a universe.

When the first aspect of the Triune God manifests as the Will to create, It arouses the second aspect (which is Wisdom) to design a plan for the future universe. This first manifestation of Force is Imagination. After this primal Force of Imagination has conceived the Idea of a universe, the third aspect (which is Activity), working in Cosmic substance, produces Motion. This is the second manifestation of Force. Motion alone, however, is not sufficient. To form a system of worlds, it must be *orderly* motion. Wisdom is therefore necessary to guide Motion in an intelligent manner to produce definite results.

Thus we find the opening sentence of the Book of Genesis tells us that in the beginning, orderly, rhythmic motion, in Cosmic Root-substance, formed the universe.

The Creative Hierarchies

The second interpretation of the opening sentence also gives us a fuller idea of God when it speaks of the "twofold energy," pointing to the positive and negative phases of the One Spirit of God in manifestation. In harmony with the teaching of occult science, God is represented as a composite Being. This is accentuated in the remaining verses of the chapter.

In addition to the creative Hierarchies which worked voluntarily in our evolution, there are seven others which belong to our evolution, and are co-workers with God in the formation of the universe. In the first chapter of Genesis these Hierarchies are called "Elohim." The name signifies a host of dual and double-sexed Beings. The first part of the word is "Eloh," which is a feminine noun, the letter "h" indicating the gender. If a single feminine Being were meant, the work "Eloh" would have been used. The feminine plural is "oth," so if the intention had been to indicate a number of Gods of the feminine gender, the correct word to use would have been "Elooth." Instead of either of those forms, however, we find the masculine plural ending, "im," added to the feminine noun, "Eloh," indicating a host of male-female, double-sexed Beings, expressions of the dual, positive-negative, creative energy.

The plurality of Creators is again implied in the latter part of the chapter, where these words are ascribed to the Elohim: "Let *us* make man in *our* image;" after which it is inconsistently added, "*He* made them male and female."

The translators have here rendered the puzzling word "Elohim" (which was decidedly not only a plural word but also *both* masculine and feminine) as being the equivalent of the singular, sexless word, "God." yet could they have done differently, even had they known? They were forbidden to disturb existing ideas. It was not truth at any price, but peace at any price that King James desired, his sole anxiety being to avoid any controversy that might create a disturbance in his kingdom.

The plural "them" is also used where the creation of man is mentioned, clearly indicating that the reference is to the creation of ADM, the human species, and not Adam, the individual.

We have shown that six creative Hierarchies (besides the Lords of Flame, the Cherubim, the Seraphim, and the two unnamed Hierarchies which have passed into liberation) were active in assisting the virgin spirits which in themselves form a seventh Hierarchy.

The Cherubim and the Seraphim had nothing to do with the creation of Form; therefore they are not mentioned in the chapter under consideration, which deals principally with the Form-side of Creation. Here we find mentioned only the seven creative Hierarchies which did the actual work of bringing man to where he acquired a dense physical form, through which the indwelling spirit could work.

After a description of each part of the work of Creation it is said: "and Elohim saw that it was good." This is said seven times, the last time being on the sixth day, when the human form had been created.

It is stated that on the seventh day "Elohim rested." This is all in accord with our occult teaching of the part taken by each of the creative Hierarchies in the work of evolution down to the present Period. It is also taught that in the present Epoch the Gods and creative Hierarchies have withdrawn from active participation, that man may work out his own salvation, leaving the necessary guidance of ordinary humanity to the "Elder Brothers," who are now the mediators between man and the Gods.

The Saturn Period

Having satisfied ourselves that the beginning of our System and the work of the creative Hierarchies, as described by occult science, harmonize with the teachings of the Bible, we will now examine the Bible account of different "Days of Creation" and see how they agree with the occult teachings relative to the Saturn, Sun, and Moon Periods; the three and one-half Revolutions of the Earth Period; and the Polarian, Hyperborean, Lemurian, and Atlantean Epochs, which have preceded the present Aryan Epoch.

Naturally, a detailed account could not be given in a few lines like the first chapter of Genesis, but the main points are there in orderly succession, very much like an algebraical formula for Creation.

The second verse proceeds: "The Earth was waste and uninhabited, and darkness rested upon the face of the deep; and the Spirits of the Elohim floated above the deep." In the beginning of manifestation that which is now the Earth was in the Saturn Period, and in exactly the condition described, as may be seen by referring to the descriptions already given of that Period. It was not "without form and void," as expressed in the King James version. It was hot, and thus well-defined and separate from the deep of space, which was cold. It is true that it was dark, but it could be dark and still be hot, for "dark" heat necessarily precedes glowing or visible heat. Above this dark Earth of the Saturn Period floated the creative Hierarchies. They worked upon it from the outside and molded it. The Bible refers to them as the "Spirits of the Elohim."

The Sun Period

The Sun Period is well described in the third verse, which says, "And the Elohim said, Let there be Light; and there was Light." This passage has been jeered at as the most ridiculous nonsense. The scornful query has been put, How could there be light upon the Earth when the Sun was not made until the fourth day? The Bible narrator, however, is not speaking of the Earth alone. He is speaking of the central "Fire-mist," from which were formed the planets of our system including the Earth. Thus when the nebula reached a state of glowing heat, which it did in the Sun Period, there was no necessity for an outside illuminant, the Light was within.

In the fourth verse we read: "The Elohim differentiated between the light and the darkness." Necessarily, for the outside space was dark, in contradistinction to the glowing nebula which existed during the Sun Period.

The Moon Period

The Moon Period is described in the sixth verse, as follows: "and Elohim said, Let there by an *expansion* (translated "firmament" in other versions) in

180

the waters, to divide the water from the water." This exactly describes conditions in the Moon Period, when the heat of the glowing fire-mist and the cold of outside space had formed a body of water around the fiery core. The contact of fire and water generated steam, which is water in expansion, as our verse describes. It was different from the comparatively cool water, which constantly gravitated toward the hot, fiery core, to replace the outrushing stream. Thus there was a constant circulation of water held in suspension, and also an expansion, as the steam, rushing outward from the fiery core, formed an atmosphere of "fire-fog" condensed by contact with outside space, returning again to the core to be reheated and perform another cycle. Thus there were two kinds of water, and a division between them, as stated in the Bible. The dense water was nearest the fiery core; the expanded water or steam was on the outside.

This also harmonizes with the scientific theory of modern times. First the dark heat; then the glowing nebula; later the outside moisture and inside heat; and, finally incrustation.

The Earth Period

The Earth Period is next described, Before we take up its description, however, we have to deal with the Recapitulations. The verses quoted and the descriptions given will also correspond to the recapitulatory Periods. Thus what is said of the Saturn Period describes also the condition of the System when it emerges from any of the rest Periods. The descriptions of the Saturn, Sun, and Moon Periods would therefore correspond to the first three Revolutions of our present Earth Period, and the following would correspond with conditions on Earth in the present Revolution.

In the ninth verse, we read: "And Elohim said, Let the waters be divided from the dry land. . . .and Elohim called the dry land Earth." This refers to the first firm incrustation. Heat and moisture had generated the solid body of our present Globe.

The Polarian Epoch: The ninth verse, which describes the Earth Period in this fourth Revolution (where the real Earth Period work commenced), also describes the formation of the mineral kingdom and the Recapitulation by man of the mineral stage in the Polarian Epoch. Each Epoch is also a Recapitulation of the previous stage. Just as there are Recapitulations of Globes, Revolutions, and Periods, so there are on each Globe, recapitulations of all that has gone before. These Recapitulations are endless. There is always a spiral within a spiral--in the atom, in the Globe, and in all other phases of evolution.

Complicated and bewildering as this may appear at first, it is really not so difficult to understand. There is an orderly method running through it all and in time one is able to perceive and follow the workings of this method, as a clue leading through a maze. Analogy is one of the best helps to an understanding of evolution.

The Hyperborean Epoch is described in verses 11 to 19, as the work of the fourth day. It is here recorded that Elohim created the plant kingdom, the Sun, the Moon, and the stars.

The Bible agrees with the teaching of modern science that plants succeeded the mineral. The difference between the two teachings is in regard to the time when the Earth was thrown off from the central mass. Science asserts that it was before the formation of any incrustation which could be called mineral and plant. If we mean such minerals and plants as we have today, that assertion is correct. There was no dense material substance, but nevertheless the first incrustation that took place in the central Sun was mineral. The Bible narrator gives only the principal incidents. It is not recorded that the incrustation melted when it was thrown off from the central mass as a ring which broke, the fragments afterward coalescing. In a body as small as our Earth, the time required for recrystallization was so comparatively short that the historian does not mention it, nor the further subsidiary fact that the melting process took place once more when the Moon was thrown off from the Earth. He probably reasons that one who is entitled to occult information is already in possession of such minor details as those.

The plants of the incrustation of the central fire-mist were ethereal, therefore the melting processes did not destroy them. As the lines of force along which the ice crystals form are present in the water, so when the Earth crystallized, were those ethereal plant-forms present in it. They were the molds which drew to themselves the dense material forming the plant-bodies of the present day and also of the plant-forms of the past, which are embedded in the geological strata of the Earth globe.

These ethereal plant-forms were aided in the formation when the heat came from outside, after the separation of the Earth from Sun and Moon. That heat gave them the vital force to draw to themselves the denser substance.

The Lemurian Epoch is described in the work of the fifth day. This Epoch, being the third, is in a sense a Recapitulation of the Moon Period, and in the Biblical narrative we find described such conditions as obtained in the Moon Period--water, fire-fog, and the first attempts at moving, breathing life.

Verses 20 and 21 tell us that "Elohim said, Let the waters bring forth life-breathing things. . .and fowl...; and Elohim formed the great amphibians and all life-breathing things according to their species, and all fowl with wings."

This also harmonizes with the teaching of material science that the amphibians preceded the birds.

The student is invited to note particularly that *the things that were formed were not Life*. it does *not* say that Life was created, but *"things" that breathe or inhale life*...The Hebrew word for that which they inhale is *nephesh*, and it should be carefully noted, as we shall meet it in a new dress later.

The Atlantean Epoch is dealt with in the work of the sixth day. In verse 24 the creation of mammals is mentioned, and there the word *nephesh* again occurs, explaining that the mammals "breathed life." "Elohim said, Let the
182

earth bring forth life-breathing things...mammals...;" and in verse 27, "Elohim formed man in their likeness; male and female made they (Elohim) them."

The Bible historian here omits the a-sexual and hermaphrodite human stages and comes to the two separate sexes, as we know them now. He could not do otherwise, as he is describing in the Atlantean Epoch, and by the time that stage in evolution was reached there were neither sexless men nor hermaphrodites, the differentiation of the sexes having taken place earlier--in the Lemurian Epoch. That which afterward became man could hardly be spoken of as man in the earlier stages of its development, as it differed but little from the animals. Therefore the Bible narrator is doing no violence to facts when he states that man was formed in the Atlantean Epoch.

In verse 28 (all versions) will be found a very small prefix, with a very great significance: "Elohim said, Be fruitful and re-plenish the earth." This plainly shows that the scribe who wrote it was cognizant of the occult teaching that the life wave had evolved here, on Globe D of the Earth Period, in previous Revolutions.

The Aryan Epoch corresponds to the seventh day of Creation, when the Elohim rested from their labors as Creators and Guides, and humanity had been launched upon an independent career.

This ends the story of the manner in which the Forms were produced. In the following chapter the story is told from the point of view which deals a little more with the Life side.

Jehovah and his Mission

There has been much learned discussion concerning the discrepancy between, and especially the authorship of the creation story of the first chapter and that which starts at the fourth verse of the second chapter. It is asserted that the two accounts were written by different men, because the Being or Beings, the name of Whom the translators have rendered as "God" in both the first and second chapters of the English version, are, in the Hebrew text, called "Elohim" in the first chapter, and "Jehovah" in the second chapter, It is argued that the same narrator would not have named God in two different ways.

Had he meant the same God in both cases, he probably would not, but he was not a monotheist. He knew better than to think of God as simply a superior Man, using the sky for a throne and the earth for a footstool. When he wrote of Jehovah he meant the Leader Who had charge of the particular part of the work of Creation which was then being described. Jehovah was and is one of the Elohim. He is the Leader of the Angels who were the humanity of the Moon Period and He is Regent of our Moon. The reader is referred to diagram 14 for an accurate understanding of the position and constitution of Jehovah.

183

As Regent of Our Moon, He has charge of the degenerate, evil Beings there, and He also rules the Angels. With Him are some of the Archangels, who were the humanity of the Sun Period. They are the "Race-Spirits".

It is the work of Jehovah to build concrete bodies or forms, by means of the hardening, crystallizing Moon forces. Therefore He is the giver of children and the Angels are His messengers in this work. It is well know to physiologists that the Moon is connected with gestation; at least, they have observed that it measures and governs the period of intra-uterine life and other physiological functions.

The Archangels, as Spirits and Leaders of a Race, are known to fight for or against a people, as the exigencies of the evolution of that Race demand. In Daniel x:20 an Archangel speaking to Daniel, says, "And now will I return to fight with the prince of Persia: and when I am gone forth, lo, the prince of Grecia shall come."

The Archangel Michael is the Race-spirit of the Jews (Daniel xii:1), but *Jehovah is not the god of the Jews alone; He is the Author of all Race-religions which led up to Christianity*. Nevertheless, it is true that He did take a special interest in the progenitors of the present degenerate Jews--the Original Semites, the "seed-race" for the seven races of the Aryan Epoch. Jehovah, of course, takes special care of a seed-race, in which are to be inculcated the embryonic faculties of the humanity of a new Epoch. For that reason He was particularly concerned with the Original Semites. They were His "chosen people"--chosen to be the seed for a new Race, which was to inherit the "Promised Land"--not merely insignificant Palestine, but the entire Earth, as it is at present.

He did not lead them out of Egypt. That story originated with their descendants and is a confused account of their journey eastward through flood and disaster out of the doomed Atlantis into the "wilderness" (the Desert of Gobi in Central Asia), there to wander during the cabalistic forty years, until they could enter the Promised Land. There is a double and peculiar significance to the descriptive word "promised" in this connection. The land was called the "promised Land" because, as land or earth suitable for human occupation, it did not exist at the time the "chosen people" were led into the "wilderness." Part of the Earth had been submerged by floods and other parts changed by volcanic eruptions, hence it was necessary that a period of time elapse before the new Earth was in a fit condition to become the possession of the Aryan Race.

The Original Semites were set apart and forbidden to marry into other tribes or peoples, but they were a stiff-necked and hard people, being yet led almost exclusively by desire and cunning, therefore they disobeyed the command. Their Bible records that the sons of God married the daughters of man--the lower grades of their Atlantean compatriots. They thus frustrated the designs of Jehovah and were cast off, the fruit of such cross-breeding being useless as seed for the coming Race.

These cross-breeds were the progenitors of the present Jews, who now speak of "lost tribes." They know that some of the original number left them
184

and went another way, but they do not know that those were the few who remained true. The story of the ten tribes being lost is a fable. Most of them perished, but the faithful ones survived, and from that faithful remnant have descended the present Aryan Races.

The contention of the opponents of the Bible, that it is a mere mutilation of the original writings, is cheerfully agreed to by occult science. Parts of it are even conceded to be entire fabrications and no attempt is made to prove its authenticity as a whole, in the form we now have it. The present effort is simply an attempt to exhume a few kernels of occult truth from the bewildering mass of misleading and incorrect interpretations under which they have been buried by the various translators and revisers.

Involution, Evolution and Epigenesis

Having in the foregoing paragraphs disentangled from the general confusion the identity and mission of Jehovah, it may be that we can now find harmony in the two seemingly contradictory accounts of the creation of man, as recorded in the first and second chapters of Genesis, in the first of which it is written that he was the last, and in the second that he was the first created of all living things.

We note that the first chapter deals chiefly with the creation of Form, the second chapter is devoted to the consideration of Life, while the fifth chapter deals with the Consciousness. The key to the meaning, then, is that we must differentiate sharply between the physical Form, and the Life that builds that Form for its own expression. Although the order of the creation of the other kingdoms is not as correctly given in the second chapter as in the first, it is true that if we consider man from the Life side, he was created *first*, but if we consider him from the standpoint of Form, as is done in the first chapter, he was created *last*.

All through the course of evolution--through Periods, Globes, Revolutions and Races--those who do not improve by the formation of *new* characteristics are held back and immediately begin to degenerate. Only that which remains plastic and pliable and adaptable for molding into new Forms suitable for the expression of the expanding consciousness; only the Life which is capable of outgrowing the possibilities for improvement inhering in the forms it ensouls, can evolve with the pioneers of any life wave. All else must straggle on behind.

This is the kernel of the occult teaching. Progress is not simply unfoldment; not simply Involution and Evolution. There is a third factor, making a triad-- Involution, Evolution, *and--Epigenesis.*

The first two words are familiar to all who have studied Life and Form, but while it is generally admitted that the involution of spirit into matter takes place in order that form may be built, it is not so commonly recognized that *the Involution of Spirit runs side by side with the Evolution of Form.*

From the very beginning of the Saturn Period up to the time in the Atlante an Epoch when "man's eyes were opened" by the Lucifer Spirits, and as a consequence the activities of man--or the Life-force which has become man-- were chiefly directed inward; that very same force which he now sends out from himself to build railways, steamboats, etc., was used internally in building a vehicle through which to manifest himself. This vehicle is threefold, like the spirit which built it.

The same power by which man is now improving outside conditions was used during Involution for purposes of internal growth.

The Form was built by Evolution, the Spirit built and entered it by Involution; but the means for devising improvements is Epigenesis.

There is a strong tendency to regard all that is, as the result of something that has been; all improvements on previously existing forms, as being present in all forms as latencies; to regard Evolution as simply the unfolding of germinal improvements. Such a conception excludes Epigenesis from the scheme of things. It allows no possibility for the building of anything *new*, no scope for originality.

The occultist believes the purpose of evolution to be the development of man from a static to a dynamic God--a Creator. If the development he is at present undergoing is to be his education and if, during its progress, he is simply unfolding latent actualities, where does He learn to *create?*

If man's development consists solely in learning to build better and better Forms, according to *models* already existing in his Creator's mind, be can become, at best, only a good *imitator*--never a *creator*.

In order that he may become an independent, original Creator, it is necessary that his training should include sufficient latitude for the exercise of the individual originality which distinguishes creation from imitation. So long as certain features of the old Form meet the requirements of progression they are retained, but at each rebirth the evolving Life adds such original improvements as are necessary for its further expression.

The pioneers of science are constantly brought face to face with Epigenesis as a fact in all departments of nature. As early as 1759, Caspar Wolff published his "Theoria Generationis," in which he shows that in the human ovum there is absolutely no trace of the coming organism; that its evolution consists of the addition of *new* formations; a building of something which is not latent in the ovum.

Haeckel (that great and fearless student of nature as he sees it, and very near to knowledge of the complete truth regarding evolution) says of the "Theoria Generationis": "Despite its small compass and difficult terminology, it is one of the most valuable works in the whole literature of biology."

Haeckel's own views we find thus stated in his "Anthropogenie": "Nowadays we are hardly justified in calling Epigenesis an hypothesis, as we have fully convinced ourselves of its being a *fact* and are able at any moment to demonstrate it by the help of the microscope."

A builder would be but a sorry craftsman were his abilities limited to the building of houses after only one particular model, which, during his apprenticeship, his master had taught him to imitate, but which he is unable to alter to meet new requirements. To be successful he must be capable of designing new and better houses, improving that which experience teaches was not serviceable in the earlier buildings. The same force which the builder now directs outward to built houses better adapted to new conditions was used in past Periods to build new and better vehicles for the evolution of the Ego.

Starting with the simplest organisms, the Life which is now Man built the Form to suit its necessities. In due time, as the entity progressed; it become evident that new improvements must be added which conflicted with the lines previously followed. A new start must be given it in a new species, where it could retrieve any previous mistakes which experience taught would preclude further development if the old lines were adhered to and thus the evolving life would be enabled to progress further in a new species. When later experience proved that the new form also was inadequate, inasmuch as it could not adapt itself to some improvement necessary to the progress of the evolving life, it too was discarded and still another departure made, in a form adaptable to the necessary improvement.

Thus by successive steps does the evolving Life improve its vehicles, and the improvements is still going on. Man, who is in the vanguard of progress, has built his bodies, from the similitude of the amoeba up to the human form of the savage, and from that up through the various grades until the most advanced races are now using the best and most highly organized bodies on Earth. Between deaths and rebirths we are constantly building bodies in which to function during our lives and a far greater degree of efficiency than the present will yet be reached. If we make mistakes in building between lives, they become evident when we are using the body in Earth life, and it is well for us if we are able to perceive and realize our mistakes, that we may avoid making them afresh life after life.

But just as the builder of houses would lag commercially if he did not constantly improve his methods to meet the exigencies of his business, so those who persistently adhere to the old forms fail to rise above the species and are left behind, as stragglers. These stragglers take the forms outgrown by the pioneers, as previously explained, and they compose the lower Races and species of any kingdom in which they are evolving. As the Life which is now Man passed through stages analogous to the mineral, plant, and animal kingdoms and through the lower human Races, stragglers were left all along the way who had failed to reach the necessary standard to keep abreast of the crestwave of evolution. They took the discarded Forms of the pioneers and used them as stepping-stones, by means of which they tried to overtake the others, but the advanced Forms did not stand still. In the progress of Evolution there is no halting-place. In evolving Life, as in commerce, there is no such thing as merely "holding your own." Progression or Retrogression is the Law. The Form that is not capable of further improvement must Degenerate.

Therefore there is one line of *improving* forms ensouled by the pioneers of the evolving Life, and another line of *degenerating* forms, outgrown by the pioneers, but ensouled by the stragglers, as long as there are any stragglers of that particular life wave to which those forms originally belonged.

When there are no more stragglers, the species gradually dies out. The Forms have been crystallized beyond the possibility of being improved by tenants of increasing inability. They therefore return to the mineral kingdom, fossilize and are added to the different strata of the Earth's crust.

The assertion of material science that man has ascended through the different kingdoms of plant and animal which exist about us now to anthropoid and thence to man, is not quite correct. Man has never inhabited forms identical with those of our present-day animals, nor the present-day anthropoid species; but he has inhabited forms which were similar to but *higher* than those of the present anthropoids.

The scientist sees that there is an anatomical likeness between man and the monkey, and as the evolutionary impulse always makes for improvement, he concludes that man must have descended from the monkey, but he is always baffled in his efforts to find the "missing link" connecting the two.

From the point where the pioneers of our life wave (The Aryan Races) occupied ape-like forms, they have *progressed* to their present stage of development, while the Forms (which were the "missing link") have *degenerated* and are now ensouled by the last stragglers of the Saturn Period.

The lower monkeys, instead of being the progenitors of the higher species, are stragglers occupying the most degenerated specimens of what was once the human form. Instead of man having ascended from the anthropoids, the reverse is true--the anthropoids have degenerated from man. Material science, dealing only with Form, has thus misled itself and drawn erroneous conclusions in this matter.

The same relative conditions are to be found in the animal kingdom. The pioneers of the life wave which entered evolution in the Sun Period are our present-day mammals. The different grades correspond to the steps once taken by man, but *the forms are all degenerating under the management of the stragglers.* Similarly, the pioneers of the life wave which entered evolution in the Moon Period are found among the fruit trees, while the stragglers of that life wave ensoul all other plant forms.

Each life wave, however remains definitely confined within its own borders. The anthropoids may overtake us and become human beings, but no other animals will reach our particular point of development. They will reach a similar stage, but under different conditions, in the Jupiter Period. The present plants will be the humanity of the Venus Period, under a still greater difference of condition, and our minerals will reach the human stage under the conditions of the Vulcan Period.

It will be noted that the modern evolutionary theory, particularly that of Haeckel, would, if it were completely reversed, be in almost perfect accord with the knowledge of occult science.

The monkey has degenerated from the man.

The polyps are the last degeneration left behind by the mammals.

The mosses are the lowest degenerations of the plant kingdom.

The mineral kingdom is the final goal of the forms of all the kingdoms when they have reached the acme of degeneration.

A corroboration of this is found in coal, which was once vegetable or plant forms; also in petrified wood and fossilized remains of various animal forms. Common stone or rock, which no scientist would admit had it origin in another kingdom, is to the occult investigator as truly mineralized plants as coal itself. The mineralogist will learnedly explain that it is composed of hornblende, feldspar, and mica, but the trained clairvoyant, who can trace it back in the memory of Nature, through millions of years, can supplement that statement by adding: Yes, and that which you call hornblende and feldspar are the leaves and stems of prehistoric flowers, and the mica is all that remains of their petals.

The occult teaching of evolution is also corroborated by the science of embryology in the ante-natal recapitulation of all past stages of development. The difference between the ovum of a human being and of some of the higher mammals, and even of the higher developments in the plant kingdom, is indistinguishable, even under the microscope. Experts are unable to tell which is animal and which is human. Even after several of the initial ante-natal stages have been passed through the experts cannot differentiate between and animal and human embryo.

But if the animal ovum is studied through the entire period of gestation, it will be observed that it passes through the mineral and plant stages only, and is born when it reaches the animal stage. This is because the Life ensouling such an ovum passed through its mineral evolution in the Sun Period, its plant life in the Moon Period, and is now forced to stop at the animal stage in the Earth Period.

On Where Epigenesis is inactive in the individual, family, nation, or Race-- there evolution ceases and degeneration commences.

A Living Soul?

Thus the two Creation stories harmonize very well.

One deals with Form, which was built up through mineral, plant and animal and reached the human *last*.

The other tells us that Life which now ensouls human forms was manifested anterior to the Life which ensouls the forms of the other kingdoms.

One of these accounts of Creation would not have been sufficient. There are important particulars hidden behind the narrative of man's creation, in the second chapter; the verse reads: "Then Jehovah formed man from the dust of the Earth, and blew into his nostrils the breath [*nephesh*], and man become a breathing creature [*nephesh chayim*]."

In other places in the King James version *nephesh* is translated "life," but in this particular instance (Gen. ii.7) it is rendered "living soul," thus conveying the idea that there was a distinction made between the life that ensouled the human form and that which ensouled inferior creations. There is no authority whatever for this difference in translation, which is purely arbitrary. The life-breath (*nephesh*) is the same in man and beast. This can be shown even to those who stand firmly upon the Bible as authority, for even the King James version distinctly states (Eccles. iii:19,20): "...as the one dieth, so dieth the other; yea, they all have one breath [*nephesh*]; so that a man hath no pre-eminence above a beast:...All go unto one place."

The animals are but our "younger brothers," and though they are not now so finely organized, they will eventually reach a state as high as our own, and we shall then have ascended higher.

If it is contended that *man* received his soul in the way described in this seventh verse of the second chapter of Genesis, and that he could have received it in no other way, it is pertinent to ask where and how *woman* received her soul?

The meaning of the chapter, and of the inspiration of the breath of life by Jehovah, is very plain and clear when we use the occult key, and it has the further and immense advantage of being logical.

The fact that the Regent of the Moon (Jehovah), with His Angels and Archangels, were the principals in this action fixes the time when this creation occurred. It was between the early and the middle parts of the Lemurian Epoch, and must have been after the Moon was thrown out from the Earth, because Jehovah had nothing to do with the generation of bodies before the Moon was thrown off. The forms were then more ethereal. There were no dense and concrete bodies. It is possible to make such bodies only by means of the hardening and crystallizing Moon-forces, It must have been in the first half of the Lemurian Epoch, because the separation of the sexes, which is recorded later, took place in the middle of that epoch.

At that time man-in-the-making had not yet commenced to breathe by means of lungs. He had the gill-like apparatus still present in the human embryo while passing through the stage of ante-natal life corresponding to that Epoch. He had no warm, red blood, for at that stage there was no individual spirit, the entire form was soft and pliable and the skeleton soft like cartilage. Before the later date, when it became necessary to separate humanity into sexes, the skeleton had grown firm and solid.

The work done by Jehovah was to build dense, hard bone substance into the soft bodies already existing. Previous to this time, i.e., during the Polarian and Hyperborean Epochs, neither animal nor man had bones.

Adam's Rib

The grotesque and impossible manner in which the separation of the sexes is said to have been accomplished (as described in the common versions of the Bible and, in this particular case, in the Masoretic text also) is another example of what may be done by changing vowels in the old Hebrew text. Read in one way, the work is "rib"; but in another, which has at least as good

190

a claim to consideration, with the additional advantage of being common-sense, it reads "side." If we interpret this to mean that man was male-female and that Jehovah caused one side or sex in each being to remain latent, we shall not be doing violence to our reason, as we would by accepting the "rib" story.

When this alternation is made, the occult teaching as previously given harmonizes with that of the Bible and both agree with the teaching of modern science that man was bi-sexual at one time, before he developed one sex at the expense of the other. In corroboration of this, it is pointed out that the fetus is bi-sexual up to a certain point; thereafter one sex predominates, while the other remains in abeyance, so that each person still has the opposite sex organs in a rudimentary form and therefore is really bi-sexual, as was primitive man.

Apparently the Bible narrator does not wish to give, in this second creation account, an accurate picture of the whole of evolution, but rather to particularize a little more what was said in the first chapter. He tells us that man did not always breathe as he does now; that there was a time when he was not separated into sexes; and that it was Jehovah Who effected the change, thus fixing the time of the occurrence. As we proceed, it will be found that much further information is given.

Guardian Angels

During the earlier Epochs and Periods the great creative Hierarchies had worked upon humanity as it was unconsciously evolving. There had been only *one common consciousness* among *all* human beings; one group-spirit for all mankind, as it were.

In the Lemurian Epoch a new step was taken. Bodies had been definitely formed, but they must have warm, red blood before they could be ensouled and become the abode of indwelling spirits.

In nature no process is sudden. We would get a wrong idea were we to imagine that air blown into the nostrils could put a soul into an image of clay and galvanize it into life as a sentient, thinking being.

The individual spirit was very weak and impotent and quite unfitted for the task of guiding its dense vehicle. In that respect it is not yet very strong. To any qualified observer, it is evident that the desire body rules the personality more than does the spirit, even at our present stage of advancement. But in the middle of the Lemurian Epoch, when the lower personality--the threefold body---was to be endowed with the light of the Ego, the latter, if left to itself, would have been absolutely powerless to guide its instrument.

Therefore it is necessary for someone much more highly evolved to help the individual spirit and gradually prepare the way for its complete union with its instruments. It was analogous to a new nation, over which, until it becomes capable of forming a stable government for itself, some stronger power establishes a protectorate, guarding it alike from external dangers and internal indiscretions. Such a protectorate was exercised over evolving humanity by the Race-spirit, and is exercised over the animals by the group-spirit, in a somewhat different way.

Jehovah is the Most High. He is Race-God, as one might express it, having dominion over all Form. He is the Chief Ruler and the highest Power in maintaining the form and exercising an orderly government over it. The Archangels are the Race-spirits, each having dominion over a certain group of people. They also have dominion over animals, while the Angels have dominion over the plants.

The Archangels have dominion over races or groups of people and also over the animals, for these two kingdoms have desire bodies and the Archangels are expert architects of desire matter, because in the Sun Period the densest globe was composed of that materials, and the humanity of that period, who are now Archangels, learned to build their densest vehicles of desire staff as we are now learning to build our bodies of the chemical elements whereof our Earth-globe is composed. Thus it will be readily understood that the Archangels are peculiarly qualified to help later life waves through the stage where they learn to build and control a desire body.

For analogous reasons the Angels work in the vital bodies of man, animal and plant. Their densest bodies are composed of ether and so was the Globe D in the Moon Period when they were human.

Jehovah and His Archangels, therefore, hold a similar relation to Races that the group-spirit does to animals. When individual members of a Race have evolved entire self-control and government, they are emancipated from the influence of the Race-spirit and kindred beings.

As we have seen, the point of vantage of the group-spirit, as of any Ego in the dense body, is in the blood. The Masoretic text shows that this knowledge was possessed by the writer of Leviticus. In the fourteenth verse of the seventeenth chapter the Jews are prohibited from eating blood because ". . .the soul of *all* flesh is in the blood...;" and in the eleventh verse of the same chapter we find these words: "...for the soul of the flesh is in the blood. . .the blood itself mediates for the soul," which shows that this applies to both man and beast, for the word here used in the Hebrew is *neshamah* and means "soul"-not "life," as it is rendered in the King James version.

The Ego works directly through the blood. The Race-spirit guides the Races by working in the blood, as the group-spirit guides the animals of its species through the blood. So also does the Ego control its own vehicle, but with a difference.

The Ego operates by means of the *heat* of the blood, while the Race (i.e., tribal, or family) spirit works by means of the *air*, as it is drawn into the lungs. That is why Jehovah, or His messengers, "breathed into man's nostrils," thereby securing admission for the Race-spirit, Community-spirits, etc.

The different classes of Race-spirits guided their peoples to various climates and different parts of the Earth. To the trained clairvoyant, a tribal-spirit appears as a cloud enveloping and permeating the atmosphere of the whole country inhabited by the people under its dominion. Thus are produced the different peoples and nations. Paul spoke of "The Prince of the Power of the Air"; or "principalities and powers," etc., showing that he knew of the Race-spirits, but now not even an attempt is made to understand what they mean, although their influence is strongly felt. Patriotism is one of the sentiments emanating from and fostered by them. It has not now so much power over people as formerly. There are some who are being liberated from the Race-spirit and can say with Thomas Paine, "The world is my country." There are those who can leave father and mother and look upon all men as brothers. They are being liberated from the Family-spirit, or spirit of the Clan which is different from the race-spirit, an etheric entity. Others again, who are deep in the toil of the Race or Family spirit, will suffer the most dreadful depression if they leave home or country and breathe the air of another Race of Family spirit.

At the time the Race-spirit entered human bodies the individualized Ego commenced to get some slight control of its vehicles. Each human entity became more and more conscious of being separate and distinct from other men, yet for ages he did not think of himself *primarily* as an individual, but as belonging to a tribe or family. The affix "son" to many present day surnames is a remnant of this feeling. A man was not simply "John," or "James." He was John Robert*son*, or James William*son*. In some countries a woman was not "Mary," or "Martha." She was Mary Marthasdaughter, Martha Mary's daughter. The custom was continued in some European countries until within a few generations of the present time; the "son" affix remains with us yet and the family name is still much honored.

Among the Jews, even down to the time of Christ, the Race-spirit was stronger than the individual spirit. Every Jew thought of himself *first* as belonging to a certain tribe or family. His proudest boast was that he was of the "Seed of Abraham." All this was the work of the Race-spirit.

Previous to the advent of Jehovah, when the Earth was yet a part of the Sun, there was one common group-spirit, composed of all the creative Hierarchies, which controlled the entire human family, but it was intended that each body should be the temple and pliable instrument of an indwelling spirit and that meant an infinite division of rulership.

Jehovah came with His Angel and Archangels and made the first great division into Races, giving to each group the guiding influence of a Race-spirit-- an Archangel. For each Ego He appointed one of the Angels to act as guardian until the individual spirit had grown strong enough to become emancipated from all outside influence.

Mixing Blood in Marriage

Christ came to prepare the way for the emancipation of humanity from the guidance of differentiating Race- and Family-spirit, and to unite the whole human family in One Universal Brotherhood.

193

He taught that "Abraham's seed" referred to the *bodies* only, and called their attention to the fact that before Abraham lived [the] "I"--the Ego--was in existence. The threefold individual spirit had its being before all Tribes and Races and it will remain when they have passed away and even the memory of them is no more.

The threefold spirit in man, the Ego, is the God within, whom the personal, bodily man must learn to follow. Therefore did Christ say that, to be His disciple, a man must forsake all he had. His teaching points to the emancipation of the God within. He calls upon man to exercise his prerogative as an individual and rise above family, tribe, and nation. Not that he is to disregard kin and country. He must fulfill all duties, but he is to cease identifying himself with part and must recognize an equal kinship with *all* the world. That is the ideal given to mankind by the Christ.

Under the rule of the Race-spirit, the nation, tribe or family was considered first--the individual last. The family must be kept intact. If any man dies without leaving offspring to perpetuate his name, his brother must "carry seed" to the widow, that there might be no dying out (Due. XXV:5-10). Marrying out of the family was regarded with horror in the earliest times. A member of one tribe could not become connected with another without losing caste in his own. It was not an easy matter to become a member of another family. Not only among the Jews and other early nations was the integrity of the family insisted upon, but also in more modern times. As previously mentioned, the Scots, even in comparatively recent times, clung tenaciously to their Clan, and the old Norse Vikings would take no one into their families without first "mixing blood" with him, for the spiritual effects of haemolysis, which are unknown to material science, were known of old.

All these customs resulted from the working of Race- and tribal-spirit in the common blood. To admit as a member one in whom that common blood did not flow would have caused "confusion of caste." The closer the inbreeding, the greater the power of the Race-spirit, and the stronger the ties that bound the individual to the tribe, because the vital force of the man is in his blood. Memory is intimately connected with the blood, which is the highest expression of the vital body.

The brain and the nervous system are the highest expression of the desire body. They call up pictures of the outside world, but in mental image-making, i.e., imagination, the blood brings the material for the pictures; therefore when the thought is active the blood flows to the head.

When the same unmixed strain of blood flows in the veins of a family for generations, the same mental pictures made by great-grandfather, grandfather and father are reproduced in the son by the family-spirit which lived in the hemoglobin of the blood. He sees himself as the continuation of a long line of ancestors who *live in him*. He sees all the events of the past lives of the family as though he had been present, therefore he does not realize himself as an Ego. He is not simply "David," but "the *son* of Abraham"; not "Joseph," but "the *son* of David."

By means of this common blood men are said to have *lived* for many generations, because through the blood their descendants had access to the memory of nature, in which the records of the lives of their ancestors were preserved. That is why, in the fifth chapter of Genesis, it is stated that the patriarchs lived for centuries. Adam, Methuselah and the other patriarchs did not *personally* attain to such great age, but they lived in the consciousness of their descendants, who saw the lives of their ancestors as if *they* had lived them. After the expiration of the period stated, the descendants did not think of themselves as Adam or Methuselah. Memory of those ancestors faded and so it is said they died.

The "second sight" of the Scotch Highlanders shows that be means of endogamy the consciousness of the inner World is retained. They have practiced marrying in the Clan until recent times; also in Gypsies, who always marry in the tribe. The smaller the tribe and the closer the inbreeding, the more pronounced is the "sight."

The earlier Races would not have dared to disobey the injunction issued by the tribal God, not to marry outside of the tribe, nor had they any inclination to do so, for they had no mind of their own.

The Original Semites were the first to evolve Will, and they at once married the daughters of the men of other tribes, frustrating temporarily the design of their Race-spirit and being promptly ejected as evil-doers who had "gone a-whoring after strange gods," thereby rendering themselves unfit to give the "seed" for the seven Races of our present Aryan Epoch. The Original Semites were, for the time being, the last Race that the Race-spirit cared to keep separate.

Later, man was given free will. The time had come when he was to be prepared for individualization. The former "common" consciousness, the involuntary clairvoyance or second-sight which constantly held before a tribesman the pictures of his ancestor's lives and caused him to feel most closely identified with the tribe or family, was to be replaced for a time by a strictly individual consciousness confined to the material world, so as to break up the nations into individuals, that the Brotherhood of Man regardless of exterior circumstances may become a fact. This is on the same principle that if we have a number of buildings and wish to make them into one large structure, it is necessary to break them up into separate bricks. Only then can the large building be constructed.

In order to accomplish this separation of nations into individuals, laws were given which prohibited endogamy or marriage in the family and henceforth incestuous marriages gradually came to be regarded with horror. Strange blood has thus been introduced into all the families of the Earth and it has gradually wiped out the involuntary clairvoyance which promoted the clannish feeling and segregated humanity into groups. Altruism is superseding patriotism, and loyalty to the family is disappearing in consequence of the mixture of blood.

Science has lately discovered that haemolysis results from the inoculation of the blood of one individual into the veins of another of a different species, causing the death of the lower of the two. Thus any animal inoculated with the blood of a man dies. The blood of a dog transfused into the veins of a bird kills the bird, but it will not hurt the dog to have the bird's blood inoculated into its veins. Science merely states the fact, the occult scientist gives the reason. The blood is the vantage ground of the spirit, as shown elsewhere. The Ego in man works in its own vehicles by means of the *heat* of the blood; the race, family or community spirit gains entrance to the blood by means of the *air* we inspire. In the animals are also both the separate spirit of the animal and the group-spirit of the species to which it belongs, but the spirit of the animal is not individualized and does not work self-consciously with its vehicles as does the Ego, hence it is altogether dominated by the group-spirit which works in the blood.

When the blood of a higher animal is inoculated into the veins of one from a lower species, the spirit in the blood of the higher animal is of course stronger than the spirit of the less evolved; hence when it endeavors to assert itself it kills the imprisoning form and liberates itself. When, on the other hand, the blood of a lower species is inoculated into the veins of a higher animal, the higher spirit is capable of ousting the less evolved spirit in the strange blood and assimilating the blood to its own purposes, therefore no visible catastrophe ensues.

The group-spirit always aims to preserve the integrity of its domain in the blood of the species under its charge. Like the human Race-God, it resents the marriage of its subjects into other species and visits the sins of the fathers upon the children as we see in the case of hybrids. Where a horse and a donkey produce a mule for instance, the mixture of strange blood destroys the propagative faculty so as not to perpetuate the hybrid which is an abomination from the standpoint of the group-spirit, for the mule is not so definitely under the dominion of the group-spirit of the horses or of the group-spirit of the donkeys as the pure breed, yet it is not so far away as to be entirely exempt from their influence. If two mules could mate, their offspring would be still less under the dominion of either of these group-spirits, and so a new species *without a group-spirit* would result. That would be anomaly in nature, an impossibility until the separate animal-spirits should have become sufficiently evolved to be *self-sufficient.* Such a species, could it be produced, would be without the guiding instinct, so-called, which is in reality the promptings of the group-spirit; they would be in an analogous position to a litter of kittens removed from the mother's womb prior to birth. They could not possibly shift for themselves, so they would die.

Therefore, as it is the group-spirit of the animals that sends the separate spirits of the animals into embodiment, it simply withholds the fertilizing seed-atom when animals of widely differing species are mated. It permits one of its charges to take advantage of an opportunity for re-embodiment where two animals of nearly the same nature are mated, but refuses to let the hybrids perpetuate themselves. Thus we see that the infusion of strange blood weakens the hold of the group-spirit and that therefore it either destroys the *form* or the propagative *faculty* where it has the power.

The human spirit is individualized, an Ego, it is evolving free will and responsibility. It is drawn to birth by the irresistible law of Consequence, so that it is beyond the power of the race, community or family spirit to keep it from returning at the present stage of human development, and by the admixture of strange blood, by intermarriage of the individuals of different tribes or nations, the leaders of man are gradually helping him to oust the family, tribal or national spirit from the blood, but with it has necessarily gone the involuntary clairvoyance which was due to its working in the blood, whereby it fostered the family traditions in its charges, and so we see that *also in the case of man a faculty was destroyed by the mixture of blood*. That loss was a gain, however, for it has concentrated man's energy on the material world and he is better able to master its lessons than if he were still distracted by the visions of the higher realms.

As man becomes emancipated he gradually ceases to think of himself as "Abraham's Seed," as a "Clan Stewart Man," as a "Brahmin" or a "Levite": he is learning to think more of himself as an individual an "I". The more he cultivates that "Self," the more he frees himself from the family and national spirit in the blood, the more he becomes a self-sufficient citizen of the world.

There is much foolish, even dangerous, talk of giving up the Self to the Not-Self; only when we have cultivated a "Self," can we sacrifice ourselves and give up the *Self* to the *whole*. So long as we can only love our own family or nation we are incapable of loving others. We are bound by the tie of kin and country. When we have burst the tie of blood and *asserted ourselves* and become self-sufficient may we become unselfish helpers of humanity. When a man has reached that stage he will find that, instead of having lost his own family, he has gained all the families in the world, for they will have become his sisters and brothers, his fathers and mothers to care for and help.

Then he will regain the viewpoint of the Spiritual World which he lost by the mixing of blood, but it will be a higher faculty, an intelligent, voluntary clairvoyance where he can see what *he* wills and not merely the negative faculty imprinted in his blood by the family spirit which bound him to the family to the exclusion of all other families. His viewpoint will be universal, to be used for universal good.

For aforementioned reasons, intertribal, and later international, marriages came gradually to be regarded as desirable and preferable to close intermarriages.

As man progressed through these stages, and gradually lost touch with the inner world, he sorrowed over the loss and longed for a return of the "inner" vision. But by degrees he forgot, and the material world gradually loomed up before his mind as the only reality, until at last he has come to scout the idea that such inner Worlds exist and to regard a belief in them as foolish superstition.

The four causes contributing to this condition were:

1. The clearing of the foggy atmosphere of the Atlantean continent.
2. The indrawing of the vital body, so that a point at the root of the nose corresponds to a similar point in the vital body.
3. The elimination of inbreeding and the substitution therefore of marriages outside the family and tribe.
4. The use of intoxicants.

The Race-spirits still exist in and work with man, but the more advanced the nation, the more freedom is given the individual. In countries where people are most fettered, the Race-spirit is strongest. The more in harmony a man is with the law of Love, and the higher his ideals, the more he frees himself from the spirit of the Races. Patriotism, while good in itself, is a tie of the Race- spirit. The ideal of Universal Brotherhood, which identifies itself with neither country nor race, is the only path which leads to emancipation.

Christ came to reunite the separated races in bonds of peace and good will, wherein all will willingly and *consciously* follow the law of Love.

The present Christianity is not even a shadow of the true religion of Christ. That will remain in abeyance until all race feeling shall have been overcome. In the Sixth Epoch there will be but one Universal Brotherhood, under the Leadership of the *Returned* Christ, but the day and the hour no man knows, for it is not fixed, but depends upon how soon a sufficient number of people shall have commenced to live the life of Fellowship and Love, which is to be the hall-mark of the new dispensation.

The Fall of Man

In connection with the analysis of Genesis, a few more words must be said about "The Fall," which is the backbone and sinew of popular Christianity. Had there been no "Fall," there would have been no need for the "plan of salvation."

When, in the middle of the Lemurian Epoch, the separation of the sexes occurred (in which work Jehovah and His Angels were active), the Ego began to work slightly upon the dense body, building organs within. Man was not at that time the wide-awake conscious being he is at present, but by means of half the sex force, he was building a brain for the expression of thought as previously described. He was more awake in the Spiritual World than in the physical; hardly saw his body and was not conscious of the act of propagation. The Bible statement that Jehovah put man to sleep when he was to bring forth is correct. There was no pain nor trouble connected with childbirth; nor (because of man's exceedingly dim consciousness of his physical surroundings) did he know anything of the loss of his dense body by death, or of his installment in a new dense vehicle at birth.

It will be remembered that the Lucifers were a part of the humanity of the Moon Period; they are the stragglers of the life wave of the Angels, too far advanced to take a dense physical body, yet they needed an "inner" organ for the acquisition of knowledge. Moreover, they could work through a physical brain, which the Angels or Jehovah could not.

These spirits entered the spinal cord and brain and spoke to the woman, whose Imagination, as explained elsewhere, had been aroused by the training of the Lemurian Race. As her consciousness was principally internal, a picture-consciousness of them was received by her, and she saw them as serpents, for they had entered her brain by the serpentine spinal cord.

The training of the women included watching the perilous feats and fights of the Men in developing Will, in which fights bodies were necessarily often killed. The dim consciousness of something unusual set the imagination of the woman to wondering why she saw these strange things. She was conscious of the spirits of those who had lost their bodies, but her imperfect sense of the Physical World failed to reveal these friends whose dense bodies had been destroyed.

The Lucifers solved the problem for her by "opening her eyes." They revealed to her her own body and that of the man and taught her how, together, they might conquer death by creating new bodies. Thus death could not touch them for they, like Jehovah, could create at will.

Lucifer opened the eyes of woman, She sought the help of man and opened his eyes. Thus, in a real though dim way, they first "knew" or became aware of one another and also of the Physical World. They became conscious of death and pain and by this knowledge they learned to differentiate between the inner man and the outer garment he wears and renews each time it is necessary to take his next step in evolution. They ceased to be automatons and became free thinking beings at the cost of freedom from pain, sickness and death.

That the interpretation of the eating of the fruit as a symbol of the generative act is not a far-fetched idea, is shown by the declaration of Jehovah (which is not a curse at all, but simply a statement of the consequences that would follow the act) that they will die and that the woman will bear her children in pain and suffering. He knew that, as man's attention had now been called to his physical garment, he would become aware of its loss by death. He also knew that man had not yet wisdom to bridle his passion and regulate sexual intercourse by the positions of the planets, therefore pain in childbirth must follow his ignorant abuse of the function.

It has always been a sore puzzle to Bible commentators what connection there could possibly be between the eating of fruit and the bearing of children, but if we understand that the eating of the fruit is symbolical of the generative act whereby man becomes "like God" inasmuch as he *knows* his kind and is thus able to generate new beings, the solution is easy.

In the latter part of the Lemurian Epoch when man arrogated to himself the prerogative of performing the generative act when he pleased, it was his then-powerful will that enable him to do so. By "eating of the tree of knowledge" at any and all times he was able to create a new body whenever he lost an old vehicle.

We usually think of death as something to be dreaded. Had man also "eaten of the tree of life," had he learned the secret of how to perpetually vitalize his body, there would have been a worse condition. We know that our bodies are not perfect today and in those ancient days they were exceedingly primitive. Therefore the anxiety of the creative Hierarchies lest man "eat of the tree of life also," and become capable of renewing his vital body, was well founded. Had he done so he would have been immortal indeed, but would never have been able to progress. The evolution of the Ego depends upon its vehicles and if it could not get new and improving ones by death and birth, there would be stagnation. It is an occult maxim that the oftener we die the better we are able to live, for every birth gives us a new chance.

We have seen that brain-knowledge, with its concomitant selfishness, was brought by man at the cost of the power to create from himself alone. He bought his free will at the cost of pain and death; but when man learns to use his intellect for the good of humanity, he will gain spiritual power over life and in addition, will be guided by an innate knowledge as much higher than the present brain-consciousness as that is higher than the lowest animal consciousness.

The fall into generation was necessary to build the brain, but that is, at best, only an indirect way of gaining knowledge and will be superseded by direct touch with the Wisdom of Nature, which man, without any co-operation, will then be able to use for the generation of new bodies. The larynx will again speak "the lost Word," the "creative Fiat," which, under the guidance of great Teachers, was used in ancient Lemuria in the creation of plants and animals.

Man will then be a creator in very truth. Not in the slow and toilsome manner of the present day, but by the use of the proper word or magical formula, will he be able to create a body.

All that was manifested during the descending period of involution remains until the corresponding point on the ascending arc of evolution has been reached. The present generative organs will degenerate and atrophy. The female organ was the first to come into existence as a separate unit and, according to the law that "the first shall be last," will be the last to atrophy. The male organ was differentiated last and is even now

Diagram 13

Life Wave   Higher Worlds

Female Organ originates . . . . Female Organ atrophies

Male Organ originates . . . . Male Organ atrophies

Involution   Evolution

Central point

Material World

commencing to divide itself from the body. Diagram 13 will make this clear.

THE SEVEN DAYS OF CREATION

STAGE OF UNCONSCIOUS INVOLUTION — STAGE OF CONSCIOUS EVOLUTION

World	Globes of the SATURN PERIOD (THRONES)	Globes of the SUN PERIOD (CHERUBIM)	Globes of the MOON PERIOD (SERAPHIM)	Globes of the EARTH PERIOD (LORDS OF FORM)	Globes of the JUPITER PERIOD	Globes of the VENUS PERIOD	Globes of the VULCAN PERIOD
	Lords of Mind were human	*Archangels were human*	*Angels were human*	*HALF We are human here*	*Animals will be human*	*Plants will be human*	*Minerals will be human*
World of Divine Spirit	awakened the Divine Spirit						We will be God-Men
World of Life Spirit	In Man and gave him the	awakened the Life Spirit			We will be Super Man and	We will be Demi-Gods	and Creators
Region of Abstract Thought — World of Thought	thought form of a	In Man and gave him a germinal	awakened the Human Spirit		extract the	and extract the	by Amalgamating the 3-fold Soul with the
Region of Concrete Thought	Dense Body	Vital Body	gave germ of Desire Body	Mind given by Lords of Mind is now a thought form	Intellectual Soul from the	Emotional Soul from the	Mind
Desire World		which was then a thought form	which was then a thought form	Conscious Soul extracted	Vital Body	Desire Body	
Etheric Region — Physical World			thought form	MARS LEFT from the Dense Body			
Chemical Region				MERCURY			

Involution brings the Spirit down into matter by crystallizing it into bodies

Growth of the 3-fold body, the focus of mind and attainment of self consciousness

Growth of the 3-fold soul by right feeling and right thought, right action

Epigenesis is the original creative activity of the spirit, is the lever and the Mind is the fulcrum upon which Involution turns to Evolution

Evolution lifts the spirit out of matter by spiritualizing the bodies into soul

Part Three – Man's Future Development and Initiation

Chapter Fifteen - Christ and His Mission

The Evolution of Religion

In the foregoing part of this work we have become familiar with the way in which our present outside world came into existence, and how man evolved the complicated organism with which he is related to outer conditions. We have also, in a measure, studied the Jewish Race-religion. We will next consider the last and greatest of the divine measures put forth for the uplifting of humanity, i.e., Christianity, which will be the Universal Religion of the future.

It is a notable fact that man and his religions have evolved side by side and in an equal degree. The earliest religion of any Race is found to be as savage as the people governed by it and as they become more civilized, their religions become more and more humane and in harmony with higher ideals.

From this fact materialists have drawn the inference that no religion has a higher origin than man itself. Their investigations into early history have resulted in a conviction that, as man progressed, he civilized his God and fashioned Him after his own pattern.

This reasoning is defective, because it fails to take into account that man is *not* the body, but an *indwelling* spirit, an Ego who uses the body with ever-increasing facility as evolution progresses.

There is no doubt that the law for the *body* is "The Survival of the Fittest." The law for the evolution of the spirit demands "Sacrifice." As long as man believes that "Might is Right," the Form prospers and waxes strong, because all obstacles are swept out of the way regardless of others. If the body were all, that manner of life would be the only one possible for man. He would be altogether incapable of any regard for others and would forcibly resist any attempt to encroach upon what he considered his rights--the right of the stronger, which is the sole standard of justice under the law of the Survival of the Fittest. He would be quite regardless of his fellow beings; absolutely insensible to any force *from without* that tended to make him act in any manner not conducive to his own momentary pleasure.

It is manifest, then, that whatever urges man toward a higher standard of conduct in his dealing with others must come *from within*, and from a source which is not identical with the body, otherwise it would not strive with the body and often prevail against its most obvious interests. Moreover, it must be a stronger force than that of the body, or it could not succeed in overcoming its desires and compelling it to make sacrifices for those who are physically weaker.

That such a force exists, surely no one will deny. We have come to that stage in our advancement where, instead of seeing in physical weakness an opportunity for easy prey, we recognize in the very frailty of another a valid claim upon our protection. Selfishness is being slowly but surely routed by Altruism.

Nature is sure to accomplish her purposes. Though slow, her progress is orderly and certain. In the breast of every man this force of Altruism works as a leaven. It is transforming the savage into the civilized man, and will in time transform the latter into a God.

Though nothing that is truly spiritual can be thoroughly comprehended, yet it may at least be apprehended by means of an illustration.

If one of two tuning-forks of exactly the same pitch is struck, the sound will induce the same vibration in the other, weak to begin with, but if the strokes are continued, the second fork will give out a louder and louder tone until it will emit a volume of sound equal to that of the first. This will happen though the forks are several feet apart, and even if one of them is encased in glass. The sound from the smitten one will penetrate the glass and the answering note be emitted by the enclosed instrument.

These invisible sound-vibrations have great power over concrete matter. They can both build and destroy. If a small quantity of very fine powder is placed upon a brass or glass plate, and a violin bow drawn across the edge, the vibrations will cause the powder to assume beautiful geometrical figures. The human voice is also capable of producing these figures; always the same figure for the same tone.

If one note or chord after another be sounded upon a musical instrument--a piano, or preferably a violin, for from it more gradations of tone can be obtained--a tone will finally be reached which will causes the hearer to feel a distinct vibration in the back of the lower part of the head. Each time that note is struck, the vibration will be felt. That note is the "key-note" of the person whom it so affects. If it is struck slowly and soothingly it will build and rest the body, tone the nerves and restore health. If, on the other hand, it be sounded in a dominant way, loud and long enough, it will kill as surely as a bullet from a pistol.

If we now apply what has been said about music or sound to the problem of how this inner force is awakened and strengthened, we may perhaps understand the matter better.

In the first place, let us particularly note the fact that the two tuning-forks were *of the same pitch*. Had this not been the case, we might have sounded and sounded one of them until the crack of doom, but the other one would have remained mute. Let us understand this thoroughly: Vibration can be induced in one tuning-fork by one of *like tone only*. Any thing, or any being, can be affected as above stated by no sound except *its own key-note*.

We know that this force of Altruism exists. We also know that it is less pronounced among uncivilized people than among people of higher social attainment, and among the very lowest races it is almost entirely lacking. The logical conclusion is that there was a time when it was altogether absent. Consequent upon this conclusion follows the natural question: What induced it?

The material personality surely had nothing to do with it; in fact, that part of man's nature was much more comfortable without it than it has been at any time since. Man must have had the force of Altruism latent *within*, otherwise it could not have been awakened. Still further, it must have been awakened by a force of the same kind--a similar force that was already active--as the second tuning-fork was started into vibration by the first *after* it was struck.

We also saw that the vibrations in the second fork become stronger and stronger under the continued impacts of sound from the first, and that a glass case was no hindrance to the induction of the sound. Under the continued impacts of a force similar to that within him, the Love of God to man has awakened this force of Altruism and is constantly increasing its potency.

It is therefore reasonable and logical to conclude that, at first, it was necessary to give man a religion commensurate with his ignorance. It would have been useless to talk to him, at that stage, of a God Who was all tenderness and love. From his viewpoint, those attributes were weaknesses and he could not have been expected to reverence a God Who possessed what were to him despicable qualities. The God to Whom he rendered obedience must be a strong God, a God to be feared, a God Who could hurl the thunderbolt and wield the flail of lightning.

Thus, man was impelled first to *fear* God and was given religions of a nature to further his spiritual well-being under the lash of fear.

The next step was to induce in him a certain kind of unselfishness, by causing him to give up part of his worldly goods--to sacrifice. This was achieved by giving him the Tribal or Race-God, Who is a jealous God, requiring of him the strictest allegiance and the sacrifice of wealth, which the growing man greatly prizes. But in return, this Race-God is a friend and mighty ally, fighting man's battles and giving him back many fold the sheep, bullocks and grain which he sacrificed. He had not yet arrived at the stage where it was possible for him to understand that all creatures are akin, but the Tribal God taught him that he must deal mercifully with his *brother tribesman* and gave laws which made for equity and fair dealing between men of the same Race.

It must not be thought that these successive steps were taken easily, nor without rebellion and lapses upon the part of primitive man. Selfishness is ingrained in the lower nature even unto this day, and there must have been many lapses and much backsliding. We have in the Jewish Bible good examples of how man forgot, and had to be patiently and persistently "prodded" again and again by the Tribal God. Only the visitations of a long-suffering Race-spirit were potent, at times, in bringing him back to the law--that law very few people have even yet learned to obey.

There are always pioneers, however, who require something higher. When they become sufficiently numerous, a new step in evolution is taken, so that several gradations always exist. There came a time, nearly two thousand years ago, when the most advanced of humanity were ready to take another step forward, and learn the religion of living a good life for the sake of future reward in a state of existence in which they must have faith.

That was a long, hard step to take. It was comparatively easy to take a sheep or a bullock to the temple and offer it as a sacrifice. If a man brought the first-fruits of his granary, his vineyards, or his flocks and herds, he still had more, and he knew that the Tribal God would refill his stores and give abundantly in return. But in this new departure, it was not a question of sacrificing his goods. It was demanded that he sacrifice *himself.* It was not even a sacrifice to be made by one supreme effort of martyrdom; that also would have been comparatively easy. Instead, it was demanded that day by day, from morning until night, he must act mercifully toward all. He must forego selfishness, and *love* his neighbor, as he had been used to loving himself. Moreover, he was not promised any immediate and visible reward, but must have faith in a future happiness.

Is it strange that people find it difficult to realize this high ideal of *continued* well-doing, made doubly hard by the fact that self-interest is entirely ignored? Sacrifice is demanded with no positive assurance of *any* reward. Surely it is much to the credit of humanity that so much altruism is practiced and that it is constantly increasing. The wise Leaders, knowing the frailness of the spirit to cope with the selfish instincts of the body, and the dangers of despondency in the face of such standards of conduct, gave another uplifting impulse when they incorporated in the new religion the doctrine of "vicarious Atonement."

This idea is scouted by some very advanced philosophers, and the law of "Consequence" made paramount. If it so happens that the reader agrees with these philosophers, we request that he await the explanation herein set forth, showing how *both* are part of the scheme of upliftment. Suffice it to say, for the present, that this doctrine of atonement gives many an earnest soul the strength to strive and, in spite of repeated failures, to bring the lower nature under subjection. Let it be remembered that, for reasons given when the laws of Rebirth and Consequence were discussed, western humanity knew practically nothing of these laws. With such a great ideal before them as the Christ, and believing they had but a few short years in which to attain to such a high degree of development as this, would it not have been the greatest imaginable cruelty to leave them without help? Therefore, the *great sacrifice* on Calvary--while it also served other purposes, as will be shown--becomes rightfully the Beacon of Hope for every earnest soul who is striving to achieve the impossible; to attain, in one short life, to the perfection demanded by the Christian religion.

Jesus and Christ-Jesus

To gain some slight insight into the Great Mystery of Golgotha, and to understand the Mission of Christ as the Founder of the Universal Religion of the future, it is necessary that we first become familiar with His exact nature and incidentally, with that of Jehovah, Who is the head of such Race-religions as Taoism, Buddhism, Hinduism, Judaism, etc.; also with the identity of "The Father," to Whom Christ is to give up the Kingdom, in due time.

In the Christian creed occurs this sentence: "Jesus Christ, the only begotten Son of God." This is generally understood to mean that a certain person Who appeared in Palestine about 2,000 years ago, Who is spoken of as Jesus Christ--one separate individual--was the only begotten Son of God.

This is a great mistake. There are three distinct and widely different Beings characterized in this sentence. It is of the greatest importance that the student should clearly understand the exact nature of these Three Great and Exalted Beings--differing vastly in glory, yet each entitled to our deepest and most devout adoration.

The student is requested to turn to diagram 6 and note that "The only begotten" ("The Word," of Who John speaks) is the second aspect of the Supreme Being.

This "Word" and It alone, is "begotten of His Father [the first aspect] before all Worlds." "Without Him was not anything made that was made," not even the third aspect of the Supreme Being, which proceeds from the two previous aspects. Therefore the "only begotten" is the exalted Being which ranks above all else in the Universe, save only the Power-aspect which created It.

The first aspect of the Supreme Being "thinks out," or imagines, the Universe before the beginning of active manifestation, everything, including the millions of Solar Systems and the great creative Hierarchies which inhabit the Cosmic Planes of existence above the seventh, which is the field of our evolution (See diagram 6). This is also the Force which dissolves everything that has crystallized beyond the possibility of further growth and at last, when the end of active manifestation has come, reabsorbs within Itself all that is, until the dawn of another Period of Manifestation.

The second aspect of the Supreme Being is that which manifests in matter as the forces of attraction and cohesion, thus giving it the capability of combining into Forms of various kinds. This is "The Word," the "creative Fiat," which molds the primordial Cosmic Root-substance in a manner similar to the formation of figures by musical vibrations, as previously mentioned, the same tone always producing the same figure. So this great primordial *"word"* brought, or "spoke," into being, in finest matter, all the different Worlds, with all their myriads of Forms, which have since been copied and worked out in detail by the innumerable creative Hierarchies.

"The Word" could not have done this, however, until the third aspect of the Supreme Being had first prepared the Cosmic Root-substance; had awakened it from its normal state of inertia and set the countless *inseparate* atoms spinning upon their axes, placing those axes at various angles with respect to each other, giving to each kind a certain "measure of vibration."

These varying angles of inclination of the axes and the measures of vibration made the Cosmic Root-substance capable of forming different combinations, which are the basis of the seven great Cosmic Planes. There is, in each of these Planes, a different inclination of the axes, and also a different measure of vibration, consequently the conditions and combinations in each one are different from those in any of the others, due to the activity of "The Only Begotten."

Diagram 14 shows us that:

"The Father" is the highest Initiate among the humanity of the Saturn Period. The ordinary humanity of that Period are now the Lords of Mind.

"The Son" (Christ) is the highest Initiate of the Sun Period. The ordinary humanity of that Period are now the Archangels.

"The Holy Spirit" (Jehovah) is the highest Initiate of the Moon Period. The ordinary humanity of that Period are now the Angels.

This diagram also shows what are the vehicles of these different orders of Beings, and upon comparison with diagram 8, it will be seen that their bodies or vehicles (indicated by squares on diagram 14) correspond to the Globes of the Period in which they were human. This is always the case so far as the ordinary humanities are concerned, for at the end of the Period during which any life wave becomes individualized as human beings, those beings retain *bodies* corresponding to the Globes on which they have functioned.

Diagram 14.   The vehicles of the highest Initiates & ordinary humanity

Zodiacal Signs	The Worlds in which these orders have corresponding vehicles	Saturn Period		Sun Period		Moon Period	
		The highest Initiate is The Father	The ordinary humanity are now Lords of Mind	The highest Initiate is Christ The Son	The ordinary humanity are now Arch-angels	The highest Initiate is Jehovah The Holy Spirit	The ordinary humanity are now Angels
13 allogether	World						
12 ♈	of						
11 ♉	God						
10 ♊	World of						
9 ♋	Virgin						
8 ♌	Spirits						
7 ♍	World of Divine Spirit						
6 ♎	World of Life Spirit						
5 ♏	Region of Abstract Thought						
4 ♐	Region of Concrete Thought						
3 ♑	Desire World						
2 ♒	Etheric Region		Jesus Bodies				
1 ♓	Chemical Region						

On the other hand, the Initiates have progressed and evolved for themselves higher vehicles, discontinuing the ordinary use of the lowest vehicle when the ability to use a new and higher one has been attained. Ordinarily, the lowest vehicle of an Archangel is the desire body, but Christ, Who is the highest Initiate of the Sun Period, ordinarily uses the life spirit as lowest vehicle, functioning as consciously in the World of Life Spirit as we do in the Physical World. The student is requested to note this point particularly, as the World of Life Spirit is the first *universal* World, as explained in the chapter on Worlds. It is the World in which differentiation ceases and unity begins to be realized, so far as out solar system is concerned.

Christ has power to build and function in a vehicle as low as the desire body, such as is used by the Archangels but *He can descend no further*. The significance of this will be seen presently.

Jesus belongs to our humanity. When the man, Jesus, is studied through the memory of nature, he can be traced back life by life, where he lived in different circumstances, under various names, in different embodiments, the same, in that respect, as any other human being. *This cannot be done with the Being, Christ. In His case can be found but one embodiment.*

It must not be supposed, however, that Jesus was an ordinary individual. He was of a singularly pure type of mind, vastly superior to the great majority of our present humanity. Through many lives had he trod the Path of Holiness and thus fitted himself for the greatest honor ever bestowed upon a

208

human being.

His mother, the Virgin Mary, was also a type of the highest human purity and because of that was selected to become the mother of Jesus. His father was a high Initiate, virgin, and capable of performing the act of fecundation as a sacrament, without personal desire or passion.

Thus the beautiful, pure and lovely spirit whom we know as Jesus of Nazareth was born into a pure and passionless body. This body was the best that could be produced on Earth and the task of Jesus, in that embodiment, was to care for it and evolve it to the highest possible degree of efficiency, in preparation for the great purpose it was to serve.

Jesus of Nazareth was born at about the time stated in the historic records, and not 105 B.C., as stated in some occult works. The name Jesus is common in the East, and an Initiate named Jesus did live 105 B.C., but he took the Egyptian Initiation, and was not Jesus of Nazareth, with whom we are concerned.

The Individual who was later born under the name of Christian Rosenkreuz, who is in the body today, was a highly evolved being when Jesus of Nazareth was born. His testimony, as well as the results of first-hand investigation by later Rosicrucians, all agree in placing the birth of Jesus of Nazareth at the beginning of the Christian Era, on about the date usually ascribed to that event.

Jesus was educated by the Essenes and reached a very high state of spiritual development during the thirty years in which he used his body.

It may be here said, parenthetically, that the Essenes were a third sect which existed in Palestine, besides the two mentioned in the New Testament--the Pharisees and the Sadducees. The Essenes were an exceedingly devout order, widely different from the materialistic Sadducees and entirely opposite to the hypocritical, publicity seeking Pharisees. They shunned all mention of themselves and their methods of study and worship. To the latter peculiarity is due the fact that almost nothing is known of them, and that they are not mentioned in the New Testament.

It is a law of the Cosmos that no Being, however high, can function in any world without a vehicle built of the material of that world (See diagram 8 and diagram 14). Therefore the desire body was the lowest vehicle of the group of spirits who had reached the human stage in the Sun Period.

Christ was one of those spirits and was consequently unable to build for Himself a vital body and a dense physical vehicle. He could have worked upon humanity in a desire body, as did His younger brothers, the Archangels, as Race-spirits. Jehovah had opened an avenue for them to enter the dense body of man by means of the air he inhaled. All Race-religions were religions of law, and creators of sin through disobedience of that law. They were under the direction of Jehovah, Whose lowest vehicle is the human spirit, correlating Him to the World of Abstract Thought, where everything is separative and therefore leads to self-seeking.

That is precisely the reason why the intervention of Christ became necessary. Under the *regime* of Jehovah unity is impossible. Therefore the Christ, Who possesses as a lowest vehicle the unifying life spirit, must enter into the dense human body. He must appear as a man among men and dwell in this body, because only from *within* is it possible to conquer the Race-religion, which influences man from *without*.

Christ could not be *born* in a dense body, because He had never passed through an evolution such as the Earth Period, therefore He would first have had to acquire the ability to build a dense body such as ours. But even had He possessed that ability, it would have been inexpedient for such an exalted Being to expend for that purpose the energy necessary for body-building through ante-natal life, childhood and youth, to bring it to sufficient maturity for use. He had ceased to use, ordinarily, vehicles such as would correspond to our human spirit, mind and desire body, although He had learned to build them in the Sun Period, and retained the ability to build and function in them whenever desired or required. He used all his own vehicles, taking only the vital and dense bodies from Jesus. When the latter was 30 years of age Christ entered these bodies and used them until the climax of His Mission on Golgotha. After the destruction of the dense body, Christ appeared among His disciples in the vital body, in which He functioned for some time. The vital body is the vehicle which He will use when He appears again, for He will never take another dense body.

It is encroaching upon a subject to be dealt with later to remark that the object of all esoteric training is to so work on the vital body that the life spirit is built up and quickened. When we come to deal with Initiation it may be possible to give more detailed explanations, but no more can be said on the subject just now. In chronicling the events incident to *post mortem* existence, this subject has been partially dealt with and the student is here asked to note that a man is supposed to have conquered his desire body to a considerable extent before attempting esotericism. His esoteric training and the earlier Initiations are devoted to work on the vital body and result in the building of the life spirit. At the time Christ entered the body of Jesus, the latter was a disciple of high degree, consequently his life spirit was well organized. Therefore, the lowest vehicle in which Christ functioned, and the best organized of the higher vehicles of Jesus, were identical; and Christ, when He took the vital body and the dense body of Jesus, was thus furnished with a complete chain of vehicles bridging the gap between the World of Life Spirit and the dense Physical World.

The significance of the fact that Jesus had passed several initiations lies in the effect that has on the vital body. Jesus' vital body was already attuned to the high vibrations of the life spirit. An ordinary man's vital body would have instantly collapsed under the terrific vibrations of the Great Spirit who entered Jesus' body. Even that body, pure and high-strung as it was, could not withstand those tremendous impacts for many years, and when we read of certain times when Christ withdrew temporarily from his disciples, as when he later walked on the sea to meet them, the esotericist knows that he drew out of Jesus' vehicles to give them a rest under the care of the Essene Brothers, who knew more of how to treat such vehicles than Christ did.

This change was consummated with the full and free consent of Jesus, who knew during this entire life that he was preparing a vehicle for Christ. He submitted gladly, that his brother humanity might receive the gigantic impetus which was given to its development by the mysterious sacrifice on Golgotha.

Thus (as shown in diagram 14) Christ Jesus possessed the twelve vehicles, which formed an unbroken chain from the Physical World to the very Throne of God. Therefore He is the only Being in the Universe in touch with both God and man and capable of mediating between them, because He has, personally and individually, experienced all conditions and knows every limitation incidental to physical existence.

Christ is unique among all Beings in all the seven Worlds. He alone possess the twelve vehicles. None save He is able to feel such compassion, nor so fully understand the position and needs of humanity; none save He is qualified to bring the relief that shall fully meet our needs.

Thus do we know the nature of Christ. He is the highest Initiate of the Sun Period and He took the dense and vital bodies of Jesus that He might function directly in the Physical World and appear as a man among men. Had He appeared in a manifestly miraculous manner, it would have been contrary to the scheme of evolution, because at the end of the Atlantean Epoch humanity had been given freedom to do right or wrong. That they might learn to become self-governing, no coercion whatever could be used. They must know good and evil through experience. Before that time they had been led willy-nilly, but at that time they were given freedom under the different Race-religions, each religion adapted to the needs of its particular Tribe or Nation.

Not Peace but a Sword

All Race-religions are of the Holy Spirit. They are insufficient, because they are based on law, which makes for sin and brings death, pain and sorrow.

All Race-spirits know this, and realize that their religions are merely steps to something better. This is shown by the fact that all Race-religions, without

211

exception, point to One Who is *to come.* The religion of the Persians pointed to Mithras; of the Chaldeans to Tammuz. The old Norse Gods foresaw the approach of "The Twilight of the Gods," when Sutr, the bright Sun-spirit, shall supersede them and a new and fairer order be established on "Gimle," the regenerated earth. The Egyptians waited for Horus, the new-born Sun. Mithras and Tammuz are also symbolized as Solar orbs and all the principal Temples were built facing the East, that the rays of the rising Sun might shine directly through the open doors; even Saint Peter's at Rome is so placed. All these facts show that it was generally known that the One Who was to come was a Sun-spirit and was to save humanity from the separative influences necessarily contained in all Race-religions.

These religions were steps which it was necessary for mankind to take to prepare for the advent of Christ. Man must first cultivate a "self" before he can become really *un*selfish and understand the higher phase of Universal Brotherhood--unity of purpose and interest--for which Christ laid the foundation at His first coming, and which He will make living realities when He returns.

As the fundamental principle of a Race-religion is separation, inculcating self-seeking at the expense of other men and nations, it is evident that if the principle is carried to its ultimate conclusion it must necessarily have an increasingly destructive tendency and finally frustrate evolution, unless succeeded by a more constructive religion.

Therefore the separative religions of the Holy Spirit must give place to the unifying religion of the Son, which is the Christian religion.

Law must give place to Love, and the separate Races and Nations be united in one Universal Brotherhood, with Christ as the Eldest Brother.

The Christian religion has not yet had time to accomplish this great object. Man is still in the toils of the dominant Race-spirit and the ideals of Christianity are yet too high for him. The intellect can see some of the beauties, and readily admits that we should love our enemies, but the passions of the desire body are still too strong. The law of the Race-spirit being "An eye for an eye," the Feeling is "I'll get even!" The heart prays for Love; the desire body hopes for Revenge. The intellect sees, *in the abstract,* the beauty of loving one's enemies but in concrete cases it allies itself with the vengeful feeling of the desire body, pleading, as an excuse for "getting even," that "the social organism must be protected."

It is a matter for congratulation, however, that society feels compelled to apologize for the retaliative methods used. Corrective methods and mercy are becoming more and more prominent in the administration of the laws, as is shown by the favorable reception which has been accorded that very modern institution, the Juvenile Court. Further manifestation of this same ten-

212

dency may be noted in the increasing frequency with which convicted prisoners are released on probation, under suspended sentence; also in the greater humanity with which prisoners of war are treated of late years. These are the vanguards of the sentiment of Universal Brotherhood, which is slowly but surely makings its influence felt.

Yet, though the world is advancing and though, for instance, it has been comparatively easy for the writer to secure a hearing for his views in the different cities where he has lectured, the daily papers sometimes devoting to his utterances whole pages (and front pages at that) so long as he confined himself to speaking of the higher worlds and the *post mortem* states, it has been very noticeable that as soon as the theme was Universal Brotherhood his articles have *always* been consigned to the waste-basket.

The world in general is very unwilling to consider anything that is, as it thinks, "too" unselfish. There must be "something in it." Nothing is regarded as an entirely natural line of conduct if it offers no opportunity for "getting the best of" one's fellowmen. Commercial undertakings are planned and conducted on that principle and, before the minds of those who are enslaved by the desire to accumulate useless wealth, the idea of Universal Brotherhood conjures up frightful visions of the abolition of capitalism and its inevitable concomitant, the exploitation of others, with the wreck of "business interests" implied thereby. The word "enslaved" exactly describes this condition. According to the Bible, man was to have dominion over the world, but in the vast majority of cases the reverse is true--it is the world which has dominion over man. Every man who has property interests will, in his saner moments, admit that they are a never-failing source of worry to him; that he is constantly scheming to hold his possessions, or at least to keep from being deprived of them by "sharp practice," knowing that others are as constantly scheming to accomplish that, to them, desirable end. The man is the slave of what, with unconscious irony, he calls "my possessions,' when in reality they possess him. Well did the Sage of Concord say, "*Things* are in the saddle and ride mankind!"

This state of affairs is the result of Race-religions, with their system of law; therefore do they all look for "One Who is to come." The Christian religion *alone* is *not* looking for One Who *is* to come, but for One Who is to come *again*. The time of this second coming depends upon when the Church can free itself from the State. The Church, especially in Europe, is bound to the Chariot of State. The ministers are fettered by economic considerations and dare not proclaim the truths that their studies have revealed to them.

A visitor to Copenhagen, Denmark, recently witnessed a church confirmation service. The Church there is under State control and all ministers are appointed by the temporal power. The parishioners have nothing whatever to say in the matter. They may attend church or not, as they please, but they are compelled to pay the taxes which support the institution.

In addition to holding office by the bounty of the State, the pastor of the particular church visited was decorated with several Orders conferred by the king, the glittering badges bearing silent but eloquent testimony as to the extent of his subservience to the State. During the ceremony, he prayed for the king and the legislators, that they might rule the country wisely. As long as kings and legislators exist, this prayer might be very appropriate, but it was a considerable shock to hear him add: "...and, almighty God, protect and strengthen our army and navy!"

Such a prayer as this shows plainly that the God worshiped is the Tribal or National God--the Race-spirit, for the last act of the gentle Christ Jesus was to stay the sword of the friend who would have protected Him therewith. Although He said He had not come to send peace, but a sword, it was because He foresaw the oceans of blood that would be spilled by the militant "Christian" nations in their mistaken understanding of His teachings and because high ideals cannot be immediately attained by humanity. The wholesale murder of war and like atrocities are harsh, but they are potent illustrations of what Love would abolish.

There is, apparently, a flat contradiction between the words of Christ Jesus, "I came not to send peace, but a sword," and the words of the celestial song which heralded the birth of Jesus, "On earth Peace, Goodwill toward men." This contradiction, however, is apparent only.

There is as great an apparent contradiction between a woman's words and her actions when she says, "I am going to clean house and tidy up," and then proceeds to take up carpets and pile chairs one upon another, producing general confusion in a previously orderly house. One observing only this aspect of the matter, would be justified in saying, "She is making matters worse instead of better," but when the purpose of her work is understood, the expediency of the temporary disorder is realized and in the end her house will be the better for the passing disturbance.

Similarly, we must bear in mind that the time which has elapsed since the coming of Christ Jesus is but little more than a moment in comparison with the duration of even one Day of Manifestation. We must learn, as did Whitman, to "know the amplitude of time," and look beyond the past and present cruelties and jealousies of the warring sects to the shining age of Universal Brotherhood, which will mark the next great step of man's progress on his long and wondrous journey from the clod to the God, from protoplasm to conscious unity with the Father, that

...one far-off, divine event
To which the whole creation moves.

It may be added that the above-mentioned pastor, during the ceremony of receiving his pupils into the Church, taught them that Jesus Christ was a composite individual; that Jesus was the mortal, human part, while Christ was the divine, immortal Spirit. Presumably, if the matter had been discussed with him, he would not have supported this statement, nevertheless in making it he stated an occult fact.

The Star of Bethlehem

The unifying influence of the Christ has been symbolized in the beautiful legend of the worship of the three magi, or "wise men of the East," so skillfully woven by General Lew Wallace into his charming story, "Ben Hur."

The three wise men--Caspar, Melchior and Balthasar--are the representatives of the white, yellow and black Races and symbolize the people of Europe, Asia and Africa, who are all led by The Star to the World-Savior, to Whom eventually "every knee shall bow," and Whom "every tongue shall confess"; Who shall unite all the scattered nations under the Banner of Peace and Goodwill; Who shall cause men to "beat their words into plowshares and their spears into pruning hooks."

The Star of Bethlehem is said to have appeared at the time of the birth of Jesus, and to have guided the three wise men to the Savior.

Much speculation has been indulged in as to the nature of this Star. Most material scientists have declared it a myth, while others have said if it were anything more than a myth, it might have been a "coincidence"--two dead Suns might have collided and caused a conflagration. Every mystic, however, knows the "Star"--yea, and the "Cross" also--not only as symbols connected with the life of Jesus and Christ Jesus, but in his own personal experience. Paul says: "Until Christ be formed in you"; and the mystic, Angelus Silesius, echoes:

Though Christ a thousand times in Bethlehem be born
And not within thyself, thy soul will be forlorn.
The Cross on Golgotha thou lookest to in vain
Unless within thyself it be set up again.

Richard Wagner shows the intuitional knowledge of the artist when, to the question of Parsifal, "Who is The Grail?" Gurnemanz answers:

That tell we not;
But if thou hast by Him been bidden,
From thee the truth will not stay hidden.
... The land to Him no path leads through,
And search but severs from Him wider
When He Himself is not the Guider.

215

Under the "old dispensation" the path to Initiation was not open. It was for only the chosen few. Some might seek the path, but only those who were guided to the Temples by the Hierophants found entrance. Previous to the advent of Christ, there was no such sweeping invitation as "Whosoever will may come."

At the moment the blood flowed on Golgotha, however, "the veil of the Temple was rent" (for reasons presently to be explained), and ever since that time, whosoever will seek admittance will surely find it.

In the Temples of Mystery the Hierophant taught his pupils that there is in the Sun a spiritual, as well as a physical force. The latter force in the rays of the Sun is the fecundating principle in nature. It causes the growth of the plant world and thereby sustains the animal and human kingdom. It is the upbuilding energy which is the source of all physical force.

This physical, solar energy reaches its highest expression in midsummer, when the days are longest and the nights are shortest, because the rays of the Sun then fall directly on the northern hemisphere. At that time the spiritual forces are the most inactive. On the other hand, in December, during the long winter nights, the physical force of the solar orb is dormant and the spiritual forces reach their maximum degree of activity.

The night between the 24th and the 25th of December is The Holy Night, *par excellence*, of the entire year. The Zodiacal sign of the immaculate celestial Virgin stands upon the eastern horizon near midnight, the Sun of the New Year is then born and starts upon his journey from the southernmost point toward the northern hemisphere, to save that part of humanity (physically) from the darkness and famine which would inevitably result if he were to remain permanently south of the equator.

To the people of the northern hemisphere, where all our present day religions originated, the Sun is directly below the Earth; and the spiritual influences are strongest, in the north, at midnight of the 24th of December.

That being the case, it follows as a matter of course that it would then be easiest for those who wished to take a definite step toward Initiation to get in conscious touch with the spiritual Sun especially for the first time.

Therefore the pupils who were ready for Initiation were taken in hand by the Hierophants of the Mysteries, and be means of ceremonies performed in the Temple, were raised to a state of exaltation wherein they transcended physical conditions. To their spiritual vision, the solid Earth become transparent and they was the Sun at midnight--"The Star!" It was not the physical Sun they saw with spiritual eyes, however, but the Spirit in the Sun--The Christ--their Spiritual Savior, as the physical Sun was their physical Savior.

This is the Star that shone on that Holy Night and that still shines for the mystic in the darkness of night. When the noise and confusion of physical

216

activity are quieted, he enters into his closet and seeks the way to the King of Peace. The Blazing Star is ever there to guide him and his soul hears the prophetic song, "On earth Peace, Goodwill toward men."

Peace and goodwill to all, without exception; no room for one single enemy or outcast! Is it any wonder that it is hard to educate humanity to such a high standard? Is there any better way to show the beauty of, and the necessity for peace, goodwill and love than by contrasting them with the present state of war, selfishness and hate? The stronger the light, the deeper the shadow it casts. The higher our ideals, the more plainly can we see our shortcomings.

Unfortunately, at the present stage of development, humanity is willing to learn only by the hardest experience. As a Race, it must become absolutely selfish to feel the bitter pangs caused by the selfishness of others, as one must know much sickness to be thoroughly thankful for health.

The religion *mis*called Christianity has therefore been the bloodiest religion known, not excepting Mohammedanism, which in this respect is somewhat akin to our malpracticed Christianity. On the battle field and in the Inquisition innumerable and unspeakable atrocities have been committed in the name of the gentle Nazarene. The Sword and the Wine Cup--the perverted Cross and Communion Chalice--have been the means by which the more powerful of the so-called Christian nations gained supremacy over the heathen peoples, and even over other but weaker nations professing the same faith as their conquerors. The most cursory reading of the history of the Greco-Latin, Teutonic and Anglo-Saxon Races will corroborate this.

While man was under the *full* sway of Race-religions each nation was a united whole. Individual interests were willingly subordinated to the community interests. All were "under the law." All were members of their respective tribes first, and individuals only secondarily.

At the present time there is a tendency toward the other extreme--to exalt "self" above all else. The result is evident in the economic and industrial problems that are facing every nation and clamoring for solution.

The state of development wherein every man feels himself an absolutely separate unit, an Ego, independently pursuing his own course, is a necessary stage. The national, tribal and family unity must first be broken up before Universal Brotherhood can become a fact. The *regime* of Paternalism has been largely superseded by the reign of Individualism. We are learning the evils of the latter more and more as our civilization advances. Our unsystematic method of distributing the products of labor, the rapacity of the few and the exploitation of many--these social crimes result in under-consumption, industrial depressions and labor disturbances, destroying internal peace. The industrial war of the present day is vastly more far-reaching and destructive than the military wars of the nations.

The Heart as an Anomaly

No lesson, though its truth may be superficially assented to, is of any real value as an active principle of the life until the heart has learned it in longing and bitterness, and the lesson man must so learn is that what is not beneficial to all can never be truly beneficial to any. For nearly 2,000 years we have lightly assented with our lips that we should govern our lives in accordance with such maxims as "Return good for evil." The Heart urges mercy and love, but the Reason urges belligerent and retaliatory measures, if not as revenge, at least as a means of preventing a repetition of hostilities. It is this divorce of head from heart that hinders the growth of a true feeling of Universal Brotherhood and the adoption of the teachings of Christ--the Lord of Love.

The mind is the focusing point by means of which the Ego becomes aware of the material universe. As an instrument for the acquisition of knowledge in those realms the mind is invaluable, but when it arrogates to itself the *role* of dictator as to the conduct of man to man, it is as though the lens should say to an astronomer who was in the act of photographing the Sun through a telescope: "You have me improperly focused. You are not looking at the Sun correctly. I do not think it is good to photograph the Sun anyway, and I want you to point me at Jupiter. The rays of the Sun heat me too much and are liable to damage me."

If the astronomer exercises his will and focuses the telescope as he desires, telling it to attend to its business of transmitting the rays that strike it, leaving the results to him, the work will proceed well, but if the lens has the stronger will and the mechanism of the telescope is in league with it, the astronomer will be seriously hampered in having to contend with a refractory instrument, and the result will be blurred pictures, of little or no value.

Thus it is with the Ego. It works with a threefold body, which it controls, or should control through the mind. But, sad to say, this body has a will of its own and is often aided and abetted by the mind, thus frustrating the purposes of the Ego.

This antagonistic "lower will" is an expression of the higher part of the desire body. When the division of the Sun, Moon, and Earth took place, in the early part of the Lemurian Epoch, the more advanced portion of humanity-in-the-making experienced a division of the desire body into a higher and a lower part. The rest of humanity did likewise in the early part of the Atlantean Epoch.

This higher part of the desire body became a sort of animal soul. It built the cerebro-spinal nervous systems and the voluntary muscles, by that means controlling the lower part of the threefold body until the link of mind was given. Then the mind "coalesced" with this animal soul and become a co-regent.

218

The mind is thus bound up in desire; is enmeshed in the selfish lower nature, making it difficult for the spirit to control the body. The focusing mind, which should be the ally of the higher nature, is alienated by and in league with the lower nature--enslaved by desire.

The law of the Race religions was given to emancipate intellect from desire. The "fear of God" was pitted against "the desires of the flesh." This, however, was not enough to enable one to become master of the body and secure its willing co-operation. It became necessary for the spirit to find in the body another point of vantage, which was not under the sway of the desire nature. All muscles are expressions of the desire body and a straight road to the capital, where the traitorous mind is wedded to desire and reigns supreme.

If the United States were at war with France, it would not land troops in England, hoping in that way to subjugate the French. It would land its soldiers directly in France, and fight there.

Like a wise general, the Ego followed a similar course of action. It did not commence its campaign by getting control of one of the glands, for they are expressions of the vital body; nor was it possible to get control of the voluntary muscles, for they are too well garrisoned by the enemy. That part of the involuntary muscular system which is controlled by the sympathetic nervous system would also be useless for the purpose. It must get into a more direct touch with the cerebro-spinal nervous system. To do this, and secure a base of operations in the enemy's country, it must control a muscle which is involuntary, and yet connected with the voluntary nervous system. Such a muscle is the heart.

We have previously spoken of the two kinds of muscles--voluntary and involuntary. The latter are formed in lengthwise stripes and are connected with functions not under the control of the will, such as digestion, respiration, excretion, etc. The voluntary muscles are those which are controlled by the will through the voluntary nervous system, such as the muscles of the hand and arm. They are striped *both* lengthwise and crosswise.

The above is true of all muscles in the body *except the heart*, which is an involuntary muscle. Ordinarily, we cannot control the circulation. Under normal conditions the heart-beat is a fixed quantity, yet to the bewilderment of physiologists, the heart is *cross*-striped like a voluntary muscle. It is the only organ in the body exhibiting this peculiarity but, sphinx-like, it refuses to give material scientists an answer to the riddle.

The occult scientist easily finds the answer in the memory of nature. >From that record he learns that when the Ego first sought a stronghold in the heart, the latter was striped lengthwise only, the same as any other involuntary muscle; but as the Ego gained more and more control over the heart, the cross-stripes have gradually developed. They are not so numerous nor so

219

well defined as on the muscles under the full control of the desire body, but as the altruistic principles of love and brotherhood increase in strength and gradually overrule the reason, which is based in desire, so will these cross stripes become more numerous and more marked.

As previously stated, the seed-atom of the dense body is located in the heart during life and withdrawn only at death. The active work of the Ego is in the blood. Now, if we except the lungs, the heart is the only organ in the body through which all the blood passes in every cycle.

The blood is the highest expression of the vital body, for it nourishes the entire physical organism. It is also, in a sense, the vehicle of the subconscious memory, and in touch with the Memory of Nature, situated in the highest division of the Etheric Region. The blood carries the pictures of life from ancestors to descendants for generations, where there is a common blood, as produced by inbreeding. There are in the head three points, each of which is the particular seat of one of the three aspects of the spirit (See diagram 17), the second and third aspects having, in addition, secondary vantage grounds.

The desire body is the perverted expression of the Ego. It converts the "Selfhood" of the spirit into "selfishness." Selfhood seeks not its own at the expense of others. Selfishness seeks gain regardless of others. The seat of the human spirit is primarily in the pineal gland and secondarily in the brain and cerebro-spinal nervous system, which controls the voluntary muscles.

The love and unity in the World of the Life Spirit find their illusory counterpart in the Etheric Region, to which we are correlated by the vital body, which latter promotes sex love and sex union. The life spirit has its seat primarily in the pituitary body and secondarily in the heart, which is the gateway of the blood that nourishes the muscles.

The actionless Divine Spirit--The Silent Watcher--finds its material expression in the passive, inert and irresponsive skeleton of the dense body, which is the obedient instrument of other bodies, but has no power to act on its own initiative. The Divine Spirit has its strong hold in the impenetrable point at the root of the nose.

In reality there is but one spirit, the Ego, but looking at it from the Physical World, it is refracted into the three aspects, which work as stated.

As the blood passes through the heart, cycle after cycle, hour after hour all through life, it engraves the pictures it carries upon the seed-atoms while they are still fresh, thus making a faithful record of the life which is indelibly impressed on the soul in the *post mortem* existence. It is always in closest touch with the life spirit, the spirit of love and unity, therefore the heart is the home of altruistic love.

As these pictures pass inward to the World of Life Spirit, in which is the true memory of nature, they do not come through the slow physical senses, but directly through the fourth ether contained in the air we breathe. In the World of Life Spirit the life spirit sees much more clearly than it can in the denser Worlds. In its high home it is in touch with the Cosmic Wisdom and in any situation it knows at once what to do and flashes the message of guidance and proper action back to the heart, which as instantaneously flashes it on to the brain through the medium of the pneumogastric nerve, resulting in "first impressions"--the intuitional impulse, which is always good, because it is drawn directly from the fountain of Cosmic Wisdom and Love.

This is all done so quickly that the heart has control before the slower reason has had time to "take in the situation," as it were. It is the thought that man "thinketh in his heart," and it is true that "so is he." Man is inherently a virgin spirit, good, noble and true in every respect. All that is not good is from the lower nature, that illusory reflection of the Ego. The virgin spirit is always giving wise counsel. If we could only follow the impulses of the heart--the first thought--Universal Brotherhood would be realized here and now.

But that is just the point where the trouble begins. After the good counsel of the first thought has been given, the mind begins to reason, with the result that, in the great majority of cases, it dominates the heart. The telescope arranges its own focus and points where it lists, despite the astronomer. The mind and the desire body frustrate the designs of the spirit by taking control and, as they lack the spirit's wisdom, both spirit and body suffer.

Physiologists note that certain areas of the brain are devoted to particular thought activities and phrenologists have carried this branch of science still further. Now, it is known that thought breaks down and destroys nerve tissues. This and all other waste of the body is replaced by the blood. When, through the development of the heart into a voluntary muscle, the circulation of the blood finally passes under the absolute control of the unifying life spirit--the Spirit of Love--it will then be within the power of that spirit to withhold the blood from those areas of the brain devoted to selfish purposes. As a result, those particular thought centers will gradually atrophy.

On the other hand, it will be possible for the spirit to increase the blood supply when the mental activities are altruistic, and thus build up the areas devoted to altruism, so that, in time, the desire nature will be conquered and the mind emancipated by Love from its bondage to desire. It is only by complete emancipation, through Love, that man can rise above the law and become a law unto himself. Having conquered himself, he will have conquered all the World.

The cross stripes of the heart may be built by certain exercises under occult training, but as some of these exercises are dangerous, they should be undertaken only under the direction of a competent teacher. That no reader of this book may be deceived by imposters professing ability and willingness to so

221

train aspirants for a consideration, it is emphatically repeated that *No true occultist ever boasts, advertises his occult power, sells occult information or lessons at so much each or for a course; nor will he consent to a theatrical display. His work is done in the most unobtrusive manner possible and solely for the purpose of legitimately helping others, without thought of self.*

As said in the beginning of this chapter, all persons earnestly desiring the higher knowledge may rest assured that if they will but seek, they will find the way open for them. Christ Himself prepared the way for "whosoever will." He will help and welcome all real seekers who are willing to work for Universal Brotherhood.

The Mystery of Golgotha

During the last 2,000 years much has been said about "the cleansing blood." The blood of Christ has been extolled from the pulpit as the sovereign remedy for sin; the *only* means of redemption and salvation.

But if the laws of Rebirth and Consequence work in such a way that the evolving beings reap as they have sown, and if the evolutionary impulse is constantly bringing humanity higher and higher, ultimately to attain perfection--where then is the need for redemption and salvation? Even if the need existed, how can the death of one individual help the rest? Would it not be nobler to suffer the consequences of one's acts than to hide behind another? These are some of the objections to the doctrine of vicarious atonement and redemption by the blood of Christ Jesus. We will try to answer them before showing the logical harmony between the operation of the law of Consequence and the Atonement by Christ.

In the first place, it is absolutely true that the evolutionary impulse does work to achieve ultimate perfection for all; yet there are some who are constantly straggling behind. At the present time, we have just passed the extreme point of materiality and are going through the sixteen Races. We are treading "the sixteen paths to destruction," and are consequently in graver danger of falling behind than at any other part of the evolutionary journey.

In the abstract, time is nothing. A number may fall behind so far that they must be abandoned, to take up their further evolution in another scheme, where they can continue their journey to perfection. Nevertheless that was not the evolution originally designed for them and it is reasonable to suppose that the exalted Intelligences in charge of our evolution use every means to bring through in safety as many as possible of the entities under their charge.

In ordinary evolution, the laws of Rebirth and Consequence are perfectly adequate for bringing the major portion of the life wave up to perfection, but they do not suffice in the case of the stragglers, who are lagging behind in the various Races. During the stage of individualism, which is the climax of the illusion of separateness, all mankind needs extra help, but for the stragglers some additional special aid must be provided.

To give that special aid, to redeem the stragglers, was the mission of Christ. He said that He came to seek and to save that which was lost. He opened the way of Initiation for all who are willing to seek it.

Objectors to vicarious atonement urge: That it is cowardly to hide behind another; that each man should be willing to take the consequence of his acts.

Let us consider an analogous case. The waters of the Great Lakes narrow into the Niagara River. For twenty miles this enormous volume of water flows rapidly toward the falls. The river bed is filled with rocks and if a person who goes beyond a certain point does not lose his life in the rapids above the cataract, he will surely do so by the plunge over the brink.

Suppose a man appeared who, in pity for the victims of the current, placed a rope above the cataract, although he knew that the conditions were such that in doing so, he himself could not by any possible chance escape death. Yet gladly and of his own free will, he sacrificed his life and placed the rope, thus modifying former conditions so that any otherwise helpless victims who would grasp the rope would be saved and thenceforward none need be lost.

What would we think of a man who had fallen into the water through his own carelessness, and was struggling madly to reach the shore, if he should say: "What! Save myself and seek to avoid penalty of my carelessness by shielding myself behind the strength of another, who suffered through no fault of his own, and gave up his life that such as I might live? No, never! That would not be "manly." I will take my deserts!" Would we not all agree that the man was a fool?

Not all are in need of salvation. Christ knew that there is a very large class who do not require salvation in this way, but just as surely as there are the ninety-and-nine who are well taken care of by the laws of Rebirth and Consequence and will reach perfection in that way, so there are the "sinners" who have become "bogged" in matter and cannot escape without a rope. Christ came to save them and to bring peace and good will to all, by raising them to the necessary point of spirituality, causing a change in their desire bodies which will make the influence of the life spirit in the heart more potent.

His younger brother Sun spirits, the Archangels, had worked as Race-spirits on the desire bodies of man, but their work had been from *without*. It was simply a reflected spiritual Sun-force and came through the Moon--as moonlight is reflected sunlight. Christ, the Chief Initiate of the Sun spirits, entered directly into the dense body of the Earth and brought the direct Sun-force, thus enabling Him to influence our desire bodies from *within*.

223

Man cannot gaze long upon the Sun without becoming blind because its vibrations are so rapid that they destroy the retina of the eye. But he can look without harmful results upon the Moon, the vibrations from which are much slower; yet they are also sunlight, but the higher vibrations have been taken up by the Moon, which then reflects the residue to us.

So it is with the spiritual impulses which help man to evolve. The reason why the Earth was thrown off from the Sun was because our humanity could not endure the Sun's tremendous physical and spiritual impulses. Even after an enormous distance had been placed between the Earth and Sun, the spiritual impulse would still have been too strong had it not been sent first to the Moon, to be used by Jehovah, the Regent of the Moon, for man's benefit. A number of Archangels (ordinary Sun spirits) were given Jehovah as helpers in reflecting these spiritual impulses from the Sun upon the humanity of the Earth, in the form of Jehovistic or Race-religions.

The lowest vehicle of the Archangels is the desire body. Our desire body was added in the Moon Period, at which time Jehovah was the highest Initiate. Therefore Jehovah is able to deal with man's desire body. Jehovah's lowest vehicle is the human spirit (see diagram 14) and its counterpart is the desire body. The Archangels are His helpers because they are able to manage the spiritual Sun forces and the desire body is their lowest vehicle. Thus they are able to work with and prepare humanity for the time when it can receive the spiritual impulses directly from the Solar Orb, without the intervention of the Moon.

Upon Christ, as the highest Initiate of the Sun Period, is laid the task of sending out this impulse. The impulse which Jehovah reflected was sent out by Christ, Who thus prepared both the Earth and humanity for His direct ingress.

The expression, "prepared the Earth," means that all evolution on a planet is accompanied by the evolution of *that planet itself.* had some observer gifted with spiritual sight watched the evolution of our Earth from some distant star, he would have noticed a gradual change taking place in the Earth's desire body.

Under the old dispensation the desire bodies of people in general were improved by means of the law. This work is still going on in the majority of people, who are thus preparing themselves for the higher life.

The higher life (Initiation) does not commence, however, until the work on the vital body begins. The means used for bringing that into activity is Love, or rather Altruism. The former word has been so abused that it no longer conveys the meaning here required.

During the old dispensation the path of Initiation was not free and open, except to the chosen few. The Hierophants of the Mysteries collected certain families about the Temples, setting them apart from all the other people. These chosen families were then rigorously guarded as to certain rites and ceremonies. Their marriages and sexual intercourse were regulated by the Hierophants.

The effect of this was to produce a race having the proper degree of laxity between the dense and vital bodies; also to wake the desire body from its state of lethargy during sleep. Thus a special few were made fit for Initiation and were given opportunities that could not be given to all. We see instances of this method among the Jews, where the tribe of Levi were the chosen Templars; also in the caste of the Brahmins, who were the only priestly class among the Hindus.

The Mission of Christ, in addition to saving the lost, was to make Initiation possible to all, therefore Jesus was not a Levite of the class to which priest-hood came by inheritance. He came from the common people and though not of the teacher class, His teaching was higher than that of Moses.

Christ Jesus did not deny Moses, the law, nor the prophets. On the contrary, He acknowledged them all and showed the people that they were His witnesses, as they all pointed to One Who was to come. He told the people that those things had served their purpose and that henceforth Love must supersede Law.

Christ Jesus was killed. In connection with this fact, we come to the supreme and fundamental difference between Him and the previous teachers, in whom the Race spirits were born. They all died and must be reborn again and again to help their peoples bear their destiny. The Archangel Michael (the Race-spirit of the Jews) raised up Moses, who was taken up to Mount Nebo to die. He was reborn as Elijah. Elijah returned as John the Baptist; Buddha died and was reborn as Shankaracharya; Shri Krishna says, "Whenever there is decay of Dharma...and...exaltation of Adharma, then I myself come forth for the protection of the good, for the destruction of evil-doers, for the sake of firmly establishing Dharma. I am born from age to age."

When death came Moses' face *shone* and Buddha's body become *alight.* They all reached the stage when the spirit begins to shine from within--but then they died.

Christ Jesus reached that stage on the Mount of Transfiguration. It is of the very highest significance that *His real work took place subsequent to that event.* He suffered; was *killed*--and *resurrected.*

Being killed is a very different thing from dying. The blood that had been the vehicle of the Race-spirit must *flow* and be cleansed of that contaminating influence. Love of father and mother, exclusive of other fathers and mothers, must go--otherwise Universal Brotherhood and an all-embracing Altruistic Love could never become an actuality.

225

The Cleansing Blood

When the Savior Christ Jesus was crucified His body was pierced in five places; in the five centers where the currents of the vital body flow; and the pressure of the crown of thorns caused a flow from the sixth also. (This is a hint to those who already know these currents. A full elucidation of this matter cannot be publicly given out at this time.)

When the blood flowed from these centers, the great Sun-spirit Christ was liberated from the physical vehicle of Jesus and found Himself *in the Earth*, with individual vehicles. The already existing planetary vehicles He permeated with His own vehicles and, in the twinkling of an eye, diffused His own desire body over the planet, which has enabled Him thenceforth to work upon the Earth and its humanity from *within*.

At that moment a tremendous wave of spiritual sunlight flooded the Earth. It rent the veil which the Race-spirit had hung before the Temple to keep out all but the chosen few, and it made the Path of Initiation free thenceforth to whomsoever will. So far as concerned the Spiritual Worlds, this wave transformed the conditions of the Earth like a flash of lightning, but the dense, concrete conditions are, of course, much more slowly affected.

Like all rapid and high vibrations of light, this great wave blinded the people by its dazzling brilliance, therefore it was said that "the Sun was darkened." The very opposite was what actually occurred. The Sun was not darkened, but shone out in glorious splendor. It was the excess of light that blinded the people, and only as the entire Earth absorbed the desire body of the bright Sun-spirit did the vibration return to a more normal rate.

The expression, "the cleansing blood of Christ Jesus," means that as the blood flowed on Calvary, it bore with it the great Sun-spirit Christ, Who by that means secured admission to the earth itself and since that moment has been its Regent. He diffused His own desire body throughout the planet, thereby cleansing it from all the vile influences which had grown up under the *regime* of the Race-spirit.

Under the law all sinned; nay, more--they could not help it. They had not evolved to where they could do right for Love's sake. The desire nature was so strong that it was an impossibility for them to rule it altogether, therefore their debts, engendered under the law of Consequence, piled up to monstrous proportions. Evolution would have been terribly delayed and many lost to our life wave altogether it some help had not been given.

Therefore did Christ come "to seek and to save that which was lost." He took away the sin of the world by His cleansing blood, which gave Him entrance to the Earth and its humanity. He purified the conditions and we owe it to Him that we are able to gather for our desire bodies purer desire-stuff than formerly, and He continues working to help us, by making our external environment constantly purer.

That this was and is done at the expense of great suffering to Himself, no one can doubt who is able to form the least conception of the limitations endured by that Great Spirit in entering the hampering conditions of physical existence, even in the best and purest vehicle possible; nor is His present limitation as Regent of the Earth must less painful. True, He is also Regent of the Sun, and therefore only partially confined to the Earth, yet the limitations set by the crampingly slow vibrations of our dense planet must be almost unendurable.

Had Christ Jesus simply died, it would have been impossible for Him to have done this work, but the Christians have a *risen* Savior; One Who is ever present to help those who call upon His Name. Having suffered like unto ourselves in all things and knowing fully our needs, He is lenient toward our mistakes and failures so long as we continue trying to live the good life. We must ever keep before our eyes the fact that *the only real failure is ceasing to try.* Upon the death of the dense body of Christ Jesus, the seed atom was returned to the original owner, Jesus of Nazareth, who for some time afterward, while functioning in a vital body which he had gathered temporarily, taught the nucleus of the new faith which Christ had left behind. Jesus of Nazareth has since had the guidance of the esoteric branches which sprang up all over Europe.

In many placed the Knights of the Round Table were high Initiates in the Mysteries of the New Dispensation. So were the Knights of The Grail--to whom was finally confided Joseph of Arimathea's Grail Cup, which was used by Christ Jesus at The Last Supper. They were afterward entrusted also with the Lance which pierced His side, and the receptacle which received the blood from the wound.

The Druids of Ireland and the Trottes of Northern Russia were esoteric schools through which the Master Jesus worked during the so-called "Dark Ages," but, dark though they were, the spiritual impulse spread, and from the standpoint of the occult scientist they were "Bright Ages" compared to the growing materialism of the last 300 years, which has increased physical knowledge immensely, but has almost extinguished the Light of the Spirit.

Tales of "The Grail," "Knights of The Round Table," etc., are now scouted as superstitions and all that cannot be materially demonstrated is regarded as unworthy of belief. Glorious as are the discoveries of modern science, they have been bought at the terrible price of crushing the spiritual intuition and, from a spiritual standpoint, no darker day than the present has ever dawned.

The Elder Brothers, Jesus among them, have striven and are striving to counteract this terrible influence, which is like that in the eyes of the snake, causing the bird to fall into its jaws. Every attempt to enlighten people and awaken in them a desire to cultivate the spiritual side of life, is an evidence of the activity of the Elder Brothers.

May their efforts be crowned with success and speed the day when modern science shall be spiritualized and conduct its investigation of matter from the standpoint of spirit, for then, and not until then, will it arrive at a true knowledge of the world.

"As Above, So Below"

GROUP NO.	1	2	3	4	5	6	7
COMBINING CAPACITY	R^2O	$R\,O$	R^2O^3	$R\,O^2$ / $R\,M4$	$R_2\,O^5$ / $R\,H3$	$R\,O^3$ / $R\,H2$	$R_2\,O^7$ / $R\,H$
ATOMIC WEIGHT	L 1.7	GL. 9	B.10.9	C. 12	N. 14	O. 16	FL. 19
DENSITY	Na 0.37	Mg 1.75	Al 2.49	Si 2.65	S 2.06	P 1.84	Cl 1.38

The world, the man and the atom are governed by the same law. Our dense earth is now in its 4th stage of consolidation. The mind, the desire body and the vital body are less solid than our 4th vehicle, the dense body. In the atomic weight of the chemical elements there is a similar arrangement. The 4th group marks the acme of density.

Chapter Sixteen - Future Development and Initiation

The Seven Days of Creation

The Rosicrucian speaks of the Earth Period as Mars-Mercury. The great creative Day of Manifestation is embodied in the names of the days of the week, for our week-days have been named after the evolutionary stages through which the virgin spirits pass in their pilgrimage through matter.

Day.	Corresponds to the	Is ruled by
Saturday	Saturn Period	Saturn
Sunday	Sun Period	The Sun
Monday	Moon Period	The Moon
Tuesday	First half of the Earth Period	Mars
Wednesday	Second half of the Earth Period	Mercury
Thursday	Jupiter Period	Jupiter
Friday	Venus Period	Venus

The Vulcan Period is the last Period of our scheme of evolution. The quintessence of all the preceding Periods is extracted by the recapitulation of spiral after spiral. No new work is done until the very last Revolution on the very last Globe and then only in the Seventh Epoch. Therefore the Vulcan Period may be said to correspond to the week, which includes all of the seven days.

The claim of astrologers that the days of the week are ruled by the particular planet for which they are named, is well-founded. The ancients were also familiar with this occult knowledge, as is shown in their mythologies, in which the names of the gods are associated with the days of the week. Saturday is plainly "Saturn's day"; Sunday is correlated to the Sun, and Monday to the Moon. The Latins call Tuesday "Dies Martis," which obviously shows its connection with Mars, the god of war. The name "Tuesday" is derived from "Tirsdag," "Tir" or "Tyr," being the name of the Norse god of war. "Wednesday" was "Wotensdag," from Woten, also a Norse god; it is called "Dies Mercurii" by the Latins, showing its association with Mercury, as given in our list.

Thursday, or "Thorsdag," is named for "Thor," the Norse god of thunder, and is called "Dies Jovis" by the Latins, after the thunder god, "Jove" or "Jupiter."

Friday is named for the Norse goddess of beauty, "Freya," and for similar reasons, the Latins call it "Dies Veneris," or Day of Venus.

These names of periods have nothing to do with the physical planets, but refer to past, present or future incarnations of the Earth; for, again applying the Hermetic axiom, "As above, so below," the macrocosm must have its incarnations as well as the microcosm, man.

Occult science teaches that there are 777 incarnations, but that does not mean that the Earth undergoes 777 metamorphoses. It means that evolving life makes 7 Revolutions around the 7 Globes of the 7 World Periods.

This pilgrimage of Involution and Evolution, including the "short cut" of Initiation, is embodied in the Caduceus, or "Staff of Mercury" (see Diagram 15), so called because this occult symbol indicates The Path of Initiation, which has been open to man only since the beginning of the Mercury half of the Earth Period. Some of the lesser mysteries were given to the earlier Lemurians and Atlanteans, but not the Four Great Initiations.

THE SEVEN DAYS OF CREATION
AND
THE FOUR GREAT INITIATIONS

DIAGRAM 15

ORDINARY HUMANITY PURSUES THE SPIRAL PATH
THE INITIATE GOES THE STRAIGHT AND NARROW WAY THAT LEADS
TO
GOD

SATURN-PERIOD
(SATURDAY)
VIOLET

VULCAN-PERIOD
THE WEEK
(EMBRACING ALL THE DAYS)
WHITE
(INCLUDING ALL THE COLORS)

VENUS-PERIOD
(FRIDAY)
RED

SUN-PERIOD
(SUNDAY)
INDIGO

MOON-PERIOD
(MONDAY)
BLUE

JUPITER-PERIOD
(THURSDAY)
ORANGE

EARTH -
MERCURY-HALF
(WEDNESDAY)-YELLOW

- PERIOD
MARS-HALF
(TUESDAY) GREEN

THE WAY OF INITIATION
THERE WAS NO INITIATION PRIOR TO THE END OF THE
MARS HALF OF THE EARTH PERIOD. THE LESSER MYS-
TERIES EMBRACE HUMAN EVOLTION IN THE MERCURY
HALF OF THE EARTH-PERIOD

230

The black serpent on diagram 15 indicates the winding, cyclic path of Involution, comprising the Saturn, Sun and Moon Periods, and the Mars half of the Earth Period, during which the evolving life built its vehicles, not becoming fully awake and clearly conscious of the outside world until the latter part of the Atlantean Epoch.

The white serpent represents the path that the human race will follow through the Mercury half of the Earth Period, and the Jupiter, Venus, and Vulcan Periods, during which pilgrimage man's consciousness will expand into that of an omniscient, Creative Intelligence.

The serpentine path is the path followed by the great majority; but the "Staff of Mercury," around which the serpents twine, shows the "straight and narrow way," the path of Initiation, which enables those who walk therein to accomplish in a few short lives that which it requires millions of years for the majority of mankind to accomplish.

It need scarcely be said that no description of the initiatory ceremonies can be given, as the first vow of the Initiate is silence; but even if permissible, it would not be important. What concerns us in getting a bird's-eye view of the evolutionary path is to ascertain the results of the ceremonies.

The whole result of initiation is to give to the spiritually aspiring an opportunity to develop the higher faculties and powers in a short time and by severe training, thereby gaining the expansion of consciousness that all mankind will surely possess eventually, but which the vast majority choose to acquire through the slow process of ordinary evolution. We may know the states of consciousness and their concomitant powers attained by the candidate as he passes through successive great Initiations provided we know what those future states and powers will be for humanity in general. Some hints have been given and more may be logically deduced by an application of the law of Correspondences, to give a fairly rounded picture of the evolution in store for all of us, and the magnitude of the great steps in Initiation. To do this it may help us to glance back over the steps by which the consciousness of man has been evolved through the various Periods.

We remember that during the Saturn Period the unconsciousness of man was similar to that of the dense body when plunged into the deepest trance condition; this was succeeded, in the Sun period, by a dreamless-sleep consciousness. In the Moon Period the first glimmering of waking showed itself in inward pictures of outward things. The entire consciousness consisted of such inward representations of external objects, colors, or sounds. At last, in the latter part of the Atlantean Epoch, this picture consciousness, in which objects could be observed outside, clearly and distinctly outlined in space. When this objective-consciousness was attained, man became aware of an outside world and for the first time thoroughly realized the difference between "self" and "others." He then realized his separateness and thenceforth the "I" consciousness, Egoism, became paramount. As previous to that time there had been no thoughts nor ideas dealing with an outside world, there had consequently been no memory of events.

The change from the internal picture consciousness to the objective-self-consciousness was effected by a very slow process, commensurate with its magnitude, lasting from the existence on Globe C in the third Revolution of the Moon Period, until the latter part of the Atlantean Epoch.

During that time the evolving life passed through four *great* stages of ani-mal-*like* development before reaching the human stage. These steps of the past correspond to four stages *yet* to be passed through, and to the *four* initi-ations.

Within these four stages of consciousness previously passed there are alto-gether thirteen steps, and from man's present state to the last of the Great Initiations there are also thirteen initiations--the nine degrees of the lesser mysteries and the four Great Initiations.

There is a similar division among our present animals which can be traced through Form, because, as the form is the expression of life, so each step in its development must necessarily show a step forward in consciousness.

Cuvier was the first to divide the animal kingdom into four primary classes, but was not so successful in his division of these classes into sub-classes. The embryologist, Karl Ernst von Baer, also Professor Agassiz and other scien-tists, classify the animal kingdom into four primary and thirteen subdivi-sions, as follows:

I.	*Radiates:*		III.	*Articulates:*	
	1.	Polyps, Sea-anemones and Coral		1.	Worms
	2.	Acalephs, or Jelly-fish		2.	Crustacea (lobsters, etc.)
	3.	Starfish, Sea-urchins		3.	Insects
II.	*Mollusks:*		IV.	*Vertebrates:*	
	1.	Acephala (oysters, etc.)		1.	Fishes
	2.	Gastropoda (snails)		2.	Reptiles
	3.	Cephalopoda		3.	Birds
				4.	Mammals

The first three divisions correspond to the remaining three Revolutions of the Mercury half of the Earth Period, and their nine steps correspond to the nine degrees of the lesser mysteries, which will have been taken by humanity in general when it has reached the middle of the last Revolutions of the Earth Period. The fourth division in the list of the advancing animal kingdom has four subdivisions: Fishes, Reptiles, Birds, and Mammals. The steps in con-sciousness thus indicated correspond to similar states of advancement to be attained by humanity at the end of the Earth, Jupiter, Venus, and Vulcan Periods and which any qualified individual may now attain by initiation. The first of the Great Initiations gives the stage of consciousness which will be attained by ordinary humanity at the end of the Earth Period; the second that to which all will attain at the end of the Jupiter Period; the third gives the extension of consciousness to be reached at the close of the Venus Period; the last brings to the initiate the power and omniscience to which the majority will attain only at the end of the Vulcan Period.

The *Objective-Consciousness* by which we obtain knowledge of the outside world is dependent upon what we perceive through the medium of the senses. This we call "real," in contradistinction to our thoughts and ideas which come to us through our inner consciousness; their reality is not apparent to us in the same as that of a book or table, or other visible or tangible object in space. Thoughts and ideas seem misty and *un*real, therefore we speak of a "mere" thought, or of "just" an idea.

The ideas and thoughts of today, however, have an evolution before them; they are destined to become as real, clear and tangible as any of the objects of the outside world which we now perceive through the physical senses. At present, when a thing or a color is thought of, the picture or color presented by the memory to our inner consciousness is but a dim and shadowy one compared with the thing thought of.

As early as the Jupiter Period there will be a marked change in this respect. Then the dream-pictures of the Moon Period will return, but they will be subject to the call of the thinker, and not mere reproductions of outer objects. Thus there will be a combination of the pictures of the Moon Period and the thoughts and ideas consciously developed during the Earth Period, that is, it will be a *Self-Consciousness Picture-Consciousness.*

When a man of the Jupiter Period says "red," or speaks the name of an object, a clear and exact reproduction of the particular shade of red of which he is thinking, or of the object to which he refers, will be presented to his inner vision and will also be quite visible to the hearer. There will be no misconception as to what is meant by the words spoken. Thoughts and ideas will be alive and visible, therefore hypocrisy and flattery will be entirely eliminated. People can be seen exactly as they are. There will be both good and bad, but the two qualities will not be mingled in the same person. There will be the thoroughly good man and the downright evil man, and one of the serious problems of that time will be how to deal with the latter. The Manichees, an Order of still higher spirituality than the Rosicrucians, are at present studying that very problem. An idea of the condition anticipated may be gained from a short resume of their legend. (All mystic orders have a legend symbolic of their ideals and aspirations.)

In the legend of the Manichees there are two kingdoms--that of the Light-Elves and that of the Night Elves. The latter attack the former, are defeated and must be punished. But, as the Light-Elves are as thoroughly good as the Night-Elves are bad, they cannot inflict evil upon their foes, so *they must be punished with Good*. Therefore a part of the kingdom of the Light-Elves is incorporated with that of the Night-Elves and in this way the evil is in time overcome. Hate which will not submit to hate, must succumb to Love.

The internal pictures of the Moon Period were a certain expression of man's external environment. In the Jupiter Period the pictures will be expressed from within; they will be an outcome of the inner life of the man. He will also possess the additional faculty, which he cultivated in the Earth Period, of seeing things in space outside of himself. In the Moon Period he did not see the concrete thing, but only its soul-qualities. In the Jupiter Period he will see both, and will thus have a thorough perception and understanding of his surroundings. At a later stage in the same Period, this perceptive ability will be succeeded by a still higher phase. His power to form clear mental conceptions of colors, objects, or tones will enable him to contact and influence supersensuous beings of various orders and to secure their obedience, employing their forces as he wishes. He will be unable to send out from himself the forces wherewith to carry out his designs, however, and will be dependent upon the help of these superphysical beings, who will then be at his service.

At the close of the Venus Period he will be able to use his own force to give his pictures life and to set them out from himself as objects in space. He will then possess an *Objective, Self-Conscious, Creative-Consciousness* .

Very little can be said about the high spiritual consciousness which will be attained at the close of the Vulcan Period; it would be quite beyond our present comprehension.

Spirals within Spirals

It must not be supposed that these states of consciousness commence at the beginning of the Periods to which they belong and last until the end. There is always the Recapitulation, and therefore there must be the corresponding stages of consciousness on an ascending scale. The Saturn Revolution of any Period, the stay on Globe A, and the first Epoch on any Globe, are repetitions of the Saturn Period states of development. The Sun Revolution, the stay on Globe B, and the second Epoch on any Globe are Recapitulations of the Sun Period states of development, and so on, all the way through. Hence it will be seen that the consciousness which is to be the especial and peculiar result or product of any Period, does not begin to be evolved until all the Recapitulations have been made. The waking-consciousness of the Earth Period was not started until the Fourth Revolution, when the life wave had

234

reached the Fourth Glove (D), and was in the Fourth or Atlantean Epoch on that Globe.

The Jupiter Consciousness will not start in the Jupiter Period until the Fifth Revolution, when the Fifth Globe (E) has been reached and the Fifth Epoch commences on that Globe.

Correspondingly, the Venus consciousness will not begin until the Sixth Revolution has come to the Sixth Globe and Epoch, and the special Vulcan work will be confined to the very last Globe and Epoch, just before the Day of Manifestation closes.

The time required for passing through these respective Periods varies greatly. The further into matter the virgin spirits descent, the slower their progress and the more numerous the steps or stages of progression. After the nadir of material existence has been passed and the life wave ascends into more tenuous and mobile conditions, the progress is gradually accelerated. The Sun Period is of somewhat longer duration that the Saturn Period, and the Moon Period is longer than the Sun Period. The Mars (or first) half of the Earth Period is the longest half of any Period. Then the time begins to shorten again, so that the Mercury half of the Earth Period the latter three and a half Revolutions, will occupy less time that the Mars half; the Jupiter Period will be shorter than the Moon Period; the Venus Period shorter than the corresponding Sun Period; and the Vulcan Period the shortest Period of them all.

The states of consciousness of the different Periods may be tabulated as follows:

Period	Corresponding consciousness
Saturn	Unconsciousness corresponding to deep trance
Sun	Unconsciousness resembling dreamless sleep
Moon	Picture consciousness corresponding to dream state
Earth	Waking, objective consciousness
Jupiter	Self-conscious picture consciousness
Venus	Objective, Self-conscious, Creative consciousness
Vulcan	Highest Spiritual Consciousness

Having taken a general survey of the states of consciousness to be developed in the next three and a half Periods, we will now study the means of attainment.

Alchemy and Soulgrowth

The dense body was started in the Saturn Period, passed through various transformations in the Sun and Moon Periods, and will reach its highest development in the Earth Period.

The vital body was started in the second Revolution of the Sun Period, was reconstructed in the Moon and Earth Periods, and will reach perfection in the

Jupiter Period, which is its fourth stage, as the Earth Period is the fourth stage for the dense body.

The desire body was started in the Moon period, reconstructed in the Earth period, will be further modified in the Jupiter Period, reaching perfection in the Venus period.

The mind was started in the Earth Period, will be modified in the Jupiter and Venus Periods, and attain perfection in the Vulcan Period.

Reference to diagram 8 will show that the lowest Globe of the Jupiter Period is located in the Etheric Region. It would therefore be impossible to use the dense physical vehicle there, as only a vital body can be used in the Etheric Region. Yet it must not be supposed that after spending the time from the beginning of the Saturn Period to the end of the Earth Period in completing and perfecting this body, it is then thrown away that man may function in a "higher" vehicle!

Nothing in Nature is wasted. In the Jupiter Period the forces of the dense body will be superimposed upon the completed vital body. That vehicle will then possess the powers of the dense body in addition to its own faculties, and will therefore be a much more valuable instrument for the expression of the threefold spirit that if built from its own forces alone.

Similarly, Globe D of the Venus Period is located in the Desire World (see Diagram 8), hence neither a dense nor a vital body could be used as an instrument of consciousness, therefore the essences of the perfected dense and vital bodies are incorporated in the completed desire body, the latter thus becoming a vehicle of transcendent qualities, marvelously adaptable and so responsive to the slightest wish of the indwelling spirit that in our present limitations, it is beyond our utmost conception.

Yet the efficiency of even this splendid vehicle will be transcended when in the Vulcan period its essence, together with the essences of the dense and vital bodies, are added to the mind body, which becomes the highest of man's vehicles, containing within itself the quintessence of all that was best in all the vehicles. The vehicle of the Venus Period being beyond our present power of conception, how much more so is that which will be at the service of the divine beings of the Vulcan Period!

During involution the creative Hierarchies assisted man to arouse into activity the threefold spirit, the Ego, to build the threefold body, and to acquire the link of mind. Now, however, on the seventh day (to use the language of the Bible), God rests. Man must work out his own salvation. The threefold spirit must complete the working out of the plan begun by the Gods.

The human spirit, which was awakened during Involution in the Moon Period, will be the most prominent of the three aspects of the spirit in the evolution of the Jupiter Period, which is the corresponding Period on the upward arc of the spiral. The life spirit, which was started into activity in the Sun Period, will manifest its principal activity in the corresponding Venus Period, and the particular influences of the Divine Spirit will be strongest in the Vulcan Period, because it was vivified in the corresponding Saturn Period.

All three aspects of the spirit are active all the time during evolution but the principal activity of each aspect will be unfolded in those particular Periods, because the work to be done there is its special work.

When the threefold spirit had evolved the threefold body and gained control of it through the focus of Mind, it commenced to evolve the threefold soul by working from within. How much or how little soul a man has depends upon the amount of work the spirit has done in the bodies. This has been explained in the chapter describing *post mortem* experiences.

As much of the desire body as has been worked upon by the Ego is transmuted into the emotional soul, and is ultimately assimilated by the human spirit, the special vehicle of which is the desire body.

As much of the vital body as has been worked upon by the life spirit, becomes the Intellectual soul, and it builds the life spirit, because that aspect of the threefold spirit has its counterpart in the vital body.

As much of the dense body as has been worked upon by the Divine Spirit is called the Conscious soul, and is ultimately merged in the Divine Spirit, because the dense body is its material emanation.

The Conscious soul grows by action, external impacts, and experience.

The Emotional soul grows by the feelings and emotions generated by actions and experiences.

The Intellectual soul, as mediator between the other two, grows by the exercise of memory, by which it links together past and present experiences and the feelings engendered thereby, thus creating "sympathy" and "antipathy," which could not exist apart from memory, because the feelings resulting from experience alone would be evanescent.

During the involution the spirit progressed by growing bodies, but evolution depends upon soul growth--the transmutation of the bodies into soul. The soul is, so to say, the quintessence, the power or force of the body, and when a body has been completely built and brought to perfection through the stages and Periods as above described, the soul is fully extracted therefrom and is absorbed by the one of the three aspects of the spirit which generated the body in the first place; thus:

The *Conscious soul* will be absorbed by the *divine spirit* in the seventh Revolution of the Jupiter Period;

The *Intellectual soul* will be absorbed by the *life spirit* in the sixth Revolution of the Venus Period;

The *Emotional soul* will be absorbed by the *human spirit* in the fifth Revolution of the Vulcan Period.

The Creative Word

The mind is the most important instrument possessed by the spirit, and its special instrument in the work of creation. The spiritualized and perfected larynx will speak the creative Word, but the perfect mind will decide as to the particular form and the volume of vibration, and will thus be the determining factor. Imagination will be the spiritualized faculty directing the work of creation.

There is a strong tendency at the present time to regard the faculty of imagination slightingly, yet it is one of the most important factors in our civilization. If it were not for the imagination, we would still be naked savages. Imagination planned our houses, our clothes and our transportation and transmission facilities. Had not the inventors of these improvements possessed the mind and imagination to form mental images, the improvements could never have become concrete realities. In our materialistic day and age there is scarcely an effort made to conceal the contempt in which the faculty of imagination is generally held, and none feel the effects of this more acutely than inventors. They are usually classed as "cranks," and yet they have been the chief factors in the subjugation of the Physical World and in making our social environment what it is today. Any improvement in spiritual or physical conditions must first be imagined as a possibility before it can become an actuality.

If the student will turn to diagram 1 this fact will become clear. In the comparison there drawn between the functions of the different human vehicles and the part of a stereopticon, the mind corresponds to the lens. It is the focusing medium whereby the ideas wrought by the imagination of the spirit are projected upon the material universe. First they are thought forms only, but when the desire to realize the imagined possibilities has set the man to work in the Physical World, they become what we call concrete "realities."

At the present time, however, the mind is not focused in a way that enables it to give a clear and true picture of what the spirit imagines. It is not one-pointed. It gives misty and clouded pictures. Hence the necessity of experiment to show the inadequacies of the first conception, and bring about new imaginings and ideas until the image produced by the spirit in mental substance has been reproduced in physical substance.

At the best, we are able to shape through the mind only such images as have to do with Form, because the human mind was not started until the Earth Period, and therefore is now in its form, or "mineral" stage, hence in our operations we are confined to forms, to minerals. We can imagine ways

238

and means of working with the mineral forms of the three lower kingdoms, but can do little or nothing with the living bodies. We may indeed graft living branch to living tree, or living part of animal or man to other living part, but it is not *life* with which we are working; it is form only. We are making different conditions, but the life which already inhabited the form continues to do so still. To create life is beyond man's power until his mind has become alive.

In the Jupiter Period the mind will be vivified to some extent and man can then imagine forms which will live and grow, like plants.

In the Venus Period, when his mind has acquired "Feeling," he can create living, growing, and *feeling* things.

When he reaches perfection, at the end of the Vulcan Period, he will be able to "imagine" into existence creatures that will live, grown, feel, and *think*.

In the Saturn Period the life wave which is now man started on its evolution. The Lords of Mind were then human. They worked with man at that Period, when he was mineral. They now have nothing to do with the lower kingdoms, but are concerned solely with our human development.

Our present animals started their mineral existence in the Sun Period, at which time the Archangels were human, therefore the Archangels are the rulers and guides of the evolution of that which is now animal, but have nothing to do with plant or mineral.

The present plants had their mineral existence in the Moon period. The Angels were then human, therefore they have special concern with the life that now inhabits the plants, to guide it up to the human stage; but they have no interest in the minerals.

Our present humanity will have to work with the new life wave, which entered evolution in the Earth Period and *now ensouls the minerals*. We are now working with it by means of the faculty of imagination, giving it form--building it into ships, bridges, railways, houses, etc.

In the Jupiter Period we shall guide the evolution of the plant kingdom, for that which is at present mineral will then have a plant-like existence and we must work with it there as the Angels are now doing with our plant kingdom. Our faculty of imagination will be so developed that we shall have the ability, not only to create forms by means of it, but to endow those forms with vitality.

In the Venus Period our present mineral life wave shall have advanced another step, and we shall be doing for the animals of that period what the Archangels are now doing for our animals--giving them living and feeling forms.

Lastly, in the Vulcan Period it will be our privilege to give them a germinal mind, as the Lords of Mind did to us. The present minerals will then have become the humanity of the Vulcan Period, and we shall have passed through stages similar to those through which the Angels and Archangels are now passing. We shall then have reached a point in evolution a little higher that that of the present Lords of Mind, for remember, there is never an exact reproduction anywhere, but always progressive improvement, because of the spiral.

The Divine Spirit will absorb the human spirit at the close of the Jupiter Period; the life spirit at the close of the Venus Period; and the perfected Mind, embodying all that it has garnered during its pilgrimage through all the seven Periods, will be absorbed by the Divine Spirit at the close of the Vulcan Period. (There is no contradiction of the foregoing in the statement made elsewhere that the Emotional soul will be absorbed by the human spirit in the fifth Revolution of the Vulcan Period, because the latter will then be within the Divine Spirit.)

Then will succeed the long interval of subjective activity during which the virgin spirit will assimilate all the fruits of the septenary Periods of active Manifestation. It is then merged in God, from Whom it came, to re-emerge at the dawn of another Great Day, as One of His glorious helpers. During its past evolution its latent possibilities have been transmuted to dynamic powers. It has acquired *Soul-power* and a *Creative Mind* as the fruitage of its pilgrimage through matter. It has advanced from *impotence to Omnipotence, from nescience to Omniscience.*

Chapter Seventeen - The Method of Acquiring First-Hand Knowledge

The First Steps

The time has now come for pointing out the way by which each individual may investigate for himself all the facts with which we have dealt thus far in our study. As stated in the beginning, there are no special "gifts" bestowed upon any. All may know for themselves the truth concerning the pilgrimage of the soul, the past evolution and future destiny of the world, without being compelled to depend upon the veracity of another. There is a method whereby this valuable faculty may be acquired, and the earnest student qualify himself to investigate those super-physical realms; a method by which, if persistently followed, the powers of a God may be developed.

A simple illustration may indicate the first steps. The very best mechanic is well-nigh helpless without the tools of his craft. Indeed it is the hall-mark of a good artisan that he is very fastidious as to the quality and condition of the tools he uses, because he knows that the work depends as much upon their excellence as upon his skill.

The Ego has several instruments--a dense body, a vital body, a desire body, and a mind. These are its tools and upon their quality and condition depends how much or how little it can accomplish in its work of gathering experience in each life. If the instruments are poor and dull there will be but little spiritual growth and the life will be a barren one, so far as the spirit is concerned.

We generally estimate a "successful" life by the bank account, the social position attained, or the happiness resulting from a carefree existence and a sheltered environment.

When life is regarded is that way all the principal things that make for permanency are forgotten; the individual is blinded by the evanescent and illusionary. A bank account seems such a very real success, the fact is forgotten that from the moment the Ego leaves the body, it has no equity in gold nor any other earthly treasure. It may even have to answer for the methods employed in amassing that hoard and suffer great pain in seeing others spend it. It is forgotten that the important social position also disappears when the silver cord is loosed. Those who once fawned may then sneer, and even those who were faithful in life might shudder at the thought of an hour spent with no company but that of the dead. All that is of this life *alone* is vanity. Only that is of true value which can be taken with us across the threshold as the treasure of the spirit.

The hot-house plant may look very beautiful as it blooms in its sheltered glass house, but should the furnace fire go out, it would wither and die, while the plant that has grown in rain and sunshine, through storm and calm, will survive the winter and bloom afresh each year. From the viewpoint of the soul, happiness and a sheltered environment are generally unfortunate circumstances. The petted and fondled lap dog is subject to diseases of which the homeless cur, which has to fight for a scrap from a garbage can, knows nothing. The cur's life is hard, but it gets experience that makes it alert, alive and resourceful. Its life is rich in events, and it reaps a harvest of experience, while the pampered lap dog drones its time away in fearful monotony.

The case of a human being is somewhat similar. It may be hard to fight poverty and hunger, but from the standpoint of the soul it is infinitely preferable to a life of idle luxury. Where wealth is nothing more than a handmaid of *well thought out* philanthropy, which helps man in such a way as to *really* uplift him, it may be a very great blessing and a means of growth for its possessor, but when used for selfish purposes and oppression, it cannot be regarded as other than an unmitigated curse.

The soul is here to acquire experience through its instruments. These are the tools furnished to each at birth, and they are good, bad or indifferent according to what we have learned through past experience in the building of them. Such as they are we must work with them, if at all.

If we have become aroused from the usual lethargy and are anxious to progress, the question naturally arises, What must I do?

Without well-kept tools the mechanic can do no effective work; similarly, the instruments of the Ego must be cleansed and sharpened; then we may commence work to some purpose. As one works with those wonderful tools they themselves improve with proper use and become more and more efficient to aid in the work. The object of this work is *Union with the Higher Self.*

There are three steps by which this work conquers the lower nature, but they are not completely taken one after the other. In a certain sense they go together, so that at the present stage the first receives the most attention, the second less, and the third least of all. In time, when the first step has been wholly taken, naturally more attention can be paid to the other two.

There are three helps given in attaining these three stages. They can be seen in the outside world, where the great Leaders of humanity have placed them.

The first help is Race religions, which by aiding humanity to *overcome the desire body*, prepare it for union with the Holy Spirit.

The full operation of this help was seen on the Day of Pentecost. As the Holy Spirit is the Race God, all languages are expressions of it. That is why the apostles, when fully united and filled with the Holy Spirit, spoke with different tongues and were able to convince their hearers. Their desire bodies had been sufficiently purified to bring about the wished-for union and this is an earnest of what the disciple will one day attain to-- the power to speak all tongues. It may also be cited as a modern, historical example, that the Comte de St. Germain (who was one of the later incarnations of Christian Rosenkreuz the founder of our sacred Order), spoke all languages, so that all to whom he spoke thought he belonged to the same nation as they. He also had achieved union with the Holy Spirit.

In the Hyperborean Epoch, before man possessed a desire body, there was but one universal mode of communication and when the desire body has become sufficiently purified, all men will again be able to understand one another, for then the separative Race differentiation will have passed away.

The second help which humanity now has is the Religion of the Son--the Christian religion, the object of which is *union with Christ* by purification and control of the vital body.

Paul refers to this future state when he says: "Until Christ be formed in you," and exhorts his followers, as men who are running a race, to rid themselves of every weight.

The fundamental principle in building the vital body is repetition. Repeated experiences work on it to create memory. The Leaders of humanity, who desired to give us unconscious help by certain exercises, instituted prayer as a means of bringing pure and lofty thought to work on the vital body, and enjoined us to "pray without ceasing." Scoffers have often asked sneeringly why it should be thought necessary to always pray, because if God is omniscient He knows our needs and if He is not, our prayers will probably never reach Him; and if not omniscient, He cannot be omnipotent, and therefore could not answer prayer in any case. Many an earnest Christian may also have thought it wrong to be continually importuning the Throne of Grace.

Such ideas are founded upon a misunderstanding of facts. Truly God is omniscient and requires no reminder of our needs, but if we pray aright, we lift ourselves up to Him, thus working upon and purifying our vital bodies. If we pray aright--but that is the great trouble. We are generally much more concerned about temporal things than we are about spiritual upliftment. Churches will hold special meetings to pray for rain! And the chaplains of opposing armies or navies will even pray before a battle that success may follow their arms!

That is prayer to the Race God, Who fights the battles of His people, gives them increase of flocks and herds, fills their granaries and caters to the material wants. Such prayers are not even purifying. They are from the desire body, which sums up the situation thus: Now Lord, I am keeping your commandments to the best of my ability and I want You to do Your part in return.

Christ gave to humanity a prayer that is, like himself, unique and all-embracing. In it there are seven distinct and separate prayers; one for each of the seven principles of man--the threefold body, the threefold spirit and the link of mind. Each prayer is peculiarly adapted to promote the progression of that part of composite man to which it refers.

The purpose of the prayer relating to the threefold body is the spiritualization of those vehicles and the extraction therefrom of the threefold soul.

The prayers relating to the threefold spirit prepare it to receive the extracted essence, the threefold soul.

The prayer for the link of mind is to keep it in its proper relation as a tie between the higher and the lower nature.

The third help to be given to humanity will be the Religion of the Father. We can have very little conception of what that will be, save that the ideal will be even higher than Brotherhood and that by it the dense body will be spiritualized.

The Religions of the Holy Spirit, the Race religions, were for the uplifting of the human race through a feeling of kinship limited to a group--family, tribe or nation.

The purpose of the Religion of The Son, Christ, is to further uplift mankind by forming it into a Universal Brotherhood of separate individuals.

The ideal of the Religion of The Father will be the elimination of all separateness, merging all into One, so that there will be no "I" nor "Thou," but all will be One *in reality*. This will not come to pass while we are still inhabitants of the physical Earth, but in a future state where we shall realize our unity with all, each having access to all the knowledge garnered by each separate individual. Just as the single facet of a diamond has access to all the light that comes through each of the other facets, is one with them, yet bounded by lines which give it a certain individuality *without separateness*, so will the individual spirit *retain the memory of its particular experiences*, while giving to all others *the fruits* of its individual existence.

These are the steps and stages through which humanity is unconsciously being led.

In past ages the Race spirit reigned alone. Man was content with a patriarchal and paternal government in which he had no part. Now all over the world we see signs of the breaking down of the old system. The caste system, which was the stronghold of England in India, is crumbling. Instead of being separated into small groups, the people are uniting in the demand that the oppressor shall depart and leave them to live in freedom under a government of, by and for the people. Russia is torn by strife for freedom from a dictatorial, autocratic government. Turkey has awakened and taken a long stride toward liberty. Here in our own land, where we are supposed to be in the actual enjoyment of such liberty as others are, as yet, only able to covet or fight for, we are not yet satisfied. We are learning that there are other oppressions than those of an autocratic monarchy. We see that we have still industrial freedom to gain. We are chafing under the yoke of the trusts and an insane system of competition. We are trending toward co-operation, which is now practiced by the trusts within their own confines for private profit. We are desirous of a state of society where "they shall sit every man under his vine and under his fig tree; and none shall make them afraid."

Thus, all over the world, the old systems of paternal government are changing. Nations, as such, have had their day and are unwittingly working toward Universal Brotherhood in accordance with the design of our invisible Leaders, who are none the less potent in shaping events because they are not officially seated in the councils of nations.

These are the slow means by which the different bodies of humanity at large are being purified, but the aspirant to the higher knowledge works *consciously* to attain to these ends, by well-defined methods, according to his constitution.

Western Methods for Western People

In India, certain methods under different systems of Yoga, are used. Yoga means Union and, as in the West, the object of the aspirant is union with the

Higher Self; but to be efficacious, the methods of seeking that union must differ. The vehicles of a Hindu are very differently constituted from those of a Caucasian. The Hindus have lived for many, many thousands of years in an environment and climate totally different from ours. They have pursued a different method of thought and their civilization, though of a very high order, is different from ours in its effects. Therefore it would be useless for us to adopt their methods, which are the outcome of the highest occult knowledge and perfectly suited to them, but as unsuitable for the people of the West as a diet of oats would be for a lion.

For instance, in some systems it is required that the yogi shall sit in certain positions, that particular cosmic currents may flow through his body in a certain way to produce certain definite results. That instruction would be altogether useless for a Caucasian, as he is absolutely impervious to those currents, because of his way of living. If he is to attain results at all, he must work in harmony with the constitution of his vehicles. That is why the "Mysteries" were established in different parts of Europe during the Middle Ages. The Alchemists were deep students of the higher occult science. The popular belief that the object of their study and experimenting was the transmutation of baser metals into gold, was because they chose that symbolic way of describing their true work, which was the transmutation of the lower nature into spirit. It was thus described to lull the suspicions of the priests, without stating a falsehood. The statement that the Rosicrucians were a society devoted to the discovery and use of the formula for the making of the "Philosopher's Stone" was and is true. It is also true that most people have handled and do often handle this wondrous stone. It is common, but of no avail to any but the individual who makes it for himself. The formula is given in the esoteric training and a Rosicrucian is no different in that respect from the occultist of any other school. All are engaged in the making of this coveted stone, each, however, using his own methods, as there are no two individuals alike and consequently really effective work is always individual in its scope.

All occult schools are divisible into seven, as are the "Rays" of Life, the virgin spirits. Each School or Order belongs to one of these seven Rays, as does each unit of our humanity. Therefore any individual seeking to unite with one of these occult groups, the "Brothers" in which do not belong to his Ray, cannot do so with benefit to himself. The members of these groups are brothers in a more intimate sense than are the rest of humanity.

Perhaps if these seven Rays are compared to the seven colors of the spectrum, their relation to one another can be better understood. For instance, if a red ray were to ally itself with a green ray, inharmony would result. The same principle applies to spirits. Each must proceed with the group to which it belongs during manifestation, yet they are all one. As all the colors are con-

245

tained in the white light, but the refractive quality of our atmosphere seems to divide it into seven colors, so the illusory conditions of concrete existence cause the virgin spirits to seem grouped and this apparent grouping will abide while we are in this state.

The Rosicrucian Order was started particularly for those whose high degree of intellectual development caused them to repudiate the heart. Intellect imperiously demands a logical explanation of everything--the world mystery, the questions of life and death. The reasons for and the *modus operandi* of existence were not explained by the priestly injunction "not to seek to know the mysteries of God."

To any man or woman who is blest, or otherwise, with such an inquiring mind it is of paramount importance that they shall receive all the information they crave, so that when the head is stilled, the heart may speak. Intellectual knowledge is but a means to an end, not the end itself. Therefore, the Rosicrucian purposes first of all to satisfy the aspirant for knowledge that everything in the universe is reasonable, thus winning over the rebellious intellect. When it has ceased to criticize and is ready to accept provisionally, as *probably* true, statements which cannot be immediately verified, then, and not until then, will esoteric training be effective in developing the higher faculties whereby man passes from faith to first-hand knowledge. Yet, even then it will be found that, as the pupil progresses in first-hand knowledge and becomes able to investigate for himself, there are always truths ahead of him that he knows to be truths, but which he is not yet advanced sufficiently to investigate.

The pupil will do well to remember that nothing that is not logical can exist in the universe and that logic is the surest guide in all the Worlds, but he must not forget that his faculties are limited and that more than his own powers of logical reasoning may be needed to solve a given problem, although it may, nevertheless, be susceptible of full explanation, but by lines of reasoning which are beyond the capacity of the pupil at that stage of his development. Another point that must be borne in mind is that unwavering confidence in the teacher is absolutely necessary.

The foregoing is recommended to the particular consideration of all who intend taking the first steps toward the higher knowledge. If the directions given are followed at all, they must be given full credence as an efficacious means to accomplish their purpose. To follow them in a half-hearted manner would be of no avail whatever. Unbelief will kill the fairest flower ever produced by the spirit.

Work on the different bodies of man is carried on synchronously. One body cannot be influenced without affecting the others, but the principal work may be done on any one of them.

If strict attention is paid to hygiene and diet, the dense body is the one principally affected, but at the same time there is also an effect on the vital body and the desire body for, as purer and better materials are built into the dense body, the particles are enveloped in purer planetary ether and desire-stuff also, therefore the planetary parts of the vital and desire bodies become purer. If attention is paid to food and hygiene only, the personal vital and desire bodies may remain almost as impure as before, but it has become just a little easier to get into touch with the good than if gross food were used.

On the other hand if, despite annoyances, an equable temper is cultivated, also literary and artistic tastes, the vital body will produce an effect of daintiness and fastidiousness in physical matters and will also engender ennobling feelings and emotions in the desire body.

Seeking to cultivate the emotions also reacts upon the other vehicles and helps to improve them.

The Science of Nutrition

If we begin with the dense vehicle and consider the physical means available to improve it and make it the best possible instrument for the spirit and afterward consider the spiritual means to the same end, we shall be including all the other vehicles as well; therefore we shall follow that method.

The first visible state of a human embryo is a small, globulous, pulpy or jelly-like substance, similar to albumen, or the white of an egg. In this pulpy globule various particles of more solid matter appear. These gradually increase in bulk and density until they come in contact with one another. The different points of contact are slowly modified into joints or hinges and thus a distinct framework of solid matter, a skeleton, is gradually formed.

During the formation of this framework the surrounding pulpy matter accumulates and changes in form until at length that degree of organization develops which is known as a fetus. This becomes larger, firmer, and more fully organized up to the time of birth, when the state of infancy begins.

The same process of consolidation which commenced with the first visible stage of existence, still continues. The being passes through the different stages of infancy, childhood, youth, manhood or womanhood, old age, and at last comes to the change that is called death.

Each of these stages is characterized by an *increasing degree of hardness and solidity.*

There is a gradual increase in density and firmness of the bones, tendons, cartilages, ligaments, tissues, membranes, the coverings and even the very substance of the stomach, liver, lungs, and other organs. The joints become rigid and dry. They begin to crack and grate when they are moved, because the synovial fluid, which oils and softens them, is diminished in quantity and rendered too thick and glutinous to serve that purpose.

The heart, the brain, and the entire muscular system, spinal cord, nerves, eyes, etc., partake of the same consolidating process, growing more and more rigid. Millions upon millions of the minute capillary vessels which ramify and spread like the branches of a tree throughout the entire body, gradually choke up and change into solid fiber, no longer pervious to the blood.

The larger blood vessels, both arteries and veins, indurate, lose their elasticity, grow smaller, and become incapable of carrying the required amount of blood. The fluids of the body thicken and become putrid, loaded with earthy matter. The skin withers and grows wrinkled and dry. The hair falls off for lack of oil. The teeth decay and drop out for lack of gelatin. The motor nerves begin to dry up and the movements of the body become awkward and slow. The senses fail; the circulation of the blood is retarded; it stagnates and congeals in the vessels. More and more the body loses its former powers. Once elastic, healthy, alert, pliable, active and sensitive, it becomes rigid, slow, and insensible. Finally, it dies of old age.

The question now arises, What is the cause of this gradual ossification of the body, bringing rigidity, decrepitude, and death?

From the purely physical standpoint, chemists seem to be unanimous in the opinion that it is principally an increase of phosphate of lime (bone matter), carbonate of lime (common chalk), and sulphate of lime (plaster of Paris), with occasionally a little magnesia and an insignificant amount of other earthy matters.

The only difference between the body of old age and that of childhood is the greater density, toughness and rigidity, caused by the greater proportion of calcareous, earthy matter entering into the composition of the former. The bones of a child are composed of three parts of gelatin to one part of earthy matter. In old age this proportion is reversed. What is the source of this death-dealing accumulation of solid matter?

It seems to be axiomatic that the entire body is nourished by the blood and that everything contained in the body, of whatever nature, has first been in the blood. Analysis shows that the blood holds earthy substances of the same kind as the solidifying agents--and mark!--the *arterial* blood contains more earthy matter than the *venous* blood.

This is highly important. It shows that in every cycle the blood deposits earthy substances. It is therefore the common carrier that chokes up the system. But its supply of earthy matter must be replenished, otherwise it could not continue to do this. Where does it renew its deadly load? There can be but one answer to that question--from the food and drink; there is absolutely no other source.

248

The food and drink which nourish the body must be, at the same time, the primary source of the calcareous, earthy matter which is deposited by the blood all over the system, causing decrepitude and finally death. To sustain physical life it is necessary that we eat and drink but as there are many kinds of food and drink, it behooves us, in the light of the above facts, to ascertain, if possible, what kinds contain the smallest proportion of destructive matter. If we can find such food we can lengthen our lives and, from an occult standpoint, it is desirable to live as long as possible in each dense body, particularly after a start has been made toward the path. So many years are required to educate, through childhood and hot youth, each body inhabited, until the spirit can at last obtain some control over it, that the longer we can retain a body that has become amenable to the spirit's promptings, the better. Therefore it is highly important that the pupil partake of such food and drink only as will deposit the least amount of hardening matter and at the same time keep the excretory organs active.

The skin and the urinary system are the saviors of man from an early grave. Were it not that by their means, most of the earthy matter taken with our food is eliminated, no one would live ten years.

It has been estimated that ordinary, undistilled spring water contains carbonate and other compounds of lime to such an extent that the average quantity used each day by one person in the form of tea, coffee, soup, etc., would in forty years be sufficient to form a block of solid chalk or marble the size of a large man. It is also a significant fact that although phosphate of lime is always found in the urine of adults, it is not found in the urine of children, because in them the rapid formation of bone requires that this salt be retained. During the period of gestation there is very little earthy matter in the urine of the mother, as it is used in the building of the fetus. In ordinary circumstances, however, earthy matter is very much in evidence in the urine of adults and to this we owe the fact that physical life reaches even its present length.

Undistilled water, when taken internally, is man's worst enemy, but used externally, it becomes his best friend. It keeps the pores of the skin open, induces circulation of the blood and prevents the stagnation which affords the best opportunity for the depositing of the earthy, death-dealing phosphate of lime.

Harvey, who discovered the circulation of the blood, said that health denotes a free circulation and disease is the result of an obstructed circulation of the blood.

The bathtub is a great aid in keeping up the health of the body and should be freely used by the aspirant to the higher life. Perspiration, sensible and insensible, carries more earthy matter out of the body than any other agency.

249

As long as fuel is supplied and the fire kept free from ashes, it will burn. The kidneys are important in carrying away the ashes from the body, but despite the great amount of earthy matter carried away by the urine, enough remains in many cases to form gravel and stone in the bladder, causing untold agony and often death.

Let no one be deceived into thinking that water contains less stone because it has been boiled. The stone that forms on the bottom of the teakettle has been left there by the evaporated water which escaped from the kettle as steam. If the steam were condensed, we should have distilled water, which is an important adjunct in keeping the body young.

There is absolutely no earthy matter in distilled water, nor in rain water, snow nor hail (except what may be gathered by contact with house-tops, etc.), but coffee, tea, or soup made with ordinary water, no matter how long boiled, is not purified of the earthy particles; on the contrary, the longer they are boiled, the more heavily charged with ash they become. Those suffering from urinary diseases should never drink any but distilled water.

It may be said generally of the solid foods we take into our system, that fresh vegetables and ripe fruits contain the greatest proportion of nutritious matter and the least of earthy substances.

As we are writing for the aspirant to the higher life and not for the general public, it may also be said that animal food should be entirely avoided, if possible. No one who kills can go very far along the path of holiness. We do even worse than if we actually killed, for in order to shield ourselves from the personal commission of the act of killing, and still reap its results, we force a fellow being, through economic necessity, to devote his entire time to murder, thereby brutalizing him to such an extent that the law will not allow him to act as a juror in cases of capital crime, because his business has so familiarized him with the taking of life.

The enlightened know the animals to be their younger brothers and that they will be human in the Jupiter Period. We shall then help them as the Angels, who were human in the Moon Period, are now helping us, and for an aspirant to high ideals to kill--either in person or by proxy--is out of the question.

Several very important food products from animals, such as milk, cheese and butter, may be used. These are the results of the *processes* of life and require no tragedies to convert them into food. Milk, which is an important food for the occult student, contains no earthy matter of any consequence and has an influence upon the body possessed by no other food.

During the Moon Period man was fed upon the milk of Nature. Universal food was absorbed by him and the use of milk has a tendency to put him in touch with the Cosmic forces and enable him to heal others.

It is popularly supposed that sugar or any saccharine substance is injurious to the general health, and particularly to the teeth, causing their decay and the resulting toothache. Only under certain circumstances is this true. It is harmful in certain diseases, such as biliousness and dyspepsia, or if held long in the mouth as candy, but if sparingly used during good health and the amount gradually increased as the stomach becomes accustomed to its use, it will be found very nourishing. The health of Negroes becomes greatly improved during the sugar-cane harvest time, notwithstanding their increased labor. This is attributed solely to their fondness for the sweet cane-juice. The same may be said of horses, cows, and other animals in those localities, which are all fond of the refuse syrup fed to them. They grow fat in harvest time, their coats becoming sleek and shining. Horses fed on boiled carrots for a few weeks will get a coat like silk, owing to the saccharine juices of that vegetable. Sugar is a nutritious and beneficial article of diet and contains no ash whatever.

Fruits are an ideal diet. They are in fact evolved by the trees to induce animal and man to eat them, so that the seed may be disseminated, as flowers entice bees for a similar purpose.

Fresh fruit contains water of the purest and best kind, capable of permeating the system in a marvelous manner. Grape juice is a particularly wonderful solvent. It thins and stimulates the blood, opening the way into capillaries already dried and choked up--if the process has not gone too far. By a course of unfermented grape-juice treatment, people with sunken eyes, wrinkled skins and poor complexions become plump, ruddy and lively. The increased permeability enables the spirit to manifest more freely and with renewed energy. The following table (Part A), (Part B), which with the exception of the last column, is taken from the publications of the United States Department of Agriculture, will give the aspirant some idea of the amount it is necessary to eat for different degrees of activity, also the constituents of the various foods named.

Considering the body from a purely physical standpoint, it is what we might call a chemical furnace, the food being the fuel. The more the body is exercised, the more fuel it requires. It would be foolish for a man to change an ordinary diet which for years had adequately nourished him, and take up a new method without due thought as to which would be the best for serving his purpose. To simply eliminate meats from the ordinary diet of meat-eaters would unquestionably undermine the health of most persons. The only safe way is to experiment and study the matter out first, using due discrimination. No fixed rules can be given, the matter of diet being as individual as any other characteristic. All that can be done is to give the table of food values and describe the general influence of each chemical element, allowing the aspirant to work out his own method.

Neither must we allow the appearance of a person to influence our judgment as to the condition of his health. Certain general ideas of how a healthy person should look are commonly accepted, but there is no valid reason for so judging. Ruddy cheeks might be an indication of health in one individual and of disease in another. There is no particular rule by which good health can be known except the feeling of comfort and well-being which is enjoyed by the individual himself, irrespective of appearances.

The table of foods here given deals with five chemical compounds.

Water is the great solvent.

Nitrogen or proteid is the essential builder of flesh, but contains some earthy matter.

Carbohydrates or sugars are the principal power-producers.

Fats are the producers of heat and the storers of reserve force.

Ash is mineral, earthy, and chokes the system. We need have no fear of not obtaining it in sufficient quantities to build the bones; on the contrary, we cannot be too careful to get as little as possible.

The calorie is the simple unit of heat, and the table shows the number contained in each article of food when bought at the market. In a pound of Brazil nuts, for instance, 49.6% of the whole is waste (shells), but the remaining 50.4% contains 1485 calories. That means that about one-half of what is bought is waste, but the remainder contains the number of calories named. That we may get the greatest amount of strength from our food we must pay attention to the number of calories it contains, for from them we obtain the energy required to perform our daily work. The number of calories necessary to sustain the body under varying conditions is shown in the following table (per day):

Man at *very* hard muscular work:	5500 Calories
Man at moderately hard muscular work:	4150 Calories
Man at moderately active muscular work:	3400 Calories
Man at moderately *light* work:	3050 Calories
Man at sedentary work:	2700 Calories
Man without muscular exercise:	2450 Calories
Woman at light to moderate manual work:	2450 Calories

	Refuse %	Water %	Proteids %	Fat %	Carbo-hydrates %	Ash %	Fuel value in Calories per lb.	Time required for digestion H. M.
FRUITS.								
Apples, dried	....	28.1	1.6	2.2	66.1	2.0	1185	
Apples, fresh	25.0	63.3	0.3	0.3	10.8	0.3	190	2 :30
Apricots, dried	....	29.4	4.7	1.0	62.5	2.4	1125	
Bananas	35.0	48.0	0.8	0.4	14.3	0.6	260	1 :45
Cucumbers	15.0	81.1	0.7	0.2	2.6	0.4	65	
Dates, dried	10.0	13.8	1.9	2.5	70.6	1.2	1275	
Figs, dried	...	18.8	4.3	0.3	74.2	2.4	1280	3 :00
Grapes	25.0	58.0	1.0	1.2	14.4	0.4	295	
Lemons	30.0	62.5	0.7	0.5	5.9	0.4	125	
Muskmelons	50.0	44.8	0.3	....	4.6	0.3	80	3 :00
Oranges	27.1	63.4	0.6	0.1	8.5	0.4	150	2 :45
Pears	10.0	76.0	0.5	0.4	12.7	0.4	230	2 :00
Persimmons (edible part)	....	66.1	0.8	0.7	31.5	0.9	550	
Raisins, dried	10.0	13.1	2.3	3.0	68.5	3.1	1265	4 :00
Raspberries	...	85.8	1.0	....	12.6	0.6	220	3 :45
Squash	50.0	44.2	0.7	0.2	4.5	0.4	100	
Strawberries	5.0	85.9	0.9	0.6	7.0	0.6	150	2 :45
Tomatoes, canned	...	94.0	1.2	0.2	4.0	0.6	95	2 :00
Tomatoes, fresh	...	94.3	0.9	0.4	3.9	0.5	100	2 :00
Watermelons	59.4	37.5	0.2	0.1	2.7	0.1	50	
NUTS.								
Almonds	45.0	2.7	11.5	30.2	9.5	1.1	1515	4 :00
Brazil nuts	49.6	2.6	8.6	33.7	3.5	2.0	1485	4 :00
Butternuts	86.4	0.6	3.8	8.3	0.5	0.4	385	4 :00
Chestnuts, dried	24.0	4.5	8.1	5.3	56.4	1.7	1385	
Chestnuts, fresh	16.0	37.0	5.2	4.5	35.4	1.1	915	
Filberts	52.1	1.8	7.5	31.3	6.2	1.1	1430	4 :00
Hickory nuts	62.2	1.4	6.8	25.3	4.3	0.8	1145	4 :00
Pecans	53.2	1.4	5.2	33.3	6.2	0.7	1465	4 :00
Walnuts, Black	74.1	0.6	7.2	14.6	3.0	0.5	730	4 :00
Walnuts, English	58.1	1.0	6.9	26.6	6.8	0.6	1250	4 :00
GRAINS.								
Bread :								
Brown	....	43.6	5.4	1.8	47.1	2.1	1040	4 :00
Graham	....	35.7	8.9	1.8	52.1	1.5	1195	4 :00
Rye	....	35.7	9.0	0.8	53.2	1.5	1170	4 :00
White, fresh	....	35.3	9.2	1.3	53.1	1.1	1200	4 :30
White, stale	....	35.3	9.2	1.3	53.1	1.1	1200	3 :30
Whole Wheat	....	38.4	9.7	0.9	49.7	1.3	1139	4 :00
Corn, green, sweet, canned	....	76.1	2.8	1.2	19.0	0.9	430	3 :45
Corn, green, sweet (edible part)	....	75.4	3.1	1.1	19.7	0.7	440	3 :45
Cornmeal	....	12.5	9.2	1.9	75.4	1.0	1635	
Flour :								
Buckwheat	....	13.6	6.4	1.2	77.9	0.9	1605	
Graham	....	11.3	13.3	1.9	71.4	1.8	1645	
Rye	....	12.9	6.8	0.9	78.7	0.7	1620	
Wheat (high grade)	....	12.0	11.4	1.0	75.1	0.5	1635	
Wheat (low grade)	....	12.0	14.0	1.9	71.2	0.9	1640	
Whole Wheat	....	11.4	13.8	1.9	71.9	1.0	1650	
Macaroni, Vermicelli, etc.	....	10.3	13.4	0.9	74.1	1.3	1645	3 :00
Oat Breakfast Food	....	7.7	16.7	7.3	66.2	2.1	1800	
Oyster Crackers	....	4.8	11.3	10.5	70.5	2.9	1910	
Rice	....	12.3	8.0	0.3	79.0	0.4	1620	1 :00
Soda Crackers	....	5.9	9.8	9.1	73.1	2.1	1875	
Starch	....	....	....	....	90.0	....	1675	
Wheat Breakfast Food	....	9.6	12.1	1.8	75.2	1.3	1680	
LEGUMES								
Beans, baked, canned	....	68.9	6.9	2.5	19.6	2.1	555	3 :45
Beans, dried	....	12.6	22.5	1.8	59.6	3.5	1520	3 :45
Beans, Lima, shelled	....	68.5	7.1	0.7	22.0	1.7	540	3 :30
Beans, String	7.0	83.0	2.1	0.3	6.9	0.7	170	
Peas, canned	....	35.3	3.6	0.2	9.8	1.1	235	
Peas, dried	....	9.5	24.6	1.0	62.0	2.9	1565	
Peas, shelled	....	74.6	7.0	0.5	16.9	1.0	440	2 :35
Peanuts	24.5	6.9	19.5	29.1	18.5	1.5	1775	
VEGETABLES.								
Beets	20.0	70.0	1.3	0.1	7.7	0.9	160	3 :45
Cabbage	15.0	77.7	1.3	0.1	4.8	0.9	115	4 :30
Celery	20.0	75.6	0.9	0.1	2.6	0.8	65	3 :15
Lettuce	15.0	80.5	1.0	0.2	2.5	0.8	65	
Onions	10.0	62.6	1.4	0.3	8.9	0.5	190	2 :05
Parsnips	20.0	66.4	1.3	0.4	10.8	1.1	230	3 :30
Potatoes	20.0	62.6	1.8	0.1	14.7	0.8	295	3 :30
Rhubarb (pie plant)	40.0	56.6	0.4	0.4	2.2	0.4	60	
Spinach	...	92.3	2.1	0.3	3.2	2.1	95	
Sweet potatoes	20.0	55.2	1.4	0.6	21.9	0.9	440	
Turnips	30.0	62.7	0.9	0.1	5.7	0.6	120	4 :00
SUGARS.								
Candy, plain	....	....	....	....	96.0	....	1680	
Honey	....	....	....	....	81.0	....	1420	
Maple Syrup	....	....	....	....	71.4	....	1250	
Molasses	....	....	....	....	70.0	....	1225	
Sugar, granulated	....	....	....	....	100.0	....	1750	
MISCELLANEOUS.								
Chocolate	....	3.5	12.9	48.7	30.3	2.2	5625	
Cocoanuts	48.8	7.2	2.9	25.9	14.3	0.9	1295	
Cocoanuts, prepared	....	3.5	6.3	57.4	31.5	1.3	2805	
Cocoa, powdered	....	4.6	21.6	28.9	37.7	7.2	2160	
Mushrooms	....	88.1	3.5	0.4	6.8	1.2	185	1 :20
Tapioca	....	11.4	0.4	0.1	88.0	0.1	1650	2 :00

According to the table, it is evident that chocolate is the most nutritious food we have; also that cocoa, in its powdered state, is the most dangerous of all foods, containing three times as much ash as most of the others, and ten times as much as many. It is a powerful food and also a powerful poison, for it chokes the system more quickly than any other substance.

Of course, it will require some study at first to secure the best nourishment, but it pays in health and longevity and secures the free use of the body, making study and application to higher things possible. After a while the aspirant will become so familiar with the subject that he will need to give it no particular attention.

While the foregoing table shows the proportion of chemical substances contained in each article of food named, it must be remembered that not all of this is available for use in the system, because there are certain portions which the body refuses to assimilate.

Of vegetables, we digest only about 83% of the proteids, 90% of the fat, and 95% of the carbohydrates.

Of fruits, we assimilate about 85% of the proteids, 90% of the fat, and 90% of the carbohydrates.

The brain is the coordinating mechanism whereby the movements of the body are controlled and our ideas are expressed. It is built of the same substances as are all other parts of the body, with the addition of phosphorus, which is peculiar to the brain alone. (As to proportion.--Ed.)

The logical conclusion is that phosphorus is the particular element by means of which the Ego is able to express thought and influence the dense physical body. It is also a fact that the proportion and variation of this substance is found to correspond to the state and stage of intelligence of the individual. Idiots have very little phosphorus; shrewd thinkers have much; and in the animal world, the degree of consciousness and intelligence is in proportion to the amount of phosphorus contained in the brain.

It is therefore of great importance that the aspirant who is to use his body for mental and spiritual work, should supply his brain with the substance necessary for that purpose. Most vegetables and fruits contain a certain amount of phosphorus, but it is a peculiar fact that the greater proportion is contained in the leaves, which are usually thrown away. It is found in considerable quantities in grapes, onions, sage, beans, cloves, pineapples, in the leaves and stalks of many vegetables, and also in sugar-cane juice, but not in refined sugar.

The following table shows the proportions of phosphoric acid in a few articles:

100,000 parts of:

Barley, dry, contain, of phosphoric acid: 210 parts

Beans:	292 parts
Beets:	167 parts
Beets, Leaves of:	690 parts
Buckwheat:	170 parts
Carrots, dry:	395 parts
Carrots, Leaves of:	963 parts
Linseed:	880 parts
Linseed, Stalks of:	118 parts
Parsnips:	111 parts
Parsnips, Leaves of:	1784 parts
Peas:	190 parts

The gist of the preceding argument may be thus succinctly stated:

1. The body, throughout the entire period of life, is subject to a process of consolidation.
2. This process consists of the depositing by the blood of earthy substances, principally phosphate and carbonate of lime, by which the various parts become ossified, converted into bone, or kindred matter.
3. This conversion into bone destroys the flexibility of the vessels, muscles and other parts of the body subject to motion. It thickens the blood and entirely chokes up the minute capillaries, so that the circulation of the fluids and the action of the system generally diminishes, the termination of this process being death.
4. This process of consolidation may be retarded and life prolonged by carefully avoiding the foods that contain much ash; by using distilled water for internal purposes; and by promotion excretion through the skin by means of frequent baths.

The foregoing explains why some religions prescribe frequent ablutions as a religious exercise, because they promote the health and purify the dense body. Fasting was also prescribed for the same purpose. They give the stomach a much-needed rest, allow the body to eliminate the *effete* matter, and thus, if not too frequent or too prolonged, promote the health, but usually as much and more can be accomplished by giving the body proper foods which are the best medicines. Always the first care of the physician is to ascertain if there is proper excretion, that being Nature's chief means for ridding the body of the poisons contained in all foods.

In conclusion, let the aspirant choose such food as is most easily digested, for the more easily the energy in food is extracted, the longer time will the system have for recuperation before it becomes necessary to replenish the supply. Milk should never be drunk as one may drink a glass of water. Taken in that way, it forms in the stomach a large cheese ball, quite impervious to the action of the gastric juices. It should be sipped, as we sip tea or coffee. It will then form many small globules in the stomach, which are easily assimilated. Properly used, it is one of the best possible articles of diet. Citrus fruits are powerful antiseptics, and cereals, particularly rice, are antitoxins of great efficiency. Having now explained, from the purely material point of view, what is necessary for the dense body, we will consider the subject from the occult side, taking into consideration the effect on the two invisible bodies which interpenetrate the dense body.

The particular stronghold of the desire body is in the muscles and the cerebro-spinal nervous system, as already shown. The energy displayed by a person when laboring under great excitement or anger is an example of this. At such times the whole muscular system is tense and no hard labor is so exhausting as a "fit of temper." It sometimes leaves the body prostrated for weeks. There can be seen the necessity for improving the desire body by controlling the temper, thus sparing the dense body the suffering resulting from the ungoverned action of the desire body.

Looking at the matter from an occult standpoint, all consciousness in the Physical World is the result of the constant war between the desire and the vital bodies.

The tendency of the vital body is to soften and build. Its chief expression is the blood and the glands, also the sympathetic nervous system, having obtained ingress into the stronghold of the desire body (the muscular and the voluntary nervous systems) when it began to develop the heart into a voluntary muscle.

The tendency of the desire body is to harden, and it in turn has invaded the realm of the vital body, gaining possession of the spleen and making the white blood corpuscles, which are not "the policemen of the system" as science now thinks, but destroyers. It uses the blood to carry these tiny destroyers all over the body. They pass through the walls of arteries and veins whenever annoyance is felt, and especially in times of great anger. Then the rush of forces in the desire body makes the arteries and veins swell and opens the way for the passage of the white corpuscles into the tissues of the body, where they form bases for the earthy matter which kills the body.

Given the same amount and kind of food, the person of serene and jovial disposition will live longer, enjoy better health, and be more active than the person who worries, or loses his temper. The latter will make and distribute through his body more destructive white corpuscles than the former. Were a scientist to analyze the bodies of these two men, he would find that there was considerably less earthy matter in the body of the kindly disposed man than in that of the scold.

This destruction is constantly going on and it is not possible to keep all the destroyers out, nor is such the intention. If the vital body had uninterrupted sway, it would build and build, using all the energy for that purpose. There would be no consciousness and thought. It is because the body checks and hardens the inner parts that consciousness develops.

There was a time in the far, far past when we set out the concretions, as do the mollusks, leaving the body soft, flexible and boneless, but at that time we had only the dull, glimmering consciousness the mollusks now have. Before we could advance, it became necessary to retain the concretions and it will be found that the stage of consciousness of any species is in proportion to the development of the bony framework *within*. The Ego must have the solid bones with the semi-fluid red marrow, in order to be able to build the red blood corpuscles for its expression.

That is the highest development of the dense body. It signifies nothing in this connection that the highest class of animals have an internal bone formation similar to man's, but still have no indwelling spirit. They belong to a different stream of evolution.

The Law of Assimilation

The law of assimilation allows no particle to be built into our bodies that we, as spirits, have not overcome and made subject to ourselves. The forces active along these lines are, as we remember, principally our "dead," who have entered "heaven" and are learning there to build bodies to use here, but they work according to certain laws that they cannot circumvent. There is life in every particle of food that we take into our bodies, and before we can build that life into our bodies by the process of assimilation, we must overcome and make it subject to ourselves. Otherwise there could be no harmony in the body. All parts would act independently, as they do when the coordinating life has been withdrawn. That would be what we call decay, the process of disintegration, which is the direct opposite of assimilation. The more individualized is the particle to be assimilated, the more energy will it require to digest it and the shorter time will it remain before seeking to reassert itself.

Human beings are not organized in such a manner that they can live upon solid minerals. When a purely mineral substance, such as salt, is eaten, it passes through the body leaving behind it but very little waste. What it does leave, however, is of a very injurious character. If it were possible for man to use minerals as food, they would be ideal for that purpose because of their stability and the little energy required to overcome and subject them to the life of the body. We should be compelled to eat very much less in quantity and also less often than we now do. Our laboratories will some time supply us with chemical food of a quality far surpassing anything that we now have, which shall be always fresh. Food obtained from the higher plants and still more from the yet higher animal kingdom, is positively nauseating because of the rapidity of decay. This process is caused by the efforts made by the individual particles to escape from the composite whole.

The plant kingdom is next above the mineral. It has an organization capable of assimilating the mineral compounds of the Earth. Man and animal can assimilate the plants and thus obtain the chemical compounds necessary to sustain their bodies and as the consciousness of the plant kingdom is that of dreamless sleep, it offers no resistance. It requires but little energy to assimilate the particles thus derived and having small individuality of their own, the life ensouling the particles does not seek to escape from our body as soon as food derived from more highly developed forms, therefore the strength derived from a diet of fruit and vegetables is more enduring than that derived from a meat diet, and the food supply does not require as frequent replenishing, besides giving more strength in proportion, because less energy is required for assimilation.

Food composed of the bodies of animals consists of particles which have been worked upon and inter-penetrated by an individual desire body, and have thus been individualized to a much greater extent than the plant particles. There is an individual cell soul, which is permeated by the passions and desires of the animal. It requires considerable energy to overcome it in the first place, so that it may be assimilated, yet it never becomes so fully incorporated into the polity of the body as do the plant constituents, which have no such strong individual tendencies. The result is that it is necessary for the flesh-eater to consume a greater weight of food than is required by the fruitarian; also he must eat oftener. Moreover, this inward strife of the particles of flesh causes greater wear and tear of the body in general, rendering the meat-eater less active and capable of endurance than the vegetarian, as all contests between advocates of the two methods have demonstrated.

Therefore, when flesh food derived from the herbivora is such an unstable diet, it is evident that if we should try to use the flesh of carnivorous animals, in which the cells are still further individualized, we would be forced to consume enormous quantities of food. Eating would occupy the greater part of our time, but notwithstanding that fact, we would always be lean and hungry. That such is its effect, can be seen in the wolf and the vulture; their leanness and hunger are proverbial. Cannibals eat human flesh, but only at long intervals and as a luxury. As man does not confine himself exclusively to a meat diet, his flesh is not that of an entirely carnivorous beast, nevertheless the hunger of the cannibal has also become the burden of a proverb.

If the flesh of the herbivora were the essence of what is good in plants, then, logically, the flesh of the carnivora should be the quintessence. The meat of wolves and vultures would thus be the *creme de la creme*, and much to be desired. This we know is not the case, but quite the reverse. The nearer we get to the plant kingdom, the more strength we derive from our food. If the reverse were the case, the flesh of carnivorous animals would be sought by other beasts of prey, but examples of "dog eat dog" are very few throughout nature.

Live and Let Live

The first law of occult science is "Thou shalt not kill," and that should have the greatest weight with the aspirant to the higher life. We cannot create so much as one particle of dust, therefore what right have we to destroy the very least form? All Form is an expression of the One Life--the Life of God. We have no right to destroy the Form through which the Life is seeking experience, and force it to build a new vehicle.

Ella Wheeler Wilcox, with the true compassion of all far advanced souls, champions this occult maxim, in the following beautiful words:

I am the voice of the voiceless;
Through me the dumb shall speak
Till a deaf world's ear
Shall be made to hear
The wrongs of the wordless weak.

The same force formed the sparrow
That fashioned man, the king.
The God *of the Whole*

Gave a spark of soul
To furred and feathered thing.

And I *am my brother's keeper*;
And I will fight his fight,
And speak the word
For beast and bird
Till the world shall set things right.

Sometimes the objection is made that life is also taken when vegetables and fruits are eaten, but that statement is based upon a complete misunderstanding of the facts. When the fruit is ripe, it has accomplished its purpose, which is to act as a womb for the ripening of the seed. If not eaten, it decays and goes to waste. Moreover, it is designed to serve as food for the animal and human kingdoms, thus affording the seed opportunities for growth by scattering it in fertile soil. Besides, just as the ovum and the semen of human beings are ineffectual without the seed-atom of the reincarnating Ego and the matrix of its vital body, so any egg or seed, of itself, is devoid of life. If it is given the proper conditions of incubator or soil, the life of the group spirit is then poured into it, thus grasping the opportunity so afforded of producing a dense body. If the egg or seed is cooked, crushed, or not given the conditions necessary for the life, the opportunity is lost, but that is all.

At the present stage of the evolutionary journey, everyone knows inherently that it is wrong to kill and man will love and protect the animals in all cases where his greed and selfish interest does not blind him to their rights. The law protects even a cat or a dog against *wanton* cruelty. Except in "sport," that most wanton of all our cruelties against the animal creation, it is always for the sake of money that animals are murdered and bred to be murdered. By the devotees of "sport" the helpless creatures are shot down to no purpose save to bolster up a false idea of prowess upon the part of the huntsman. It is hard to understand how people who appear otherwise sane and kindly can, for the time, trample upon all their gentler instincts and revert to bloodthirsty savagery, killing for the sheer lust of blood and joy in destruction. It is certainly a reversion to the lowest savage animal instincts, and can never be dignified into the remotest semblance of anything "manly", even though practiced and defended by the otherwise humane and worthy temporary head of a mighty nation.

How much more beautiful it would be for man to play the role of friend and protector of the weak. Who does not love to visit Central Park in New York City and pet, stroke and feed the hundreds of squirrels which are running about secure in the knowledge that they will not be molested? And who is not glad, for the sake of the squirrels, to see the sign, "Dogs found chasing the squirrels will be shot." This is hard on the dogs, but it is to be commended as an evidence of the growth of the sentiment favoring the protection of the weak against the unreasoning or merciless strong. Nothing is said on the sign about the squirrels being injured by men, because that would be unthinkable. So strong is the influence of the trust the little animals repose in the kindness of man, that no one would violate it.

The Lord's Prayer

Returning to our consideration of the spiritual aids to human progress, the Lord's Prayer, which may be considered as an abstract, algebraical formula for the upliftment and purification of all the vehicles of man, the idea of taking proper care of the dense body is expressed in the words: "Give us this day our daily bread."

The prayer dealing with the needs of the vital body is, "Forgive us our trespasses, as we forgive those who trespass against us."

The vital body is the seat of memory. In it are stored the sub-conscious records of all the past events of our life, good or ill, including all injuries inflicted or sustained and benefits received, or bestowed. We remember that the record of the life is taken from those pictures immediately after leaving the dense body at death, and that all the sufferings of *post mortem* existence are the results of the events these pictures portray.

260

If, by continual prayer, we obtain forgiveness for the injuries we have inflicted upon others and if we make all the restitution possible, purify our vital bodies by forgiving those who have wronged us, and eliminate all ill feeling, we save ourselves much *post mortem* misery, besides preparing the way for Universal Brotherhood, which is particularly dependent upon the victory of the vital body over the desire body. In the form of memory, the desire body impresses upon the vital body the idea of revenge. An even temper amid the various annoyances of daily life indicates such a victory, therefore the aspirant should cultivate control of the temper, as it includes work on both bodies. The Lord's Prayer includes this also, for when we see that we are injuring others, we look about and try to find the cause. Loss of temper is one of the causes and it originates in the desire body.

Most people leave physical life with the same temperament they bring into it, but the aspirant must systematically conquer all attempts of the desire body to assume mastery. That can be done by concentration upon high ideals, which strengthens the vital body and is much more efficacious than the common prayers of the Church. The *occult scientist* uses concentration in preference to prayer, because the former is accomplished by the aid of the mind, which is cold and unfeeling, whereas prayer is usually dictated by emotion. Where it is dictated by a pure unselfish devotion to high ideals prayer is much higher than cold concentration. It can never be cold, but bears upon the pinions of Love the outpourings of the mystic to the Deity.

The prayer for the desire body is, "Lead us not into temptation." Desire is the great tempter of mankind. It is the great incentive to all action, and in so far as the actions subserve the purposes of the spirit, it is good; but where the desire is for something degrading, something that debases the nature, it is indeed meet that we pray not to be led into temptation.

Love, Wealth, Power, and Fame!--These are the four great motives of human action. Desire for one or more of these is the motive for all that man does or leaves undone. The great Leaders of humanity have wisely given them as incentives to action, that man may gain experience and learn thereby. They are necessary, and the aspirant may safely continue to use them as motives for action, but he must transmute them into something higher. He must overcome with nobler aspirations the selfish love which seeks the ownership of another body, and all desires for wealth, power and fame for narrow and personal reasons.

The Love for which he must long is that only which is of the soul and embraces all beings, high and low, increasing in proportion to the needs of the recipient;

The Wealth, that which consists solely of abundance of opportunities to serve his fellow men;

The Power, that alone which makes for the upliftment of humanity;

The Fame, none save that which increases his ability to spread the good news, that all who suffer may thus quickly find solace for the heart's grief.

The prayer for the mind is "Deliver us from evil." We have seen that mind is the link between the higher and the lower natures. Animals are permitted to follow desire without any restriction whatever. In their case, there is neither good nor evil, because they lack mind, the faculty of discrimination. The method of self-protection which we pursue in regard to animals which kill and steal is different from that which we use in relation to human beings who do the same things. Even a human being who is bereft of mind is not held accountable. The fact is recognized that he does not know he is doing wrong, therefore he is simply restrained.

It was only when his mental eyes were opened that man came to know good and evil. When the link of mind becomes allied to the Higher Self and does its bidding, we have the high-minded person. On the contrary, the coalition of the mind with the lower desire nature produces the low-minded person; therefore the meaning of this prayer is that we may be delivered from the experience resulting from the alliance of the mind with the desire body, with all thereby implied.

The aspirant to the higher life accomplishes the union of the higher and the lower natures by means of Meditation on lofty subjects. This union is further cemented by Contemplation, and both these states are transcended by Adoration, which lifts the spirit to the very Throne.

The Lord's Prayer, given for the general use of the Church, gives Adoration first place, in order to reach the spiritual exaltation necessary to proffer a petition representing the needs of the lower vehicles. Each aspect of the threefold spirit, commencing with the lowest, raises itself in adoration to its corresponding aspect of Deity. When the three aspects of the spirit are all arrayed before the Throne of Grace, each utters the prayer appropriate to the needs of its material counterpart, all three joining in the closing prayer for the mind.

The human spirit soars to its counterpart, the Holy Spirit (Jehovah), saying "Hallowed be Thy Name."

The life spirit bows before its counterpart, The Son (Christ), saying "Thy Kingdom Come."

The divine spirit kneels before its counterpart, The Father, with the prayer, "Thy Will be done."

Then the highest, the divine spirit, petitions the highest aspect of the Deity, the Father, for its counterpart, the dense body: "Give us this day our daily bread."

The next highest, the life spirit, prays to its counterpart, the Son, for its counterpart in the lower nature, the vital body: "Forgive us our trespasses as we forgive those who trespass against us."

The lowest aspect of the spirit, the human spirit, next offers its petition to the lowest aspect of Deity for the highest of the threefold bodies, the desire body: "Lead us not into temptation."

Lastly, in unison, all three aspects of the threefold spirit in man join in the most important of the prayers, the petition for the mind, in the words: "Deliver us from evil."

The introduction, "Our Father Who art in Heaven," is merely as the address on an envelope. The addition, "For Thine is the Kingdom, and the Power, and the Glory, forever. Amen," was not given by Christ, but is very appropriate as the parting adoration of the threefold spirit as it closes its direct address to the Deity.

Diagram 16 illustrates the foregoing explanation in a simple and easily remembered manner, showing the connection between the different prayers and the corresponding vehicles, which are similarly colored.

The Vow of Celibacy

The sex-pervert, or sex-maniac, is a proof of the correctness of the contention of occultists that one part of the sex-force builds the brain. He becomes an idiot, unable to think because of drawing and sending out, not only the negative or positive part of the sex force (according to whether male or female) which is normally to be used through the sex-organ for propagation, but in addition to that, some of the force which should build up the brain, enabling it to produce thought--hence the mental deficiency.

On the other hand, if the person is given to spiritual thought, the tendency to use the sex force for propagation is slight, and whatever part of it is not used in that way may be transmuted into spiritual force.

That is why the initiate, at a certain stage of development, takes the vow of celibacy. It is not an easy vow, nor one to be lightly taken by one desirous of spiritual advancement. Many people who are not yet ripe for the higher life have ignorantly bound themselves to a life of asceticism. They are as dangerous to the community and to themselves on the one hand as is the imbecile sex-maniac on the other.

At the present stage of human evolution the sex function is the means whereby bodies are provided, through which the spirit can gain experience. The people who are most prolific and follow the creative impulse unreservedly are the lowest classes; thus it is difficult for incoming entities to find good vehicles amid environments enabling them to unfold their faculties in such a manner as to permanently benefit themselves and the rest of humanity, for among the wealthier classes who could furnish more favorable conditions many have few or no children. It is not because they live abstemious sex-lives, but for the entirely selfish reasons that they may have more ease and leisure and indulge in unlimited sex-gratification without the burden of a family. Among the less wealthy middle class, families are also restricted, but in their case partially for economic reasons, that they may give one or two children educational and other advantages that their means would not permit them to give to four or five.

Thus man exercises his divine prerogative of bringing disorder into nature. Incoming Egos must take the opportunities offered them sometimes under unfavorable circumstances. Other Egos who cannot do that, must wait till favorable environment offers. Thus do we affect one another by our actions and thus are the sins of the fathers visited upon the children, for as the Holy Spirit is the creative energy in nature, the sex energy is its reflection in man, and misuse or abuse of that power is the sin that is not forgiven, but must be expiated in impaired efficiency of the vehicles, in order to thoroughly teach us the sanctity of the creative force.

Aspirants to the higher life, filled with an earnest desire to live a noble spiritual life, often regard the sex-function with horror, because of the harvest of misery which humanity has reaped as a result of its abuse. They are apt to turn in disgust from what they regard as impurity, overlooking the fact that it is precisely such people as they who (having brought their vehicles into good condition by means of proper sanitary food, high and lofty thought, and pure and spiritual lives) are best fitted to generate the dense bodies essential to the development of entities seeking incarnation. It is common knowledge among occult scientists that, to the detriment of the race, many high class Egos are kept out of incarnation at the present time solely because parents cannot be found who are pure enough to provide them with the necessary physical vehicles.

Persons who, for the reason above mentioned, refrain from doing their duty to humanity, are magnifying the sun spots to such an extent that they forget to see the Sun itself! The sex function has its great place in the economy of the world. When properly used, there is no greater boon to the Ego, for it then provides pure and healthful bodies such as man needs for his development; conversely, when abused, there is no greater curse, for it is then the source of the worst ills to which flesh is heir.

It is a truism that "no man liveth unto himself." By our words and acts we are constantly affecting others. By the proper performance, or the neglect of our duty, we make or mar the lives, first, of those in our immediate environment, but ultimately of all the inhabitants of the Earth, and more. No one has a right to seek the higher life without having performed his duty to his family, his country, and the human race. To selfishly set aside everything else and live solely for one's own spiritual advancement, is as reprehensible as not to care for the spiritual life at all. Nay, it is worse; for those who do their duty in the ordinary life to the best of their ability, devoting themselves to the welfare of those dependent upon them, are cultivating the essential quality of faithfulness. They will certainly advance in due time to a point where they will become awake to spiritual necessities, and will carry to that work the faithfulness developed elsewhere. The man who deliberately turns his back upon his present duties to take up the spiritual life will surely be forced back into the path of duty from which he has mistakenly diverged, with no possible means of escape until the lesson has been learned.

Certain tribes of India make the following excellent division of life. The first twenty years are spent in obtaining an education; the years from 20 to 40 are devoted to the duty of raising a family; and the remaining time is devoted to spiritual development, without any physical cares to harass or distract the mind.

During the first period the child is supported by its parents; during the second period the man, in addition to supporting his own family, cares for his parents while they are giving their attention to higher things; and during the balance of his life, he is in turn supported by his children.

This seems a very sensible method, and is quite satisfactory in a country where all, from the cradle to the grave, feel the spiritual need, to such degree that they mistakenly neglect material development except as impelled by the lash of direst need, and where the children cheerfully support their parents, secure in the knowledge that they will be supported in turn and thus be enabled to devote themselves entirely to the higher life after having performed their duty to their country and to humanity. In the Western World, however, where no spiritual need is at present felt by the average man because he is properly following material lines of development, such a mode of life would be impossible of realization.

Spiritual desire never comes until the time is ripe, and always when the particular conditions obtain under which we must seek its gratification, if at all. Whatever duties exist which are apparent restrictions must be borne. If the care of a family prevents the complete consecration desired, the aspirant would certainly not be justified in neglecting duty and devoting the entire time and energy to spiritual purposes. An effort must be made to gratify such aspirations without interfering with duty to family.

If the desire to live a celibate life comes to a person who holds marriage relations with another, the obligations of such relations are not to be forgotten. It would be very wrong, by practicing celibacy under such circumstances, to endeavor to escape from the *proper* performance of duty. As to what constitutes duty in regard to coition, however, there is a standard for aspirants to the higher life different from that of the ordinary man or woman.

Most people regard marriage as sanctioning unlimited license for the gratification of sexual desire. In the eyes of statute law, perhaps it does so, but no man-made law nor custom has any right to govern this matter. Occult science teaches that the sex-function should *never* be used for sense-gratification, but for propagation *only*. Therefore an aspirant to the higher life would be justified in refusing coition with the marriage partner unless the object were the begetting of a child, and then only if both parties were in perfect health--physically, morally and mentally--as otherwise the union would be likely to result in the generation of a feeble or degenerate body.

Each person owns his or her body, and is responsible to the law of Consequence for any misuse resulting from the weak willed abandonment of that body to another.

In the light of the foregoing, and looking at the matter from the viewpoint of occult science, it is both a duty and a privilege (to be exercised with thanks for the opportunity) for all persons who are healthy and of sound mind to provide vehicles for as many entities as is consistent with their health and ability to care for the same. And, as previously stated, most particularly are aspirants to the higher life under obligation in this respect, on account of the purification which their purer lives have wrought in their bodies, because of which they are better qualified than ordinary humanity to generate pure vehicles. Thus they enable high-class entities to find suitable vehicles and help humanity to advance by affording these waiting Egos opportunities to incarnate and exercise their influence at an earlier period than would otherwise be possible.

If the sex force is used in the way indicated, coition will take place but few times in a life, and practically the entire sex force may be used for spiritual purposes. It is not the use, but the abuse that causes all the trouble and interferes with the spiritual life, so there is no need for anyone to abandon the higher life because he or she cannot be celibate. It is not necessary to be strictly celibate while going through the lesser Initiations. The vow of absolute celibacy applies to the greater Initiations only, and even then a single act of fecundation may sometimes be necessary as an act of sacrifice, as was the case in providing a body for Christ.

It may also be said that it is worse to suffer from a burning desire, to be constantly thinking vividly of the gratification of sense, than to live the married life in moderation. Christ taught that unchaste thoughts are as bad as, and even worse than unchaste acts, because thoughts may be repeated indefinitely, whereas there is at least some limit to acts.

The aspirant to the higher life can be successful only in proportion to the extent of the subjugation of the lower nature, but should beware of the other extreme.

The Pituitary Body and the Pineal Gland

In the brain, and in approximately the positions shown in diagram 17, are two small organs called the pituitary body and the pineal gland. Medical science knows but little about these, or the other ductless glands of the body. It calls the pineal gland "the atrophied third eye," yet neither it nor the pituitary body are atrophying. This is very perplexing to scientists, for nature retains nothing useless. All over the body we find organs which are either atrophying or developing, the former being milestones, as it were, along the path which man has traveled to reach his present stage of development, the latter pointing out the lines for future improvement and development. For instance, the muscles which animals use to move the ears are present in man also, but as they are atrophying, few people can use them. The heart belongs to the class indicating future development; as already shown, it is becoming a voluntary muscle.

The pituitary body and the pineal gland belong to still another class of organs, which at the present time are neither evolving nor degenerating, but are dormant. In the far past, when man was in touch with the "inner" Worlds, these organs were his means of ingress thereto, and they will again serve that purpose at a later stage. They were connected with the involuntary or sympathetic nervous system. Man then saw the inner Worlds, as in the Moon Period and the latter part of the Lemurian and early Atlantean Epochs. Pictures presented themselves quite independent of his will. The sense centers of his desire body were spinning around counter-clockwise (following negatively the motion of the Earth, which revolves on its axis in that direction) as the sense centers of "mediums" do to this day. In most people these sense-centers are inactive, but true development will set them spinning clockwise, as explained elsewhere. That is the difficult feature in the development of positive clairvoyance.

The development of mediumship is much easier, because it is merely a revival of the mirror-like function possessed by man in the far past, by which the outside world was involuntarily reflected in him, and which function was afterward retained by inbreeding. With present day mediums this power is intermittent, which explains why they can sometimes "see" and at other times, for no apparent reason, fail utterly. Occasionally, the strong desire of the client enables them to get into touch with the information he is seeking, on which occasions they see correctly, but they are not always honest. Office rent and other expenses must be paid, so when the power (over which they have no conscious control) fails them, some resort to fraud and utter any absurdity that occurs to their minds, in order to satisfy their client and get his money, thus casting discredit upon what they really do see at other times.

The aspirate to true spiritual sight and insight must first of all give proof of unselfishness, because the trained clairvoyant has no "off days." He is not in the least mirror-like, dependent upon the reflections which may happen to come his way. He is able to reach out at any time and in any direction, and read the thoughts and plans of others, provided he particularly turns his attention that way--not otherwise.

The great danger to society which would result from the indiscriminate use of this power if possessed by an unworthy individual, can be easily understood. He would be able to read the

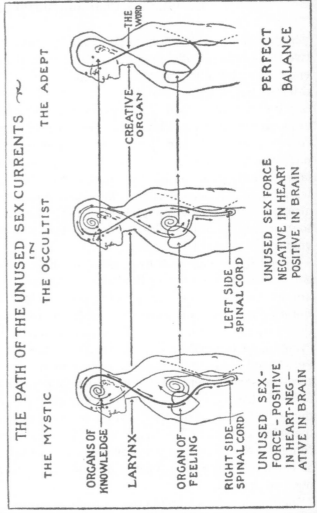

most secret thought. Therefore the initiate is bound by the most solemn vows never to use this power to serve his individual interest in the slightest degree, nor to save himself a pang. He may feed five thousand others if he will, but he must not turn a stone into bread to appease his own hunger. He may heal others of palsy and leprosy, but by the Law of the Universe, he is forbidden to stanch his own mortal wounds. Because he is bound by his vow of absolute unselfishness, it is ever true of the Initiate that although he saves others, himself he cannot save.

So the trained clairvoyant who really has something to give will never hang out a sign offering to exercise his gifts for a fee, but will give and give freely where he considers it consistent with the ripe destiny generated under the law of consequence by the person to be helped.

Trained clairvoyance is the kind used for investigating occult facts, and it is the only kind that is of any use for that purpose. Therefore the aspirant must feel, not a wish to gratify an idle curiosity, but a holy and unselfish desire to help humanity. Until such a desire exists, no progress can be made in the attainment of positive clairvoyance.

In the ages that have passed since the Lemurian Epoch humanity has been gradually building the cerebro-spinal nervous system, which is under the control of the will. In the latter part of the Atlantean Epoch, this was so far evolved that it became possible for the Ego to take full possession of the dense body. That was the time (previously described) when the point in the vital body came into correspondence with the point at the root of the nose in the dense body and the indwelling spirit became awake in the Physical World but, so far as the greater part of humanity was concerned, lost consciousness of the inner Worlds.

Since then, the connection of the pineal gland and the pituitary body with the cerebro-spinal nervous system has been slowly building, and is now all but complete.

To regain contact with the inner Worlds, all that remains to be done is the reawakening of the pituitary body and the pineal gland. When that is accomplished, man will again possess the faculty of perception in the higher worlds, but on a grander scale than formerly, because it will be in connection with the voluntary nervous system and therefore under the control of his Will. Through this inner perceptive facility all avenues of knowledge will be opened to him and he will have at his service a means of acquiring information compared with which all other methods of investigation are but child's play.

The awakening of these organs is accomplished by Esoteric Training, which we will now describe, as far as may be done in public.

Esoteric Training

In the majority of people, the greater part of the sex force which may legitimately be used through the creative organs is expended for sense-gratification; therefore in such people there is very little of the ascending current shown in diagram 17.

When the aspirant to the higher life begins to curb these excesses more and more, and to devote his attention to spiritual thoughts and efforts, the trained clairvoyant can perceive the unused sex force commencing to ascend.

269

It surges upward in stronger and stronger volume, along the path indicated by the arrows in diagram 17, traversing the heart and the larynx or the spinal cord and the larynx or both, and then passing directly between the pituitary body and the pineal gland toward the dark point at the root of the nose where "The Silent Watcher," the highest spirit, has its seat.

These currents do not usually take one of the two paths indicated in the diagram to the entire exclusion of the other, but generally one path is traveled by the greater volume of the sex-currents, according to the temperament of the aspirant. In one who is seeking enlightenment along purely intellectual lines the current travels particularly over the spinal cord and only a small part goes over the path through the heart. In the mystic who feels rather than knows, the currents find their way upwards through the heart.

Both are developing abnormally, and each must sometime take up the development he has neglected, so as to become fully rounded. Therefore the Rosicrucians aim to give a teaching that will satisfy both classes, although their main efforts are expended in reaching the intellectually minded, for their need is the greater.

This current of itself, however, even though it assumes the proportions of a Niagara and flows until the crack of doom, will be useless. But still, as it is not only a necessary accompaniment, but a pre-requisite to self-conscious work in the inner World, it must be cultivated to some extent before the real esoteric training can begin. It will thus be seen that a moral life devoted to spiritual thought must be lived by the aspirant for a certain length of time before it is possible to commence the work that will give him first-hand knowledge of the super-physical realms and enable him to become, in the truest sense, a helper of humanity.

When the candidate has lived such a life for a time sufficient to establish the current of spiritual force, and is found worthy and qualified to receive esoteric instruction, he is taught certain exercises, to set the pituitary body in vibration. This vibration causes the pituitary body to impinge upon and slightly defect the nearest line of force (See diagram 17). This, in turn, impinges upon the line next to it, and so the process continues until the force of the vibration has been spent. It is similar to the way in which the striking of one note on a piano will produce a number of overtones, by setting up a vibration in the other strings which are at proper intervals of pitch.

When by the increased vibration of the pituitary body, the lines of force have been deflected sufficiently to reach the pineal gland, the object has been accomplished, the gap between these two organs has been bridged. This is the bridge between the World of Sense and the World of Desire. From the time it is built, man becomes clairvoyant and able to direct his gaze where he will. Solid objects are seen both inside and out. To him space and solidity, as

270

hindrances to observation, have ceased to exist.

He is not yet a *trained* clairvoyant, but he *is* a clairvoyant *at will*, a voluntary clairvoyant. He is a very different faculty from that possessed by the medium, who is usually an involuntary clairvoyant and can see only what comes; or who has, at best, very little more than the purely negative faculty. But the person in whom this bridge is once built is always in sure touch with the inner Worlds, the connection being made and broken at his will. By degrees, the observer learns to control the vibration of the pituitary body in a manner enabling him to get in touch with any of the regions of the inner Worlds which he desires to visit. The faculty is completely under the control of his will. It is not necessary for him to go into a trance or do anything abnormal, to raise his consciousness to the Desire World. He simply *wills* to see, and sees.

As we explained in the earlier part of this work, the neophyte must learn to see in the Desire World, or rather, he must learn how to understand what he sees there. In the Physical World objects are dense, solid, and do not change in the twinkling of an eye. In the Desire World they change in the most erratic manner. This is a source of endless confusion to the negative involuntary clairvoyant, and even to the neophyte who enters under the guidance of a teacher, but the teaching soon brings the pupil to a point where the Form may change as often as it will; he can perceive the Life that causes the change, and knows it for what it is, despite all possible and puzzling changes.

There is also another and most important distinction to be made. The power which enables one to *perceive* the objects in a world is *not* identical with the power of *entering* that world and *functioning* there. The voluntary clairvoyant, though he may have received some training, and is able to distinguish the true from the false in the Desire World, is in practically the same relation to it as a prisoner behind a barred window is to the outside world-- he can see it, but cannot function therein. Therefore esoteric training not only opens up the inner vision of the aspirant, but at the proper time further exercises are given to furnish him with a vehicle in which he can function in the inner Worlds in a perfectly self-conscious manner.

How the Inner Vehicle is Built

In ordinary life most people live to eat, they drink, gratify the sex-passion in an unrestrained manner, and lose their tempers on the slightest provocation. Though outwardly these people may be very "respectable," they are, nearly every day of their lives, causing almost utter confusion in their organization. The entire period of sleep is spent by the desire and the vital bodies in repairing the damage done in the day time, leaving no time for outside work of any kind. But as the individual begins to feel the needs of the higher life, control sex force, and temper, and cultivate a serene disposition, there is less disturbance caused in the vehicles during waking hours; consequently less time is required to repair the damage during sleep. Thus it becomes possible to leave the dense body for long periods during sleeping hours, and function in the inner Worlds in the higher vehicles. As the desire body and the mind are not yet organized, they are of no use as separate vehicles of consciousness. Neither can the vital body leave the dense body, as that would cause death, so it is evident that measures must be taken to provide an organized vehicle which is fluidic and so constructed that it will meet the needs of the Ego in the inner Worlds as does the dense body in the Physical World.

The vital body is such an organized vehicle, and if some means could be found to loosen it from the dense body without causing death, the problem would be solved. Besides, the vital body is the seat of memory, without which it would be impossible to bring back into our physical consciousness the remembrance of super-physical experiences and thus obtain the full benefit of them.

We remember that the Hierophants of the old Mystery Temples segregated some of the people into castes and tribes such as the Brahmins and the Levites, for the purpose of providing bodies for use of such Egos as were advanced enough to be ready for Initiation. This was done in such a manner that the vital body became separable into two parts, as were the desire bodies of all humanity at the beginning of the Earth Period. When the Hierophant took the pupils out of their bodies he left one part of the vital body, comprising the first and second ethers, to perform the purely animal functions (they are the only ones active during sleep), the pupil taking with him a vehicle capable of perception, because of its connection with the sense-centers of the dense body; and also capable of memory. It possessed these capabilities because it was composed of the third and fourth ethers, which are the mediums of sense-perception and memory.

This is, in fact, that part of the vital body which the aspirant retains from life to life, and immortalizes as the Intellectual Soul.

Since Christ came and "took away the sin of the world," (not of the individual) purifying the desire body of our planet, the connection between all human dense and vital bodies has been loosened to such an extent that, by training, they are capable of separation as above described. Therefore Initiation is open to all.   The finer part of the desire body, which constitutes the Emotional Soul, is capable of separation in most people (in fact, it possessed that capability even before Christ came) and thus when, by concentration and the use of the proper formula, the finer parts of the vehicles have been segregated for use during sleep, or at any other time, the lower parts of the

272

desire and vital bodies are still left to carry on the processes of restoration in the dense vehicle, the mere animal part.

That part of the vital body which goes out is highly organized, as we have seen. It is an exact counterpart of the dense body. The desire body and the mind, not being organized, are of use only because they are connected with the highly organized dense body. When separated from it they are but poor instruments, therefore before man can withdraw from the dense body, the sense-centers of the desire body must be awakened.

In ordinary life the Ego is *inside* its bodies and its force is directed *outward*. All man's will and energy are bent upon the task of subduing the outside world. At no time is he able to get away from the impressions of his outside environment and thus be free to work on himself in his waking hours. During sleep, when such an opportunity is afforded, because of the dense body having lost consciousness of the world, the Ego is *outside* his bodies. If man is to work on his vehicle at all, it must be when the outside world is shut out as in sleep, but yet the spirit still remains within and in full control of the faculties, as it is in the waking state. Not until such a state can be attained will it be possible for the spirit to work inwardly and properly sensitize its vehicles.

Concentration is such a state. When in it, the senses are stilled and a person is outwardly in the same condition as in the deepest sleep, yet the spirit remains within and fully conscious. Most people have experienced this state, at least in some degree, when they have become interested in absorption in a book. At such times they live in the scenes depicted by the author and are lost to their environment. When spoken to, they are oblivious to the sound, so to all else transpiring around them, yet they are fully awake to all they are reading, to the invisible world created by the author, living there and feeling the heart-beats of all the different characters in the story. They are not independent, but are bound in the life which some one has created from them in the book.

The aspirant to the higher life cultivates the faculty of becoming absorbed *at will* in any subject he chooses, or rather not a subject usually, but a very simple object, which he imagines. Thus when the proper condition or point of absorption has been reached where his senses are absolutely still, he concentrates his thought upon the different sense centers of the desire body and *they start to revolve.*

At first their motion is slow and hard to bring about, but by degrees the sense centers of the desire body will make places for themselves within the dense and vital bodies, which learn to accommodate themselves to this new activity. Then some day, when the proper life has developed the requisite cleavage between the higher and lower parts of the vital body, there is a supreme effort of the will; a spiral motion in many directions takes place, and the aspirant stands *outside his dense body*. He looks at it as at another person. The door of this prison house has been opened. He is free to come and go, as much at liberty in the inner worlds as in the Physical World, functioning at will, in the inner or outer World, a helper of all desiring his services in any of them.

Before the aspirant learns to voluntarily leave the body, he may have worked in the desire body during sleep, for in some people the desire body becomes organized before the separation can be brought about in the vital body. Under those conditions it is impossible to bring back these subjective experiences to waking consciousness, but generally in such cases it will be noticed, as the first sign of development, that all confused dreams will cease. Then, after a while, the dreams will become more vivid and perfectly logical. The aspirant will dream of being in places and with people (whether known to him in waking hours or not matters little), conducting himself in as reasonable a way as if he were in the waking state. If the place of which he dreams is accessible to him in waking hours, he may sometimes get proof of the reality of his dream if he will note some physical detail of the scene and verify his nocturnal impression next day.

He will next find that he can, during sleeping hours, visit any place he desires upon the face of the Earth and investigate it a great deal more thoroughly than if he had gone there in the dense body, because in his desire body he has access to all places, regardless of locks and bars. If he persists, there will at last come a day when he need not wait for sleep to dissolve the connection between his vehicles, but can consciously set himself free.

Specific directions for freeing the higher vehicles cannot be given indiscriminately. The separation is brought about, not by a set formula of *words*, but rather by *an act of will*, yet the manner in which the will is directed is individual, and can therefore be given only by a competent teacher. Like all other real esoteric information, it is never sold, but comes only as a result of the pupil qualifying himself to receive it. All that can be done here is to give an indication of the first steps which lead up to the acquirement of the faculty of voluntary clairvoyance.

The most favorable time to exercise is on first awakening in the morning, before any of the worries and cares of daily life have entered the mind. At that time one is fresh from the inner Worlds and therefore more easily brought back into touch with them than at any other time of the day. Do not wait to dress, or sit up in bed, but relax the body perfectly and let the exercises be the first waking thought. Relaxation does not mean simply a comfortable position; it is possible to have every muscle tense *with expectation* and that of itself frustrates the object, for in that condition the desire body is gripping the muscles. It cannot do otherwise till we calm the mind.

Concentration

The first thing to practice is fixing one's thoughts upon some ideal and holding them there *without letting them swerve*. It is an exceedingly hard task, but, to some extend at least, it must be accomplished before it is possible to make any further progress. Thought is the power we use in making images, pictures, thought forms, according to ideas from within. It is our principal power, and we must learn to have absolute control of it, so that what we produce is not wild illusion induced by outside conditions, but true imagination generated by the spirit from within (see diagram 1).

Skeptics say that it is *all* imagination but, as said before, if the inventor had not been able to imagine the telephone, etc., we would not today possess those things. His imaginings were not generally correct or true at first, otherwise the inventions would have worked successfully from the beginning, without the many failures and apparently useless experiments that have nearly always preceded the production of the practical and serviceable instrument or machine. Neither is the imagination of the budding occult scientist correct at first. The only way to make it true is by uninterrupted practice, day after day, exercising the will to keep the thought focused upon one subject, object, or idea, exclusive all else. Thought is a great power which we have been accustomed to waste. It has been allowed to flow on aimlessly, as water flows over a precipice before it is made to turn the wheel.

The rays of the Sun, diffused over the entire surface of the Earth, produce only a moderate warmth, but if even a few of them are concentrated by means of a glass, they are capable of producing fire at the focusing point.

Thought-force is the most powerful means of obtaining knowledge. If it is concentrated upon a subject, it will burn its way through any obstacle and solve the problem. If the requisite amount of thought-force is brought to bear, there is nothing that is beyond the power of human comprehension. So long as we scatter it, thought-force is of little use to us, but as soon as we are prepared to take the trouble necessary to harness it, all knowledge is ours.

We often hear people exclaim petulantly, "Oh, I cannot think of a hundred things at once!" when really that is exactly what they have been doing, and what has caused the very trouble of which they complain. People are constantly thinking of a hundred things other than the one they have in hand. Every success has been accomplished by persistent concentration upon the desired end.

This is something the aspirant to the higher life must positively learn to do. There is no other way. At first he will find himself thinking of everything under the sun instead of the ideal upon which he has decided to concentrate, but he must not let that discourage him. In time he will find it easier to still his senses and hold his thoughts steady. Persistence, *persistence*, and always *persistence* will win at last. Without that, however, no results can be expected. It is of no use to perform the exercises for two or three mornings or weeks and then neglect them for as long. To be effective they must be done faithfully every morning without fail.

Any subject may be selected, according to the temperament and mental persuasion of the aspirant, so long as it is pure and mentally uplifting in its tendency. Christ will do for some; others, who love flowers particularly, are most easily helped by taking one as the subject of concentration. The object matters little, but whatever it is we must imagine it true to life in all details. If it is Christ, we must imagine a real Christ, with mobile features, life in His eyes, and an expression that is not stony and dead. We must build a living ideal, not a statue. If it is a flower, we must, in imagination, take the seed and having buried it in the ground, fix our mind upon it steadily. Presently we shall see it burst, shooting forth its roots, which penetrate the Earth in a spiral manner. From the main branches of the roots we watch the myriads of minute rootlets, as they branch out and ramify in all directions. Then the stem begins to shoot upward, bursting through the surface of the earth and coming forth as a tiny green stalk. It grows, presently there is an off-set; a tiny twig shoots out from the main stem. It grows; another off-set and a branch appears; from the branches, little stalks with buds at the end shoot out; presently there are a number of leaves. Then comes a bud at the top; it grow larger until it begins to burst and the red leaves of the rose show beneath the green. It unfolds in the air, emitting an exquisite perfume, which we sense perfectly as it is wafted to us on the balmy summer breeze which gently sways the beautiful creation before the mind's eye.

Only when we "imagine" in such clear and complete outlines as these, do we enter into the spirit of concentration. There must be no shadowy, faint resemblance.

Those who have traveled in India have told of fakirs showing them a seed, which was planted and grew before the eyes of the astonished witness, bearing fruit which the traveler tasted. That was done by concentration so intense that the picture was visible, not only to the fakir himself, but also the spectators. A case is recorded where the members of a committee of scientist all saw the wonderful things done before their eyes, under conditions where sleight-of-hand was impossible, yet the photographs which they obtained while the experiment was in progress, came to naught. There was no impression on the sensitive plates, because there had been no material, concrete objects. At first the pictures which the aspirant builds will be but shadowy and poor likenesses, but in the end he can, by concentration, conjure up an image more real and alive than things in the Physical World.

When the aspirant has become able to form such pictures and has succeeded in holding his mind upon the picture thus created, he may try to drop the picture suddenly and, holding his mind steady without any thought, wait to see what comes into the vacuum.

For a long time nothing may appear and the aspirant must carefully guard against making visions for himself, but if he keeps on faithfully and patiently every morning, there will come a time when, the moment he has let the imaged picture drop, in a flash the surrounding Desire World will open up to his inner eye. At first it may be but a mere glimpse, but it is an earnest of what will later come at will.

Meditation

When the aspirant has practiced concentration for some time, focusing the mind upon some simple object, building a living thought form by means of the imaginative faculty, he will, by means of Meditation, learn all about the object thus created.

Supposing that the aspirant has, by concentration, called up the image of the Christ. It is very easy to meditatively recall the incidents of His life, suffering and resurrection, but much beyond that can be learned by meditation. Knowledge never before dreamed of will flood the soul with a glorious light. Yet something that is uninteresting and does not of itself suggest anything marvelous, is better for practice. Try to find out all about--say, a match, or a common table.

When the image of the table has been clearly formed in the mind, think what kind of wood it is and whence it came. Go back to the time when, as a tiny seed, the tree from which the wood was cut first fell into the forest soil. Watch it grow from year to year, covered by the snows of winter and warmed by the summer Sun, steadily growing upward--its roots meanwhile constantly spreading under the ground. First it is a tender sapling, swaying in the breeze; then, as a young tree, it gradually stretches higher and higher toward the air and the sunshine. As the years pass, its girth becomes greater and greater, until at last one day the logger comes, with his axe and saw gleaming as they reflect the rays of the winter Sun. Our tree is felled and shorn of its branches, leaving but the trunk; that is cut into logs, which are hauled over the frozen roads to the river bank, there to await the springtime when the melting snow swells the streams. A great raft of the logs is made, the pieces of our tree being among them. We know every little peculiarity about them and would recognize them instantly among thousand, so clearly have we marked them in our mind. We follow the raft down the stream, noting the passing landscape and become familiar with the men who have the care of the raft and who sleep upon little huts built upon their floating charge. At last we see it arrive at a sawmill and disbanded. One by one the logs are grasped by prongs on an endless chain and hauled out of the water.

Here comes one of our logs, the widest part of which will be made into the top of our table. It is hauled out of the water to the log deck and rolled about by men with peavies. We hear the hungry whine of the great circular saws as they revolve so fast that they appear as mere blurs before our eyes. Our log is placed upon a carriage which is propelled toward one of them, and in a moment those teeth of steel are tearing their way through its body and dividing it into boards and planks. Some of the wood is selected to form part of a building, but the best of it is taken to a furniture factory and put into a kiln, where it is dried by steam so that it will not shrink after it has been made into furniture. Then it is taken out and put through a great planing machine with many sharp knives, which makes it smooth. Next it is sawn off into different lengths and glued together to form table-tops. The legs are turned from thicker pieces and set into the frame which supports the top; then the whole article is smoothed again with sandpaper, varnished and polished, thus completing the table in every respect. It is next sent out, with other furniture, to the store where we bought it, and we follow it as it is carted from that place to our home and left in our dining room.

Thus, by meditation, we have become conversant with the various branches of industry necessary to convert a forest tree into a piece of furniture. We have seen all the machines and the men, and noted the peculiarities of the various places. We have even followed the life process whereby that tree has grown from a tiny seed, and have learned that back of seemingly very commonplace things there is a great and absorbingly interesting history. A pin; the match with which we light the gas; the gas itself; and the room in which that gas is burned--all have interesting histories, well worth learning.

Observation

One of the most important aids to the aspirant in his efforts is observation. Most people go through life blind-folded. Of them it is literally true that they "have eyes, and see not; . . . have ears, and hear not." Upon the part of the majority of humanity there is a deplorable lack of observation.

Most people are, to some extent, excusable for this, because their sight is not normal. Urban life has caused untold damage to the eyes. In the country the child learns to use the muscles of the eye to the full extent, relaxing or contracting them as required to see objects at considerable distances in the open, or close at hand in and about the house. But the city-bred child sees practically *everything* close at hand and the muscles of its eyes are seldom used to observe objects at any great distance, therefore that faculty is to a great extent lost, resulting in a prevalence of near-sightedness and other eye troubles.

It is very important to one aspiring to the higher life that he be able to see all things about him in clear, definite outlines, and in full detail. To one suffering from defective sight, the use of glasses is like opening up a new world. Instead of the former mistiness, everything is seen clearly and definitely. If the condition of the sight requires the use of two foci, one should not be content with having two pairs of glasses, one for near and one for far seeing, thus necessitating frequent changes. Not only are the changes wearisome, but one is very apt to forget one pair when leaving home. The two foci can be had in one pair of bi-focal glasses, and such should be worn, to facilitate observation of the minutest details.

Discrimination

When the aspirant has attended to his eyesight, he should systematically observe everything and everybody, drawing conclusions from actions, to cultivate the faculty of logical reasoning. Logic is the best teacher in the Physical World, as well as the safest and surest guide in any world.

While practicing this method of observation, it should always be kept in mind that it must be used only to gather facts and not for purposes of criticism, at least not wanton criticism. Constructive criticism, which points out defects and the means of remedying them, is the basis of progress; but destructive criticism, which vandalistically demolishes good and bad alike without aiming at any higher attainment, is an ulcer on the character and must be eradicated. Gossip and idle tale-bearing are clogs and hindrances. While it is not required that we shall say that black is white and overlook manifestly wrong conduct, criticism should be made for the purpose of helping, not to wantonly besmirch the character of a fellow-being because we have found a little stain. Remembering the parable of the mote and the beam, we should turn our most unsparing criticism toward ourselves. None is so perfect that there is no room for improvement. The more blameless the man, the less prone he is to find fault and cast the first stone at another. If we point out faults and suggest ways for improvement, it must be done without personal feeling. We must always seek the good which is hidden in everything. The cultivation of this attitude of discrimination is particularly important.

When the aspirant to first-hand knowledge has practiced concentration and meditation exercises for some time, and has become fairly proficient in them, there is a still higher step to be taken.

We have seen that concentration is focusing thought upon a single object. It is the means whereby we build a clear, objective, and living image of the form about which we wish to acquire knowledge.

Meditation is the exercise whereby the history of the object of our investigation is traced and, so to say, entered into, to pick out of it every shred of evidence as to its relation to the world in general.

These two mental exercises deal, in the deepest and most thorough manner imaginable, with *things*. They lead up to a higher, deeper and more subtle stage of mental development, which deals with the very *soul of things*.

The name of that stage is Contemplation.

Contemplation

In contemplation there is no reaching out in thought or imagination for the sake of getting information, as was the case in Meditation. It is simply the holding of the object before our mental vision and letting the soul of it speak to us. We repose quietly and relaxed upon a couch or bed--not negatively, but thoroughly on the alert--watching for the information that will surely come if we have reached the proper development. Then the *Form* of the object seems to vanish and we see only the *Life* at work. Contemplation will teach us about the Life side, as Meditation taught us about the Form side.

When we reach this stage and have before us, say, a tree in the forest, we lose sight of the Form entirely, and see only the Life, which in this case is a group spirit. We shall find, to our astonishment, that the group spirit of the tree includes the various insects which feed upon it; that the parasite and its host are emanations from one and the same group spirit, for the higher we ascend in the invisible realms, the fewer the separate and distinct forms, and the more completely the One Life predominates, impressing upon the investigator the supreme fact that there is but the One Life--the Universal Life of God, in Whom it is an actual fact that "we live, and move, and have our being." Mineral, plant, animal, and man--all, without exception--are manifestations of God, and this fact furnishes the true basis of brotherhood--a brotherhood which includes everything from the atom to the Sun, because all are emanations from God. Conceptions of brotherhood based upon any other foundation, such as class distinctions, Race affinity, similarity of occupation, etc., fall far short of this true basis, as the occult scientist clearly realizes when he sees the Universal Life flowing in all that exists.

Adoration

When this height has been reached by Contemplation, and the aspirant has realized that he is in truth beholding God in the Life that permeates all things, there remains still to be taken the highest step, Adoration, whereby he unites himself with the Source of all things, reaching by that act the highest goal possible of attainment by man until the time when the permanent union takes place at the end of the great Day of Manifestation.

It is the writer's opinion that neither the heights of Contemplation, nor the final step of Adoration can be attained without the aid of a teacher. The aspirant need never fear, however, that for want of a teacher he will be delayed in taking these steps; nor need he be concerned about looking for a teacher. All that is necessary for him to do is start to improve himself, and to earnestly and *persistently* continue therein. In that way he will purify his vehicles. They will commence to shine in the inner Worlds, and cannot fail to attract the attention of the teachers, who are always watching for just such cases and are more than eager and glad to help those who, because of their earnest efforts to purify themselves, have won the right to receive help. Humanity is sorely in need of helpers who are able to work from the inner Worlds, therefore "seek and ye shall find," but let us not imagine that by going about from one professed teacher to another, we are seeking. "Seeking," in that sense of the word, will avail nothing in this dark world. We ourselves must kindle the light--the light which invariably radiates from the vehicles of the earnest aspirant. That is the star which will lead us to the teacher, or rather the teacher to us.

The time required to bring results from the performance of the exercises varies with each individual and is dependent upon his application, his stage in evolution and his record in the book of destiny; therefore no general time can be set. Some, who are almost ready, obtain results in a few days or weeks; others have to work months, years, and even their whole life without *visible* results, yet the results will be there, and the aspirant who faithfully persists will some day, in this or a future life, behold his patience and faithfulness rewarded and the inner Worlds open to his gaze, finding himself a citizen of realms where the opportunities are immeasurably greater than in the Physical World only.

From that time--awake or asleep, through what men call life, and through what men call death--his consciousness will be unbroken. He will lead a consciously continuous existence, having the benefit of all the conditions which make for more rapid advancement to every higher positions of trust, to be used in the uplifting of the race.

Chapter Eighteen - The Constitution of the Earth and Volcanic Eruptions

Even among occult scientists it is counted amount the most difficult problems to investigate the mysterious construction of the Earth. Every occult scientist knows how much easier it is to thoroughly and accurately investigate the Desire World and the Region of Concrete Thought and bring back the results into the Physical World than to investigate completely the secrets of our physical planet, because to do that fully, one must have passed through the nine lesser Mysteries and the first of the Great Initiations.

Modern scientists know very little about this matter. So far as seismic phenomena are concerned, they very frequently change their theories, because they are constantly discovering reasons why their previous hypotheses were untenable. They have, with all their usual splendid care, investigated the very outside shell, but only to an insignificant depth. As for volcanic eruptions, they try to understand them as they try to understand everything else, in a purely mechanical way, depicting the center of the Earth as a fiery furnace and concluding that the eruptions are caused by the accidental admission of water and in other similar ways.

In a certain sense, their theories have some foundation, but in this case they are, as always, neglecting the spiritual causes which to the occultist appear to be the true ones. To him, the world is far from being "dead." On the contrary, its every nook and crevice is permeated by spirit, which is the leaven that causes changes in and upon the planet.

The different kinds of quartz, the metals, the disposition of the various strata--all have a much higher significance than the materialistic investigator has ever been able to grasp. To the occult scientists, the way in which these materials are arranged is full of meaning. On this subject, as on every other, occult science stands in the same relation to modern science as physiology does to anatomy. Anatomy states with minute detail the exact position of every bone, muscle, ligament, nerve, etc., their relative positions to one another and so forth, but does not give any clue to the use of any one of the different parts of which the body is composed. Physiology, on the other hand, not only states the position and structure of every part of the body, but also tells their use in the body.

To know the different strata of the Earth and the relative positions of the planets in the sky without having also a knowledge of their use and meaning in the life and purpose of the Cosmos, is as useless as to know merely the positions of bones, nerves, etc., without understanding also their use in the functional economy of the body.

The Number of the Beast

To the trained clairvoyant sight, of the Initiate of the various degrees of the Mysteries, the Earth appears built in strata, something like an onion, one layer or stratum outside another. There are nine such strata and the central core, making ten in all. These strata are revealed to the Initiate gradually. One stratum becomes accessible to him at each Initiation, so that at the end of the nine lesser Initiations he is master of all the layers, but has not yet access to the secrets of the core.

In ancient parlance these nine steps are called the "lesser Mysteries." They take the neophyte consciously through all that relates to his past evolution, through the activities of involuntary existence, so that he is able to under-stand the manner and meaning of the work he then performed unconscious-ly. He is shown how the present ninefold constitution (the threefold body, the threefold soul, and the threefold spirit) was brought into existence; how the great creative Hierarchies worked on the virgin spirit, awakening in it the Ego, helping it to form the body; and also the work he himself has done, to extract from the threefold body as much of the threefold soul as he now pos-sesses. One step at a time is he led through the nine steps of the lesser mys-teries, the nine strata.

This number nine is the root number of our present stage of evolution. It bears a significance in our system that no other number does. It is the num-ber of Adam, the life which commenced its evolution as Man, which reached the human stage during the Earth Period. In the Hebrew, as in the Greek, there are no numerals, but each letter has a numerical value. In Hebrew "Ad-am" is called "ADM." The value of "A" is 1; of "D," 4; and of "M," 40. If we add these figures, we get 1+4+4+0=9--the number of Adam, or humanity.

If we turn from the Book of Genesis, which deals with the creation of man in the hoary past, to the Book of Revelation, which deals with his future at-tainment, we find that the number of the beast which hinders is 666. Adding these figures, 6+6+6=18; and further, 1+8=9--we have again the number of humanity, which is itself the cause of all the evil which hinders its own pro-gress. Going further, to the point where the number of those who are to be saved is stated, we find it to be 144,000. Adding as before, 1+4+4+000=9--again the number of humanity, showing that practically it will be saved in its totality, the number incapable of progress in our present evolution being negligible in comparison to the grand total, and even the few who fail are not lost, but will progress in a later scheme.

The consciousness of the mineral and the plant is really unconsciousness. The first glimmering dawn of consciousness begins with the animal kingdom. We have seen also that according to the most modern classification, there are thirteen steps in the animal kingdom: three classes of Radiates; three classes of Mollusks; three classes of Articulates; and four classes of Vertebrates.

If we regard ordinary man as a step by himself, and remember that there are thirteen Initiations from man to God, or from the time he commenced to qualify himself for becoming a self-conscious Creative Intelligence, we have again the same number, Nine: 13+1+13=27 2+7=9.

The number 9 is also hidden in the age of Christ Jesus, 33; 3x3=9, and in a similar manner in the 33 degrees of Masonry. In olden times Masonry was a system of Initiation into the lesser Mysteries which, as we have seen, have 9 degrees, but the Initiates often wrote it as 33. Similarly we read of the 18th degree of the Rosicrucians, which was only a "blind" for the uninitiated, because there are never more than 9 degrees in any lesser Mystery, and the Masons of today have but very little of the occult ritual left in their degrees.

We have also the nine months of gestation, during which the body is built up to its present efficiency; and there are in the body nine perforations-two eyes, two nostrils, two ears, one mouth, and the two lower orifices.

When the advancing man has passed through the nine lesser Initiations, gaining thereby entrance to all the layers of the Earth, entrance into the core is yet to be won. That is opened to him by the first of the four Great Initiation, in which he learns to know the mystery of the mind, that part of his being begun on Earth. When he is ready for the first Great Initiation he has developed his mind to the degree all men are destined to attain to at the end of the Earth Period. In that Initiation he is given the key to the next stage, and all work done by him after that will be such as humanity in general will do in the Jupiter Period, and does not concern us at present.

After his first Great Initiation, he is an Adept. The second, third and fourth Initiations pertain to the stages of development to be arrived at by ordinary humanity in the Jupiter, Venus, and Vulcan Periods.

These thirteen Initiations are symbolically represented in the Christ and His twelve Apostles. Judas Iscariot is the traitorous propensities of the lower nature of the neophyte. The beloved John is the Venus Initiation, and Christ Himself symbolizes the Divine Initiate of the Vulcan Period.

In different schools of occult science the rites of Initiation vary, also their statement of the number of Initiations, but that is merely a matter of classification. It will be observed that such vague descriptions as can be given become more vague as one proceeds higher and higher. Where seven or more degrees are spoken of, almost nothing is said of the sixth Initiation, and nothing whatever of the ones beyond. That is because of another division--the six steps of "Preparation." and the four Initiations which bring the candidate to the end of the Earth Period, to Adeptship. Then there must always be three more, if the philosophy of the school or society goes so far. The writer, however, knows of none but the Rosicrucians who have anything to say of the three Periods which preceded the Earth Period, save the bare statement that there were such Periods. They are not brought very definitely into relationship with our present phase of existence, however. Likewise, other occult teachings simply state that there will be three more schemes of evolution, but no particulars are given. Of course, under those circumstances, the three last Initiations are not mentioned.

Diagram 18 will give an idea of the arrangement of the Earth's strata, the central core being omitted to indicate more clearly the lemniscate formation of the currents in the ninth stratum. In the diagram the strata are represent-

284

ed as being of equal thickness, thought in reality some are much thinner than other. Beginning at the outside, they appear in the following order:

1. **The Mineral Earth:** This is the stony crust of the Earth, with which Geology deals as far as it is able to penetrate.
2. **The Fluid Stratum:** The matter of this stratum is more fluid than that of the outside crust, yet it is not watery, but rather more like a thick paste. It has the quality of expansion, like that of an exceedingly explosive gas, and is kept in place only by the enormous pressure of the outer crust. Were that removed, the whole of the fluid stratum would disappear in space with a tremendous explosion. These correspond to the Chemical and Etheric Regions of the Physical World.
3. **Vapor Stratum:** In the first and second strata there is really no conscious life. But in this stratum there is an even-flowing and pulsating life, as in the Desire World surrounding and inter-penetrating our Earth.
4. **Water Stratum:** In this stratum are the germinal possibilities of all that exists upon the surface of the Earth. Here are the archetypal forces which are back of the group spirits; also the archetypal forces of the minerals, for this is the direct physical expression of the Region of Concrete Thought.
5. **Seed Stratum:** Material scientists have been baffled in their efforts to discover the origin of life, how the first living things came forth from previously dead matter.

In reality, according to the occult explanation of evolution, the question should be how the "dead" things originated. *The Life was there previous to the dead Forms.* It built its bodies from the attenuated, vaporous substance long before it condensed into the Earth's solid crust. *Only when the life had left the forms could they crystallize and become hard and dead.*

Coal is but crystallized plant bodies; coral is also the crystallization of animal forms. The life leaves the *forms* and the *forms* die. Life never came into a form to awaken it to life. Life departed from the forms and the forms died. Thus did "dead" things come to be.

In this fifth stratum is the primordial fount of life from which came the impetus that built all the forms on Earth. It corresponds to the Region of Abstract Thought.

6. **Fiery Stratum:** Strange as it may seem, this stratum is possessed of sensation. Pleasure and pain, sympathy and antipathy have here their effect on the Earth. It is generally supposed that under no possible circumstances can the Earth have any sensation whatever. The occult scientist, however, as he watches the harvesting of the ripe grain and the gathering of fruit from the trees in the autumn, or the plucking of flowers, knows the pleasure experienced by the Earth itself. It is similar to the

pleasure felt by the cow when its bursting udders are being relieved by the sucking calf. The Earth feels the delight of having yielded nourishment for its progeny of Forms, this delight reaching its culmination in the harvest time.

On the other hand, when plants are torn out by the roots, it is patent to the occult scientist that the Earth senses a sting of pain. For that reason he does not eat the plant-foods which grow under the Earth. In the first place they are full of the Earth force and deficient in Sun force, and are additionally poisoned by being pulled up by the roots. The only exception to this rule is that he may partake sparingly of the potato, which originally grew on the surface of the earth, and has only in comparatively recent times grown beneath the soil. Occultists endeavor to nourish their bodies on fruits which grow toward the Sun, because they contain more of the higher Sun force, and have not caused the Earth pain.

It might be supposed that mining operations would be very painful to the Earth, but the reverse is the case. Every disintegration of the hard crust causes a sensation of relief and every solidification is a source of pain. Where a mountain torrent washes away the soil and carries it toward the plains, the earth feels freer. Where the disintegrated matter is again deposited, as in a bar outside the mouth of a great river, there is a corresponding sense of uneasiness.

As sensation in animals and men is due to their separate vital bodies, so the feeling of the Earth is particularly active in this sixth stratum, which corresponds to the World of Life Spirit. To understand the pleasure felt when mining operations are disintegrating the hard rock, and the pain when deposits gather, we must remember that the Earth is the dense body of a Great Spirit, and to furnish us with an environment in which we could live and gather experience, it had to crystallize this body into its present solid condition.

As evolution proceeds, however, and man learns the lessons pertaining to this acme of concretion, the Earth will become softer and its spirit more and more liberated. This is what Paul meant when he spoke of the whole creation groaning and travailing, waiting for the day of liberation.

7. **Refracting Stratum:** This part of the Earth corresponds to the World of Divine Spirit. There are, in occult science what are known as "The Seven Unspeakable Secrets." For those who are not acquainted with these secrets, or have not as least an inkling of their import, the properties of this stratum must seem particularly absurd and grotesque. In it all the forces which are known to us as the "Laws of Nature" exist as moral, or rather immoral forces. In the beginning of the conscious career of man they were much worse than at present. But it appears that as humanity progresses in morals, these forces improve correspondingly; also that any

lapse in morals has a tendency to unleash these Nature forces and causes them to create havoc upon the Earth; while the striving for higher ideals makes them less inimical to man.

The forces in this stratum are thus, at any time, an exact reflection of the existing moral status of mankind. From the occult point of view, the "hand of God" which smites a Sodom or a Gomorrah is not a foolish superstition, for as surely as there is individual responsibility to the law of Consequence which brings to each person the just results of his deeds whether for good or evil, so is there also community and national responsibility, which brings upon groups of men corresponding results for their collective acts. Nature forces are the general agents of such retributive justice, causing floods, or earthquakes, or the beneficent formation of oil or coal for various groups, according to their deserts.

8. **Atomistic Stratum:** This is the name given by the Rosicrucians to the eighth layer of the Earth, which is the expression of the World of Virgin Spirits. It seems to have the property of multiplying many fold the things in it; this applies, however, only to those things which have been definitely formed. An unshapen piece of wood, or an unhewn stone has not existence there, but upon anything which has been shaped, or has life and form (such as a flower or a picture), this stratum has the effect of multiplication to an astonishing degree.

9. **Material Expression of the Earth spirit:** There are here lemniscate currents, which are intimately connected with the brain, heart and sex organs of the human race. It corresponds to the World of God.

10. **Center of Being of the Earth spirit:** Nothing more can be said about this at present except that it is the ultimate seed ground of all that is in and on Earth, and corresponds to the Absolute.

From the sixth or fiery stratum to the surface of the Earth are a number of shafts in different places. The outer ends of these are called "volcanic craters." When the Nature forces in the seventh stratum are unleashed so that they can express themselves through a volcanic outburst, they set the (sixth) fiery stratum in motion and the agitation spreads outward to the mouth of the crater. The bulk of the material is taken from the substance of the second stratum, for that is the denser counterpart of the sixth stratum as the vital body, the second vehicle of man, is the denser counterpart of the life Spirit, the sixth principle. This fluidic stratum, with its expansive and highly explosive quality, insures an unlimited supply of material at the point of eruption. The contact with the outer atmosphere hardens that part of it which is not blown away into space, thus forming a lava and dust, until, as the blood from a wound congeals and stanches the flow, so the lava finally seals the aperture from the inner parts of the Earth.

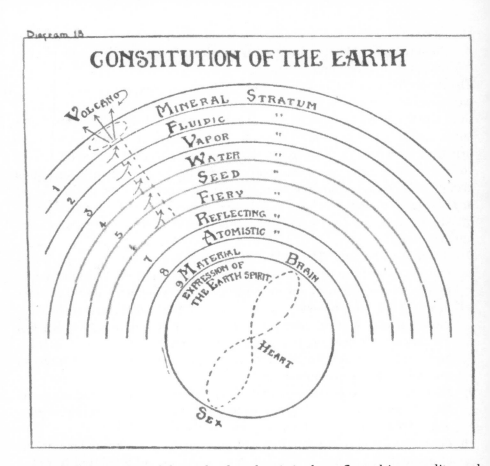

Diagram 18

CONSTITUTION OF THE EARTH

Volcano

Mineral Stratum

Fluidic "

Vapor "

Water "

Seed "

Fiery "

Reflecting "

Atomistic "

Material Expression of the Earth Spirit

Brain

Heart

Sex

1 2 3 4 5 6 7 8 9

As might be gathered from the fact that it is the reflected immorality and anti-spiritual tendencies of mankind which arouse the Nature-forces in the seventh stratum to destructive activity, it is generally profligate and degenerate peoples who succumb to these catastrophes. They, together with others whose destiny, self-generated under the law of consequence, for various reasons, involves a violent death, are gathered from many lands by the superhuman forces, to the point where the eruption is to occur. To the thoughtful, the volcanic outbursts of Vesuvius, for instance, will afford corroboration of this statement.

A list of these outbursts during the last 2,000 years shows that their frequency has been increasing with the growth of materialism. In the last sixty years, especially, in the ratio that materialistic science has grown arrogant in its absolute and sweeping denial of everything spiritual, have the eruption increase in frequency. While there were but six eruptions in the first 1,000 years after Christ, the last five have taken place within 51 years, as will be shown.

288

The first eruption during the Christian Era was that which destroyed the cities of Herculaneum and Pompeii, in which the elder Pliny perished, A. D. 79. The older eruptions followed in A. D. 203, 472, 512, 652, 982, 1036, 1158, 1500, 1631, 1737, 1794, 1822, 1855, 1872, 1855, 1891, 1906.

In the first thousand years, there were six eruptions; in the second thousand there have been twelve, the last five occurring in a period of 51 years, as before stated.

Of the entire number of 18 eruptions, the first nine occurred in the so-called "dark ages," that is to say, the 1600 years during which the Western World was dominated by what are commonly termed the "heathen," or by the Roman Church. The remainder have taken place in the last three hundred years, during which the advent and rise of Modern Science, with its materializing tendencies, has driven almost the last vestige of spiritually to the wall, particularly in the last half of the 19th Century. Therefore the eruptions for that period comprise nearly one-third of the total number that have taken place in our Era.

To counteract this demoralizing influence, a great deal of occult information has been given out during that time by the Elder Brothers of Wisdom, who are ever working for the benefit of humanity. It is thought that by giving out this knowledge and educating the few who will still receive it, it may be possible to stem the tide of materialism, which otherwise may bring about very serious consequences to its advocates who, having so long denied the existence of the spiritual, may be unable to find their balance when they discover that though still living, they have been deprived of the dense body. Such persons may meet a fate too sad to contemplate with equanimity. One of the causes of the dread "white plague" is this materialism, not traceable to the present incarnation perhaps, but the result of previous materialistic beliefs and affirmations.

We have spoken of the demise of the elder Pliny, at the time of the destruction of Pompeii. It is interesting to follow the fate of such a scientist, not so much for the sake of that particular individual as for the light it throws upon the manner in which the memory of Nature is read by the occult scientist, how the impressions are made upon it, and the effect of past traits upon present tendencies.

When a man dies, his dense body disintegrates, but the sum total of its forces can be found in the seventh or reflecting stratum of the Earth, which may be said to constitute a reservoir in which, as forces, past forms are stored. If, knowing the time of the death of a man, we search this reservoir, it is possible to find his form there. Not only is it stored in the seventh stratum, but the eighth or atomistic stratum multiplies it, so that any one type may be reproduced and modified by others. Thus it is used over and over again in the formation of other bodies. The brain-tendencies of such a man as Pliny the elder may have been reproduced a thousand years afterwards, and have been partly the cause of the present crop of materialistic scientists.

There is still much for modern, material scientists to learn and to unlearn. Though they fight to the last ditch what they sneeringly term the "illusionary ideas" of the occult scientist, they are being compelled to acknowledge their truth and accept them one by one, and it is only a matter of time when they will have been compelled to accept them all.

Mesmer, who was sent by the Elder Brother, was worse than ridiculed, but when materialists had changed the name of the force discovered by him, calling it "hypnotism" instead of "Mesmerism," it at once became "scientific."

Twenty years ago Madame Blavatsky, a faithful pupil of Eastern Masters, said that the Earth had a third movement, in addition to the two producing day and night and the seasons. She pointed out that the inclination of the Earth's axis is caused by a movement which, in due time, brings the north pole to where the equator is now and still later, to the place now occupied by the south pole. This, she said, was known to the ancient Egyptians, the famous planisphere at Dendera showing that they had records of three such revolutions. These statements, in common with the whole of her unexcelled work, "The Secret Doctrine," were hooted at.

A few years ago, an astronomer, Mr. G. E. Sutcliffe, of Bombay, discovered and mathematically demonstrated that Laplace had made a mistake in his calculations. The discovery and rectification of this error confirmed by mathematical demonstration the existence of the third motion of the Earth, as claimed by Madame Blavatsky. It also afforded an explanation of the theretofore puzzling fact that tropical plants and fossils are found in the polar regions, as such a movement would necessarily produce, in due time, tropical and glacial periods on all parts of the Earth, corresponding to its changed position in relation to the Sun. Mr. Sutcliffe sent his letter and demonstration to *Nature*, but that journal refused to publish them, and when the author made public the discovery by means of a pamphlet, he drew upon himself an appalling storm of vituperation. However, he is an avowed and a deep student of "The Secret Doctrine," and that explains the hostile reception according his discovery and its inevitable corollaries.

Later, however, a Frenchman, not an astronomer, but a mechanic, constructed an apparatus demonstrating the ample possibility of the existence of such a movement. The apparatus was exhibited at the Louisiana Purchase Exhibition at Saint Louis, and was warmly endorsed by M. Camille Flammarion, as worthy of investigation. Here was something concrete, something "mechanical," and the editor of *The Monist*, thought he described the inventor as a man laboring somewhat under "mystic illusions" (because of his belief that the ancient Egyptians knew of this third motion), nevertheless magnanimously overlooked that feature of the case and said that he had not lost faith in M. Beziau's theory on that account. He published an explanation and an essay by M. Beziau, wherein the motion and its effects upon the surface of the Earth were described in terms similar to those used by Madame Blavatsky and Mr. Sutcliffe. M. Beziau is not definitely "billed" as an occultist, therefore his discovery may be countenanced.

Many instances might be cited showing how occult information has been corroborated later by material science. One of them is the atomistic theory, which is advocated in the Greek philosophies and later in "The Secret Doctrine." It was "discovered" in 1897, by Professor Thomson.

In Mr. A. P. Sinnett's valuable work, "The Growth of the Soul," published in 1896, the author stated that there are two planets beyond the orbit of Neptune, only one of which, he thought, would be discovered by modern astronomers. In *Nature* for August, 1906, the statement is made that Professor Barnard, through the 36-inch Lick refractor, had discovered such a planet in 1892. There had been no mistake about it, yet he waited fourteen years before he announced his discovery! One need not be concerned about that, however. The main point is that the planet is there, and that Mr. Sinnett's book said so ten years before Professor Barnard's claim to prior discovery. Probably, previous to 1906 the announcement of the newly discovered planet might have tended to disarrange some popularly accepted theory!

There are many such theories. The Copernican theory is not altogether correct, and there are many facts that cannot be accounted for by the lauded Nebular theory alone. Tyco Brahe, the famous Danish astronomer, refused to accept the Copernican theory. He had a very good reason for remaining true to the Ptolemaic theory because, as he said, by it the movements of the planets figured out correctly, while with the Copernican theory, it is necessary to use a table of corrections. The Ptolemaic system is correct from the standpoint of the Desire World, and it has points that are needed in the Physical World.

By many the statements made in the foregoing pages will be considered fantastic. Be it so. Time will bring to all a knowledge of the facts herein set forth. This book is only for the few who, having freed their minds from the shackles of orthodox science and religion, are ready to accept this until they have proven it wrong.

Chapter Nineteen - Christian Rosenkreuz and the Order of Rosicrucians

Ancient Truths in Modern Dress

Having encountered among the public a widespread desire to learn something of the Order of Rosicrucians, and as there is a lack of understanding of the important place occupied by the Brothers of the Rose Cross in our Western civilization, even among our students, it may be well to furnish authentic information upon the subject.

Everything in the world is subject to law, even our evolution is thus encompassed; spiritual and physical progression go hand in hand. The sun is the physical light bringer and, as we know, it apparently travels from east to west bringing light and life to one part of the earth after another. But the visible sun is only a part of the sun as the visible body is a small part of composite man. There is an invisible and spiritual sun whose rays promote soul growth upon one part of the earth after another as the physical sun promotes the growth of form, and this spiritual impulse also travels in the same direction as the physical sun; from east to west.

Six or seven hundred years B.C., a new wave of spirituality was started near the western shores of the Pacific Ocean to give enlightenment to the Chinese nation and the religion of Confucius is embraced to this day by many millions in the celestial kingdom. Later we note the effect of this wave in the religion of Buddha, a teaching designed to stir the aspirations of millions of Hindus and western Chinese. In its westward course it appears among the more intellectual Greeks in the lofty philosophies of Pythagoras and Plato, and at last it sweeps over the western world, among the pioneers of the human race, where it takes the lofty form of the Christian religion.

The Christian religion has gradually worked its way to the westward, even to the shores of the Pacific Ocean and thither the spiritual aspirations are being massed and concentrated. There they will reach a point of culmination, prior to taking a new leap across the ocean and inaugurating a higher and more lofty spiritual awakening in the Orient than now exists in that part of the earth.

Just as day and night, summer and winter, ebb and flood, follow each other in unbroken sequence according to the law of alternating cycles, so also the appearance of a wave of spiritual awakening in any part of the world is followed by a period of material reactions, so that our development may not become one-sided.

Religion, Art and Science are the three most important means of human education, and they are a trinity in unity which cannot be separated without distorting our viewpoint of whatever we may investigate. *True Religion* embodies both science and art, for it teaches a beautiful life in harmony with the laws of nature.

True Science is artistic and religious in the highest sense, for it teaches us to reverence and conform to laws governing our well-being and explains why the religious life is conducive to health and beauty.

True Art is as educational as science and as uplifting in its influence as religion. In architecture we have a most sublime presentation of cosmic lines of force in the universe. It fills the spiritual beholder with a powerful devotion and adoration born of an awe-inspiring conception of the overwhelming grandeur and majesty of Deity. Sculpture and painting, music and literature inspire us with a sense of transcendent loveliness of God, the immutable source and goal of all this beautiful world.

Nothing short of such an all-embracing teaching will answer the needs of humanity permanently. There was a time, even as late as Greece, when *Religion, Art* and *Science* were taught unitedly in Mystery temples. But it was necessary to the better development of each that they should separate for a time.

Religion held sole sway in the so-called "dark ages." During that time it bound both Science and Art hand and foot. Then came the period of Renaissance and *Art* came to the fore in all its branches. Religion was strong as yet, however, and Art was only too often prostituted in the service of Religion. Last came the wave of modern *Science*, and with iron hand it has subjugated Religion.

It was a detriment to the world when Religion shackled Science. *Ignorance* and *Superstition* caused untold woe, nevertheless man cherished a lofty spiritual ideal then; he hoped for a higher and better life. It is infinitely more disastrous that Science is killing Religion, for now even *Hope*, the only gift of the gods left in Pandora's box, may vanish before *Materialism* and *Agnosticism*.

Such a state cannot continue. Reaction must set in. If it does not, Anarchy will rend the Cosmos. To avert a calamity *Religion, Science* and *Art* must reunite in a higher expression of the *Good*, the *True* and the *Beautiful* than obtained before the separation.

Coming events cast their shadows before, and when the Great Leaders of humanity saw the tendency towards ultra-materialism which is now rampant in the Western World, they took certain steps to counteract and transmute it at the auspicious time. They did not wish to kill the budding Science as the latter has strangled Religion, for they saw the ultimate good which will result when an advanced Science has again become the co-worker of Religion. A spiritual Religion, however, cannot blend with a materialistic Science any more than oil can mix with water. Therefore steps were taken to spiritualize Science and make Religion scientific.

In the thirteenth century a high spiritual teacher, having the symbolical name Christian Rosenkreuz--Christian: Rose: Cross--appeared in Europe to commence that work. He founded the mysterious Order of Rosicrucians with the object of throwing occult light upon the misunderstood Christian Religion and to explain the mystery of Life and Being from the scientific standpoint in harmony with Religion.

Many centuries have rolled by since the birth, as Christian Rosenkreuz, of the Founder of the Rosicrucian Mystery School, and by many his existence is even regarded as a myth. But his birth as Christian Rosenkreuz marked the beginning of a new epoch in spiritual life of the Western World. That particular Ego has also been in continuous physical existence ever since, in one or another of the European Countries. He has taken a new body when his successive vehicles have outlived their usefulness, or circumstances rendered it expedient that he changes the scene of his activities. Moreover, he is embodied today--an Initiate of high degree, an active and potent factor in all affairs of the West--although unknown to the World.

He labored with the Alchemists centuries before the advent of modern science. He, through an intermediary, inspired the now mutilated works of Bacon. Jacob Boehme and others received through him the inspiration which makes their works so spiritually illuminating. In the works of the immortal Goethe and the masterpieces of Wagner the same influence meets us. All undaunted spirits who refuse to be fettered by either orthodox science or orthodox religion, who fling away the husks and penetrate to the spiritual kernel regardless of vilification or of flattery, draw their inspiration from the same fountain as did and does the great spirit which animated Christian Rosenkreuz.

His very name is an embodiment of the manner and the means by which the present day man is transformed into the Divine Superman. This symbol,

"Christian Rosen Kreuz"
[The] Christian Rose Cross,

shows the end and aim of human evolution, the road to be traveled, and the means whereby that end is gained. The black cross, the twining green stem of the plant, the thorns, the blood red roses--in these is hidden the solution of the World Mystery--Man's past evolution, present constitution, and particularly the secret of his future development.

It hides from the profane, but reveals to the Initiate the more clearly how he is to labor day by day to make for himself that choicest of all gems, the Philosopher's Stone--more precious than the Kohinoor; nay, than the sum of all earthly wealth! It reminds him how mankind, in its ignorance, is hourly wasting the actual concrete material that might be used in the formation of this priceless treasure.

To keep him steadfast and true through every adversity, the Rose cross holds aloft, as an inspiration, the glorious consummation in store for him that overcometh, and points to Christ as the Star of Hope, the "first fruits," Who wrought this marvelous Stone while inhabiting the body of Jesus.

Upon investigation it has been found that there was in all systems of Religion a teaching reserved for the Priest-craft and not given to the multitude. The Christ also spoke to the multitude in parables, but explained the inner meaning of these parables to the disciples, to give them an understanding more suited to their developed minds.

Paul gave "milk" to the *babes* or younger members of the community, but "meat" to the *strong* who had studied more deeply. Thus there has always been an *inner* and an *outer teaching*, and this inner teaching was given in so-called Mystery Schools which have changed from time to time to suit the needs of the people among whom they were designed to work.

The Order of Rosicrucians is not merely a secret society; it is one of the Mystery Schools, and the Brothers are Hierophants of the lesser Mysteries, Custodians of the Sacred Teachings and a spiritual Power more potent in the life of the Western World than any of the visible Governments, though they may not interfere with humanity so as to deprive them of their free will.

As the path of development in all cases depends upon the temperament of the aspirant, there are two paths, *the mystic* and *the intellectual*. The Mystic is usually devoid of intellectual knowledge; he follows the dictates of his heart and strives to do the will of God as he *feels* it, lifting himself upward without being conscious if any definite goal, and in the end he attains knowledge. In the middle ages people were not as intellectual as we are nowadays, and those who felt the call of a higher life usually followed the mystic path. But in the last few hundred years, since the advent of modern science, a more *intellectual* humanity has peopled the earth; the head has completely overruled the heart, materialism has dominated all spiritual impulse and the majority of the thinking people do not believe anything they cannot touch, taste or handle. Therefore, it is necessary that appeal should be made to their intellect in order that the heart may be allowed to believe what the intellect has sanctioned. As a response to this demand the Rosicrucian Mystery teachings aim to correlate scientific facts to spiritual verities.

In the past these have been kept secret from all but a few Initiates, and even today they are among the most mysterious and secret in the Western World. All so-called "discoveries" of the past which have professed to reveal the Rosicrucian secrets, have been either fraudulent, or the result or treachery upon the part of some outsider who may, accidentally or otherwise, have overheard fragments of conversation, unintelligible to all but those who have the key. It is possible to live under the same roof and on terms of the closest intimacy with an Initiate of any school, yet his secret will always remain hidden in his breast until the friend has reached the point where he can become a Brother Initiate. The revealing of secrets does not depend upon the Will of the Initiate, but upon the qualifications of the aspirant.

Like all other Mystery Orders, the Order of Rosicrucians is formed on cosmic lines: If we take balls of even size and try how many it will take to cover one and hide it from view, we shall find that it will require 12 to conceal a thirteenth ball. The ultimate division of physical matter, the true atom, found in interplanetary space, is thus grouped in twelve around one. The twelve signs of the Zodiac enveloping our Solar System, the twelve semi-tones of the musical scale comprising the octave, the twelve Apostles who clustered around the Christ, etc., are other examples of this grouping of 12 and 1. The Rosicrucian Order is therefore also composed of 12 Brothers and a 13th.

There are other divisions to be noted, however. We have seen that of the Heavenly Host of twelve Creative Hierarchies who were active in our scheme of evolution, five have withdrawn to liberation, leaving only seven to busy themselves with our further progress. It is in harmony with this fact that the man of today, the indwelling Ego, the microcosm, works outwards through seven visible orifices in his body: 2 eyes, 2 ears, 2 nostrils and a mouth, while five more orifices are wholly or partially closed. the mammae, the umbilicus and two excretory organs.

The seven roses which garnish our beautiful emblem and the five pointed radiating star behind, are emblematical of the twelve Great Creative Hierarchies which have assisted the evolving human spirit through the previous conditions as mineral, plant and animal, when it was devoid of self-consciousness and unable to care for itself in the slightest degree. Of these twelve hosts of Great Beings, three classes worked upon and with man of their own free wills and without any obligation whatever.

These are symbolized by the three points in the star upon our emblem which points upwards. Two more of the Great Hierarchies are upon the point of withdrawal, and these are pictured in the two points of the star which radiate downward from the center. The seven roses reveal the fact that there are still seven Great Creative Hierarchies active in the development of the beings upon earth, and as all of these various classes from the smallest to the greatest are but parts of One Great Whole whom we call God, the whole emblem is a symbol of God in manifestation.

The Hermetic axiom says: "As above so below," and the lesser teachers of mankind are also grouped upon the same cosmic lines of 7, 5 and 1. There are upon earth seven schools of the lesser Mysteries, five of the Greater Mysteries and the whole is grouped under one Central Head Who is called the Liberator.

In the Order of Rosicrucians seven Brothers go out into the World whenever occasion requires; appearing as men among other men or working in their invisible vehicles with or upon others as needed; yet it must be strictly kept in mind that they never influence people against their will or contrary to their desires; but only strengthen good wherever found.

The remaining five Brothers never leave the temple; and though they do possess physical bodies all their work is done from the inner Worlds.

The Thirteenth is Head of the Order, the link with a higher Central Council composed of the Hierophant of the Greater Mysteries, who do not deal with ordinary humanity at all, but only with graduates of the lesser Mysteries.

The Head of the Order is hidden from the outside world by the twelve Brothers, as the central ball mentioned in our illustration. Even the pupils of the School never see him, but at the nightly Services in the Temple His presence is *felt* by all, whenever He enters, and is the signal for the commencement of the ceremony.

Gathered around the Brothers of the Rose Cross, as their pupils, are a number of "lay brothers"; people who live in various parts of the Western World, but are able to leave their bodies consciously, attend the services and participate in the spiritual work at the temple; they having each and every one been "initiated" in the method of so doing by one of the Elder Brothers. Most of them are able to remember all that happens, but there are a few cases where the faculty of leaving the body was acquired in a previous life of welldoing and where a drug habit or a sickness contracted in the present existence has unfitted the brain to receive impression of the work done by the man when away.

Initiation

The general idea of initiation is that it is merely a ceremony which makes one a member of a secret society; that it may be conferred upon anyone willing to pay a certain price, a sum of money in most cases.

While that is true of the so-called initiation of fraternal orders and also in most pseudo-occult orders, it is altogether an erroneous idea when applied to initiations into various degrees of truly occult Brotherhoods, as a little understanding of the real requirements and of their reasonableness will readily make clear.

In the first place there is no golden key to the temple; merit counts but not money. Merit is not acquired in a day; it is the cumulative product of past good action. The Candidate for initiation is usually totally unconscious that he is a candidate, he is usually living his life in the community and serving his fellow man for days and years without any ulterior thought until one day there appears in his life the teacher, a Hierophant of the lesser Mysteries appropriate to the country in which he resides. By this time the candidate has cultivated within himself certain faculties, stored up certain powers for service and help, of which he is usually unconscious or which he does not know how to properly utilize. The task of the initiator will now be plain; he shows the candidate the latent faculties, the dormant powers and initiates him into their use; explains or demonstrates to him *for the first time* how the candidate may awaken the static energy into dynamic power.

Initiation may be accomplished by a ceremony, or not, but let it be particularly observed, that while Initiation is the inevitable culmination of prolonged spiritual endeavor, whether conscious or the reverse upon the part of the candidate, it can positively never take place till the requisite inner development has accumulated the latent powers which Initiation teaches how to use dynamically, any more than pulling the trigger can cause an explosion in a gun that has not first been loaded.

Neither is there any danger that the teacher may overlook anyone who has attained the requisite development. Each good and unselfish deed increases the luminosity and vibrant power of the candidate's aura enormously, and as surely as the magnet attracts the needle, so will the brilliancy of that auric light bring the teacher.

It is, of course, impossible to describe in a book intended for the general public the stages of the Rosicrucian Initiation; to do so would be a breach of faith and it would also be impossible for lack of words to adequately express oneself. But it is permissible to give an outline and to show the purpose of initiation.

The lesser Mysteries deal only with evolution of mankind during the Earth Period. In the first three and one-half Revolutions of the life wave around the seven globes the Virgin Spirits had not yet attained consciousness. In consequence of this fact we are ignorant of how we came to be as we are today. The candidate is to have light upon that subject so by the spell of the Hierophants during the period of initiation into the first degree his consciousness is turned towards that page of the memory of nature bearing the records of the first revolution when we recapitulated the development of the Saturn Period. He is still in full possession of his every-day consciousness; he knows and remembers the facts of twentieth Century life, but he is now consciously watching the progress of the evolving host of Virgin Spirits of which he formed one unit during the Saturn Revolution. Thus he learns how the first steps were taken in the Earth Period towards the goal of attainment which will be revealed to him in a later step.

Having learned the lesson as practically described in Chapter X, the candidate has acquired first-hand knowledge upon this subject and has come into direct touch with the Creative Hierarchies in their work with and upon man; he is therefore able to appreciate their beneficent labors in the World and is in measure able to range himself in line with them; becoming thus far their co-worker.

When the time has arrived for him to take the second degree, he is similarly caused to turn his attention to the conditions of the second Revolution of the Earth Period, and as depicted in the memory of nature; then he watches in full consciousness the progress made at that time by the Virgin Spirits, much as Peter Ibbetson, the hero of a book, "Peter Ibbetson," by George du Maurier; it is well worth reading, for it is a graphic description of certain phases of subconsciousness--watched his child life during the nights when he "dreamed true." In the third degree he follows the evolution of the third or Moon, Revolution, and in the fourth degree he sees the progress made in the half-Revolution we have made of the fourth.

There is, however, a further step taken in each degree; the pupil sees in addition to the work done in each revolution also the work accomplished in the corresponding Epoch during our present stay upon globe D, the Earth.

During the first degree he follows the work of the Saturn Revolution and its latest consummation in the Polarian Epoch.

In the second degree he follows the work of the Sun Revolution and its replica: the Hyperborean Epoch.

During the third degree he watches the work as performed in the Moon Revolution and sees how that was the basis of life in the Lemurian Epoch.

During the fourth degree he sees the evolution of the last half Revolution with its corresponding period of time in our present stay on Earth; the first half of the Atlantean Epoch which ended when the dense foggy atmosphere subsided, and the sun first shone upon land and sea; then the night of unconsciousness was over, the eyes of the indwelling Ego were fully opened, and he was able to turn the Light of Reason upon the problem of conquering the World. That was the time when a man as we now know him was first born.

When in the olden system of initiation we hear that the candidate was entranced for a period of three and one-half days, reference is had to the part of initiation just described, and the three and one-half days refer to the stages gone through, they are not by any means days of twenty-four hours; the actual time varies with each candidate, but in all cases he is taken through the unconsciousness development of mankind during the past Revolutions, and when it is said that he is awakened at the time of sunrise on the fourth day that is the mystical way of expressing that his initiation into the work of the involutionary career of man ceases at the time when the sun rose above the clear atmosphere of Atlantis. Then the candidate is also hailed as a "first-born."

Having become familiar with the road we have traveled in the past, the fifth degree takes the candidate to the very end of the Earth Period, when a glorious humanity is gathering the fruits of this Period and taking it away from the seven globes upon which we evolve during each day of manifestation, into the first of the five dark globes which are our habitation during the Cosmic nights. The densest of these is located in the Region of Abstract Thought, and is in reality the "Chaos" spoken of in Chapter XI and in the following pages. This globe is also the Third Heaven, and when Paul speaks of being caught up into the Third Heaven and of seeing things there which he could not lawfully reveal, he was referring to the experiences of an equivalent of this fifth degree in the present Rosicrucian Mysteries.

After being shown the end in the fifth degree, the candidate is made acquainted with the means whereby that end is attained during the remaining three and one-half Revolutions of the Earth Period; the four remaining degrees being devoted to his enlightenment in that respect. By the insight he has thus acquired he is able to intelligently co-operate with the Powers that work for Good, and thus he will help to hasten the day of our emancipation.

In order to rout a common misconception we wish to make clear to students that we are not Rosicrucians because we study their teachings, nor does even admission to the temple entitle us to call ourselves by that name. The writer, for instance, is only a lay brother, a pupil, and would under no circumstances call himself a Rosicrucian.

We know well, that when a boy has graduated from grammar school he is not therefore fitted to teach. He must first go through high school and college, and even then he may not feel the call to be a school teacher. Similarly in the school of life, because a man has graduated from the Rosicrucian Mystery School he is not even then a Rosicrucian. Graduates from the various schools of the lesser mysteries advance into five schools of the greater mysteries. In the first four they pass the four Great Initiations and at last reach the Liberator, where they receive a knowledge concerning other evolutions and are given the choice of remaining here to assist their brothers or enter other evolutions as Helpers. Those who elect to stay here as helpers are given various positions according to their tastes and natural bent. The Brothers of the Rose Cross are among those Compassionate Ones, and it is a sacrilege to drag the Rosicrucian name in the mire by applying it to ourselves when we are merely students of their lofty teachings.

During the past few centuries the Brothers have worked for humanity in secret; each night at midnight there is a Service at the temple where the Elder Brothers, assisted by the lay brothers who are able to leave their work in the World (for many of them reside in places where it is yet day when it is midnight in the location of the temple of the Rose Cross), gather up from everywhere in the Western World the thoughts of sensuality, greed, selfishness and materialism. These they seek to transmute into pure love, benevolence, altruism and spiritual aspirations sending them back to the World to uplift and encourage all Good. Were it not for this potent source of spiritual vibration materialism must long ago have totally squelched all spiritual effort, for there has never been a darker age from the spiritual standpoint than the last three hundred years of materialism.

Now the time has come, however, when the method of secret endeavor is to be supplemented with a more direct effort to promulgate a definite, logical and sequential teaching concerning the origin, evolution and future development of the World and man, showing both the spiritual and the scientific aspect: a teaching which makes no statements that are not supported by reason and logic; a teaching which is satisfying to the mind, for it holds out a reasonable solution to all mysteries; it neither begs nor evades questions and its explanations are both profound and lucid.

But, and this is a very important "But," *The Rosicrucians do not regard an intellectual understanding of God and the Universe as an end in itself; far from it!* The greater the intellect, the greater the danger of its misuse. Therefore, *this scientific, logical and exhaustive teaching is given in order that man may believe in his heart that which his head has sanctioned and start to live the religious life.*

The Rosicrucian Fellowship

In order to promulgate this teaching the Rosicrucian Fellowship has been formed, and anyone who is not a *hypnotist, professional medium, clairvoyant, palmist or astrologer,* may enroll as a *Preliminary Course Student* by writing to the General Secretary. There is no fee for Initiation, or dues. Money cannot buy our teaching, advancement depends on merit.

After completing the Preliminary Course one is put on the Regular Student list for a period of two years, after which if he has become so imbued with the verity of the Rosicrucian teachings that he is prepared to sever his connection with all other occult or religious orders--*the Christian Churches and Fraternal Orders are excepted*--he may assume the Obligation which admits him to the degree of *Probationer.*

We do not mean to insinuate by the foregoing clause that all other schools of occultism are of no account--far from it--many roads lead to Rome, but we shall attain with much less effort it we follow one of them than if we zigzag from path to path. Our time and energy are limited in the first place, and are still further curtailed by family and social duties not to be neglected for self-development. It is to husband the minim of energy which we may legitimately expend upon ourselves, and to avoid waste of scanty moments at our disposal, that resignation from all other Orders is insisted upon by the leaders.

The world is an aggregate of opportunities, but to take advantage of any one of them we must possess efficiency in a certain line of endeavor. Development of our spiritual powers will enable us to help or harm our weaker brothers. It is only justifiable when efficiency in Service of Humanity is the object.

The Rosicrucian method of attainment differs from other systems in one especial particular: It aims, even at the very start, to emancipate the pupil from dependence upon others, to make him *Self-Reliant* in the very highest degree, so that he may be able to stand alone under all circumstances and cope with all conditions. Only one who is thus strongly poised can help the weak.

When a number of people meet in a class or circle for self-development along *Negative* lines, result are usually achieved in a short time on the principle that it is easier to drift with the tide than to breast the current. The medium is not master of his actions, however, but the slave of a spirit control. Hence such gatherings must be shunned by Probationers.

Even classes which meet in positive attitude of mind are not advised by the Elder Brothers, because the latent powers of all members are massed and visions of the inner worlds obtained by anyone there, are partly due to the faculties of others. The heat of coal in the center of a fire is enhanced by surrounding coals, and the clairvoyant produced in a circle, be it ever so positive, is a hot-house plant, too dependent himself to be trusted with the care of others.

Therefore each Probationer in the Rosicrucian Fellowship performs his exercises in the seclusion and privacy of his room. Results may be obtained more slowly by the system, but when they appear, they will be manifest as powers cultivated by himself, useable independently of all others. Besides, the Rosicrucian methods build character at the same time that they develop spiritual faculties and thus safeguard the pupil against yielding to temptation to prostitute divine powers for worldly prestige.

When the Probationer has complied with the necessary requirements and completed the term of probation, he may send request for individual instruction by the Elder Brothers through the General Secretary.

When this request has been granted the Probationer becomes a *Disciple* and is gradually fitted for work as an Invisible Helper.

Rays from the Rose Cross

The Rosicrucian Fellowship has, among other activities, a correspondence course of monthly letters and lessons for *Students*. The lessons are contained in little pamphlets entitled *"Rays from the Rose Cross,"* and bound in durable paper covers with our beautiful symbolical cover design. In the letters Mr. Heindel takes up and emphasizes points in the lesson, which is thus thoroughly impressed upon the consciousness of the *Student.*

There is also an advanced correspondence course open to Probationers to help them derive the greatest possible benefit from their exercises and advance them upon the path to *Discipleship.*

Upon request, the General Secretary Rosicrucian Fellowship (Esoteric Section), P. O. Box 866, Ocean Park, Cal., will send application blank for the elementary correspondence course to anyone who wishes to study the Rosicrucian teachings directly with Mr. Heindel. When that is filled out and returned, the applicant's name will be placed upon Mr. Heindel's correspondence list and he will receive the letters and lessons in due time.

These letters and lessons are not sold, *the Rosicrucian teachings are free,* but the expenses incidental to their production and distribution are met by free will offerings from grateful students according to ability. From one comes "the widow's mite," from another a munificent donation, but all receive the same teaching and attention irrespective of whether they are able to contribute or not.

The Symbolism of the Rose Cross

When inquiring into the meaning of any myth, legend or symbol of occult value, it is an absolute necessity that we should understand that, as any object in the three-dimensional world may, or rather must, be viewed from all points to obtain a full and complete comprehension thereof, so all symbols have a number of aspects. Each viewpoint reveals a different phase from the others, and all have an equal claim to consideration.

Viewed in its fullness, this wonderful symbol contains the key to man's past evolution, his present constitution and future development, together with the method of attainment. In the form where it is represented with a single rose in the center it symbolizes the spirit radiating from itself the four vehicles: the dense, vital and desire bodies plus the mind; where the spirit has drawn *into* its instruments and become the *indwelling* human spirit. But

303

there was a time when that condition did not obtain, a time when the three-fold spirit hovered above its vehicles and was unable to enter. Then the cross stood alone without the rose, symbolizing the condition which prevailed in the early third of Atlantis. There was even a time when the upper limb of the cross was lacking and man's constitution was represented by the Tau (T) that was in the Lemurian epoch when he had only the dense, vital and desire bodies, but lacked the mind. Then the animal nature was paramount. Man followed desire without reserve. At a still earlier time, in the Hyperborean Epoch, he was also minus the desire body and possessed only the dense and vital bodies. Then man-in-the-making was like the plants: chaste and devoid of desire. At that time his constitution could not have been represented by a cross. It was symbolized by a straight shaft, a pillar (I).

This symbol has been considered phallic, an emblem showing the licentiousness of the people who worshiped it. Truly it is a symbol of generation, but generation is by no means synonymous with degradation--far from it--the pillar is the lower limb of the cross, symbolical of man-in-the-making when he was plantlike. The plant is unconscious of passion, desire, innocent of evil. It generates and perpetuates its species in a manner so pure, so chaste, that properly understood, it is a model for fallen and passionate humanity to worship as an ideal and it was given to earlier races with that intent. The Phallus and Yona used in the Greek mystery temples were given by the hierophants in that spirit, and over the temple was placed the enigmatical words: "Man, know thyself," which motto, properly understood, is similar to that of the Rose Cross, for it shows the reason for man's fall into desire, passion and sin, and gives the key to his liberation in the same way that the roses upon the cross indicate the path of liberation.

The plant is innocent, *but not virtuous*; it has neither desire not choice. Man has both. He may follow desire or not as he wishes, that he may learn to master himself.

While he was plant-like, a hermaphrodite, he could generate *from himself* without the help of another, but though he was as chaste and as innocent as the plants, he was also as unconscious and inert. In order to advance he must have desire to spur him on, and a mind to guide him, and therefore half his creative force was retained for the purpose of building a brain and a larynx. He had at that time a round shape similar to that of the embryo, and the present larynx was a part of the creative organ which adhered to the head when the body straightened out. The connection between the two is seen even today in the fact that the boy, who expresses the positive pole of the generative force, changes his voice at puberty. That the same force which builds another body when it is sent *outwards* builds the brain when *retained* is equally clear when we consider that sex mania leads to insanity, while the profound thinker will feel little inclination for amorous practices. He uses all his creative force to generate thought instead of wasting it in sense gratification.

At the time when man commenced to withhold half his creative force for the above-mentioned purpose, his consciousness was directed *inwards* to build organs. He was capable of *seeing* these organs and he used the same creative force then under the direction of Creative Hierarchies in planning and in executing plans of organs, that he now uses in the *outer* world to build airships, houses, automobiles, telephones, etc. Then he was unconscious of how that half of the creative force was used which was sent *outwards* for generation of another body.

Generation was carried on under the guidance of Angels. At certain times of the year they herded the growing man together in great temples and there the generative act was performed. Man was unconscious of the fact. His eyes had not yet been opened, and though it was necessary for him to have a partner who had the half or other pole of the creative force available for generation which he retained to build organs within, he did not at first *know* his wife. In ordinary life he was shut within himself so far as the Physical World was concerned, but it was different when he was brought into such intimate and close touch with another, as in the case of the generative act. Then for the moment the spirit pierced the veil of flesh and Adam *knew* his wife. He had ceased to *know himself*--thus his consciousness became more and more and more and more centered outside himself in the *outside world* and he lost his *inner perception*. That cannot be fully regained until he has passed to the stage where it is no longer necessary to have a partner in generation, and he has reached the development where he can again utilize his *whole* creative force at will. Then he will again *know himself* as he did during his stage of plant-like existence, but with this all-important difference that he will use his creative faculty consciously, and will not be restricted to using it solely for the pro-creation of his own species, but may create whatever he will. Neither will he use his present organs of generation, but the larynx will *speak* the creative *word* as directed by the spirit through the coordinating mechanism of the brain. Thus the two organs built by half the creative force will in time be the means whereby man will eventually become an independent self-conscious creator.

Even at the present time man molds matter both by thought and voice, as instanced in scientific experiments where thoughts have created an image on photographic plates, and where the human voice has created geometrical figures in sand, etc. In proportion as man becomes unselfish he will release the creative force held in leash. That will give him added thought power and enable him to utilize it for upliftment of others instead of to plan how to degrade and subject others to his will. He will learn how to master *himself* and cease to try to master others, except it be done temporarily *for their good*, but never for selfish ends. Only one who has mastered himself is qualified to rule others, and competent to judge when that should be done, and what is best for them.

Thus we see that in time the present passionate mode of generation will be again superseded by a pure and more efficient method than the present, and that also is symbolized in the Rose Cross where the rose is placed in the center between the four arms. The long limb represents the body, the two horizontals, the two arms, and the short upper limb, the head. *The rose is in place of the larynx.*

The rose, like any other flower, is the generative organ of the plant. Its green stem carries the colorless, passionless plant blood. The blood red rose shows the passion filled blood of the human race, but in the rose the vital fluid is not sensuous, it is chaste and pure. Thus it is an excellent symbol of the generative organ in the pure and holy state to which man will attain when he has cleansed and purified his blood from desire, when he has become chaste, pure and Christ-like.

Therefore the Rosicrucians look ardently forward to the day when the roses shall bloom upon the cross of humanity, therefore the Elder Brothers greet the aspiring soul with the words of the Rosicrucian Greeting: "May the Roses bloom upon your Cross," and therefore the greeting is given in the meetings of the Fellowship Centers by the leader to the assembled students, probationers and disciples who respond to the greeting by saying "And on yours, also."

John speaks of his purification (1st epistle, iii, 9) and says that he who is born of God cannot sin, *for he keepeth his seed within him.* It is an absolute necessity to progress that the aspirant should be chaste. Yet it must be borne in mind, that absolute celibacy is not required of man until he has reached a point where he is ready for the great initiations, and that it is a duty we owe to the whole to perpetuate the race. If we are mentally, morally, physically and financially able, we may approach the act of generation as a holy sacrifice laid upon the altar of humanity, but not for sensual pleasure. Neither should it be performed in an austere, forbidding frame of mind, but in glad giving up of oneself for the privilege of furnishing a friend seeking rebirth with the body and environment he needs for development. Thus we shall also help him cultivate the blooming roses upon his cross.